FOUNDING OF THE
AMERICAN PUBLIC SCHOOL SYSTEM

THE MACMILLAN COMPANY
NEW YORK · BOSTON · CHICAGO · DALLAS
ATLANTA · SAN FRANCISCO

MACMILLAN AND CO., Limited
LONDON · BOMBAY · CALCUTTA · MADRAS
MELBOURNE

THE MACMILLAN COMPANY
OF CANADA, Limited
TORONTO

Founding of the American Public School System

A HISTORY OF EDUCATION IN THE UNITED STATES

From the Early Settlements to the
Close of the Civil War Period

BY PAUL MONROE, PH.D., LL.D.

Emeritus Professor of Education, Teachers College, Columbia University,
President of the World Federation of Education Associations.

This publication was made possible by funds granted by Carnegie Corporation of New York. That Corporation is not, however, the author, owner, publisher, or proprietor of this publication, and is not to be understood as approving by virtue of its grant any of the statements made or views expressed therein.

Volume I

THE MACMILLAN COMPANY · NEW YORK
1940

Copyright, 1940, by
PAUL MONROE

All rights reserved—no part of this book may be reproduced in any form without permission in writing from the publisher, except by a reviewer who wishes to quote brief passages in connection with a review written for inclusion in magazine or newspaper.

Printed in the United States of America

Published February, 1940

TO MY FORMER STUDENTS

whose work, unidentified, enters into these volumes

INTRODUCTION

To give a clear view of all the forces shaping the attitudes and activities of any generation, a complete survey of the entire institutional structure of the society of that period would be required; for all institutions and social activities conduce to shape the ideals and ideas of the youth of the times. The present volume has no such ambitious aim. It explains the more commonplace idea of education as a school process, and aims to give an idea of the general laws and local regulations creating social institutions which establish educational customs and conventional standards. The conventional standards of that period, however, are not the conventional standards of the present: some institutions then bulked largely that have since disappeared. Such was the apprentice system.

Even the very restricted standard of a single colony is so complex that only an outline can be presented. The text reproduces at times only a very sketchy account. No attempt is made to go into detail.

However, one other attempt is made. The writing of the text involved the examination of a vast amount of documentary evidence, much of which is not readily accessible. It seemed fair to assume that many students would be interested in an examination of this material; so an effort has been made in a second volume, *Readings in the Founding of the American Public School System,* to present enough of the quotations from this mass of documentary evidence to illustrate at least all the major conclusions made by the author.

Then a further difficulty presented itself. Even this collection made a more extensive mass of material than many students would have the time to use. Consequently both the textbook and the source book have been limited in extent, and the source material issued by a new mode of publication—microfilm.

The use of microfilm as an aid to research is not new. To date,

INTRODUCTION

however, its use as an alternative to printing has been restricted, and as far as can be discovered, the present instance is the first in which the two processes have both been used in the original publication of a single work. The film copy furnished as Volume Two is a positive microfilm on 35 mm safety base, made from a negative kept on file. The author's manuscript is used as a photographic copy.

Most of the American libraries which serve research students are already equipped with the relatively inexpensive "readers" required for the use of microfilmed material. These readers are simple to operate, and the projected image is sufficiently large and clear to make reading easy.

While the problems of microfilm production have been largely solved, the problems of distribution are only now being studied. In the present instance, the filmed material has been made immediately available by depositing copies of it in strategically located libraries which already possess facilities for its use. A list of these libraries is appended.

Educational Institutions

Arkansas
    University of Arkansas

California
    Stanford University
    University of California at Berkeley
    University of California at Los Angeles

Canada
    University of Toronto

Connecticut
    Yale University

District of Columbia
    Catholic University of America
    Howard University

INTRODUCTION

Illinois
    Illinois State Normal University
    Northwestern University
    University of Chicago
    University of Illinois
    Western Illinois State Teachers College

Indiana
    Ball State Teachers College

Iowa
    State University of Iowa

Kansas
    University of Kansas

Kentucky
    Eastern Kentucky State Teachers College
    Western Kentucky State Teachers College

Maryland
    Johns Hopkins University

Massachusetts
    Clark University
    Harvard University
    Massachusetts Institute of Technology
    Smith College
    Wellesley College

Michigan
    Michigan State Normal College

Minnesota
    State Teachers College, St. Cloud
    University of Minnesota

Missouri
    Central Missouri State Teachers College
    Northeast Missouri State Teachers College
    University of Missouri

Nebraska
    Nebraska State Teachers College
    University of Nebraska

INTRODUCTION

New Jersey
    New Jersey State Teachers College, Montclair
    Princeton University

New York
    Cornell University
    New York University
    Teachers College, Columbia University
    Vassar College

North Carolina
    East Carolina Teachers College

Ohio
    Ohio University

Oklahoma
    East Central State Teachers College

Pennsylvania
    University of Pennsylvania

Rhode Island
    Brown University

Tennessee
    Joint University Libraries, Nashville

Texas
    North Texas State Teachers College
    University of Texas

Virginia
    Hampton Institute
    State Teachers College, Farmville

Washington
    University of Washington

Wisconsin
    State Teachers College, Milwaukee
    University of Wisconsin

INTRODUCTION

Public Libraries

Colorado
 Public Library, Denver

Georgia
 Carnegie Library, Atlanta

Iowa
 Public Library, Des Moines

Maryland
 Enoch Pratt Free Library, Baltimore

Massachusetts
 Public Library, Boston

New York
 Public Library, New York
 Public Library, Rochester

Pennsylvania
 Carnegie Library, Pittsburgh
 Free Library, Philadelphia

Texas
 Public Library, Houston

Other libraries or individuals may purchase microfilm copies, or secure further information, from University Microfilms, 313 North First Street, Ann Arbor, Michigan.

Paul Monroe

CONTENTS

	PAGE
INTRODUCTION	vii

PART I. EDUCATION UNIVERSALIZED

CHAPTER
- I. EUROPEAN ANTECEDENTS OF AMERICAN EDUCATION . . 3
- II. APPRENTICE EDUCATION IN THE COLONIES 34
- III. THE ENGLISH SCHEME OF EDUCATION IN VIRGINIA AND THE SOUTH 53
- IV. THE CHURCH-STATE SCHOOL SYSTEM OF THE MIDDLE COLONIES 69
- V. THE TOWN SCHOOLS OF NEW ENGLAND 105
- VI. THE LATIN GRAMMAR SCHOOL, AND SECONDARY EDUCATION IN THE COLONIES 136
- VII. THE COLONIAL COLLEGE 165

PART II. THE EARLY NATIONAL PERIOD TO THE CLOSE OF THE CIVIL WAR

EDUCATION NATIONALIZED, DEMOCRATIZED, AND MADE FREE

- VIII. EDUCATION NATIONALIZED 185
- IX. EDUCATION NATIONALIZED. DEVELOPMENT OF SCHOOL SYSTEMS FROM 1830 TO THE CIVIL WAR 222
- X. EDUCATION MADE FREE 295
- XI. EDUCATION DEMOCRATIZED THROUGH ORGANIZATION, METHOD, AND CURRICULUM 338

CONTENTS

CHAPTER	PAGE
XII. Secondary Education, the Dominance of the Academy and the Rise of the High School	390
XIII. Higher Education	420
XIV. The Education of Girls and Women	445
XV. The Teaching Profession	482
Index	509

PART I

EDUCATION UNIVERSALIZED

Chapter I

EUROPEAN ANTECEDENTS OF AMERICAN EDUCATION

Character of the Colonists and of the Colonial Period.— The men and women who founded Colonial America were cast in heroic mold. Their education was not primarily the education of the school. Their training was in the world: in the church, on the sea, in the ships, on the land. Their generation had inherited two dominant ideas and two great forces of recent origin. These were the Renaissance and the Reformation.

To the sixteenth and seventeenth centuries had been revealed "a new heaven and a new earth." Copernicus had laid bare the design of an infinite starry universe, now no longer a mere shell to cover the earth. Tycho Brahe had calculated the movements of the heavenly bodies, and declared a mechanism beyond the imagination of man. Kepler had formulated the principles according to which the planets move, and had given a new conception of physical law. The telescope invented in 1610 revealed a new heaven; the microscope, invented two years earlier, revealed a new earth. Columbus, Vespucci, the Cabots, had found a new world; Da Gama, Magellan, Frobisher had taken it from the speculations of philosophers and the dreams of poets and fixed it in the scheme of realities.

To these men and women of the sixteenth century came also a new revelation. To the hardy Protestants of the North, who approached the divine through reason and the suppression of the emotions, the papacy appeared as the "great beast" of the Apocalypse. To the adherents of the erstwhile universal church, who approached the divine through authoritative representatives who alone could administer the sacrament, no vision of the Seer could sufficiently characterize the sinfulness of those who rebelled against the mother church. Both sides had the courage of their convictions and the cruelty born of the hardness of their everyday life. One is in turn aroused to admiration by their unsurpassed fortitude and shocked beyond measure by their acts of cruelty committed in the name of religion. The Elizabethan explorers may be considered pirates or Christian knights, empire-builders or ravaging freebooters, with equal show of evidence. Of their manhood, their faith in God, their loyalty to King or Queen, there could be no question. They hewed out empires with a handful of men, and sailed the seas in pygmy vessels which could be dropped into the hatchways of a modern transatlantic liner and lost like a pebble in a well. When Sir Humphrey Gilbert, conquered only by the tempestuous Atlantic seas in his "frigate" of ten tons, was besought by his devoted followers to seek the refuge of the "great ship" of forty tons—little larger than a lifeboat of a modern liner—he replied, "Heaven is as near by sea as by land." The last glimpse of the gallant knight—whose fortune and life were devoted to the expansion of knowledge for his fellowmen and of territory and power for his Queen—showed him seated in the stern of his little vessel "reading a book."

But the education of the book was a small part of the schooling of these generations of colonizers. Behind the leaders were the mass of their followers. Leaders and men were sometimes charmed by the revelation of the "wealth of Ormuz and of Ind," sometimes by the promise of release from the restrictions at home. The movable Western frontier has ever proved a safety valve for the mechanism of Anglo-Saxon society. The education of books made no widespread appeal to this age of action and of opportunity. Literary education was the accomplishment of a gentleman, the professional equipment of a churchman. Education for the people must be of sterner stuff. For the leader it was the education of activity,—of the world. For the masses it was an education through industry, or the everyday activities of life as organized into institutions—the shop, the smithy, the office, the farm, the coach, or the sailing vessel. Intellectual insight and spiritual leadership were due from the church. It is true that some had begun to say that the people had in reality been deprived of this insight and leadership because of their inability to read the Scriptures themselves. These malcontents began an insistent demand for a new type of education for the masses—that of books. In England they were but a handful, for the most part Puritans. Those of Scotland and the Protestant lands of the Continent who agreed with them were more numerous or at least more powerful. For in these lands they were in control and shaped the education of the people while the Puritans of England were able to do so for less than a score of years.

It was a select lot of these men and women of the early seventeenth century, inheriting the traditions and aspirations of one of the most glorious periods in English history, who severed the ties with the home land and ventured into an unknown country, the domain of savage tribes. They were moved by a variety of motives; in few indeed was there a singleness of purpose. All perhaps shared to some slight extent in the highest purposes and in the most worldly. The savages themselves had a place in these plans, for there was an abiding hope of the conversion of the natives in the minds of the early colonists. A new route to the old Indies still beckoned. No one was entirely proof against the lure of easy wealth of gold and spices and fur and land. Freedom of opportunity, freedom from the harsh economic restrictions of home conditions appealed to all; freedom of religion appealed to some. The spirit of adventure moved in all; and the earliest organized colonization was by the "merchant adventurers." Whatever their motives for coming, from whatever land or whatever stratum of society they came, these men and women continued to act and think regarding the fundamentals of life in America much as they did at home. Such individual habits of thinking and acting become what we call the institution of society. So this period of colonization is but the time when European institutions were transplanted to American soil. Here, during the century and a half of the Colonial period, they were slowly modified by the stress of new conditions. Among these institutions our special interest lies in those we term educational.

To understand at all the educational ideas and customs of later times, or even of the Colonial period, it is necessary to see in general outline the educational institutions which are brought over. Hence our first problem is the study of the educational ideas and customs

FOUNDING OF AMERICAN SCHOOL SYSTEM

of that period in England, and to a lesser extent those of other peoples, which influenced American Colonial life.

The Question of the Origin of the American School.— The question whether American education had its source in England or in Holland has frequently been discussed. The chief difficulty in conceding an English origin lies in the fact that England had no system of state-supported schools and had enacted no laws whatever on the subject of literary education for the masses. This statement concerning the indifference of the English government to education is quite true. It may even be claimed that during this period the English people felt little interest in education, except as it related to the small favored class in society. Within this group social pride and the prevalence of class privilege were supposed to supply sufficient motive, and education was left to the care of individual effort alone. Nevertheless it may also be true that the institutional germs from which American educational ideals and the American school system developed were, for the most part, of English origin.

A comparison of conditions in England with the conduct of the colonists shows: First, that the dominant attitude in most of the colonies was that of English society, a disbelief in governmental action regarding schooling for the masses and a general dependence on individual initiative and effort for the education of the selected few who were to be leaders. Second, the education provided for the great mass of the people was to be social or moral and vocational, secured through the apprentice system. Though similar systems existed in other European countries, this working principle came to America direct from England. Third, in addition to these two principles, the Puritans of New England brought with them the idea of state-supported schools for every community and for every child. This ideal was common to all the Calvinistic branches of the Protestant church. The Puritans shared it with the Reformed church of Scotland, of the Netherlands, of the German Rhine States, and of the Swiss in Geneva. The idea was quite as much English as it was Dutch or Scottish, only there had been no opportunity for the Puritans to act on it in England. It was in order to work out

[6]

this and related ideas that they came to America. This educational idea belonged to no nation. It belonged to a religious group or sect and was rooted in fundamental religious and moral and political principles.

The basis for these views is now to be sought in English custom.

The Apprentice System.—This system was common to all countries of Western Europe. It was an outgrowth of the late Middle Ages, which organized so many of the institutions fundamental to modern society. While the apprentice system was primarily economic in character and grew up with the handicraft system of industry, then universal, its social, moral, and educational aspects were quite as real and quite as important.

In the form into which it had developed at the time of the settlement of the American Colonies, it had long been established by statute. This law provided that no one could enter into industry, trade, or even agriculture, without a preliminary period of service of from three to ten years, during which time the apprentice must serve his master without remuneration. In return his master must give him food, clothing, and lodging, must teach him his trade or mystery, and must be responsible for his moral conduct and training.

The English statutes of artificers, apprentices, or labor, as they are variously called, go back to Edward III, following the Black Death of the middle fourteenth century. The system was finally formulated for the generation of the colonists by a Statute of Queen Elizabeth (5th of Eliz. Ch. IV. See Quotation 1) in 1562.

This statute had many provisions, among which the following are of significance for our study. The fundamental feature was that every person entering into industry or not possessing an independent income should pass through seven years of apprentice training. The exact wording of the statute is "it shall not be lawful to any person or persons . . . to set up, occupy, use or exercise any craft, mystery, or occupation within the realm of England or Wales except he shall have been brought up therein seven years at least as an apprentice." This had been a custom in England for many generations, but a custom which had many local variations. After 1562 these variations were removed and the custom became uniform throughout the country, on the basis of the customs prevalent among the London gilds. Each of these gilds was an organization of all master workmen engaged in a certain handicraft in a given town or locality. Under the master were journeymen and apprentices. The journeymen were those who had passed through the apprentice stage and now worked for wages. The apprentices were the youth under twenty-four or twenty-one who served without wage. On the continent the custom of requiring all apprentices to serve

FIG. 1. A European portrayal of the apprentice system. A master cordwainer with journeyman and two apprentices. (From *Album Historique*, Vol. III, p. 125.)

as journeymen before they could become master workmen was fixed. In England this regulation never became binding, but the workman who had served his apprenticeship might become a master by purchase or by inheritance.

During this seven or more years the apprentice must serve his master faithfully and industriously, obey his order, and commit no infringement of moral or civil law or of decency. In return the master was to furnish food, clothing, and shelter, to teach him the art or mystery of the craft, and to equip him at the expiration of the

EUROPEAN ANTECEDENTS

term of service with two new suits of apparel, one for work days, one for Sunday. In practice the apprentice became a member of his master's family, serving him without pay for seven or more years in return for his maintenance and his industrial or vocational education. The same system applied to husbandry or farming. By the Statute of Artificers all persons not engaged in any other art, craft, or mystery, and not of independent income were compelled to serve in husbandry.

The same general regulations applied to all engaged in trade and commerce. Naturally the merchant gilds were much stronger and wealthier than the craft gilds and exercised greater social, political, and financial power. But since the chief and at times the only entrance into the freemanship of the city was through the gilds, either craft or merchant, these organizations became an essential part of the political and social structure. The gilds also constituted the foundation of local government, since the franchise for municipal and indirectly for national government was thus obtained.

The educational significance of this custom of apprenticeship is further indicated by the fact that youth of the wealthier classes were frequently educated under the same system. This was particularly true of the entire merchant class. Sir Thomas Gresham, one of the leading men of the sixteenth century, a merchant prince in a literal sense, thus writes of his own education, in a letter to the Duke of Northumberland.

> "I myself was bound prentisse VIII years, to come by the experience and knowledge that I have. Nevertheless I need not to have been prentisse, for that I was free by my father's coppy; albeit my father, Sir Richard Gresham, being a wise man, knew, although I was free by his coppy, it was to no purpose, except I were bound prentisse to the same whereby to come by the experience and knowledge of all kinds of merchandise."

The English Poor Law and the Machinery of School Support.—In the rural regions of almost any American commonwealth there will be found even yet some connection between school authorities and authorities having charge of poor relief. In a number of states these local officials are identical. Some further inquiry into the early school customs of almost any of the states east of the Mississippi River will reveal a time when schools which charged no fee for tuition were called charity schools. Even now there is a popular prejudice in many regions against public free schools on the ground that they are only for the poorer classes of the people.

The origin of this situation is found in sixteenth century English local government procedure. Here was worked out a system of public taxation for the support of the poor, which was later applied to the schools. It will be found that the earlier forms of free education were for indigent children, and were paid for from the funds raised for the relief of the poor. Later, the first use of public taxation for the support of education was to raise funds to provide for the tuition of poor children. In many of the communities the forerunner of state systems of free public education was the free tuition of those who could not afford to pay. This is the historical connection between education and poor relief. This relation indicates the chief reason why English poor law procedure should be considered an educational precedent.

The Protestant Reformation in England swept away the system of monasteries and chantry foundations, and limited and weakened if it did not destroy the social and industrial gilds or labor organizations. The monasteries were religious orders owing direct allegiance to the papacy and hence formed an obstacle to the development of a national church. Chantry foundations provided, among other things, for prayers for the souls of the dead and therefore were considered superstitious institutions which were to be suppressed. Gilds usually had chantry foundations or foundations for priests connected with them, and thus added the accusation of superstition to the economic and political considerations which aroused the opposition of the government. All of these organizations had distinct educational influences. The larger monasteries usually sheltered schools, many of them for children not destined for the orders. Many chantry priests had to teach schools by a provision of their foundation. Practically all gilds had funds for

EUROPEAN ANTECEDENTS

the education or apprenticeship of children of their members. Many of them supported schoolmasters. All of them also made provision for the relief of poverty.

These institutions were swept away by Henry VIII in his laws of 1535 and 1537 and by Edward VI in 1547. There were many reasons, real and assigned, for the suppression of these institutions and many forces were at work resulting in the various destructive and constructive acts. They may all be summed up in terms of the Reformation movement in religion and the growing sense of nationalism in politics. The monastic orders owed their allegiance directly to the pope and hence hindered the development of a national church. They were accused of many abuses, justly in some cases, unjustly in others. The great variety of ecclesiastical foundations had tied up a large part of the property of the kingdom and exempted it from bearing its share of the national support. Forms of worship and religious ideas no longer held by great masses of the people were bound up in these foundations. Suppression and reorganization were the means chosen. The poor laws of Queen Elizabeth's reign effected a reorganization of those activities of the old ecclesiastical institutions which related to the relief of the indigent and the helping of the inefficient classes of society. As the apprentice laws provided for the organization and education of the self-supporting portion of the masses of the people, so did the poor laws supply the organization and education of those not capable of self-support.

Among the provisions of the poor law there were several features which had educational significance. Since it was customary for a master to charge a substantial fee, usually about five pounds, for receiving an apprentice, the law provided for the payment of that sum from the poor funds in cases of the parents' inability. Thus the poor law became a scheme of taxation to secure the education of the poor. In a similar way these laws authorized the poor relief authorities to expend funds to give the poor an industrial training. The quaint phraseology of the statutes of 1597 and 1601 runs, "A convenient stock of flax, hemp, wool, thread, iron, and other necessary ware and stuff to set the poor on work." This is the origin of

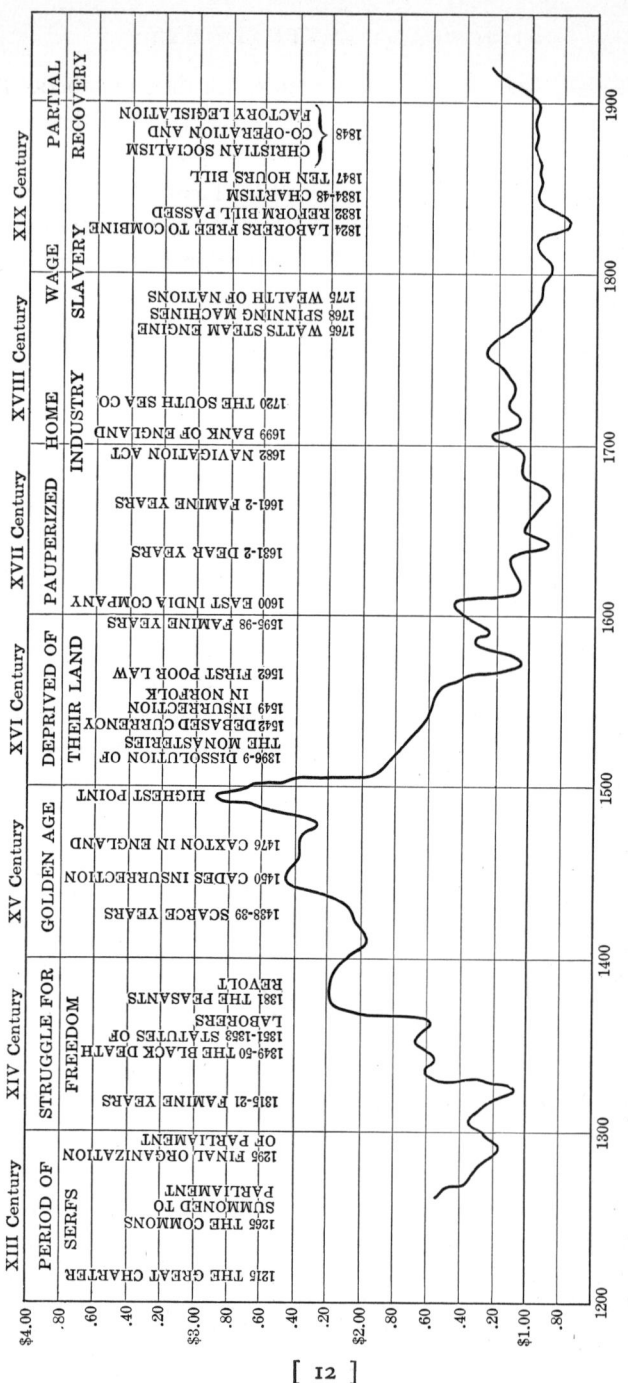

CHART I. Wages of an English carpenter compared with cost of living. 13th to 19th centuries. (Based on Roger, *Work and Wages*.)

EUROPEAN ANTECEDENTS

the workhouse school still prevalent in Great Britain. While this provision long persisted, it was probably not taken very seriously in most places. Yet the quaint wording of the provision reappears over and over again in American Colonial statutes.

The main provision of the poor laws which had educational significance was the financial one. By a statute of Edward VI (1553, Doc. 2) two collectors were to be appointed in every parish to solicit alms for the poor. In 1562 a statute of Elizabeth (Doc. 3), which was a complement of the Statute of Artificers and was passed at the same time, provided that those persons able to contribute but unwilling to do so were to be summoned before the Justices of the Quarter Sessions. Here they must submit to a tax or be imprisoned. By a somewhat euphemistic use of terms this was called a "voluntary contribution." Justices were also given power either to levy an assessment to provide for the poor or to license them to beg. In 1597 (Quo. 4) the justices were "to raise weekly or otherwise, by taxation of every inhabitant," sums for the education and the relief of the poor. Poor relief officers, constituted of church wardens and overseers of the poor, were authorized to apprentice out all children who could not be cared for and educated vocationally by their parents. In 1601 the justices were required to levy such tax annually as well as to make provision for the care of the poor and the vocational education of their children.

The generation that saw the culmination of this far-reaching Elizabethan social policy was the same that founded Jamestown, Plymouth, Salem, and Boston. From the time of Elizabeth to that of Victoria, these two statutes constituted the foundation of English social policy.

The English Government and Education.—The German, Dutch, and French Protestant governments of the sixteenth and seventeenth centuries fostered education as they did the Reformed church. It is, therefore, surprising to find that the English government did practically nothing in the way of direct encouragement to education during this long period covering the American Colonial period. Protective acts by way of prohibition were more numerous. These facts reveal the attitude maintained by the English until near the close of the nineteenth century—that literary education is a matter of concern to the individual only.

The chantry suppression acts under Edward VI specified that grammar schools were to be refounded out of the escheated funds. But far more were destroyed than were founded. The Artificers Act of 1562 provided that scholars in universities and schools should be exempt from its provisions. In 1558 all schools were exempted from paying tithes—the tenth part of their revenues due to the crown from ecclesiastical foundations on specified occasions. Schoolmasters were ordinarily freed from taxation. In subsequent acts suppressing ecclesiastical foundations (1558), schools were specifically exempted. A new body,—commissioners for charitable uses,—was created and placed in authority over all of the endowed schools, and endowed schools constituted practically the entire school system. However, through the courts of appeal these foundations were gradually perverted and in time came to be of use chiefly to the wealthier classes.

The Commonwealth passed an act in 1649 that had educational significance for Wales but not for England. This statute gave schoolmasters a share in the revenues of the national church. By the same act these revenues were to be augmented by funds from the gross income of the government. This would have constituted direct taxation for the support of education. While this statute is significant in revealing the attitude of the English Puritans towards education, there is no evidence that any such sums were ever appropriated or that the act had any practical influence.

The restored Stuart monarch was responsible for many repressive and reactionary statutes relating to schools and schoolmasters. But as these were not enforced in America and came not only after the establishment of English institutions in America but after the great influx of English to the Colonies had ceased, they concern us but slightly here. The traditions, institutions, and laws brought over were largely those of an earlier period. An early act of Charles (1662) was repeated through subsequent reigns. It required that every schoolmaster should take the oath of allegiance to the monarch and should subscribe to a declaration that he would conform to the confession of faith and to the liturgy of the established church. The one educational principle of this period which was of significance was that education should be under the control of the church.

The English Church and Education.—According to the views of today even the interest of the church would appear very limited. Schoolmasters should be orthodox in religion, moral in

FIG. 2. Catechetical instruction in a Protestant church. (From a 17th century woodcut.)

conduct, loyal in politics. Schools should be supported in connection with cathedral and collegiate churches, and where private bequests had provided an endowment for the support of a schoolmaster and perhaps of his pupils. Such schools were numerous enough to recruit the clergy and to afford opportunity to ambitious boys. From such would be selected the rulers in church and state. Government, however, was the function of the ruling class, and families of the ruling class could see to the education of their own children if they so desired. There was no widespread belief in the need and

[15]

FOUNDING OF AMERICAN SCHOOL SYSTEM

the virtue of a literary education for the people, as in Scotland, and no enlightened policy of the ruling class, as with the Dutch and German states. Rare indeed was the enlightened theorist of education or of society who, like Mulcaster, believed in the education of the masses in the vernacular.

Under each monarch a council of the church was convened to formulate its constitution and canons which contained the provi-

FIG. 3. Catechetical instruction in a Roman Catholic church. (From a 16th century woodcut.)

sion concerning education. From Mary to the Commonwealth these scarcely varied. The essential one was that "No man shall teach either in public school or private house but such as shall be allowed by the Bishop of the Diocese, or Ordinary of the place under his hand and seal." (Quo. 6.) This licensing by the church required an oath of loyalty to the reigning monarch and a sub-

[16]

scription to the articles of faith of the established church. Though modified by judicial decisions of the late seventeenth century and by lax enforcement throughout the eighteenth, this provision was

> ***Canons Ecclesiasticall.***
>
> calling, the Churchwardens of the Parish where they dwell shall present to the Bishop of the Diocesse, or to the Ordinarie of the place, hauing Episcopall Iurisdiction.
>
> ¶ **Schoolemasters.**
>
> LXXVII.
>
> *None to teach Schoole without Licence.*
>
> NO man shall teach either in publike Schoole, or priuate house, but such as shall bee allowed by the Bishop of the Diocesse, or Ordinary of the place vnder his Hand and Seale, being found meete aswell for his learning & dexteritie in teaching, as for sober and honest conuersation, and also for right vnderstanding of Gods true Religion, and also except he shal first subscribe to the first and third Articles aforementioned simply, and to the two first clauses of the second Article.

FIG. 4. Regulations from the Constitution and Canons of the English Church adopted 1604.

legally valid throughout the Colonial period and applied to the royal Colonies in America. Additional canonical provisions secured a monopoly of teaching to minor church officials when they desired

[17]

to exercise this claim, and required the use of an orthodox Latin grammar, that of Henry VIII. The schoolmaster's creed of the time is therefore said to have been one catechism, one grammar, one ferule for all.

Under these general constitutions of the church, various archbishops and bishops revealed a varying interest in the work of the schools. Many of these formulated "articles of visitation" which showed keen and intelligent purposes in education. The injunctions which often followed such visitations sometimes manifested a determination to enforce a broad and enlightened educational policy. The vast majority of the churchmen, however, did not go beyond the perfunctory enforcement of the provisions made in the foundations. In these various provisions it is obvious that zeal for the established church, whether it be Roman Catholic, Episcopal, Presbyterian, or Separatist, was the determining motive. Education was a handmaid to religion, rather than of value for itself.

Attitude of the Ruling Class towards Education Is Revealed in These Laws Provided for the Lower Classes.—The forty shillings income, above which the Statute of Artificers did not apply, marks the boundary of economic independenec. To all children of a family having less than forty shillings income the law did apply and secured their education. The inference of English law and custom was that all persons receiving this income should have sufficient means and sufficient motive to give their children the education demanded by their class. If not so situated they would fall below the standard of the law and come under the apprentice regulation. The education demanded by those of independent means was chiefly social, moral, and economic and was given for the most part by tutors. Schools offered literary education to the few who for professional reasons demanded it. Such schools were sufficient in number and were provided with adequate funds to make sure that every boy who had the ability and who desired this peculiar limited type of education might gain it. All of these forms of education for the higher classes were special and did not need the attention of the government or legal control. The individualism of the English people held in practice as well as in theory that all

EUROPEAN ANTECEDENTS

such affairs should be left to the choice and the initiative of each person concerned.

The entire philosophy of society and of education is expressed in a few sentences by a writer on education of this period:

> "In a free nation where slaves are not allowed of, the surest wealth consists in a multitude of laborious poor; for that they are the never failing nursery of fleets and armies, without them there could be no enjoyment and no product of any country could be valuable. To make the society happy and people easy under the meanest circumstances, it is requisite that great numbers of them should be ignorant as well as poor. Knowledge both enlarges and multiplies our desires. . . . Reading, writing, and arithmetic are very necessary to those whose business requires such qualifications; but where peoples livelihood has no dependence on these arts, they are very pernicious to the poor, who are forced to get their daily bread by their daily labor. . . . Reading and writing I would treat as we do music and dancing, I would not hinder them, nor force them upon society; as long as there was anything to be got by them, there would be masters enough to teach them; but nothing should be taught for nothing but at church." [1]

Perhaps these views are somewhat more frankly even cynically stated than would have been by many, but Mandeville gave clearly the working theory of his times and the views of the dominant ruling class of the latter half of the seventeenth century and all of the eighteenth.

Higher Schools.—To the Englishman of the seventeenth and eighteenth centuries, as to all people of those centuries, the really essential parts of an educational system were the Latin grammar school and the university. Elementary schools were necessary to give a brief preparation for the study of Latin, to train boys to assist in church service and perhaps even to teach writing and reckoning for business. This latter training, however, was given chiefly in the shop itself; to a less extent in private "writing schools." Education was not essentially a matter of the schools; training for the professions was. The Englishman of the sixteenth and seventeenth

---

[1] Mandeville, *Fable of the Bees*, vol. 1, 328–29 (Ed. of 1724).

centuries no more thought of the education of the masses as connected with schools and with literary training than we now think of it as connected with vocational training in handicrafts and merchandise. But the Englishmen of that time did think of education for the masses wholly in terms of the handicraft or vocational training, while we today think of education wholly in terms of book learning. Schooling meant essentially the study of Latin as a preparation for the universities or for a profession, or as the proper attainment or polish of a gentleman. Latin grammar schools were therefore essential and existed in sufficient numbers to recruit all these professions as well as to afford the opportunity to any youth of sufficient ability and ambition to obtain the desired training.

A chronicler of Elizabeth's time wrote, "There are not many corporate towns now under the Queen's domain that hath not one grammar school at the least." Investigations have shown that during the early sixteenth century there were about 300 such schools in England, or one to about 8300 population. The survey made by Parliament in 1869 revealed one such school for every 23,000 population. So sixteenth century England was much better supplied with secondary schools than was nineteenth century England, and believed much more thoroughly in them.

For the select boys who went to them, these schools gave a complete schooling. *"Ludus Literarius* or the Grammar School, showing how to proceed from the first entrance into learning to the highest perfection required in grammar schools,"[1] is the title to one of the best books of the period on the work of these schools. The title in itself indicates the scope of this work.

Into these schools boys entered at the age of six to nine and remained until sixteen or seventeen, when they were ready for the university. There was one dominant subject—Latin. In addition, Greek—sometimes some Hebrew also—was taught. In the first year there was perhaps enough vernacular to assist in beginning Latin. To this was added religious instruction. One of the characters of Brinsley's book mentioned above complains, "you shall have scholars, almost ready to go to the university, who yet can hardly

[1] By John Brinsley, published 1612.

EUROPEAN ANTECEDENTS

tell you the number of the pages, sections, chapters or other divisions of their books, to find what they should." "You shall find few good writers in grammar schools, unless either they have been taught by scriveners or be themselves marvelously apt hereunto and very apt." But they could converse—poorly, no doubt—in Latin, could write Latin prose and compose doggerel verse. Even Brinsley questions the general use of Latin by the pupil and believes "that without great severity they will not be brought unto; but they will speak English and one will wink at another, if they be out of the master's hearing." The few who succeeded did make rare scholars; for such was "a grammarian, a philosopher, an historian, a stylist and a sage in one." Most fell into the conventional routine of the formalist who acquired sufficient knowledge to enter the universities or the professions and to mark him off from the great mass of the unlearned. From these the clergy, the public official with clerical duties, and the professions in general were recruited. The English universities, Oxford and Cambridge, during most of this period gave an education of no greater breadth or vitality than that of the grammar schools. During the latter half of the sixteenth and the first half of the seventeenth they were the seats of active linguistic studies and of theological investigations and controversies. During the latter half of the seventeenth and all of the eighteenth they lost even the interest and life of religious controversy. After the Restoration (1661) all dissenters were excluded, and this kept out the great middle class with its solid worth and intellectual progressiveness. They remained the hospitable home of the scholarly recluse, the training school of the clergy of the established church, and the pleasant abode of the gentry where social standing could be proclaimed, social polish acquired with the accomplishments or vices which would render tolerable a life of leisure. From the gentry were drawn those who carried on the affairs of state, as from the clergy were drawn those who gave force and reality to the work of the church. But in each case these were but a limited few of the entire body of students. Perhaps they were leaders through sheer force of native ability. But the universities did give the traditional training which in those cases made up in intensity and perfection of

FIG. 5. The great schoolroom in the Winchester Latin Grammar School. (From Ackerman, *Public Schools of England*.)

scholarship what it lacked in breadth. The universities were vital organs of the church and of the state and component parts of a formal and non-progressive society. They were not centers of a new intellectual life as was Leyden or later Göttingen or Edinburgh. Even in the late sixteenth century Bacon wrote of the university students: "They learn nothing there but to believe: first, to believe that others know that which they know not; and after, that themselves know that which they know not."

Nevertheless the influence of the English universities was profound; they reflected as well as directed the life and thought of their time. Englishmen of the ruling class believed in them with entire devotion; and the colonists shared this belief, only differing perhaps in regard to which church should control the schools.

Scotch Precedents.—The influence of the Scots on American political life and educational practices during the Colonial period has often been overlooked, because it was exerted in no one particular region. The Scots, constituting no inconsiderable portion of the Colonial population, were scattered throughout the colonies from Massachusetts to North Carolina. Large numbers of them had settled in the north of Ireland throughout the seventeenth century and the eighteenth century saw scores of thousands of these hardiest, thriftiest, and most independent subjects of the English monarch driven to the American Colonies through unjust and imbecile political and religious persecution. To these were added later numerous exiles from Scotland, deported because of chivalric loyalty to a lost political cause, or for more humdrum violation of civic ordinance. To these elements was added the irregular but continuous immigration motivated by desire of better worldly conditions, by love of adventure or change, by imitation or through personal ties.

Scotch migration to the Colonies was practically limited to the eighteenth century. For the two preceding centuries Scottish history finds its explanation quite as much in religious as in political activities and interests, its center quite as much in the church as in the state. But the conflict in Scotland had been settled and there as nowhere else had peculiar religious doctrine entered into the intellectual make-up of the people and determined their educational practices. The conflicts of the seventeenth and eighteenth centuries were those against restrictions from without on religious privileges. From the point of view of our study, in fact for all purposes of interpretation of American history, the Scots and the Scotch-Irish element may be considered a unit — Calvinist in theology, Presbyterian in polity.

The schools of Scotland preceding the Reformation resembled those of Holland more than those of England. In every city and large town there were grammar schools. The municipal authorities claimed and usually exercised the "patronage" of these, that is, the right to appoint the master; the church, as ever, reserved the right of "visitation" or supervision. An act of Parliament of 1496 enjoined "barons and freeholders that are of substance to put their eldest sons and heirs of nine years of age to remain at the grammar school until they be completely founded and have perfect Latin."

John Knox, the great reformer of Scotland, returned from his labors with Calvin at Geneva and issued the Book of Discipline of the Scottish Church (Quo. 19) in the same year that Calvin founded his academy. The fundamental tenet is the statement that "no father of what state or condition whatever he may be, may use his children at his own fantasy, especially in their youth, but all must be compelled to bring up their children in learning and virtue." Every church was commanded to have a schoolmaster and "if the town be of any reputation" one that could teach Latin. In every "notable town" there was to be a "college," or as we would say a secondary school, teaching the classics. Regarding the support of education, it was ordered that "the children of the poor must be sustained on the charge of the church till trial be taken whether the spirit of docility (teachableness) be found in them or not." But of the well-to-do it was specified "this they must do at their own expense, because they are able." But Knox's plan was not enacted into law by Parliament. Numerous subsequent acts of Parliament (Quos. 12–17) give to the church the right of visitation and, more important still, the right to certify all teachers. The cities or towns retained the control they had previously had over the "burgh" schools, subject to the visitation right mentioned above. But over

EUROPEAN ANTECEDENTS

the parochial schools the church was supreme. Various statutes of the seventeenth century (1616–96, Quo. 12) gave government sanction to this scheme and attempted to elaborate an adequate national system, but no general scheme of government support was worked out.

The contributions of the Scots to colonial American education were not those of administration or of state support, or of system. The great factors emphasized by this element in our population were the need of the universality of education; the significance of learning and intelligence for healthy political or religious conditions; the importance of individual effort; the willingness to make any sacrifice for education; the educational function of the ministry; the building up of schools under church or ministry, independent of state aid or control, and having no relation to any system; of superiority of education itself to any particular scheme of curriculum or method. The freedom declared in politics by the English element, in religion by the various dissenting bodies, was by the Scots declared in education.

Dutch Precedents.—These are of importance because the Dutch exerted an educational influence over the Puritans in England, as well as over the Pilgrims who settled Plymouth; and because they established a distinct type of school in their colony of New Amsterdam. The Dutch were then the leading commercial people of the world. Wealth, enterprise, knowledge, were concentrated in this little country, which, however, at this time had a population about equal to that of England. Its shadowy allegiance to the Holy Roman Empire along with the contested power of Spain had permitted a development of local or municipal freedom beyond that of any other country. This municipal freedom is to be sharply distinguished from the freedom of the individual citizen, the chief birthright of the Anglo-Saxon. Nowhere was this distinction more clearly revealed than in the settlement of New Amsterdam. The suzerain nobles were not powerful; the middle class burghers increased their rights. As the center of commerce of the world, and favorably situated with regard to the raw materials of all the great industries, the Netherlands developed a commercial

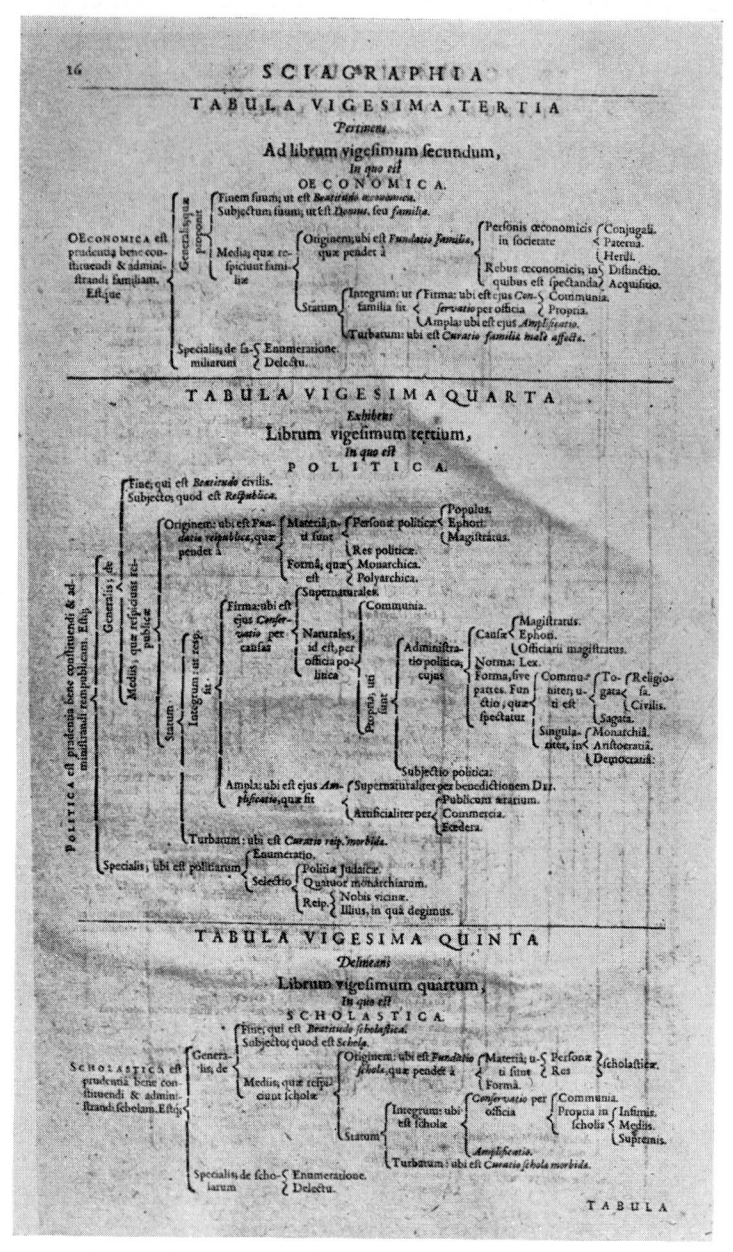

FIG. 6. Analysis of learning from the *Encyclopedia Universale* of Johann Heinrich Alsted. The *Encyclopedia* was the chief of his 120 works, published in the latter 16th and early 17th centuries.

EUROPEAN ANTECEDENTS

and industrial power and its burghers an intelligence, influence, and sturdy independence not equaled even in England.

The Netherlands were the home of the arts—of painting, of music, of architecture. Their painters revealed the national interest in home life and the importance of the burgher class. In general intelligence and education of the masses, probably no country in Europe equaled the Dutch part of the Netherlands. In higher learning also they were not surpassed. For a century after its founding in 1575 the University of Leyden stood at the head of all universities in its freedom of thought and in the influence it exerted. The origin of this university furnishes the best illustration of the esteem in which these people held learning. After a most heroic defense against the Spaniards, the government offered the citizens as a reward the choice between a university and exemption from taxation for a long term of years. Though impoverished beyond measure, they chose the university, to the everlasting honor of the city.

From the Netherlands came some of the most significant discoveries and inventions of this period,—the telescope, the microscope, the thermometer, the pendulum clock. Among her sons were the leading men of the age in science, in jurisprudence, and in general scholarship. Not only were the printing presses of the Netherlands the most numerous among all European countries, but among them were the most famous. The most influential man of letters of the preceding century—perhaps of all centuries—Erasmus,—was a Dutchman and was educated chiefly in Dutch schools. It is to be expected that such a people would exercise great influence in shaping the educational ideals and practices of a new people. At the least, a survey of Dutch educational customs is necessary to an understanding of the schools of the Dutch colony of New Netherland as well as of later conditions in New York. However, their influence on education in America has been greatly exaggerated.

It is often stated that even the Dutch peasants of this period could read and write; it is sometimes stated that there were practically none that could not do so. The latter is not true even in the present day, for Holland has a higher rate of illiteracy than several other countries. The former statement would make them quite superior to any other people of that period.

The Dutch population was more largely urban than that of any other country. Even those engaged in agriculture lived in villages. There was a large element of intelligent and highly skilled workmen in the various handicrafts, for the finest of wares in almost every line came from Holland. Commerce and trade have ever developed intelligence and a need for literary training, and Holland led the world in these lines.

Religious struggles had been fierce, keen, and cruel. A generation earlier this struggle had been settled in favor of the Protestants who now controlled the land, though they probably were as yet a minority of the population. The generation which settled New Netherland saw the great Synod of Dort (1618-19) which gave Holland to the Calvinists and settled the policy of her schools. As in England, the apprenticeship system prevailed and furnished to the great mass of the people a practical industrial or vocational training. The very high development of their industries and their trade indicates the effectiveness of this system. But the Dutch had a profound belief in the value and necessity of a literary education for the masses and insisted through their church organizations on a very general scheme of universal education.

During the two or three centuries preceding the departure of the Dutch colonists to America, a network of schools had grown up all over Holland. As the relationship of these to church and state varied from place to place, this congeries of schools can hardly be called a system. Many of them, especially the Latin grammar schools, were supported and controlled directly by the cities in which they existed. Many had been founded by municipal authorities. Some were under the control of local nobles or gentry or churchmen much like the "livings" in the Church of England. Some were schools of religious orders. Many, especially of the elementary class, were under the control of local churches or under joint control of local church and local government. Many of these elementary schools were private.

The interest in the schools and the responsibility for them were

EUROPEAN ANTECEDENTS

more evenly divided between the church and the government than in England, and the church was more independent of the state. A few words of explanation concerning the Dutch Reformed Church are necessary in order to explain the school system. Its organization was similar to that of the Presbyterian Church or of the Dutch Reformed Church in America today, with the very important exception of dependence upon the government. The local church was governed by a consistory of minister, elders, and deacons. As a rule these elders and deacons selected their successors or virtually did so. Hence the church was not a democracy. A group of local churches constituted a classis, and a number of classes a synod. A general or national synod included all the local synods.

The church had a very definite policy concerning schools, which it pursued and developed until its complete adoption at the Synod of Dort in 1619. This policy was designed to take the power of selecting and appointing the schoolmaster and of determining the curriculum and school procedure from the local government and to place it in the hands of the church; and to place on the local government the obligation of support. Such power was of very great significance for the church, enabling it to secure a more general religious attitude and knowledge and to develop or to preserve the orthodoxy of the people.

To the classis was given the power of examining and licensing and often of appointing the master; to the consistory the right of supervision if not of appointment. The Synod (of Dort) (Quo. 23) commanded that the schools should be established in all places, including country villages; that religious instruction be given in all schools; that only orthodox persons be allowed to teach; that the magistrates should support the schools; that children of the poor should be instructed free. The local government in many places did not agree with this policy; and for some years the conflict of the preceding century between church and local government for control of the schools was continued. But this was the policy adopted, and represented substantially the national policy. This was the system transplanted to America.

While there is no means of demonstration that such a system

was fully carried out, both probability and evidence would indicate that it was as well enforced as in any state system or any specific local law in the United States at the present time. At all events we may accept the statement that at this time educational opportunity was more general, achievement more common, and literacy more nearly universal in Holland than in any other country. The essential thing to note is that there was developed a public elementary school system, free to the poor, supported by the state, supervised by the church, with the possibility of variation to suit local needs and traditions.

To the Latin grammar school the Dutch showed as great devotion as did the English. The origin of many of these schools is lost in the obscurity of the Middle Ages. Among them were some which drew students from every European country. Being in the center of European teaching and travel, the home of the greatest intelligence and tolerance, some of these schools formed the intellectual vanguard in that age. They had been the home of the "new learning" of the Renaissance. Religious orders, chief among which was the famous "Brethren of the Common Life," had fostered the intellectual life and intellectual freedom. Many of these schools had been founded by princes or nobles of earlier centuries. By the time of American colonization practically all had passed into the hands of the cities, often after local contests with the church lasting through centuries. The conception, purpose, studies, and methods of these Latin schools did not differ from those of England and other European countries.

The Universities.—No part of the Dutch system of education was more famous or more influential during the seventeenth century than its universities. Previous to the period of their independence (about 1575), the Dutch had depended on the universities of other countries, chiefly Louvain—in Roman Catholic Netherlands—and Paris. Upon achieving their freedom and adopting Protestantism they determined to furnish their own higher education. The circumstances which led to the founding of the first of the Dutch universities have been mentioned. During the early years of national independence, these others were founded: Francker in 1586,

EUROPEAN ANTECEDENTS

Groningen in 1614, and Utrecht in 1636. These four well-endowed and flourishing institutions compare most favorably with the two conservative ones of England or those of any other country. Unhampered by tradition and inspired by their recent history and future opportunity, they gave color to the intellectual life of all Europe for this century. Especially did Leyden become the center of advanced research and free thought. After the Restoration, when Oxford and Cambridge were closed to all dissenters, the Dutch universities were most frequented. In all of them, but especially in Leyden, medical education and scientific investigation were more advanced than in any other country. Here lived and worked such scholars as Grotius, the great jurist; Scaliger, the great classicist; Spinoza, the philosopher; Descartes, the mathematician and philosopher; Arminius, the theologian, and many others whose names are not so familiar today, but whose work has greatly benefited mankind.

It is unquestionably true that in the Netherlands was centered the most advanced of the learning of the world for the greater part of the seventeenth century.

Calvin and the French Protestant Influence on Education.—No survey of the European antecedents of American education can be complete without a consideration of the influence of Calvinistic views. As a matter of fact the preceding survey of education antecedents in Holland, Scotland, and among the Puritans of England is really a study of the Calvinistic influence. Calvinistic ideas had intensified the earlier belief of these peoples in the value of education. But a brief description of the source of this influence is desirable. In the Calvinist scheme of thought there were fundamental social and political principles which give peculiar force and backing to their education ideas. The fundamental equality of all men appeared as a religious truth, to which the political application was secondary. The separation of church and state was proclaimed, but seldom practiced. Religious tolerance did not appear as a virtue, except when required of a hostile government. But the frequency and the virulence of such hostility led the Calvinists to justify the right of revolt as fundamental. In their thought education was essential; in the Calvinistic scheme of society schools were indispensable. To many men ignorance seemed the most secure basis of piety; to Calvin piety was based upon intelligence. Calvinists shared with most other branches of the church a belief in a learned ministry, since a knowledge of languages and of philology was the chief defense of revelation. But the Calvinists went beyond all other divisions of the church in holding that nothing should come between the individual and the source of religious truth—the Scriptures. Inability to read and to understand was therefore the chief source of impiety, irreligion, and heretical belief. Consequently the emphasis on education and schools was fundamental with all peoples among whom the Calvinistic faith predominated.

Calvin's own school system at Geneva never had the greatest success or influence. It was patterned largely after the far more famous one of Sturm at Strassburg. But it was through these Calvinistic centers of Geneva, Strassburg, Lausanne, Neuchatel, Frankfort, Leyden; through such leaders as Corderius, the textbook writer, Sturm the educational statesman, Ramus the university reformer, and Beza and the other university teachers, that the Calvinistic ideas concerning education were formulated and organized, and it was through the Calvinists in Scotland, Holland, and New England that these ideas were worked out. To the Genevan Academy founded in 1559 (Quo. 20) came students from England, Scotland, Netherlands, France, Germany, Switzerland, and Italy. From it went out the leaders of Calvinistic thought who were to carry the idea of universal education into all parts of the world. Advocates of this idea were to be found in several American colonies.

Under the academy belonged the elementary school (Quo. 16). Its essential feature was the Latin grammar school with its course of seven years. Above it was the school of theology, which was also a school of languages. After Calvin's death the schools of law and medicine were added. All of these were later organized into the University of Geneva. In this famous institution then were combined the three essential features of an educational system, the vernacular school for all, the Latin grammar school for the boys of ability, the university for the professional leaders of society.

EUROPEAN ANTECEDENTS

Summary.—The colonists of the seventeenth century brought with them the educational ideas and institutions of their home countries. The most fundamental of these were that education is primarily a training through the home, the industrial organization, and that schools with their literary education were for a selected class. The apprentice system of industry and trade together with the system of poor relief provided for the education of the masses. In England, the government did little for education beyond this. Connected with the church or on special foundations there were numerous schools, chiefly of secondary grade, and also the universities. Canons of the church required all schoolmasters to be licensed by church authorities. In Holland both church and state went further in the establishment of a system of elementary as well as of Latin schools. These the government supported and the church supervised. In Scotland a similar system was provided, though its development occurred chiefly during the seventeenth century and adequate support by the state came later. In all of these countries the underlying principles of Calvinism formulated the foundation of a system of schools in which state and church cooperated.

Chapter II

APPRENTICE EDUCATION IN THE COLONIES

Apprentice Education Fundamental.—Training through apprenticeship was the fundamental plan of education in all of the colonies during the seventeenth century. The conception of education which the colonists brought over and maintained for several generations was that education consists of a training in some handicraft or vocation through the relation of apprentice and master. Our forefathers would have found it difficult to think of education in terms of books alone, as our own generation finds it difficult to think of it in terms of vocational training. Reading and writing were desirable accomplishments to be added if possible and if the child was of a position in society where he would need them. To the Puritans and some other minor religious bodies, reading was essential for reasons of religion. But among the Puritans, as with all the colonists, education was far broader than literary instruction. Even literary instruction was provided much more generally through the apprentice relation than through the schools. The earlier educational laws in all the colonies related to apprenticeship.

Character of the Apprentice System.—The system of apprentice education is so simple that a few words of description will suffice. Children whose parents were able to give them a literary education, and whose wealth would keep them from want, were exempt. All other children must receive a training in some vocation. This training was secured by binding the youth as an apprentice to some master for a term of years. This period was usually seven years, though it must last until the boy was 21 or the girl 18. In agriculture the older English custom had required apprenticeship until 25. On the Continent the age might be 22 or 23. There were numerous variations of the custom. The apprentice was bound to serve his master for this period, without wage, in all the activities of the craft or industry and, within limits, in all other things as well. He was responsible solely to his master in all things instead of to his parents. On the other hand the master was responsible for the apprentice's technical education in the handicraft or trade or vocation, was obligated to furnish him a home and adequate food and clothing, and to train him in the industry so that at the end of the term of service the apprentice would become a self-supporting workman. In time the requirement was added that the master should teach him, or see that he be taught, to read and write. This general plan applied to such unorganized forms of labor as agriculture, shipping, and household service, to such commercial activities as merchandising, and even to the professional activities of lawyer, physician, and schoolmaster. In fact, long after the decline of the apprentice system of education in industry, it remained as a custom in the education of the lawyer and the physician, though the legal form of indenture was no longer retained. While the system of education is so simple that it calls for little description, it is important to notice the evidence of its fundamental character and its universality.

Origins of the Servant Class in the Colonies.—The indentured servant class in the Colonies was recruited from a variety of sources. The basal element was that furnished by the personal and household servants, the latter including all apprentices to masters in any handicraft or industry. This also constituted the largest element. But in addition journeymen workmen who came to the colony were usually bound out either to a master on contract, to a ship owner or adventurer for their passage, or to a trading company. All such were included in the servant class. In the rural regions, especially in the plantations of the South, the handicraftsmen as well as the laborers of the field were bound by agreement for a period of years and hence were servants. Even more important is it for us to note the sources of population from which these servants were drawn; for not all of them came from the working classes. Conditions in England during the seventeenth century favored the emigration of the laboring class. Great economic, social, and political changes were in progress. But the

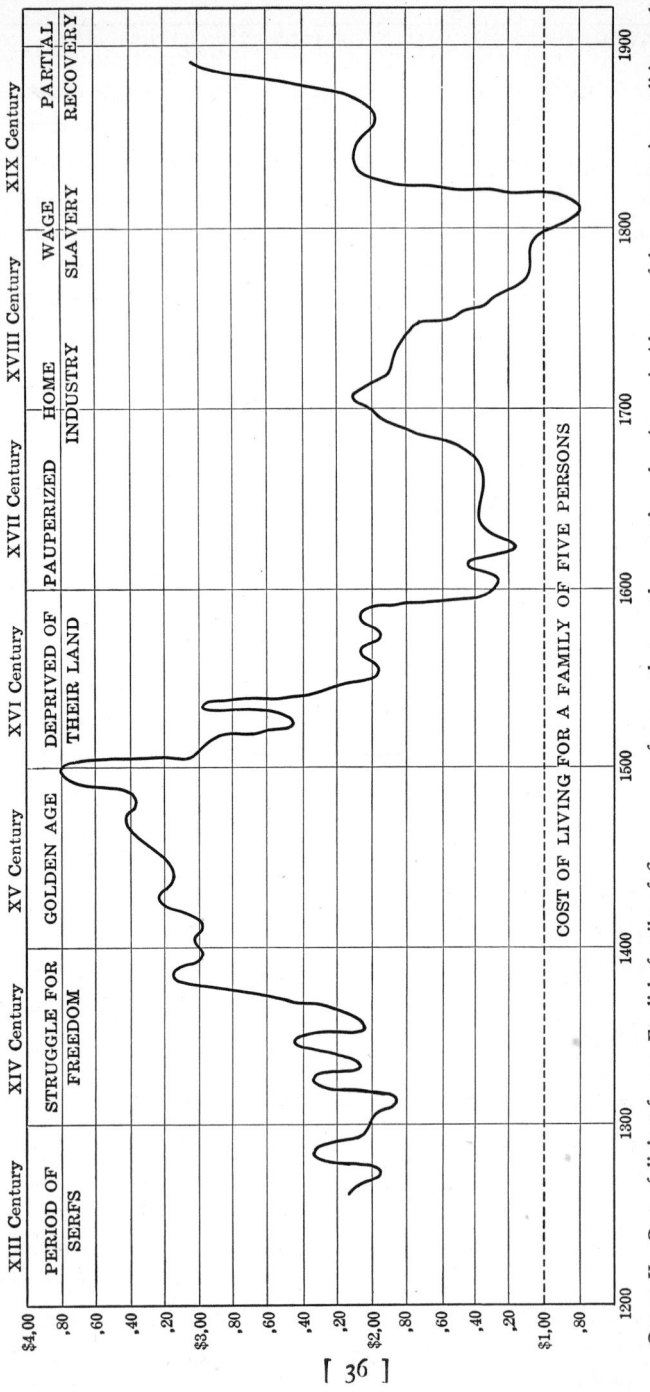

CHART II. Cost of living for an English family of five persons, from 13th to 19th centuries, showing coincidence of low economic conditions of early 17th century with period of colonization of America. (Based on Roger, *Work and Wages*.)

APPRENTICE EDUCATION IN COLONIES

advance in trade, commerce, and industry had made but slight improvement in the condition of the laboring classes. The apprenticeship system included all forms of labor and was applied to the handicrafts through the gilds. These gilds—both handicraft and merchant—exercised monopolies, kept up the price of commodities, and kept down the supply of labor. The poverty of the great masses was distressing. Unemployment was increasing. The wages of labor were at the bare subsistence point. Labor had few privileges and many restrictions. The laborer could not remove his place of residence without the consent of a justice of the peace. The economic theory of the day raised no objection to the migration of these unemployed and poverty-stricken laborers from the country while the political policy favored it. The virgin lands of America promised an abundant living—in a few years, freedom; in time, wealth.

One large element of the indentured servant class, and quite the most valuable one, was composed of those deported for political offense. These came at numerous periods. After the defeat of the Irish rebels by Cromwell's forces at Drogheda in 1649, all the officers, as well as every tenth private, were shot and the remainder were transported to America. During the following years numerous adherents of Charles II were in various ways transported to America. The tables were turned after the Restoration. By 1663 enough of Cromwell's followers were transported to Virginia to engage in a conspiracy to overthrow the government in Virginia and set up a commonwealth in its place.

During the eighteenth century the great stream of immigrants forced out by political oppression was added to the limited number actually deported. Among these the most numerous were the Scotch-Irish from the north of Ireland. Of these, though many were prosperous, many also went to swell the servant class. They went chiefly to the middle and Southern colonies.

A less desirable but large element consisted of deported criminals. Despite Colonial legislation against it, this type of immigration continued in several of the colonies quite up to the Revolutionary War. It is to be remembered, however, that during the seventeenth century there were one hundred crimes on the English statute books pun-

FOUNDING OF AMERICAN SCHOOL SYSTEM

ishable by death. Deportation was the only means at hand of tempering the severity of the law. Many of these offenses were trivial,—the burning of a hayrick or a third conviction for unauthorized begging. Criminals were deported to Virginia for offenses ranging from "preaching abroad" to piracy.

Abducted children formed a large portion of the indentured class. The "spiriting away" of children and even of adults was a recognized business during the seventeenth century. The "spirits" were a well-known class in London and other English seaports. In a petition of English merchants to Parliament it was stated that scarcely a vessel sailed for America without carrying a number of persons who were taken by force or who claimed to be so detained. In 1664 a government registrar was appointed who was to keep a record of every person who went out bound by terms of contract. It is significant of the spirit of the times that the chief reason for establishing this office was not because of the number abducted, but because of the constant frauds committed by those who claimed to have been "spirited" only after they had received clothing and food for a long period at the expense of the merchant adventurers.

This last term indicates another source of recruits for this class. The transporting of servants became a profitable part of the business of every shipowner and master. These men became regular brokers of servants. This was a recognized and reputable business on both sides of the Atlantic during the Colonial centuries. It is to be remembered in this connection that it was reputable on the part of the servant as well. Very few laborers of any standing came except under indenture. This was the customary way of paying for the ocean passage. Carpenters, tailors, and other handicraftsmen were frequently under bond of service for five or seven years. In other words, this class included journeymen as well as apprentices. Where rural rather than town life prevailed, journeymen merged into the servant class. One of the chief objections offered to negro slavery was that for every negro brought in one white servant was kept out.

John Harrower, a schoolmaster, who voluntarily sold himself into servitude to secure his passage, wrote in his diary: "This day several came on board to purchase servant indentures, and among them

[38]

APPRENTICE EDUCATION IN COLONIES

were two soul drivers. They are men who make a business to go on board all ships which have either servants or convicts and buy sometimes a parcel of them as they can agree, and then drive them through the country like a parcel of sheep until they can sell to advantage." (Quo. 84.) Harrower had previously recorded that there were seventy of this class on the vessel with him. This was in Virginia as late as 1774.

One other important source of Colonial servants was the English poor. These were not necessarily the undesirable and utterly ineffi-

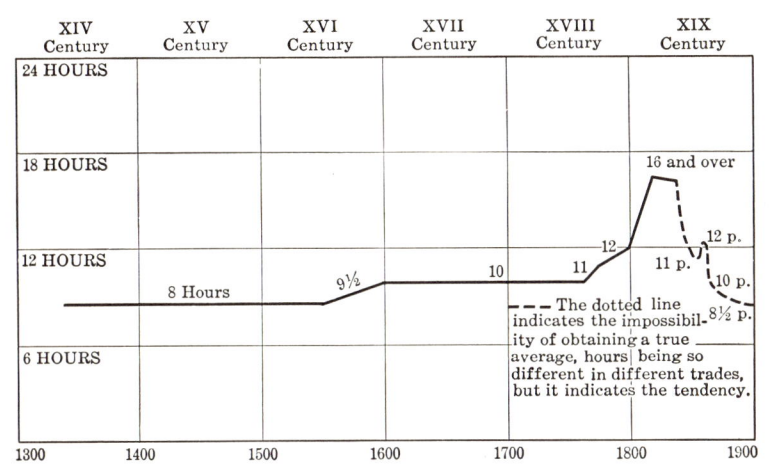

	XIV Century	XV Century	XVI Century	XVII Century	XVIII Century	XIX Century
24 HOURS						
18 HOURS						16 and over
12 HOURS		8 Hours	9½	10	12 — 11	11 p. 12 p. 10 p. 8½ p.
6 HOURS					— — — The dotted line indicates the impossibility of obtaining a true average, hours being so different in different trades, but it indicates the tendency.	
	1300	1400	1500	1600	1700	1800 1900

CHART III. Hours of labor of an English working man, 14th to 19th centuries. (Based on Roger, *Work and Wages*.)

cient and dependent paupers. The cost of living had greatly increased, especially during the seventeenth century, the price for necessities becoming quite fourfold. The influx of precious metals from America was one cause of this change. But the rate of wage was fixed by local government boards and had been changed but slightly. It was barely possible for the most industrious workmen to exist without governmental aid. Consequently when unemployment or irregularity of employment greatly increased, as it did during the seventeenth century, poverty and pauperism became appalling. The governing class of the time, which did not see the economic value of the working class to the home country, valued the Colonies highly if not chiefly as a source of relief from this class of unemployed or "paupers." In 1620 the Virginia Company appointed a committee to obtain from the justice of the peace of the various shires of England all those above fifteen years of age who were a burden to their families. In time, however, the colony turned against this policy, as it objected to the reception of "jail birds," as they were termed. But the policy of the home government often overrode that of the Colonies.

The Apprentice System in the Colonies.—The colonists brought with them not only the customs of Europe but also its laws. In the earliest stages the Colonies were merely commercial companies, existing under special charters or privileges but bound by home laws. Consequently general legislation was not necessary. Some of the earliest activities of the colonists indicate the existence of the apprentice system. The Virginia Company in London in 1609 forwarded to Virginia one hundred children who had been taken from the poor authorities of London. For each of them they received the customary five pounds (or marks). The same authorities paid for the indenture and education of each of these but drew the customary fee (five marks) which in this case paid the cost of transportation to the Colonies. Upon reaching Virginia a demand was found for the children and they were "bound" or "sold" to the planters. Thus, instead of making a payment to dispose of the apprentices, the Company received a sum. The transaction thus being found profitable, it was repeated in at least one additional shipment. While the Company itself did not continue this business, private parties, usually shipowners, did. To bring over such dependent children, as well as debtors, the unemployed, unfortunates, or undesirables who sought refuge from punishment for offenses, criminals deported usually for minor offenses—became a regular and profitable part of the shipping business. One of the earliest New England pamphlets argues against this custom, saying: "It seems to be a common and gross error that colonies ought to be emunctories or sinks of states, to drain away their filth." All such immigrants became indentured servants; and, if minors, subject to the educational provisions of the apprentice system.

APPRENTICE EDUCATION IN COLONIES

The early evidence in New England is found in the experience of the Salem colony in 1632. Among the early colonists were numerous servants of the Company. The winter proving extremely severe and the permanent hardships of frontier life burdensome, it seemed easier to throw the responsibility of livelihood directly upon the servants themselves. So they received their freedom and a share in the common land while the Company was relieved of its responsibility as master. There are numerous records in various towns of granting allotments of land to servants. A much larger proportion of the early colonists than we often realize were of this servant or indentured class even in New England. Most were adults and hence had no immediate connection with the educational policy. But their existence in such numbers is an evidence of the vitality of the apprentice system and of its continuance as an educational system for those who came under its provisions.

The lot of the apprentice and the indentured servant was much easier in America than in Europe. The inevitable hardships of frontier life, shared by master and servant alike, put all more nearly on a plane of equality. The opportunity for a livelihood where land was so abundant as to be had for the clearing and wealth was gained by farming or other manual work, ameliorated the condition of the servant class. These conditions gradually wore away the class distinctions which were to disappear entirely before the coming flood of new immigration of the early nineteenth century. The opportunities for this class of indentured servants and the improvement which so many were able to make in their fortunes are cited among the evidences of the Divine favor shown to New England. About 1650 Johnson, in his *Wonder-working Providence,* says, "There are many hundreds of laboring men who had not enough to bring them over, yet now worth scores and some hundreds of pounds."

Until the middle of the eighteenth century newspapers in all of the colonies continued to advertise indentured boys and girls as for sale. The *Boston News Letter* of 1746 advertises "a few servants indentured for seven years and girls for four years." The unexpired services of such indentured children were offered for sale like any

[41]

material article. The services of indentured schoolmasters were similarly offered. The document reproduced (p. 48) shows the indenture of a youth to a schoolmaster to be taught the "mystery" of teaching.

There are numerous records, especially in the Southern colonies, showing that the sons of the gentry were often placed under indenture. Lawyers were spoken of as "servants" of their clients. In fact, the term "servant" was a very much broader one than now and the indenture system included much more than manual labor. It is to this latter, however, that it was particularly applied. Throughout most of the seventeenth century the "servant class"—indentured laborers, handicraftsmen, and farmers—composed the larger part of the population of Virginia. Until the opening of the eighteenth century they formed a more numerous body of laborers in that colony than did the negro slaves.

The chief educational problem for the Colonies related to this class, for they formed a large part of the population throughout the period. In general the home system was transplanted bodily, oftentimes without any conscious provision for it by enactment. Never did the home system become as effective here, for there were no gilds. Thus the system of monopoly and the chief agency for the enforcement of the apprentice system were wanting.

Apprentice Education in Virginia and the South.—The simplest and clearest illustration of the transfer of this system to the Colonies is found in the early Virginia enactment, "The Statutes for Artificers and Workmen are thought fit to be published in this colony." (Quo. 27.) This one sentence is all that there was of the enactment, but it was sufficient. Indeed, even this was not essential, as the custom was substantially in force. But again in 1646 a statute (Quo. 28) which established a school for poor apprentices reaffirmed the law. After referring to the precedents in the Act of Parliament, it provided "that justices of the peace should, at their discretion, bind out children to husbandmen or tradesmen to be brought up in some good or lawful calling." In 1672 the general assembly enacted a law (Quo. 29) empowering the county courts "to place out all children whose parents are not able to bring them up apprentices

APPRENTICE EDUCATION IN COLONIES

to tradesmen, the males till one and twenty years of age, and the females to other necessary employment, till eighteen years of age and no longer." The church wardens of every parish were obligated to give an annual report of all such apprentices to the county court.

In 1701 (Quo. 30), an enactment concerning orphans covering the provisions of similar laws of previous reigns added the requirement "and the master of every such orphan shall be obliged to teach him to read and write." This is the first Virginia requirement of any literary element in the training of an apprentice. By an inclusive phrase of one of the statutes concerning orphans, passed about the middle of the eighteenth century, the requirement of reading and writing seems to be extended to include all apprentices, but there is no specific enactment to this effect.

The laws and customs of the other Southern colonies were quite similar, but some of these laws are more specific. A Maryland statute of 1715 requires that the justices of the county court are to inquire yearly "whether apprentices are taught their trade or rigorously turned to common labor at the ax or hoe, instead of learning their trade. And if they find that orphans are not maintained and educated according to their estate or apprentices neglected to be taught their trades, upon pretence that the last year is enough to learn their trade, that they remove them to other guardians and masters."

This statute indicates one of the commonest abuses of the apprentice system of education. In a new country where common labor was in great demand and skilled labor of no general value except as a phase of plantation economy, the master was tempted to put off the teaching of the trade until the last few months of the term of service. In all of the colonies the same abuse existed, especially in the teaching of reading and writing where this was required.

Apprentice Education in Pennsylvania.—The earliest educational laws of the Province of Pennsylvania (1682 to 1683) contain far more explicit references (Quo. 158). One provision guards against the abuse just referred to in the phrase "shall cause such to be able to read the Scriptures; and to write by the time they attain

This Indenture

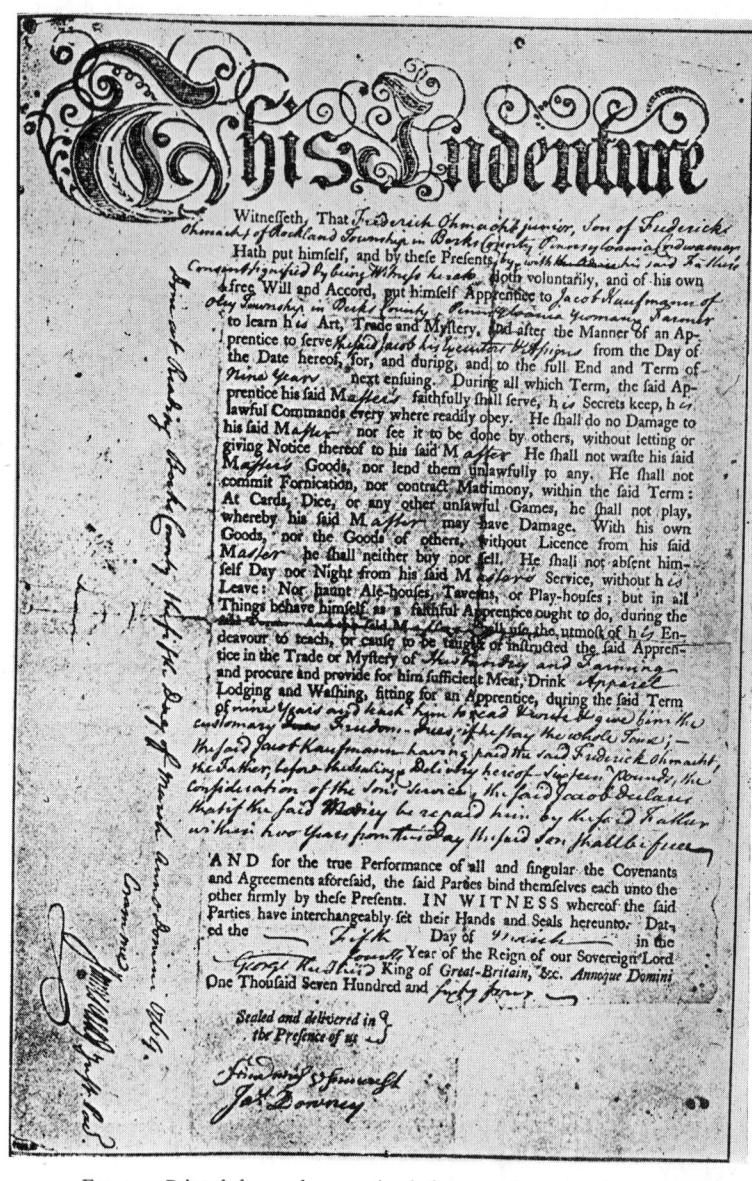

Witnesseth, That Frederick Ohmacht junior, Son of Fredericks Ohmacht of Rockland Township in Berks County, Pennsylvania (a waggoner) Hath put himself, and by these Presents, by with the consent of his said Father Consent signified by being Witness hereto, doth voluntarily, and of his own free Will and Accord, put himself Apprentice to Jacob Kauffmagen of Oley Township in Berks County, Pennsylvania yeomany Farmer to learn his Art, Trade and Mystery, and after the Manner of an Apprentice to serve said Jacob his executors & assigns from the Day of the Date hereof, for, and during, and to the full End and Term of Nine Years next ensuing. During all which Term, the said Apprentice his said Master faithfully shall serve, his Secrets keep, his lawful Commands every where readily obey. He shall do no Damage to his said Master, nor see it to be done by others, without letting or giving Notice thereof to his said Master. He shall not waste his said Master's Goods, nor lend them unlawfully to any. He shall not commit Fornication, nor contract Matrimony, within the said Term: At Cards, Dice, or any other unlawful Games, he shall not play, whereby his said Master may have Damage. With his own Goods, nor the Goods of others, without Licence from his said Master he shall neither buy nor sell. He shall not absent himself Day nor Night from his said Masters Service, without his Leave: Nor haunt Ale-houses, Taverns, or Play-houses; but in all Things behave himself as a faithful Apprentice ought to do, during the said Term. And the said Master shall use the utmost of his Endeavour to teach, or cause to be taught or instructed the said Apprentice in the Trade or Mystery of Husbandry and Farming and procure and provide for him sufficient Meat, Drink Apparell Lodging and Washing, fitting for an Apprentice, during the said Term of nine years and teach him to read & write & give him the customary two Suits Freedom Dues, if he stay the whole Term;— the said Jacob Kauffmann having paid the said Frederick Ohmacht the Father, before the sealing & delivery hereof Sixteen Pounds, the consideration of the said service, the said Jacob declares that if the said Money be repaid him by his s'd Father within two years from this day the said Son shall be free

AND for the true Performance of all and singular the Covenants and Agreements aforesaid, the said Parties bind themselves each unto the other firmly by these Presents. IN WITNESS whereof the said Parties have interchangeably set their Hands and Seals hereunto. Dated the _____ Fifth _____ Day of _____ March _____ in the _____ Fourth _____ Year of the Reign of our Sovereign Lord George the Second King of Great-Britain, &c. Annoque Domini One Thousand Seven Hundred and _____ fifty four _____

Sealed and delivered in the Presence of us

Friedrich Ohmacht
Jac. Downey

FIG. 7. Printed form of apprentice indenture. Pennsylvania, 1754.

[44]

APPRENTICE EDUCATION IN COLONIES

to twelve years of age." The penalty of five pounds was assessed for any violation of this law. This is the most specific enactment to be found on the Colonial statute books, but it soon ceased to be operative because of change in the form of government. However, it expressed an ideal. But that these rulers of Pennsylvania also looked upon education primarily as a system of vocational training is shown by the sentence following the one quoted above, "And that they be taught some useful trade and skill, that the poor may work to live, and the rich, if they become poor, may not want." As becomes a colony that was founded as a social or philanthropic experiment, this statute contains not only the provision but the social theory back of it. This economic theory constituted the very foundation of society: "that the poor may work to live," and that poverty and unemployment be not increased by such thrusting down of the derelicts of the upper class as was occurring at this period on a large scale in England.

Apprentice Education in New York.—New York Colony introduced an additional feature of the gild system of Europe and thus established an additional relationship of this system of education to public welfare in general. This came about naturally, for the city of New Amsterdam—and after it, New York—was a commercial and industrial community. During both the Dutch and the English period, merchants and master workmen could do business in the city only if they were possessed of the burgher's or citizen's rights. As in Europe one could become a burgher only through inheritance, purchase or apprenticeship. This custom grew up during the early Dutch period when it was desired to restrict the rights of trade to those under control of the company or later of the city. Documents show the operation of the system in the colonies in both the seventeenth and the eighteenth centuries. The city of Albany had adopted the same regulation (Quo. 40).

These ordinances do not require the teaching of reading and writing to the apprentice. But masters were obliged to file indentures with the city clerk, and these papers show that a provision requiring reading and writing was usually inserted (Quos. 37–42). Furthermore, in the eighteenth century records there are numerous

FOUNDING OF AMERICAN SCHOOL SYSTEM

references to evening schools or "apprentice schools," kept by private parties to instruct apprentices in reading and writing and thus affording masters the opportunity to delegate the performance of this requirement of custom or indenture, if they so desired.

The universality of this custom of apprentice education in the Dutch period is further borne out by the numerous records of orphans' courts and of contracts of remarriage. In the latter case the parties contracting the marriage gave bond to provide for the

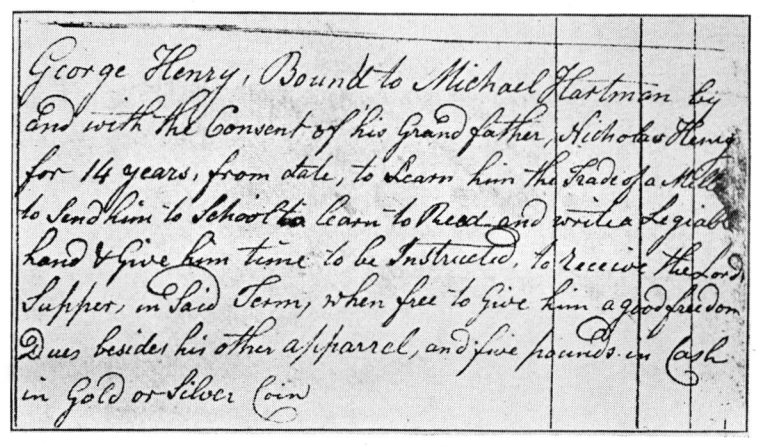

FIG. 8. Simple form of apprentice indenture.

education of any children of the previous marriage. This was usually done by means of apprenticeship (Quos. 119-120—121).

Apprentice Education in New England.—Evidences of the educational character of the apprentice system in New England are also abundant. But the school system was so much better developed in these colonies than elsewhere that the apprentice system is not so conspicuously an educational institution. However, the general statement that the earliest educational laws are apprentice and not school laws holds true in New England as well as in the other colonies. The first general enactment concerning education in Massachusetts Bay Colony was the famous Law of 1642 (Quo. 46). This has frequently been considered the foundation of our school system, but it has no word to say about schools. There exists no better evidence than this law that our forefathers thought of education as something distinguishable from schooling. The occasion for the law was "the great neglect in many parents and masters in training up their children in learning and labor and other employments which may be profitable to the commonwealth." The law required that the prudential men of each town should "take account from time to time of their parents and masters and of their children, concerning their calling and employment of their children, especially of their ability to read and understand the principles of religion and the capital laws of the country." They were authorized to take children or apprentices from parents or masters who neglected them and to apprentice all such children to other masters. Such a provision is about as stringent as laws can be made. Local records bear evidence that these provisions were enforced (Quos. 52, 53, 54, 55, 56). The law further provides that the selectmen were to divide the town into districts and that each selectman was to be responsible for the oversight of a small group of families. One familiar provision which binds this law to the apprentice and poor laws of England is to the effect that the authorities must see "that a sufficient quantity of materials, as hemp, flax, etc., may be raised in their several towns," and tools and implements provided for working out the same. Thus the industrial or vocational character of this law is stamped. Though enacted at first for but two years, its provisions remained long in force, as is evidenced by the records of the various towns. In fact it is the local records in all the colonies that prove the effectiveness and the generality of these laws or customs in providing an education for the masses of the people.

The Boston Town Records of 1656 bear evidence that "it is agreed that the complaint against the son of Goodwife Samon, living without a calling, that if she dispose not of him in some way of employment before next meeting," that then the townsmen will dispose of him to service according to law. Plymouth Town Records of the same year contain the item, "I, Jonathan Briggs, do most thankfully certify that I have received full satisfaction of William Hailstone of the sum of fifteen pounds, which was awarded to me by you for his neglect and wrong done to me in not instructing me in

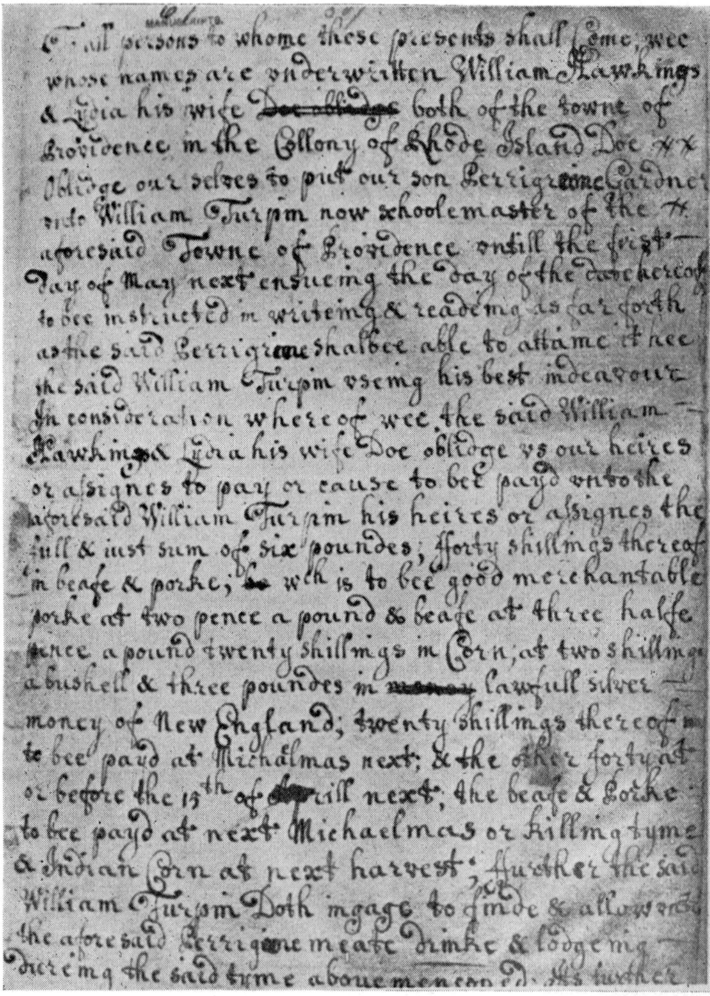
To all persons to whome these presents shall come, wee whose names are underwritten William Hawkings & Lydia his wife ~~Doe obliedge~~ both of the towne of Providence in the Collony of Rhode Island Doe obliedge our selves to put our son Perrigreene Gardner unto William Turpin now schoolemaster of the aforesaid Towne of Providence untill the first day of May next ensueing the day of the date hereof to bee instructed in writeing & readeing as far forth as the said Perrigreene shalbee able to attaine it hee the said William Turpin useing his best indeavour In consideration whereof wee the said William Hawkings & Lydia his wife Doe obliedge us our heires or assignes to pay or cause to bee payd unto the aforesaid William Turpin his heires or assignes the full & just sum of six poundes; fforty shillings thereof in beafe & porke; wch is to bee good merchantable porke at two pence a pound & beafe at three halfe pence a pound twenty shillings in Corn; at two shillings a bushell & three poundes in ~~money~~ lawfull silver money of New England; twenty shillings thereof to bee payd at Michalmas next; & the other forty at or before the 15th of Aprill next; the beafe & Porke to bee payd at next Michaelmas or killing tyme & Indian Corn at next harvest; further the said William Turpin Doth ingage to finde & allow unto the aforesaid Perrigreene meate drinke & lodgeing dureing the said tyme abovemencioned. It's further

FIG. 9. Indenture of a youth bound to a schoolmaster to learn the art and mystery of school teaching. Rhode Island, 1684.

FOUNDING OF AMERICAN SCHOOL SYSTEM

the mystery of a tailor according to his engagement." A county court of Virginia in 1717 "ordered that the sheriff summon George Smyth to the next court to answer the complaint of his apprentice, Richard Williams, and show reasons why he does not teach him to read as by indenture he is obliged."

Such evidence could be accumulated indefinitely.

Benjamin Franklin's Account of His Apprenticeship.— The life of an apprentice is not often described in literature, least of all by an eye witness. Yet the most famous, or at least the most typical, American of the Colonial period has left us a brief account of his own experience. His narrative (Quo. 61) indicates clearly that the apprentice system and the school system were alternative and parallel schemes of education. "My elder brothers," he says, "were all put apprentices to different trades. I was put to grammar school at eight years of age, my father intending to devote me, as a tithe of his sons, to the service of the church." This plan proving unattractive to the son and burdensome to the father, recourse was had to the other system of education. Accordingly Benjamin became an assistant to his father in the candle-making industry,— "a business he was not bred to (by apprenticeship in England) but had assumed on his arrival in New England and on finding that his dyeing trade would not maintain his family, being in little request." This occupation did not satisfy the restless boy, nor did two others proposed. Longing for the sea and interest in books distracted him. "This bookish inclination," Franklin says, "at last determined my father to make me a printer, though he had already one son of that profession. . . . I stood out some time, but at last was persuaded and signed the indentures when I was yet but twelve years old. I was to serve as an apprentice till I was twenty-one years of age, only I was to be allowed journeyman's wages during the last year." Franklin's entire account of his apprentice experience (Doc. 61) illuminates this phase of Colonial education.

Decline of the System.—The system had begun to lose its force in England during the latter half of the seventeenth century. The civil wars had much to do with this. The government no longer desired to keep up the monopoly of the gilds. The municipal courts were quite indifferent. The gilds remained the chief agent for putting into effect the law which was based on national customs of centuries' growth. But except in London the gilds had been shorn of all legal power. In the Colonies they did not exist. Unemploy-

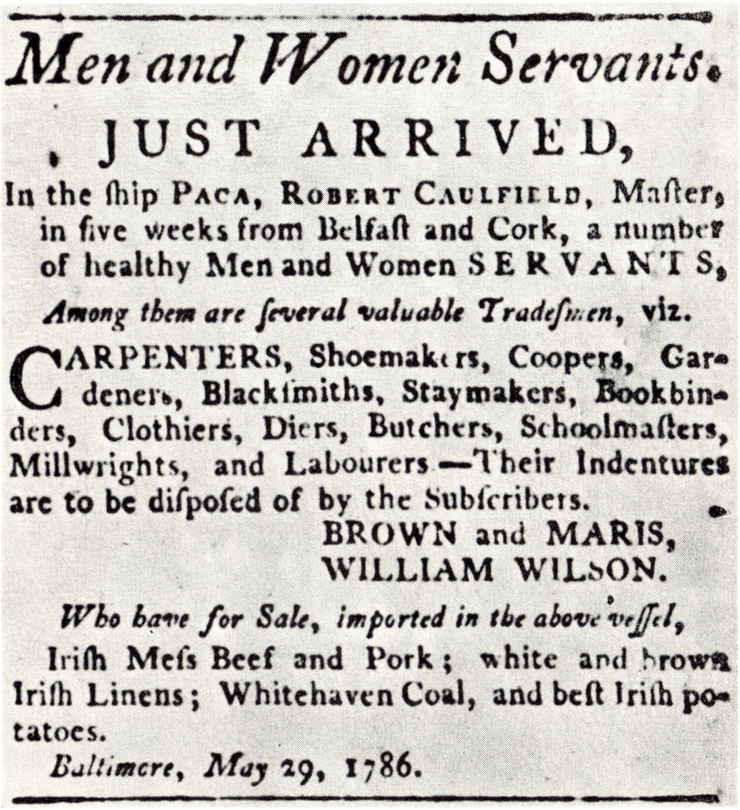

> *Men and Women Servants.*
>
> **JUST ARRIVED,**
>
> In the ship PACA, ROBERT CAULFIELD, Master, in five weeks from Belfast and Cork, a number of healthy Men and Women SERVANTS, *Among them are several valuable Tradesmen,* viz.
>
> CARPENTERS, Shoemakers, Coopers, Gardeners, Blacksmiths, Staymakers, Bookbinders, Clothiers, Diers, Butchers, Schoolmasters, Millwrights, and Labourers.—Their Indentures are to be disposed of by the Subscribers.
>
> BROWN and MARIS,
> WILLIAM WILSON.
>
> *Who have for Sale, imported in the above vessel,* Irish Mess Beef and Pork; white and brown Irish Linens; Whitehaven Coal, and best Irish potatoes.
>
> *Baltimore, May* 29, 1786.

FIG. 10. A schoolmaster auctioned as a white slave or an indentured servant. (From the Maryland *Gazette,* 1786.)

ment and poverty were evils too pressing to be further aggravated by artificial restrictions on labor. The spirit of individual liberty was rapidly developing. Some of these conditions were true also in the Colonies. Others there were even more inimical to the apprentice system. Labor was much more fluid; gilds did not exist;

[51]

land was abundant; natural sources of wealth were readily available; opportunities for trade were numerous and profitable; the spirit of the frontier bred intolerance of restrictions; the spirit of individual freedom was developing. In general the economic and social conditions supporting the apprentice system, which was a system of "status," were passing away. Meanwhile the system served its purpose as the educational foundation of Colonial society.

Summary.—Training through the apprentice system was the fundamental plan of education accepted by all the colonists. The earliest educational laws of all the colonies were apprenticeship laws. This system of training required a period of years, usually seven, in which the youth should be trained by a master in all the skills and secrets of a trade. This system was established in the English laws brought over by the colonists; but most of the colonies enacted some legislation of their own. In Virginia and the South generally this appears at first in legislation for orphans; by the middle of the eighteenth century all apprentices were included under these laws which now required reading and writing as well as the art of the craft. Pennsylvania included such a provision in its fundamental law formulated at the founding of the colony. This required a knowledge of reading and writing. Both the Dutch and the English in New York made these requirements through local ordinance. Burgher or citizen rights could be obtained by the working classes chiefly through apprenticeship. Such laws were enacted by all the New England colonies. In 1642 Massachusetts Bay enacted a very stringent law bringing all children under the provision of this apprentice system and establishing the requirements of reading and writing. This was enforced by dividing the oversight of the families of a town among the selectmen. Thus the apprentice system became a means for universal literary education. A school law soon followed. Meanwhile during the late eighteenth and the early nineteenth century the apprentice system lost its general significance as an educational scheme.

Chapter III

THE ENGLISH SCHEME OF EDUCATION IN VIRGINIA AND THE SOUTH

The Spirit of Virginia Education.—The best description of the Virginia scheme of education is that given by Governor Berkeley in 1671 (Quo. 79). The home government had sent over "articles of inquiry" long used in England to discover social and cultural conditions. The last question was, "What course is taken about instructing the people within your government in the Christian religion?" To this the governor replied, "The same course that is taken in England out of towns, every man according to his ability instructing his children. . . . But I thank God there are no free schools or printing, and I hope we shall not have them these hundred years, for learning has brought disobedience and heresy and sects into the world and printing has divulged them and libels against the best government. God keep us from both." The negative part of this reply is often quoted. But the partial quotation is not only misleading but is probably inaccurate, for there are documents which seem to indicate that there were "free schools" in operation at that time. In spirit at least the statement is misleading concerning education in Virginia, though not concerning the governor's fervent loyalty to the Stuart monarch from whom came all political gifts. For the governor himself had but a short time before made a generous contribution to a free school.

The significant part of the governor's reply, seldom quoted, lies in the positive statement that the same course regarding education was pursued in Virginia as "is taken in England out of towns." This tells the whole story of Colonial education in Virginia and in other Southern colonies as well. Cranshaw, in his famous sermon preached before Lord Delaware on the eve of that governor's departure for the colony, bore similar testimony concerning the makeup of the population. Denouncing the slander that the population of Virginia consisted of the refuse of England, he said, "They are like those left behind, even of all sorts, better and worse."

The English Social System Set Up in Virginia.—To better their lot in an established scheme of society, not to escape from or overthrow that system, brought the Virginia settlers to America. In the Southern colonies there was little or none of the element of reform or of dissent that motivated all the colonies of the North except New York. Even the numerous servants came merely to better themselves, not because of dissatisfaction with the scheme of things. This large servant element among the emigrants was due to the fact that agriculture of a very limited type formed the only profitable industry in the Colonies. These two conditions together accounted largely for the perpetuation of the English social scheme. In Europe during the seventeenth century practically all of the initiative, revolt, and progress came from towns. The towns were the homes of industries. The Virginia Company and the home government anticipated the establishment of life in towns in the colony. They expected to establish highly specialized and intensive forms of subtropical agriculture, such as silk and tea. The one thing which did prove profitable was the discovery of tobacco. By 1619 the colony was definitely committed to its cultivation. Throughout the Colonial period this was the determining economic fact. Tobacco culture demanded not only large acreage but the constant use of virgin soil, since no processes of fertilization were used. Under this necessity and with large areas available, the tendency to build up large estates was strong and that towards a scattered population and a rural life irresistible. The average acreage of the land holdings previous to 1650 was about 450. During the generation following, this average was doubled. Before the close of the century a population equal to that of a London parish owned land of greater area than all England. Large estates and crowding of the poorer people onto the poorer lands continued for several generations.

Large land holdings necessitated a large class of laborers—the servant class. For the most part these were bond servants, sold into servitude for a term of years because of social delinquency, political

EDUCATION IN VIRGINIA AND THE SOUTH

offense or debt, or merely self-committed to obtain their ocean passage or a betterment of their economic condition.

The social stratification of England was further paralleled by the differentiation of a small group of large land-owners from the ordinary land-holders or freemen. One of these estates comprised nearly 200,000 acres—a principality in itself. As in England this small, landed aristocracy came to control and direct public affairs. Towns hardly existed in such a scheme of society; but the general social relations of rural England were readily adaptable to such slight changes of conditions as developed. During the seventeenth century Jamestown was the chief town. At the time of its burning in 1676 it numbered about a dozen houses; later in the century, after its restoration, not over twenty. The plantation was the real unit of population and center of life.

The population scattered over this vast territory numbered about 1,200 in 1624, 5,000 in 1634, 15,000 in 1650, 38,000 in 1670, 72,000 in 1700, 137,000 in 1750, and 200,000 in 1770.

Education of the Lower Classes through the Apprentice System and the Workhouse Schools.—To understand the importance of this, the most fundamental and important phase of education in Virginia, a few facts should be considered in addition to those discussed in the preceding chapter. Throughout much of the Colonial period the servant class composed of white maids and men who labored on the plantations numbered quite half of the population. Until well into the eighteenth century the indentured servants outnumbered the negro slaves. In 1671, in the replies to the Commissioner's inquiries referred to at the opening of this chapter, Governor Berkeley estimated the total population at about 40,000, the indentured servants at 6,000, the negro slaves at 2,000. The servant or laboring class, however, included many who were not indentured. Most colonial educational legislation was for the benefit of this class or for orphaned or illegitimate children.

The education of this large class was provided for chiefly by the laws relating to orphans and to apprentices, as described in the preceding chapter. A large proportion of the imported immigrant servant class were youth. Examination of the shipping records and the records of the "head right" on the basis of which planters and merchants obtained new land grants, show the great number of youth. Because of ease of discipline, smaller cost of maintenance, more profitable labor, and probable longer term of service, youths from fifteen to twenty were preferred above all others. Thus the law for orphans covered this large group as it did the offspring of the large proportion of the servant class, to whom a family life was denied. During the eighteenth century the apprentices were added to the orphans and provided for, so far as education was concerned, under the same law.

There was one additional provision for the education of these young people which bulked larger in the seventeenth century legislation than it did in the actual life of the colony. This was the workhouse type of school (Quos. 70, 71). The poor laws of England provided funds for the industrial training of poor youth. So schools grew up, in connection with the "poor houses" or "work houses," for the training of the children of the inmates there cared for. One such school was founded in the colony by the Law of 1646 (also, Quo. 70). Because of the detailed provisions of this law, it plays a large part in the usual accounts of Virginia educational history. The preamble cites the wise precedent of the English law and states that the law is especially designed "for the relief of such parents whose property extends not to give them (their children) breeding." Besides authorizing apprentice education in general, the law decreed that "according to the laudable custom of England" a workhouse school should be established at James City, to which the commissioners of each county were to send two children "to be employed in the public flax house under such master and mistress as there shall be appointed, in carding, knitting, and spinning." The respective counties were to provide each child with "six barrels of corn, two coverlets, or one rug and one blanket, one bed, one wooden bowl or tray, two pewter spoons, a sow shote of six months old, two laying hens, with convenient apparel both linen and woolen, with hose and shoes." The Assembly contracted with the governor to erect this schoolhouse. The records give in detail the earliest description of a Virginia schoolhouse which we have, but they

EDUCATION IN VIRGINIA AND THE SOUTH

give us no further information, and it is not now known how long the school operated.

In 1668 the legislature authorized the county and parishes to establish such schools (Quo. 70). The purpose of the bill was "to endeavor to propagation and increase of all manufactures conducing to the necessities of their subsistence." The law gives the local authorities power to erect houses "for the educating and instructing of poor children in the knowledge of spinning, weaving, and other useful occupations and trades." It also repeated the authorization previously given "to take poor children from indigent parents to place them to work in those houses."

How general the response was to this authorization is not known. The local records give little evidence of any response. Yet there was some. The vestry book of Bristol Parish (Quo. 71) shows that in 1755-7 at the initiation of that parish, two adjoining ones entered into agreement with it and built such a school. This was in connection with the poorhouses. As other parishes erected poorhouses, it is fair to assume that at least in some of them some kind of instruction or schooling was carried on. Undoubtedly, however, this type of school never commended itself greatly to the colonists. Undoubtedly also, along with the entire apprentice system, it became of small importance during the later eighteenth century.

The Church and Education.—One large factor in determining the English character of society in Virginia and the other Southern colonies was the dominance of the Church of England as an established church. The educational function of the Church of England was confined to religious instruction through a catechizing of the youth (Quos. 67, 68) and the licensing of all teachers to assure their orthodoxy and loyalty. In Virginia the parish system prevailed with its vestry board in control of both religion and secular affairs. The support of the ministry was required by the Colonial government and paid for by the local. The instructions to Governor Yeardley in 1618 provided that "to the intent that godly, learned, and painful ministers may be placed there for the service of Almighty God and for the spiritual benefit and comfort of the people," every parish or every hundred should set aside one hundred acres of land for the minister and should raise by taxation £200 or more per annum for his salary. This salary was excessive and could not be maintained. There were many problems connected with the maintenance of the church during the Colonial period, not the least among them being that the ministry, like the other professional classes in Colonial society, was to a considerable extent recruited from the undesirables of their class at home. The roughness and hardships of frontier life and the scattered population were conditions with which the home clergy had had no experience.

A statute of 1631 (Quo. 67) laid on the minister the obligation "to examine, catechise and instruct the youth and ignorant persons of his parish" in the catechism and Book of Common Prayer, on every Sunday. The same statute required "all fathers, mothers, masters and mistresses to instruct their children and servants or apprentices in these matters or send them to the church for this purpose. Failure to do either was to be punished by public censure by the court. In 1641 a statute was passed renewing previous requirements of this character and assessing a penalty of 500 pounds of tobacco on every minister who failed to attend to this catechetical visitation every Sunday afternoon. In the later seventeenth century there was a great dearth of ministers. A statute of 1661 (Quo. 69) authorized the employment of a reader where there was no minister. He was to hold the usual services and "to catechise children and servants." The statutes indicate that this appointment of readers was a custom in England "in the time of Queen Elizabeth when there was a scarcity of orthodox reformed ministers to supply the congregation."

The vestry records indicate that the local churches were as faithful in the educational phase of their duty as in any other. The degree of that faithfulness varied with time and place. There is little to indicate that the churches were greatly concerned with education beyond these religious limits. Some concern was shown for charity schools and there was considerable interest in the university.

Visitation inquiries were sent out from the church in England during the eighteenth century. To one of these made in 1724 (Quo. 84) to the Archbishop of Canterbury there were replies from 29

EDUCATION IN VIRGINIA AND THE SOUTH

parishes. This was more than half the number of parishes in Virginia at that time. One of the questions was, "Have you in your parish any public school for the instruction of youth? If you have, is it endowed? Who is the master?" In answer, 4 parishes report a public school, one of these being the grammar school at the University; two of the other three were for reading, writing, and arithmetic only. Thirteen parishes report private schools or "little schools" but no public schools. Thirteen others report no schools at all. Only one of the five schools reported was directly under the control of the local church. The vestry books of the eighteenth century occasionally report the effort to support a charity school. But it is quite evident that the church did not conceive it part of her duty to support or even to encourage charity schools.

Charity Schools.—Many of these local church or private schools permitted poor children to attend gratis. In some instances the local poor authorities, practically identical with the authorities controlling church and school, would pay for the tuition of certain poor children. There is no evidence to show, however, that these authorities considered it necessary to give such a literary education to all children, no matter how poor.

The most important part of the charity school system was that supported during the eighteenth century by the missionary body of the Church of England called "The Society for the Propagation of the Gospel in Foreign Parts." This society was very active in the royal Colonies, though its operations were more extensive in New York than in Virginia. Besides supporting schools, the Society paid the stipends of ministers, gave libraries, sent out traveling missionaries, and contributed to the university. Probably no more than eight or ten masters were supported at any one time for the fifty or sixty parishes of Virginia. However, the activities of the Society in the case of well-to-do communities were limited to securing and forwarding the schoolmaster from England.

Private System of Education; Private Schools.—The survey of 1724 indicates that private schools existed in at least half the parishes of Virginia—perhaps more. The character of these schools is quite clearly indicated. The minister of Bristol Parish reported,

"There is no public school in the parish but there are several private ones to teach children to read, write, and cipher, and the children's fathers hire those schools and pay out of their own pockets." Westover Parish reported, "We have no public school for the instruction of the youth but two private ones for to teach reading and writing; consisting of about 35 scholars; both are very indifferently attended by the masters." Another one reports "little schools, where they teach to read, write, and arithmetic, are set up." Such schools, called "little schools" or "small schools," are frequently found, and with the growth of towns in the eighteenth century they multiplied. The first Virginia newspaper was issued in 1736. By the middle of the century the files of the newspapers became a record of great numbers of such schools.

After the Restoration in 1660, successive governors were directed, as in other royal colonies, to require that all schoolmasters be certified by them. Orders were sent out to the county courts concerning this requirement. One governor, Howard, required the presence of all schoolmasters at James City at the session of the general court (1686) to secure this official approval. Compliance with this demand being quite impossible in some cases, the result was the withdrawal of a number of the small class of teachers.

Old Field Schools.—Out of this condition of widely scattered population grew a type of elementary or ungraded private school peculiar, in name at least, to Virginia. Because of the frequent location of the schoolhouses in some abandoned field, they came to be called "old field schools." These originated in the latter part of the seventeenth century and persisted till the middle of the nineteenth century. In Colonial times some of these were taught by the parish minister or by a minister without a charge, some by the "readers" of the church; some by the wandering schoolmasters, usually Scotch-Irish, or by others of the redemptionist class.

It is quite impossible to give any accurate statement of the extent or ramification of this system, for reports were required only on rare occasions and none of these are extant. But by numerous entries of payments to such schoolmasters in the accounts of various estates all over Virginia, by the local records of parish or county,

EDUCATION IN VIRGINIA AND THE SOUTH

by wills and similar documents, the existence of these schools in every section of Virginia is indicated. For the most part such schoolmasters confined their instruction to the rudiments of reading, writing, and ciphering. Some are on record as giving instruction in French or Latin; some in higher mathematics, as surveying; some in "finishing" subjects. Occasionally they prepared the exceptional youth for college.

Tutorial Education.—Allied to the private schools was tutorial instruction in the home. This was the normal form of education for the upper class as apprentice education was for the lower. Berkeley's reply to the home government in 1671 stated "Every man according to his ability instructing his children." During a considerable part of the seventeenth, and throughout the eighteenth century this meant the private tutor in all families of means. This was the English custom. Some of the reports of 1724 state that "care is generally taken by parents that their children be taught to read."

The widespread employment of the family tutor is attested by very numerous references from many sources. Many of these tutors were indentured servants. As such, they were bought and sold. There are wills recorded which make provision for the purchase of servants as tutors for children of the deceased. Harrower, the redemptioner of the year 1774, wrote in his diary: "At 11 a.m. Mr. Anderson begged to settle as schoolmaster with a friend of his—one Col. Daingerfield. At the same time all the rest of the servants were ordered ashore to a tent at Fredericksburg and several of their indentures were then sold. About 4 p.m. I was brought to Col. Daingerfield, when we immediately agreed and my indenture for four years was then delivered him" (Quo. 84). But college students were a more fruitful source of supply. Especially did the Princeton tutor become a factor in the quarter century preceding the Revolution. Some of the most vivid pictures we have of the social life of that period are to be found in the records of such tutors. Moreover, ministers or those trained for the clergy found similar occupation.

In many cases a family tutor had charge of the education of children of relatives or neighbors. Often this led to the boarding of children of such parents in the home on a large estate. Thus arose a condition similar to that in the homes of the gentry or nobles under feudalism, when a "court" became a center of training for the youth of a number of families. Sometimes a schoolhouse was erected for the accommodation of the children. In case of such groups, French or Latin, or even Greek, and a number of accomplishments or advanced studies, were taught. When this stage was reached, the resulting institution differed little from the private school or even the academy.

Closely allied to this custom is the similar one of sending the young men to England to finish their education. Hugh Jones in his description of Virginia in 1724 (Quo. 83) wrote: "As for education, several are sent to England for it; though the Virginians, being naturally of good parts, neither require nor admire as much learning as we do in Britain; yet more would be sent over were they not afraid of the smallpox, which most commonly proves fatal to them." Jones describes how the Virginian youth are put to tutors "that know little of this temper, who keep them drudging in what is of least use to them, or in pedantic methods too tedious for their volatile genius." The account sounds as if Mr. Jones had had some experience as a tutor with the Virginia youth. He agrees that the grammar learning was no more beneficial than delightful to them, and recommends greater liberty of action and liberality of study. Thackeray, in *The Virginians,* clothes this custom with flesh and blood and gives a vision of its effect both in the Colonies and in the mother country.

The upper classes in England had long been accustomed to send their sons to the Continent to acquire a finishing culture: to the colonists, denied all contact with culture, the custom of a "finish" abroad seemed even more desirable. It was not so much Oxford and Cambridge which cared for these students as again the private tutor or the law courts or schools of London. At the Middle Temple or Inns of Court was completed the training of many an American youth who was to become a political leader at home, even a leader against the mother country which educated him. Between 1760 and the outbreak of the Revolution 115 American colonists were enrolled in the Inns of Court as students of law. During the same

EDUCATION IN VIRGINIA AND THE SOUTH

period 63 Americans took the degree in medicine at the University of Edinburgh. Practically all of these were from the Southern colonies. This training in the principles of common law gave to these youths a conception of English liberty which was to enter into the structure of the New Republic.

The Free School.—The most conspicuous school of Colonial Virginia, because of the prominent and permanent place given to it in the public records which have come down to us, is the free or endowed school. This is the "public school" referred to in the visitation inquiry of 1671 (Quo. 79) and of 1724 (Quo. 83). In 1724 there were six schools reported as endowed, though some "very meanly." These schools furnish the clearest indication of the similarity of the Virginia attitude towards education with that of the home country. The Elizabethan period had witnessed a great popular movement for the founding of such schools. Their number and influence was one reason for the indifference or inaction of the government regarding education. The provision of such schools in numbers sufficient to give every boy of ability and ambition a literary education was considered a social and religious obligation. This done through the establishment of endowments for the support of such schools, government and church need take no further thought concerning education.

It is important to notice the use of the terms "free" and "endowed" as alternative. Endowment provided for the living of the master, often for that of a certain number of pupils also. All were free at least of charges for tuition. Consequently such schools were free in the modern sense.

There was one great difference between the Colonies and the mother country in relation to these schools. In England the endowments were almost always in the form of land and the equipment of the land. Few other permanent forms of wealth existed. None was more stable or more certain to rise in value as time passed. Naturally the colonists followed home custom and gave of the chief form in which wealth existed for them—that is, land. But nothing was more abundant in the new country than land. It was to be had almost for the asking. It was of agricultural value only for a few years; then it must be abandoned for new acres of cultivation. Land was a source of wealth only as it was made productive by hard labor under constant intelligent oversight. Such supervision could hardly be expected in a new country. Therefore, few of these land endowments possessed a permanent value; most of them rapidly depreciated; in the course of time nearly all disappeared. Besides the grammar school of William and Mary, which had other sources of income and did not stand by itself, only one of these has survived to our own times, now merged in a modern high school.

The first of these, the Indian School, was an ill-starred missionary venture. In 1619-20 there was placed in the hands of the London Company, by an anonymous donor, five hundred pounds to found a school for a "convenient number of Indian youth." They were to be instructed in reading and the principles of the Christian religion, and after they were fourteen years old were to be taught some handicraft. The sum was finally placed in the hands of Southampton Hundred, which decided, after the manner of many modern boards of trustees, in favor of a community enterprise as a form of investment. The entire sum was devoted to the erection of an iron foundry and the importation of men to operate it. After some difficulties the plant was erected and gave promise of successful operation. But with peculiar inappropriateness, the Indian massacre of 1622 concentrated its fury on the little settlement and destroyed it completely. Thus the entire fund was dissipated.

The East India School.—The second foundation was also an ill-fated missionary effort of the same period (Quo. 65). In 1620 or 1621 Rev. Mr. Copeland, a chaplain on an East Indian Company ship returning from a voyage to India, took up a collection for some good enterprise in the West Indies under the London Company. To the sum thus obtained the chaplain added several substantial contributions from friends in India. It was decided to make this gift the foundation of a school, which the London Company called "The East India School." The following year Mr. Copeland was chosen rector and a Mr. Dike, usher. The latter was sent out as was also a carpenter to erect the building. Mr. Dike was to secure

EDUCATION IN VIRGINIA AND THE SOUTH

someone who could give instruction in writing and arithmetic. The expense was to be borne by the Company. Charles City was chosen as a site. The Indian massacre put an end to the immediate execution of the project, though the plan is mentioned again in 1625 in a letter by the governor, who expressed the view that it would come to nothing. The governor's prophetic vision seems to have been justified, for no further mention of it occurs.

The Symms School.—In 1643 the General Assembly passed a bill authorizing the establishment of a free school in accordance with the provisions of a will drawn in 1635 (Quo. 72). The donor was a planter, Benjamin Symms. The gift was of 200 acres of land and a small herd of cows. A schoolhouse was to be erected and the proceeds of the farm were to supply the running means for the school. The building was situated in Elizabeth City and tuition was to be free only for the children of Elizabeth City County. The first report of its operation in 1647 shows a herd of forty cows as a part of the endowment. Occasional records give fragmentary glimpses of the school at various periods during the seventeenth and eighteenth centuries (Quo. 73).

The Eaton Free School was likewise established in the seventeenth century at Elizabeth City for the children of that community (Quo. 74). Its foundation was much more elaborate than that of the Symms School, consisting of cattle and negro slaves, and 500 acres of land. The trustees were to be the clergyman, church wardens, and justices of the peace.

Little evidence is to be found concerning the early work of these free schools. It was provided that the Eaton schoolmaster was to teach "English grammar." This probably indicates that the English elements as well as Latin entered into the curriculum. In the opening years of the nineteenth century (1805), the two schools were united as the Hampton Academy. At the opening of the twentieth century (1902), a portion of the endowment was used to erect The Symms-Eaton Academy, a part of the public school system.

Other Endowed Schools.—There were numerous other foundations of this character, made at various times during the seventeenth

E. ARMSTON (or perhaps better known by the Name of GARDNER) continues the School at *Point Pleasant*, *Norfolk* Borough, where is a large and convenient House proper to accommodate young Ladies as Boarders; at which School is taught Petit Point in Flowers, Fruit, Landscapes, and Sculpture, Nuns Work, Embroidery in Silk, Gold, Silver, Pearls, or embossed, Shading of all Kinds, in the various Works in Vogue, *Dresden* Point Work, Lace Ditto, Catgut in different Modes, flourishing Muslin, after the newest Taste, and most elegant Pattern, Waxwork in Figure, Fruit, or Flowers, Shell Ditto, or grotesque, Painting in Water Colours and Mezzotinto; also the Art of taking off Foilage, with several other Embellishments necessary for the Amusement of Persons of Fortune who have Taste. Specimens of the Subscriber's Work may be seen at her House, as also of her Scholars; having taught several Years in *Norfolk*, and else where, to general Satisfaction. She flatters herself that those Gentlemen and Ladies who have hitherto employed her will grant her their farther Indulgence, as no Endeavours shall be wanting to complete what is above mentioned, with a strict Attention to the Behaviour of those Ladies intrusted to her Care.

Reading will be her peculiar Care; Writing and Arithmetick will be taught by a Master properly qualified; and, if desired, will engage Proficients in Musick and Dancing.

Fig. 11. A Virginia private school of the late 18th century.

[66]

EDUCATION IN VIRGINIA AND THE SOUTH

and eighteenth centuries. Beverley, writing in 1705, describes this phase of Virginia's educational institutions (Quo. 81).

Many bequests for endowed schools are shown to have been made in the wills which are on record. Some of these bequests relate to endowments for a stipulated number of children. Such gifts may have occasioned a small local school through sufficient payment of fees to locate a master. Occasional bequests were made for the education of poor children. In 1655 the will of John Moon states (Quo. 75): "Also I give and bequeath four female cattle to remain for a stock forever for poor fatherless children that hath nothing left them to bring them up." According to the English custom, some wills include provision for the relief of the poor, of old people, of the sick or injured, as does this Moon bequest. But all such small bequests tend to disappear in time as the origin and purpose of the funds are forgotten by succeeding generations.

The University, described in Chapter VII, crowned the system. Plans for such an institution were discussed from the earliest year. In 1692 a charter was given and William and Mary College was founded. For a decade or two it was little more than a grammar school, but for much of the eighteenth century it flourished and influenced Colonial life by training its leaders in church and state.

Summary.—In habits of living and organization of society Virginia more nearly resembled England—that is rural England—than did the other colonies. The Carolinas and Maryland approximated Virginia in this; and their educational customs and organization were substantially the same. There was universal belief in the importance of education, and in the need of some form of education—not necessarily literary—for all people. For the masses of the people —including all who worked at manual labor—the apprentices and journeymen laborers at handicraft, the farm laborer, the household servant — as well as the assistant to merchant, professional man or plantation owner—education came through the provisions of the laws for artificers, apprentices, orphans, or paupers. Education for vocation must be universal. Religious education must be universal. This latter was the duty of the church through its ministers. As for schools—opportunity for literary education must be universal.

So there were founded private schools, charity schools, free endowed schools. The education of the gentry must be universal—so there grew up the custom of employing tutors in the homes. The education of the professions must be universal—so there was established the university. Universal individual responsibility, universal opportunity for schooling, universal training for vocation—this was the English conception of education as worked out in Virginia and the South.

Chapter IV

THE CHURCH–STATE SCHOOL SYSTEM OF THE MIDDLE COLONIES

The Dutch Colony of New Netherland, 1609–64 and 1673–74, was more completely an outgrowth of commercial interests than any other of the original colonies. The settlers came with no purpose of reform, were moved by no spirit of protest. As traders, merchants, and the craftsmen and workers subordinate to these, they would naturally reproduce the life and institutions with which they were familiar at home. So we should expect to find in New Netherland a more complete transplanting of European institutions than elsewhere. But throughout its existence, the colony was only a commercial trading company's settlement. For many years it was merely an outpost, concerned chiefly in obtaining furs from savages. Long after a permanent community was planted on Manhattan, this settlement was composed chiefly of the officers and servants of the company, of traders, sailors, and longshore population, or of the restless, adventurous, shiftless, and rough characters of a frontier or foreign shipping port.

Hudson discovered in 1609 the river which bears his name. The Dutch West India Company was not organized, however, until 1621, and the first permanent settlement was not made until 1623. Manhattan was purchased and Fort Amsterdam built in 1626. Under the first two directors-general—as the governors of the colony, acting as agents for the company, were called—few representatives of the better element of Dutch society entered into its population. Protests of the settlers against the arbitrary government of an unintelligent despot, fear on the part of the home government of the growing power of the English settlements, realization of the shortsighted commercial policy of the company, danger from the Indians, threats of the settlers to return to Holland if their protests against

FOUNDING OF AMERICAN SCHOOL SYSTEM

misgovernment were not heeded (1634), led to a better type of director-general, reforms in administration, and after a few years to some participation of the settlers in local government. This last did not occur until the Great Remonstrance of 1649 (Quos. 113, 114–115, 116–117) had forced concessions which went into effect in 1653.

Fig. 12. The Town Hall of New York, in which the local town school was held by consent of the local government; corner of Pearl St. and Coenties Alley, 1652.

After these reforms, in fact earlier after the adoption of a more liberal policy about 1636, more of the better home element came out.

Meanwhile another phase of the colony's organization began to attract a very different type of settlers. Beginning with the overthrow of the Spanish control (about 1579), the Netherlands had been an asylum for the persecuted religious sects of Europe. Much of Dutch prosperity was due to the thrift, skill, and intelligence

SCHOOL SYSTEM OF THE MIDDLE COLONIES

of these people, who usually belonged to the most progressive if not the most cultured element of the peoples who drove them out. Much of the Dutch influence on other European countries at this time was due to the return of these exiles, when persecution abated. The Dutch colony of New Netherland pursued the same liberal course as the home country concerning religious refugees, and only when these became so numerous as to be somewhat significant politically, were they required to take the oath of allegiance to Holland. Even then they were not obliged to adopt her state religion (Quo. 88). Thus numbers of intelligent, thrifty, resourceful, determined people were added to the population of New Netherland. Among these the French Huguenots were probably the most important element. The French names of many families prominent in New York throughout the Colonial and all succeeding times bear witness to this fact, as do the names of such places as New Rochelle. Allied to the Huguenots were Waldensian refugees from north Italy, Moravians, and other persecuted sects from Teutonic lands, Baptists and Quakers from England and New England, Jews from various places. The village of Harlem was settled in 1658. By 1661 there were 32 adult male residents of whom 11 were French, 4 Waldenses, 7 Dutch, 4 Danish, 3 Swedish, and 3 German. From New England came Anne Hutchinson of Boston fame, Captain John Underhill, the hero of the Pequot War, and others who stamped their name and influence on this Dutch period of New York history. So numerous were these settlers that an English secretary was added to the Company's staff. For the most part these people settled in the region north of Manhattan or on Long Island. These, added to the shifting population of traders—who during the Dutch period were termed "Scotchmen"—gave thus early to this community the cosmopolitan character which it has ever retained. It is estimated that before the end of the Dutch period fifteen languages could be heard in New Amsterdam.

Some further consideration of the character of the government of New Netherland is necessary in order to understand the educational history and influence of the colony. By the charter of 1621 this colony was entirely under the control of the Dutch West India

Company. The States-General of the United States of the Netherlands which granted the charter reserved the right of confirming the appointee to the governorship of the colony, and of declaring war. Beyond this the company was supreme. The Dutch West India Company was a stock company controlled by an executive committee, called the College of Nineteen, selected from the five separate boards or chambers which represented the different sections of the Netherlands. The principal executive officer of the company in New Netherland was the director-general or, as we would say, governor. The laws governing the colony were made by the West India Company, chiefly by the Amsterdam chamber, and the director-general was merely their agent. He was to be assisted by a council of five members, with combined legislative, executive, and judicial powers. Members of this council were often, if not usually, chosen from subordinate officers of the company. One director-general—Kieft (1636–1646)—appointed but one member to this council besides himself, and so became a virtual despot. Arbitrary government may be necessary for the conduct of a trading post and the protection of a frontier settlement, but it will not attract settlers or build up a permanent community in a new land. As an outcome of the struggle between the citizens and this despotic and often unintelligent and brutal government, a struggle, in other words, with successive directors-general, New Amsterdam was incorporated as a city in 1653. The director still retained the power to appoint the two burgomasters, the councilors, and other officials and of issuing ordinances or interdicts binding on the inhabitants. After repeated objections and petitions (1556) the outgoing burgomasters and aldermen were allowed to nominate double their number, from which list the director-general appointed those who actually served. The government of the other villages of the colony was similar to that of New Amsterdam. The director-general originally appointed the officers, jointly administrative, judicial, and executive; thereafter the outgoing officials nominated double their number and the director-general appointed from this body. Such was the extent of their self-government.

One other phase of the government which had educational signifi-

SCHOOL SYSTEM OF THE MIDDLE COLONIES

cance was the patroon system, introduced in 1629. In order to attract settlers and build up the colony, the Company granted to all those who would "plant there within four years" a colony of fifty souls upwards of fifteen years old practical feudal rights over an estate fronting sixteen miles on a river or waterway and extending indefinitely into the wilderness. The period of limitation was later extended. Manhattan was exempted from such settlements. Many such feudal estates were started: only two became of such permanent importance as to have an educational history. These were the Van Rensselaer estate founded in 1630 (see pp. 77-78) and one founded much later by the city of Amsterdam in what is now the state of Delaware (see p. 78).

Further insight into the character of the colony and the degree of its educational importance is gained from a consideration of the population of the colony. New Amsterdam itself had a population of 220 in 1628; and in 1643, shortly after the first school was founded, of 400. By 1652, just before the municipal government was established, New Amsterdam had grown to 700. A census was taken in 1656 which showed 120 houses and 1000 inhabitants. When the English took control in 1664 the city had grown to about 1500 souls. The population of the colony at this time was but little over 6000 while Massachusetts Bay had grown to 25,000 and Virginia to 33,000.

The First School in New Amsterdam.—Much has been written about the first school of New Amsterdam. It has often been claimed that this school was the first permanent one founded within the thirteen original colonies. On the existence of this school has been built a structure of assumption which would make it the foundation of the present school system of the United States. The claim of establishing the first permanent school has likewise been advanced for the colonies of Massachusetts Bay, Rhode Island, Connecticut, and Virginia. Mere priority does not concern us, for it signifies little. But proper interpretation of historic evidence, the elimination of myth and fiction in our educational history, do concern us, as do antecedents of the influences which shaped our educational traditions.

FOUNDING OF AMERICAN SCHOOL SYSTEM

It is stated in practically all accounts dealing with this subject that the first school of New Amsterdam was founded in 1633. The sole evidence for this is an affidavit made in a police court in 1638 by one Adam Roelantsen, who gave his occupation as schoolmaster, that in 1633 he was on the strand in New Amsterdam and heard certain slanderous conversation. In 1637 Adam Roelantsen was licensed to teach school by the classis at Amsterdam—as according to Dutch law all schoolmasters must be who were going to the

FIG. 13. A Dutch elementary school. (From a painting by Ostade, 1676.)

Colonies. Roelantsen was authorized to teach in New Netherland. He is shown to have been in New Amsterdam in 1638 and to have signed himself as schoolmaster. There are no records of his teaching, but another teacher was at work in 1642, so Roelantsen's term of service probably lasted the customary four years' contract. The income and the social standing of the schoolmaster are shown by a court record in which he sues a patron for a year's charges for "washing defendant's linen" (Quo. 302). While this humble avocational activity, though menial, is no discredit to the schoolmaster,

[74]

SCHOOL SYSTEM OF THE MIDDLE COLONIES

numerous other records, chiefly of police court character, reveal our hero in far less pleasant light. For one of these offenses he is sentenced to be publicly whipped and banished from the settlement. If Roelantsen is to be considered the cornerstone of the public school system, we are unfortunate; for he makes a better hero for the pen of a Diedrich Knickerbocker than the patron saint for the teacher's profession in America.

Character of the School of New Amsterdam.—Roelantsen's successor was Jan Stevenson, who taught "for six or seven years"—or until 1648. A succession of teachers, most of them serving for five or six years, make an unbroken record until the colony passed into English hands (1664). A detailed account of this school is possible, and shows it to have been practically a reproduction of the parochial school system of Holland. (See Kilpatrick, *The Dutch Schools of New Netherlands and New York*.) Such a description will serve for the schools of the remaining villages or towns, in which it is known that schools existed.

The classis of the church at Amsterdam retained full power in the selection of schoolmasters, as of ministers and of comforters of the sick—subordinate but none the less essential church officials. It examined and certified such masters; selected and recommended them to the authorities in New Amsterdam upon request: and at least occasionally authorized them to go out. For these purposes there was a standing committee. The request to the classis for a schoolmaster might come from the minister in New Amsterdam, from the church (consistory) in New Amsterdam, from the director-general in New Amsterdam, or from the Lords Directors in Amsterdam. In some cases it came from all. It is by this latter body that the appointment was usually made, though independent appointment by the synod of the church also occurred. It was also by the Lords Directors in Amsterdam—that is, by the West India Company, acting as the political government—that the salary was paid. Upon the arrival in America the schoolmaster was again under many authorities (Quos. 99–112 incl.). The local church through its consistory, church masters—appointed by the director-general—or the minister had the right or duty of supervision or inspection (Quo. 96). This power was of variable degree, at times quite extensive, but for the most part slight. The schoolmaster was also a church official—the *voorlezer* and *voorsanger*—who read the services, led the singing, and in the absence of a minister conducted the service. In fact the schoolmaster is included in the official term "ecclesiastical establishment."

If the authority of the church was the somewhat remote one of examining and selecting teachers, and that of the local church the somewhat hazy, indefinite one of supervision, the obligation of the company was the very definite and substantial one of support (Quos. 97, 98). It had been proposed as early as 1638 (Quo. 87) and at intervals thereafter that every householder should be taxed for schools as for other public charges, but the proposal was rejected by the States-General. This rejected proposition is often erroneously cited as the earliest case in America of school support by public taxation. The municipal government which was formed for New Amsterdam in 1653 agreed to take over from the company the support of the minister and schoolmaster if the funds from the sale of liquor licenses were also turned over to them. These charges would about balance each other. But a dispute arising between the burgomaster of the city and the director-general, over the extent of these excise rights, the agreement was withdrawn after one year (Quos. 104–109). So the municipal support of schools continued but one year—and was partial and inadequate during that short period. The company continued to pay the salary while it remained in power. The city government did furnish and maintain a schoolhouse or, since the schoolmaster often taught in his own home, made contribution for the maintenance of the schoolmaster's house.

Thus the West India Company assumed practically the same relation to the Colonial schools as did the state or local government to those of Holland. The interest of the Lords Directors sometimes extended into numberless details (Quos. 99–103). They purchased schoolbooks and writing materials, and charged Stuyvesant with their distribution. The "Grand Duke of Muscovy" kept an account of the school children's copy paper and authorized the use of state-supplied textbooks. He and his august council drew up

SCHOOL SYSTEM OF THE MIDDLE COLONIES

rules for the conduct of the schoolmaster, as the latter in turn did for the school children. The charges for the school were sometimes paid in the Netherlands by the Lords Directors, ofttimes in the colony by the director-general. This obligation seems to have been assumed as one of the functions of government. Several early documents are often erroneously quoted to prove that this obligation was definitely laid upon the colony or the people. The privileges and exemptions of 1629 (Doc. 85) founding the patroon system and requiring the support of ministers and schoolmasters by the patroons, particularly exempted Manhattan. The "charter of freedoms and exemptions" of 1638 was never adopted (Quos. 86, 87); the one of 1640 which contained a similar provision passed (Quo. 88), but as it was designed to promote colonization Manhattan was again exempted.

However, the policy is clear; the company assumed as a matter of course the obligation concerning their chief settlement, and required it of the patroons and Colonies founded or encouraged under its authority. In these latter the States-General co-operated at least by tacit approval. As the church itself supervised, inspected, and controlled the "ecclesiastical establishment," the system of church-state schools was operative throughout the Dutch period.

One of the last acts of the Dutch government (1664. Doc. 103) was an ordinance framed by the Dutch director-general and his council requiring the public catechizing of the children on Wednesday and Saturday by the schoolmaster and minister and the granting of a half holiday following this act. The supervision of instruction and other churchly authority over the schools was undoubtedly a traditional affair. But this civil ordinance is merely another indication of the joint authority of church and state, or the effort of an aristocratic ruler to make himself head of the local church as well as of the state.

Schools in Other Dutch Settlements.—Similar to the situation in New Amsterdam was that in the other Dutch villages—Beverwyck (now Albany) (in Renssaelerwick); Brooklyn, Flatbush, Flatlands, Newcastle (Delaware), Harlem, Bergen (now Newark, N. J.), Bushwick, New Utrecht, and Kingston. Of these

FOUNDING OF AMERICAN SCHOOL SYSTEM

Beverwyck and Delaware were patroon estates; the latter was founded by the city of Amsterdam. In time all of them had schools. In practically all, church and state co-operated on terms similar to those of New Amsterdam (Quo. 118). In Beverwyck, the patroons took the place of the company and gave very tardy support to a school. The grant was made in 1630, but it does not appear that the patroon supported a schoolmaster until twenty years later. Voluntary contributions of citizens and a high rate of payment for tuition by the pupils maintained the school. When the English took charge, however, the schoolmaster was one of the officials regularly supported by the local Dutch government. Brooklyn was granted a charter in 1646; but nineteen years later the village numbered only thirty-one households and 134 people. With the aid of a contribution from the company, a schoolmaster was employed in 1661 by joint action of the local government and the church. The colony of New Amstel (or Newcastle) in Delaware, settled by the city of Amsterdam as patroon in 1656, would give the best illustration of Dutch practices. In the draft of its charter it is provided "that the city of Amsterdam shall send thither a proper person for schoolmaster, who shall also read the Holy Scriptures and set the psalms." This was done in the first shipload of settlers. A house was built by the patroon and the teacher is found at work the first year. The salary paid was generous and the school continued as a city or public school as long as the Dutch ruled.

Character of the School.—While the New Amsterdam school was supported by the company or the city or both and supervised by the church, yet it was not a free school in the modern sense. The master was allowed to supplement his stipend from the company by charges for tuition of the children. Such charges were regulated by the authorities and "the poor and needy, who ask to be taught for God's sake, he shall teach for nothing." This was a common European attitude which was long perpetuated in America. The master's charges were moderate and varied according to the subjects taught (Quo. 111). Sometimes they are stated and paid in beaver skins, wampum, or other local forms of money.

SCHOOL SYSTEM OF THE MIDDLE COLONIES

School accommodation itself was very simple. Almost invariably sessions were held in the master's house. This house was built or furnished by the community, usually by the municipal government, occasionally by the church. The room was ridiculously small, and must have been crowded far beyond comfort. Its equipment included rough benches, and tables for writing. Pen, paper, slates, books were in the earlier days furnished by the company.

Sessions were held both forenoon and afternoon except that Wednesday and Saturday afternoons were free. The term continued throughout the year except on the occasional church holidays. The usual hours of session were from eight to eleven and from one to four. Both boys and girls attended. The subjects taught were the usual essential rudiments with great stress on religious instruction. Frequently the instruction of the girls was limited to reading and sewing or to reading and household duties. The order of the classis of Amsterdam of 1636 gives a concise statement of the curriculum, which was at least approximated by the various schools. This order was prepared for masters going to the East or the West Indies and read:

"He is to instruct the youth, in reading, writing, ciphering, and arithmetic, with all zeal and diligence; he is also to implant the fundamental principles of the true Christian Religion and salvation, by means of catechizing; he is to teach them the customary forms of prayers, and also accustom them to pray; he is to give heed to their manners and bring these as far as possible to modesty and propriety."

The teachers belonged to a distinct professional class (Quo. Ch. X). Whether teaching in a private or a public school, they must be licensed. They were recognized as public and as church officials. As such their names appear on all lists of officers. They were seldom learned men; there is no evidence of their being university men. Some few in addition to the earliest one were not of the highest character, but were men of the type that would seek or be driven to laxly governed settlements of the frontier. Of one it is recorded that "he behaved most shamefully here, drinking, cheating, forging other people's writings, so that he was forbidden not only to preach, but even to teach school." The qualifying "even" is quite suggestive of the status of the school. The teacher's duties were manifold. Of the one at Flatbush it was required that he serve "as process-server for the schepen's court . . . also to serve the church, leading the singing and in reading, to arrange the seats, to ring the bell, and furthermore to hold school, to dig graves, and to look after everything else that is needful thereto" (Quo. 304). In addition he often drew up papers for the local court and thus served as an embryo lawyer. Some such formula as this is found in the contract of many of them. Such was the character of the Dutch schools, which changed but little even under English rule. Schools founded later under the English differed little from the Dutch ones.

Dutch Schools under English Rule (Quos. 135–142).—When the English took over the authority in 1664 as little change as possible was made in Dutch customs. The government of New York City acknowledged its responsibility for the rent of the schoolhouse and for at least part payment of the master's salary. This it did until after the brief restoration of Dutch rule in 1673–1674. Upon the re-establishment of the English authority in the latter year, the government ceased to recognize any responsibility for the support of the Dutch church or school. The school thereby became dependent upon the church for its support and thus passed under church control, as it has remained until the present day. The city mayor and council, however, and later the governor continued to exercise the right of licensing schoolmasters, all of whom had now become private. In a charter given to the church by the English the minister, elders, and deacons were authorized "to nominate and appoint a clerk, schoolmaster, bell ringer or sexton, and to make rate or assessment upon every one of the members in communion of said church for the raising of money for the yearly stipends and salaries of the aforesaid officers of the said school." Thus the school became a parochial institution supported by rates assessed by church officials and collected by authority of civil law. This stipend paid by the church includes tuition charges for the poor children—often a stipulated number only. Otherwise pupils are to pay a certain rate for tuition. Here again we have the co-operation of state and

SCHOOL SYSTEM OF THE MIDDLE COLONIES

church in the control and support of the school, but on a novel plan (Quos. 135-142).

During the greater part of the eighteenth century these schools of the Dutch churches were concerned chiefly with the preservation of the Dutch tongue. Though English came to be the language of commerce and of general public life, early in the eighteenth century the conservative party of the Dutch succeeded in retaining the Dutch tongue in their churches and schools almost until the Revolutionary War. Thereby these schools came to have a still narrower function than they exercised as parochial schools when the population was largely Dutch, becoming little more than charity schools for a limited portion of the population.

In the remaining Dutch villages, the English population and the English influence were less prominent. The history of the schools in these communities is of far greater significance than that of the Dutch school in New York City. To the original eleven villages chartered under Dutch rule were added a number in towns with a mixed Dutch and English population. Among these were Kinderhook, Poughkeepsie, Fishkill, Hackensack, Hopeful, Catskill, Tappan, and others. For in all of these towns schools continued to exist or were built up according to the Dutch custom. In all of them church and local government participated. The salary of the schoolmaster continued to be paid in large part by the town officials. The town government consisted of a local court consisting of *schout* or constable and *schepens* or overseers (selectmen). This court was usually self-perpetuating, but as the power of the people continued to develop, the town meeting in a few places came to exercise this authority over schools. In the early period of English rule, the government in several cases, notably Harlem and Bergen, supported the local Dutch or town government in its insistence that all inhabitants should contribute by rate to the support of schools. This rate was primarily a voluntary contribution; but by court decision reluctant inhabitants could be forced to pay the voluntary rate on penalty of distraint by the constable.

Local Customs Varied.—In the main the old customs prevailed (Quos. 135-142); the town government furnished the house, contributed a large portion of the salary; employed the teacher. The church contributed in payment for some of the services of the schoolmaster, since he also was a church official—reader and precenter (*voorlezer* and *voorsanger*). Inspection was by church officials; school children were taught the catechism and church service and repeated these in public service or on public occasions under supervision of church officials. In one instance (Albany, 1744) the village schools numbered at least 200 children. In some English began to be taught with Dutch early in the eighteenth century. In others Dutch was used exclusively until near the Revolutionary War. At all times the English governor claimed the right of licensing such teachers and on occasion exercised this right to the chagrin, often as they thought to the danger, of the Dutch community. In some communities, as in Flatbush, the control had practically passed into the hands of the town meeting by Revolutionary War time (Quo. 304).

The significant fact in regard to this system of parish schools is the marked contrast which it offers to the villages or towns where English customs prevailed. In all of these Dutch settlements a community school existed as one essential part of the structure of society and of the local system of government. While church and town government co-operated, these were essentially town schools supported as a town charge. To the Dutch a church was essentially a part of the local government scheme. The "church masters" were selected by the town government. So while the school was immediately under the church, it was essentially a town school. In the early national period these schools continued to form the basis or nucleus of a system of public schools. Undoubtedly the traditions represented by these state-church or parish schools, and the actual working system which they presented were a leading factor in the establishment of the first system of public schools created after the Revolution (New York, 1795) (Quo. 379).

Other Phases of the Dutch School System.—In the rejoinder (Quo. 115) made in 1650 to the Great Remonstrance it was stated in refuting the charge of neglect of education "the other schoolmasters keep school in hired houses, so that the youth, con-

SCHOOL SYSTEM OF THE MIDDLE COLONIES

sidering the circumstances of the country, are not in want of schools." Such private schoolmasters taught throughout the Colonial period. Some of these were private tutors in the family of the governor or other prominent citizens. Some tutored the children of the well-to-do. Of one of these (Cortelyou, 1652) it is recorded that "he had studied philosophy in his youth and spoke Latin and good French. He was a mathematician and a sworn land surveyor. He had also formerly learned several sciences, and had some knowledge of medicine. The worst of it was he was a good Cartesian and not a good Christian, regulating himself in all externals by reason and justice only."

From time to time license to keep private schools was granted by the director and council. In one case (Doc. 127–129) the director closed the school until such license had been granted. Police court records showed that the children of such masters were as mischievous and troublesome as school boys of a later age. Some of these masters taught the higher branches.

Presumably there were dame schools in the colony as there were in Holland, though there is no direct evidence of their existence during the Dutch rule. Only infrequent mention of them occurs in the records of the Dutch communities under English rule. Among the English communities, they are more common, owing no doubt to the absence of town or community schools.

A type of school occurring far more frequently was the evening school. This may seem quite a modern development, but the Colonial institution was quite different from the evening school of the present. It finds its explanation in the universal existence of the apprentice system. For the pupils in these evening schools were apprentices who were busy with their industrial obligations during the day. So the almost universal requirement that masters teach their apprentices to read and write, or have them so taught, necessitated some such institution.

From the instructions to the official schoolmaster in 1661 (Doc. 102) we learn that he was permitted to hold such a school, being allowed to charge "those who come in the evening and between times pro rata a fair sum." This permission appears frequently throughout the later seventeenth and a greater part of the eighteenth century, even as late as 1772, showing that the evening or apprentice school was a fixed institution in the Dutch communities and in New York City. For these the town had no responsibility except that of supervision. Numerous apprentice indentures show that the obligation of payment for such schooling rested upon the master; occasionally it was assumed by the parents. In most cases it was only reading and writing that were to be taught. Sometimes ciphering or arithmetic or both are added. Rarely ciphering stands as the only requirement.

The English Colonial Government and Education.—The activities of the English government concerning education are briefly recounted. The "Duke's laws" (Quo. 36), formulated in 1665, included a provision for the oversight of children according to the apprentice system (Ch. 2). Constables and overseers were to see that children and apprentices were brought up in "some honest lawful calling, labor, or employment." As we have previously seen, the Dutch system of schools continued to operate with little interference until after the second occupation (1674). Thereafter instructions to the governors of the colony included a provision that all schoolmasters coming from England were first to be authorized by officials of the church there; and all teachers residing in the colony, by the governor of the colony as representing the established church (Quos. 124, 125). Records for several decades reveal considerable activity on the part of the governors in licensing teachers for private schools and for the Dutch schools. After the beginning of the work of the foreign missionary society of the church of England, in the first decade of the eighteenth century, interest on the part of the governors was rare.

Cornbury was the only governor who showed especial interest in education. Aside from the futile efforts concerning the Latin school (Ch. 6), neither the governor nor the Colonial government took any further action concerning schools. The reason for this was the existence of the Dutch town schools and the work of the missionary society referred to above. Thus dependence was placed chiefly upon private venture schools or upon charity or church schools.

SCHOOL SYSTEM OF THE MIDDLE COLONIES

Schools of the S.P.G. in Colonial New York.—The Society for the Propagation of the Gospel in Foreign Parts, more briefly known as the S.P.G., was the foreign missionary society of the Church of England, founded in 1701. This society was greatly in-

Fig. 14. Bookplate of the S.P.G., 1721. (From the Columbia University Library.)

terested in the American Colonies, especially in those under direct royal control. Its efforts were directed to the supply and support of ministers, of schoolmasters, and of libraries. Its interest included the colonists and the "heathen nations" alike. The records indicate a number of children of Indian blood attending schools. The early confidence in the desire of these heathen nations for learning and the gospel is indicated in the society's coat of arms given above. The

[85]

society was greatly interested in the christianizing of America and in the upbuilding of the Church of England; and as such naturally had an aggressive even a proselyting spirit. New York and New Jersey, then under the same administration, were the home of sectaries. As early as 1687 Governor Dongan wrote (Quo. 126):

> "Every town ought to have a minister. New York has first a chaplain belonging to the fort, of the church of England; secondly, a Dutch Calvinist; thirdly, a French Calvinist; fourthly, a Dutch Lutheran. . . . Here be not many of the church of England; few Roman Catholics; abundance of Quakers, preachers, men, and women, especially; singing Quakers, ranting Quakers; Sabbatarians, Anti-sabbatarians, some Anabaptists, some Independents, some Jews—in short, of all sorts of opinions there are some. . . . The great church which serves both the English and the Dutch is within the fort, which is found to be very inconvenient. The most prevailing opinion is that of the Dutch Calvinist."

Later, in addition to these were found Mennonites, Moravians, New Born, Dunkards, Seceders, New Lights, Covenanters, Mountain Men, all contending for existence if not for proselytes.

Especially against the Quakers did the S.P.G.'s work, and the Quakers were particularly strong in these colonies. Many of the colonists, liberal in their religious attitude, felt a genuine fear of the building up of an established church. For this reason and because there was opposition to a state-church system of schools like that of the Dutch, the work of the S.P.G. met with hostility throughout the period. But the schools of the society did constitute a system, did supply the communities of the colony with schools, so far as these existed outside the Dutch villages. The church of England examined and supported the teachers, the governor licensed and approved. So there was, to all intents and purposes, an English state-church system parallel to the Dutch.

The society began work in New York City in 1703. Trinity Church, the first congregation of the Church of England, was organized in 1697. It supported the school of a Mr. Huddlestone, who had begun teaching ten years earlier. The society in 1706 assumed the support of Mr. Huddlestone, stipulating after 1710 that he

SCHOOL SYSTEM OF THE MIDDLE COLONIES

should teach forty poor children gratis (Quo. 152). The usual result followed. Soon afterwards it was reported that "he had not above seven scholars, except those he teaches on the society's bounty, for the townspeople have taken away their children, being unwilling to send them to a charity school." This condition finally brought about the establishment of a parish school by Trinity Church, distinct from the charity school.

For the most part the schools of the society were "charity schools"; that is, the master was subsidized by the society on condition that he be an adherent of the Church of England and teach so many children free. In the smaller places, however, the opposition to the charity feature could not be so strong; consequently such schools served both elements of a community. Practically all of the English villages of the colony were assisted by the society. Schools were established in Rye, Westchester, Yonkers, New Rochelle, Staten Island, Hempstead, Oyster Bay, Jamaica, South Haven, Brookhaven, New Windsor, Newburgh, Albany, Schenectady, Poughkeepsie, and Johnstone. Some of these will be recognized as Dutch villages, where the society's schools were in competition with those of the original settlers. Schools were also maintained for the negroes by an affiliated society, and missionaries and teachers were sent out among the Indians (Quos. 148–153). While not all of these schools were in continuous operation, the society kept eight or ten open throughout the eighteenth century until the close of the Revolutionary War. These schools were an object of special concern to the English Colonial administration; the governor stood as patron; the mayor of New York and the public officials of other towns inspected them and certified their character and verified the report of the teachers to the society's secretary (see illustration, p. 88).

Character of the S.P.G. Schools.—The work and routine of these schools varied little from that of the Dutch schools previously described. They were in session the year round except on church holidays. The day's session was from five to eight hours in length depending on the season and the density of settlement.

The subjects of study were the usual reading, writing and sometimes arithmetic, with the catechism and religious instruction first of all. One master writes that he taught "Church of England catechism, as also what other learning he had, to render them able to know their duty to God by reading the Scriptures" and "as much reading and writing and arithmetic as may relieve the common occasions of vulgar people, which is the most the people aspire to."

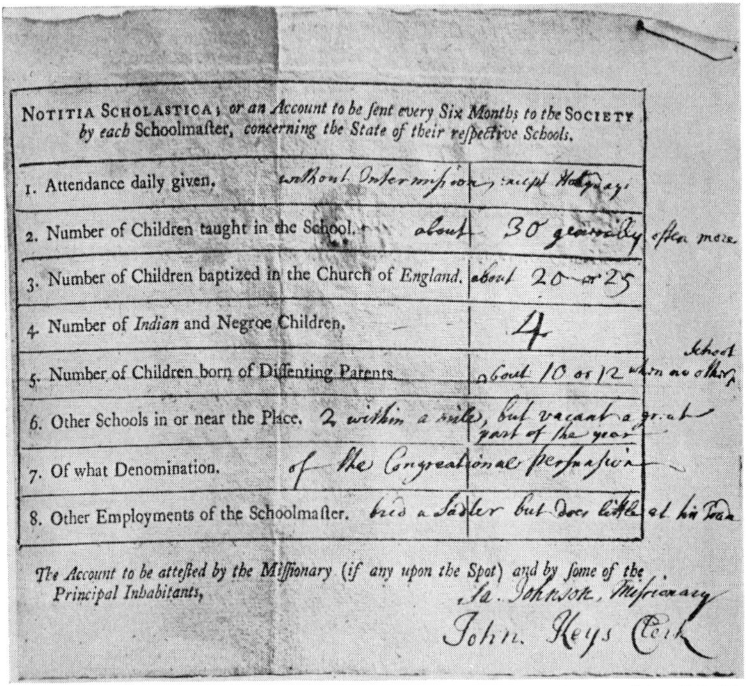

NOTITIA SCHOLASTICA; *or an Account to be sent every Six Months to the* SOCIETY *by each* Schoolmaster, *concerning the State of their respective Schools.*

1. Attendance daily given,	without Intermission except Holydays
2. Number of Children taught in the School.	about 30 generally often more
3. Number of Children baptized in the Church of *England*.	about 20 or 25
4. Number of *Indian* and Negroe Children.	4
5. Number of Children born of Dissenting Parents.	about 10 or 12 when no other School
6. Other Schools in or near the Place.	2 within a mile, but vacant a great part of the year
7. Of what Denomination.	of the Congregational persuasion
8. Other Employments of the Schoolmaster.	bred a Sadler but does little at his Trade

The Account to be attested by the Missionary (if any upon the Spot) and by some of the Principal Inhabitants,

Sa. Johnson, Missionary

John. Keys Clerk

FIG. 15. Report made by teacher of the S.P.G. school to the home office. "Notitia Scholastica" of Jos. Brown, schoolmaster at Stratford, Conn. 1739. (From Pascoe, *Two Hundred Years of the S.P.G.*)

On rare occasions this aim was enlarged: as for instance one teacher reports "several scholars are not only qualified for country employments, but for other business, for I teach all of the rules of vulgar and decimal arithmetic, and Mr. Barstow's eldest son is now about to learn geometry, trigonometry, surveying and other branches of the mathematics." Whether young Barstow ever did learn these higher branches of the mathematics is not known;

but the aspiration even is quite unique. Among the texts authorized were spellers, readers, grammars, elementary history books—all permeated with the same religious spirit. The list of textbooks authorized for all (Quo. Ch. X) in these schools and sent over by the society shows that the religious purpose permeates all instruction, while the reports of the masters indicate that the schools were typical "charity schools," attended for the most part by children of poorer people. Teaching followed the formal, superficial, memoriter methods of the day. The reports of some of the teachers describe these in full (Quo. 145), giving also the routine and daily program of the school (Quos. 148, 151).

Schools of Other Religious Sects.—The scheme of education adopted by the two dominant elements—the Dutch and the English—was naturally imitated so far as possible by other religious groups. Many of the sects previously mentioned maintained schools. Even the small body of Jews supported one from 1751. Most important of all, however, was the system of the Society of Friends. The Quakers were strong and very active throughout the middle colonies, and were objects of the special antipathy of the Church of England. Hence they labored under great difficulties in New York. However, this sect built up a system of schools practically coextensive with the system of churches. As this system was more highly elaborated in Pennsylvania and New Jersey, a further description will be given in connection with this region. (See p. 95.)

While these sectarian schools were not supported by the government, they were tolerated, and the nominal right of the governor to examine and license all teachers persisted. As the government did nothing directly for education, but depended on these various parochial systems of schools, it is obvious that the state-church conception of education was even more definitely formulated here than in England.

Schools in New Jersey Follow the New York Type.—The colony of New Jersey was formed in 1665 by a grant of the Duke of York who held all of the Dutch colony of New Netherland, including the coast lands to the present state of Maryland. The original proprietors, holders of this grant, issued "concessions and

BOOKS
Proper to be used in
CHARITY-SCHOOLS.

A Bible, New Testament, and Common-Prayer-Book.
The Church-Catechism.
Bishop *Gastrel*'s Christian Institutes.
The Church-Catechism broke into short Questions.
Lewis's Exposition of the Church-Catechism.
Archbishop *Wake*'s Commentary on the Church-Catechism.
Dr. *Worthington*'s Scripture-Catechism.
The first Principles of Practical Christianity.
Dr. *Woodward*'s Short Catechism, with an Explanation of divers hard Words.
A New Method of Catechizing.
Prayers for the Charity-Schools.
The Christian Scholar.
An Exercise for Charity-Schools upon Confirmation.
Pastoral Advice before, and after Confirmation.
The Whole Duty of Man, by way of Question and Answer.
An Abridgment of the History of the Bible, which may be bound up at the Beginning, or End of the Bible.
The Anatomy of Orthography: Or, a practical Introduction to the Art of Spelling and Reading *English*.
Monro's Essay on Christian Education.
Dr. *Talbot*'s Christian Shoolmaster.
Lessons for Children, Historical and Practical, &c.
An Exercise against Lying.
An Exercise against Taking God's Name in Vain.
A Serious Exhortation to Parents, in Relation to their Children, especially those who are educated in Charity-Schools.
The Way of Living in a Method and by Rule: Or a regular Way of Employing our Time.
Directions for the Devout and Proper Use of the Common Prayer, in the daily Service of the Church.
Cautions and Directions for the more devout Performance of the Publick Worship of God.
The Devout Psalmodist.

FIG. 16. List of books authorized for use in S.P.G. schools. (From Pascoe, *Two Hundred Years of the S.P.G.*)

SCHOOL SYSTEM OF THE MIDDLE COLONIES

agreements" which guaranteed among other things liberty of conscience. Consequently the colony became, as New Netherland had been under the Dutch, the resort of sectaries. To most of these groups of religious devotees, the school was as essential to the maintenance of their denominational entity as was the church.

West Jersey, including the southern half, eventually (in 1677) became the property of William Penn and four other Quakers, who reasserted the doctrine of religious freedom. In 1682 Penn and others—not all Quakers—purchased East Jersey. But after the English Revolution of 1688, the proprietors did not resume their political authority and the two provinces were annexed to New York (1702). Religious liberty was again conceded to all "except papist." Meanwhile large numbers of Scots had come over, especially to East Jersey. Here also were strong settlements of Puritans from New England, desirous of greater religious liberty than they had at home. Constant conflict with the governor over his restriction of their religious liberty and his arbitrary exercise of power led to the separation of New Jersey from New York in 1738. The original Dutch and Swedish elements of population were soon absorbed. The Scots or Scotch-Irish element and that from New England grew strong in comparison with the Quaker and the Episcopalian.

While the settlers from New England came to exercise increasing power, their educational policy was carried out only in their own communities. There town schools were built up. During this period of conflict over the character of the Colonial government, following the Revolution of 1688, the legislature passed a bill, in 1693, authorizing a system of town schools, when the inhabitants "think meet and convenient." Two years later the legislature acknowledged this plan to be a failure and decreed "that three men be chosen yearly and every year in each respective town in this province to appoint and agree with a schoolmaster." This no longer specified that their control of schools should be by town meeting. Practically it authorized the control of schools by church congregations. However, to most people of this period the function of the schools was peculiarly that of religious instruction. Hence with the guarantee of religious freedom went the right of the

[39]

Numb. III.

An ACCOUNT of the RATES of Cloathing Poor Children belonging to CHARITY-SCHOOLS.

The Charge of Cloathing a BOY.

	l.	s.	d.
A Yard half-quarter and Nail of Grey *Yorkshire* Broad-Cloth, 6 quarters wide, at 3 s. 6 d. per Yard, makes a Coat for a Boy 9 Years old	00	04	02
Making the Coat, with Pewter Buttons, and all other Materials	00	01	00
A Waistcoat of the same Cloth lined	00	04	04
A pair of Breeches of Cloth or Leather lined	00	03	00
1 Knit Cap, with Tuft and String, of any Colour	00	00	10
1 Band	00	00	02
1 Shirt	00	01	06
1 Pair of Woollen Stockings	00	00	10
1 Pair of Shoes	00	02	00
1 Pair of Buckles	00	00	01
1 Pair of Knit or Wash-Leather Gloves	00	00	07
The Total	00	18	06

Note. *A Suit of Blue Kersey is of the same price as Grey Broad-Cloth.*

The Charge of Cloathing a GIRL.

	l.	s.	d.
4 Yards of blue long Ells, about yard wide, at 18 d. p. Yard, makes a Gown and Petticoat for a Girl 9 Years old	00	06	00
Making thereof, Strings, Body-lining, and other Materials,	00	01	00
A Coif and Band of fine Ghenting	00	01	00
A Shift	00	01	06
A White, Blue, or Checquer'd Apron	00	01	00
A pair of Leather Bodice and Stomacher	00	02	06
1 Pair of Woollen Stockings	00	00	10
1 Pair of Shoes	00	01	10
A Pair of Pattens	00	00	09
1 Pair of Buckles	00	00	01
1 Pair of Knit or Wash Leather Gloves	00	00	07
The Total	00	17	01

N. B *The different Stature of Children is allowed for here ; and 50 Children, between the Ages of 7 and 12, (where there are as many from 7 to 9, as from 9 to 12 Years old) may be cloathed at these Rates.*

If the Length of the Boys Coats and the Girls Gowns and Petticoats, with the Girt of their Breast and Waste, be sent in Feet and Inches, the Children will be exactly fitted.

Where the Cloathing of a Boy or Girl is to last them for one Year, there must be an Allowance made of 1 Shirt and 1 Band more for the Boys, and of 1 Shift, 1 Coif, 1 Band, and 1 Apron, more for the Girls. And so of Stockings, Shoes, and Gloves, &c. for both Boys and Girls, where found necessary.

The Particulars abovementioned may be had at Mr. Richard Parker's, in Queen's-Court

FIG. 17. List of Equipment for S.P.G. Pupils. (From Pascoe, *Two Hundred Years of the S.P.G.*)

SCHOOL SYSTEM OF THE MIDDLE COLONIES

churches to control the schools. So it remained in New Jersey. There was no other Colonial legislation referring to elementary education. The governor of the colony claimed the same right as the governor of New York to license all schoolmasters, and to a slight extent exercised this right. The chief interest of the Colonial government concerned a college. This concern was really an outgrowth of religious controversy between the governor and the council, in sympathy with the Church of England on the one hand, and on the other the assembly, controlled by Quakers and other dissenters. The independent Colonial government beginning in 1738 gave marked encouragement to this movement, and finally the two factions agreed. The result was the founding of Princeton in 1746 and 1748, with a board of joint control. In reality the dissenters were in majority, as will be seen later (p. 168).

Church Control of Schools in the Colony of Pennsylvania.—The most extreme case of relinquishing all control of the school system to the churches occurred in Pennsylvania. In reality the customs in this colony were very similar to those of New Jersey, and the legal plans adopted quite similar. Pennsylvania was founded in 1681 by the great protagonist of that age of liberty of conscience and democracy of government. Naturally the broad principle of religious toleration was adopted as the cornerstone of the Colonial structure. And following the English conception of the times, education went with the church. For the original "frame of government" given by Penn to the colonists gave to the governor and his council the privilege and duty "to erect and order all public schools" and maintain a committee "of manners, education, and arts." In the first year of Colonial life (1682) the general statute of apprentice education discussed in Chapter 2 was passed by both council and assembly. In pursuance of authority granted to the council in 1698, that body gave the Quakers the right to set up a school "where poor children may be freely maintained, taught, and educated in good literature, until they be fit to be put out apprentices, or capable to be masters or ushers in said schools," and also to set up a public school "where all children and servants, male and female, whose guardians and masters be willing to sub-

[11]

The present State of the CHARITY-SCHOOLS in and about LONDON and WESTMINSTER, May 1715.

This Mark * denotes Schools set up since the last Year's Account, or not mentioned therein for want of Information. C. signifies Cloath'd. pt. Cl. part Cloathed. C & B. Caps and Bands. M. Maintained and set to Work. W. Set to Work only.

CHARITY - SCHOOLS in the Parishes of	No. of Sch.	BOYS	GIRLS	Voluntary Subscriptions about per Annum	Collections at Sermons & Sacraments about p. An num	Gifts to each School from the Beginning	Boys & Girls put out Apprentices from the Beginning
				l. s. d.	l. s. d.	l. s. d.	Boys Girls
ST. Allhallows Lombard-street C.	1	40			78 12 2		6
St. Andrew Holborn C.	2	80	80	291 10	87 1 8	580 5	137 116
In the same Parish, at St. George's Chappel C.	2	50	40	143	118 18 7	119 1 6	29 9
St. Anne Alderfgate C.	1	20	10	18 4	81 3 6		
St. Anne Blackfriars, endowed by a private Person C.	2	40	40				
St. Anne Westminster C.	2	50	50	89 7	136 5 2	391 2 6	89 50
* Billinsgate Ward C.		40		30	60	16 2 6	3
St. Botolph Alderfgate C.	2	50	50	100	23	163	18 20
St. Botolph Aldgate C.	5	115	80	122	50	278	92 92
*St. Botolph Bishopsgate C.	2	30	6	21 10	37	20	
St. Brides Parish C.	2	50	50	215	70	68	2 5
Broad-Street Ward, C. To which Schools there is 5l. per Annum left for 16 Years, to place out an Apprentice	2	50	30	67	20	500	64
Camberwell in Surry	1	20	20	50	40	11 1 6	
Castle Baynard Ward Cl.	1	30		50	50		
Chelsea in Middlesex C.	1	26		10	34	400	17
In the same Parish, Cl. Another Sch. chiefly supported by Ladies and Gentlewomen, 7 of whom are Trustees	1		30	50			4
Christ-Church in Surry C.	1	30		43	40	304 19	
St. Clement Dane, C.	2	70	40	111 19	44 7 3	993 16 4	106 53
*Cordwainers Ward Cl.	2	50	20	70	60	44 15 6	35
Cornhill-Ward C.	2	50	20	42 10	6 135 3 9	172 5 1	
*Cripplegate ward within including the School in the Parish of St. Alphage, C.	2	50	25	117 7	18	343 7 9	
* Deptford in Kent,	4	55		25			
	41	990	616	1642 7	6 1183 12 1	4405 16 8	598 349

FIG. 18. List of charity schools in London. (From Pascoe, *Two Hundred Years of the S.P.G.*)

ject them to the rules and orders of such schools." (Quo. 159.) Here is an institution which is at once both a charity school and a public school, an elementary and a secondary school, a school for males and for females. By the law the Monthly Meeting was given full power to admit pupils, and to appoint masters and ushers as well as "to remove and displace them." Out of this grew the Penn Charter School, which still exists.

The authority of the Colonial government extended over all teachers, as in other colonies. As early as 1689 a private school teacher "was told (by governor and council) that he must not

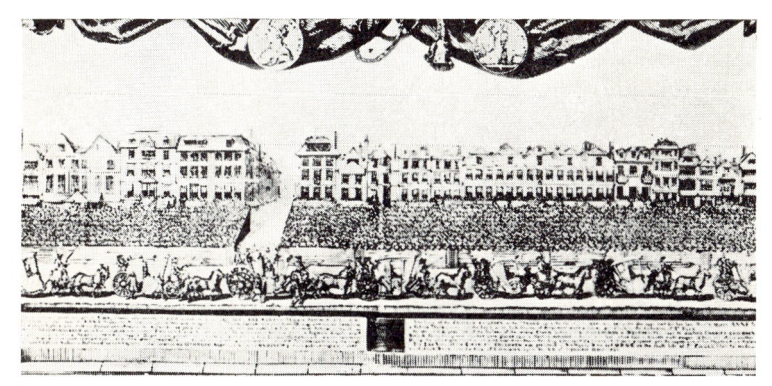

FIG. 19. Children of the charity schools at the public Thanksgiving for the Peace of Utrecht July 7, 1713. (From Allen & McClure, *Two Hundred Years: The History of the Society for Promoting Christian Knowledge.*)

teach school without a license." But "a certificate of his ability, learning, and diligence from the inhabitants of note of this town" was sufficient to obtain such permission. Here was no narrow sectarian restriction. A charter of 1701 reconferred the privileges and gave to the same Society of Friends the authority to erect such schools in the town or county.

Meanwhile a new frame of government had been given, which remained in force until the Revolution. In this the provisions for education found in the earlier "frame" were omitted. But the policy begun with the Quaker schools was soon made the policy of the colony for all of its inhabitants. It was enacted "that it shall and may be lawful to and for all religious societies or assem-

FOUNDING OF AMERICAN SCHOOL SYSTEM

blies, and congregations of Protestants, within this province, to purchase any lands or tenements for burying grounds and for erecting houses of religious worship, schools, and hospitals." The act gave them authority to collect and receive money and bequests for any of these purposes. A subsequent act (1731) (Quo. 161) prevented the alienation of such funds or property from the purposes for which they were given by trustees who might change their religious views.

Thus to these religious bodies was given the entire responsibility for the educational efforts of the community. A Quaker system of schools grew up, as in New Jersey; a few schools of the church of England were fostered by the S.P.G., as in New York. Above all the various German sects, grown numerous by the middle eighteenth century, reproduced their own schemes of education. As the various sectaries of England revolted against an established church and sought to buttress their own views and the faith of coming generations by schools, so did these German sects. A difference lies in the fact that these latter had the tradition of schools, but revolted against an orthodox state school as well as an orthodox state church, and strove with unquenchable zeal to protect, develop, and perpetuate as a part of their very existence an orthodox school of their own making. This liberty of schools, given as a part of the liberty of conscience of the early eighteenth century, was preserved by some of these communities, as we shall see, until the late nineteenth century.

These Germans numbered from one third to one half the population of the province from 1740 to 1783. In earlier years the Mennonites (German Quakers), Dunkards, and similar sects predominated. After 1740 the Lutherans and Moravians, the sects of the German Protestants holding less extreme social views, became the more numerous. The Lutherans under the Synod of Halle sent over more than twenty schoolmasters. The Moravians were largely a proselyting body greatly interested in a unification of the whole Christian church under their banner. From the time of Comenius, their great bishop and a patron saint of education, they were active in education. In Bethlehem, Nazareth, and neighboring towns of Pennsylvania, they built up schools of permanent influence. Through them came the first higher education of women in America. Moreover, because of their communistic form of

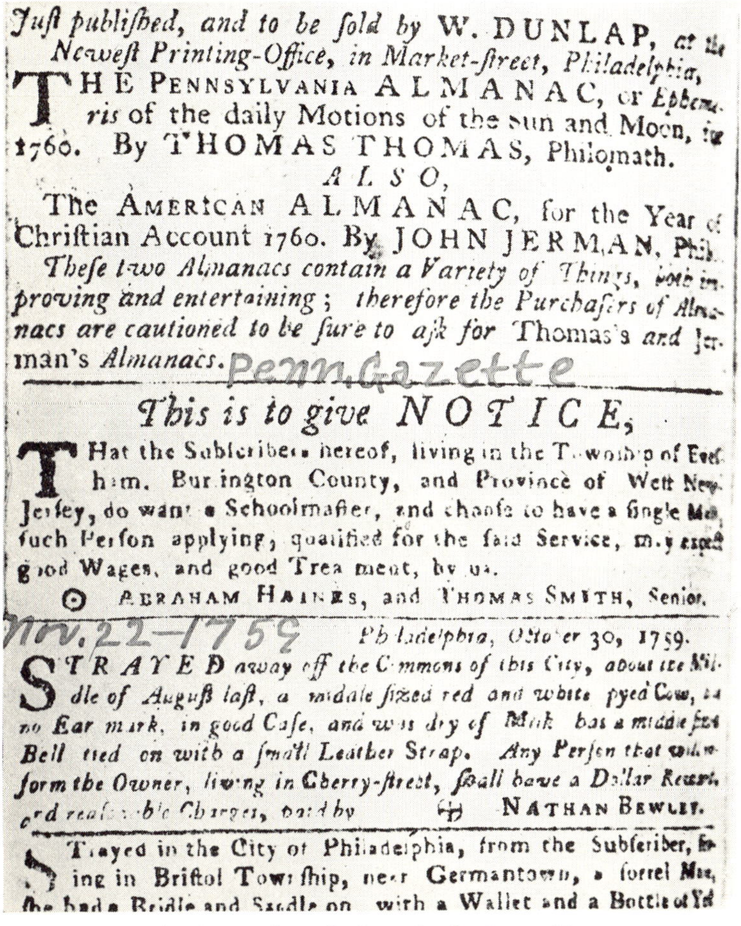

> *Just published, and to be sold by* W. DUNLAP, *at the Newest Printing-Office, in Market-street, Philadelphia,*
> THE PENNSYLVANIA ALMANAC, or Ephemeris of the daily Motions of the Sun and Moon, for 1760. By THOMAS THOMAS, Philomath.
> ALSO,
> The AMERICAN ALMANAC, for the Year of Christian Account 1760. By JOHN JERMAN, Phil.
> These two Almanacs contain a Variety of Things, both improving and entertaining; therefore the Purchasers of Almanacs are cautioned to be sure to ask for Thomas's and Jerman's Almanacs.
>
> ---
>
> *This is to give* NOTICE,
> THat the Subscribers hereof, living in the Township of Evesham, Burlington County, and Province of West New Jersey, do want a Schoolmaster, and chuse to have a single Man, such Person applying, qualified for the said Service, may expect good Wages, and good Treatment, by us.
> ABRAHAM HAINES, and THOMAS SMITH, Senior.
>
> Philadelphia, October 30, 1759.
> STRAYED away off the Commons of this City, about the Middle of August last, a middle sized red and white pyed Cow, no Ear mark, in good Case, and was dry of Milk, has a middle sized Bell tied on with a small Leather Strap. Any Person that will inform the Owner, living in Cherry-street, shall have a Dollar Reward and reasonable Charges, paid by NATHAN BEWLEY.
>
> STrayed in the City of Philadelphia, from the Subscriber, living in Bristol Township, near Germantown, a sorrel Mare, she had a Bridle and Saddle on, with a Wallet and a Bottle of ...

FIG. 20. Advertisement from the Pennsylvania *Gazette*, Nov. 22, 1759.

society, they conducted a "nursery school" from 1750 to 1764. Therefore to the Moravians belongs also the credit of the first infant school, a forerunner of the kindergarten.

Conditions were not always so good, however. Writing to the

[97]

Halle Synod in 1742 the Lutheran representative said, "Finally there are many hirelings and vagrants who in our town, from being shoemakers, tailors or linen weavers, become ministers, and who because of the lack of other men, are metamorphosed by the helpless people. But most of them came very humbly to me and agreed to lay down their office if I could . . . secure them an opportunity to teach school."

In subject matter the custom of these schools did not vary much from those of the church schools already described. In method and organization they preserved much of the traditions peculiar to

Fig. 21. Church, schoolhouse and parsonage of a Pennsylvania German village. (From *The Pennsylvania German*, vol. 4, page 273.)

their fatherland. Almost without exception they were appendages of the church, and the master was a church official. Like the Dutch schoolmaster, he was usually an assistant to the pastor.

At a Synod of the Lutheran churches in 1760 an enlightened discussion of educational conditions and methods took place, resulting in this conclusion: "It has been the custom in the past in the schools to teach the children reading and spelling out of the Bible or testaments or psalm-books, and occasionally also to scold and

SCHOOL SYSTEM OF THE MIDDLE COLONIES

beat the children, whereby the Word of God was made disagreeable and hateful to them in later life, especially since there already pre-exists in depraved nature a hatred of divine truth. The Bible must be used indeed, but in reference to youth it must be used with discretion as the holiest of holy things, which when it is opened before the children, they may feel in their youthful sensu-

FIG. 22. A Moravian schoolhouse and church. (From *The Pennsylvania German*, vol. 3, page 130.)

ousness as if a box of sugar or something of that sort had been opened for distribution."

Similar views are given by Christopher Dock, the greatest of these Colonial schoolmasters, who taught from 1718 to 1771. His *Hundred Rules for the Conduct of Children* is one of the earliest of American works on education (Quo. 289). One thing which Dock notes is of significance. He "confessed" that in the treatment of children, teachers must be less severe in America than in Germany, both because they have less authority there and because of the prevalence of humanitarian sentiments.

FOUNDING OF AMERICAN SCHOOL SYSTEM

Among all the various religious bodies which played a part in developing Colonial America, perhaps none were more devoted to educational endeavor or made greater sacrifices in its support than the German sectaries. For these people were probably the poorest equipped in worldly goods of all the Colonial groups. They were the persecuted of their own land, and were now set down in the midst of a population alien in language, in customs, and in cultural ideals. A very large number of them came over as redemptioners, bound for years to servile labor. It is rather because of

FIG. 23. A church-school building at Bethlehem, Pa. (From *The Pennsylvania German*, vol. 8, page 301.)

their devoted attachment to education and their sacrifices for it, than because they made any permanent contribution to system or method that these people are of significance in our educational history.

The Colony of Delaware.—Delaware was first settled in 1638 by the Swedes. The charter of this colony contained an educational provision similar to that of the Dutch colony (p. 73). The region was taken by the Dutch in 1654, whose principal settlement, New Amstel, has been previously noted as having a school from the first (p. 73). The English took possession in 1664 but allowed the

SCHOOL SYSTEM OF THE MIDDLE COLONIES

Dutch laws to stand until 1674. In 1682 they turned the region over to William Penn. The charters and laws of Pennsylvania were valid until 1702 when a separate legislature was granted. The only educational legislation of the colony was a law (1743) similar to the Pennsylvanian enactment of 1731, confirming religious bodies in their right to maintain schools and in the possession of all property raised or given for this purpose.

Secondary and Higher Education in the Middle Colonies.—As in the other colonies the Latin school was included within the

FIG. 24. Town of Bethlehem, Pa., with its seminary. (From Reichel, *History of Bethlehem Seminary*.)

institutional and social scheme of the Dutch, of the English, and of the sectarian groups of the middle colonies. The same long struggle occurred in New Amsterdam and in New York as in the other colonies. After repeated complaints on the part of the people, the Dutch company made appropriation for a Latin teacher in 1652 which proved of temporary success. Six years later the company sent over a learned "professor" and the school thus founded continued under its patronage during the Dutch rule.

FOUNDING OF AMERICAN SCHOOL SYSTEM

A generation passed under the English rule before any action revealed a concern in education. In Governor Cornbury's first address to the general assembly in 1702, he recommended a law "for the erecting of public schools in proper places." What he had in mind by "public schools" was probably the traditional Latin school of the upper class Englishmen. After prolonged bickerings between houses of the legislature and the governor, such a school was established, to have the joint support of the Colonial and the city government for one year, and to be taught by a master licensed by the governor and appointed by the city council. Not for a generation did this matter come up again. In 1732 another attempt was made and a Latin grammar school was established and operated with Colonial support for five years. Again the matter fell into abeyance until the grammar school preparatory to King's College, now Columbia University, was founded, after the middle of the century. (See Ch. VII.)

Fig. 25. An octagonal school house, Northampton County, Pennsylvania. Early 19th century. (From *The Pennsylvania German*, vol. 4, page 273.)

In Pennsylvania the Penn Charter School as organized in 1701 was probably a Latin school from the first. While this religious organization was devoted to education, having no ministry they were not in such need of these schools as other sects and so did not seek to multiply them. With other religious bodies rudimentary schools of this type were started by the ministry. Since it was well into the eighteenth century before any progress was made with these, they tended to develop along the new lines of greater freedom ultimately resulting in the academies. In each of the middle colonies such rudimentary schools of the new type flourished.

Of the colleges to be discussed in Chapter VII, New York and Pennsylvania developed one and New Jersey two. A long preparatory period of discussion was necessary and the institution did not

SCHOOL SYSTEM OF THE MIDDLE COLONIES

take shape until the generation preceding the Revolution. In New York and New Jersey these colleges were supported by religious denominations, and chartered by the state. In Pennsylvania, the institution owed its origin to private initiative and was more nearly an expression of forces tending for social ends than occurred in any other colony. Religious toleration was exercised by all; gov-

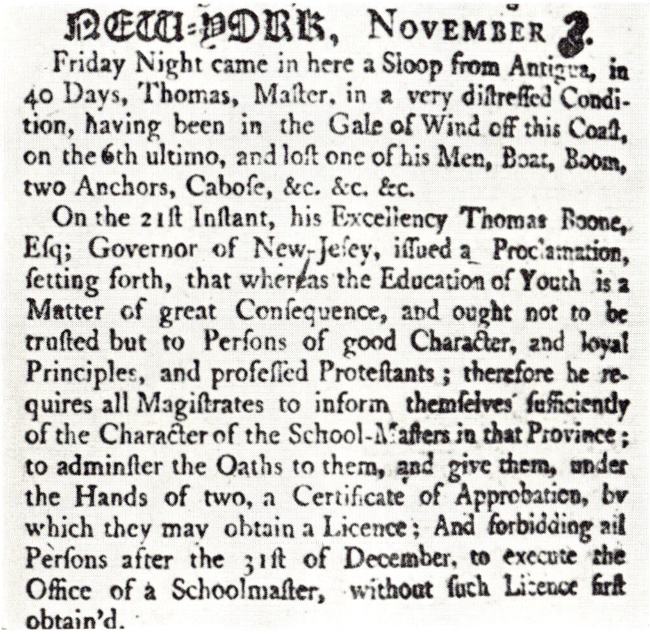

> **NEW-YORK, NOVEMBER 3.**
> Friday Night came in here a Sloop from Antigua, in 40 Days, Thomas, Master, in a very diftreffed Condition, having been in the Gale of Wind off this Coaft, on the 6th ultimo, and loft one of his Men, Boat, Boom, two Anchors, Caboſe, &c. &c. &c.
> On the 21ſt Inſtant, his Excellency Thomas Boone, Efq; Governor of New-Jefey, iffued a Proclamation, ſetting forth, that whereas the Education of Youth is a Matter of great Confequence, and ought not to be trufted but to Perfons of good Character, and loyal Principles, and profeffed Proteftants; therefore he requires all Magiftrates to inform themfelves fufficiently of the Character of the School-Mafters in that Province; to adminfter the Oaths to them, and give them, under the Hands of two, a Certificate of Approbation, by which they may obtain a Licence; And forbidding all Perfons after the 31ft of December, to execute the Office of a Schoolmafter, without fuch Licence firft obtain'd.

FIG. 26. A governor's proclamation requiring the licencing of school teachers. (From *New York Mercury*, Nov. 4, 1760.)

ernment contributions to support were slight; government participation in control still slighter.

Summary.—The middle colonies attempted a universal scheme of education through the churches. The government supported, contributed, supervised, authorized, or tolerated these schools as the case might be; but in no case assumed the ultimate responsibility. The Dutch government of New Amsterdam, which was primarily a trading corporation, assumed the support of schools throughout its existence. The Dutch church in the home country

[103]

FOUNDING OF AMERICAN SCHOOL SYSTEM

licensed and the local church supervised. The West India Company contributed to schools in other settlements and expected the local government and patroons to do likewise. For a short time only the municipal government of New Amsterdam assumed support and control of the schools. Under the English rule in the Dutch communities these schools survived. Frequently church and school came to be supported by the town on the general tax rate and so approximated the town system of New England. Under the English rule the interest of the government was limited to the licensing of teachers to assure their orthodoxy and loyalty. In the absence of town schools or of any Colonial support of schools, a system of church schools was built up in English towns by the Society for the Propagation of the Gospel in Foreign Parts. Other religious denominations likewise supported their own schools. In New Jersey conditions were similar. Dutch and New England communities built up their church-town schools. The Quakers usually established a school in connection with each "meeting house." The Scotch Presbyterians frequently developed schools around their minister. Private schools flourished. In Pennsylvania the colony early authorized each religious body to build up its own school system and took no further interest itself. In Delaware the same policy was followed. Secondary schools and colleges developed quite late, were found in each of the colonies except Delaware, where a famous academy flourished. These higher institutions were for the most part also founded and supported by the religious organizations.

Chapter V

THE TOWN SCHOOLS OF NEW ENGLAND

Early Apprenticeship Laws and Education.—As has been seen, the early educational laws of the New England colonies, like those of the other colonies, were primarily apprenticeship laws. But the glory of Massachusetts was that she made of this apprenticeship law, which by tradition related only to training for vocation, an educational law to cover literary learning as well. By all English practice and ideas, the literary arts of reading and writing had hitherto been based upon the initiative of the individual and the favor of social position and wealth. New England now universalized them by attaching to them a national tradition of universal application and of legal compulsion.

What a few other peoples had done on a religious basis, Massachusetts did in 1642 on the basis of social worth and individual right. It was "the training up of children in learning and labor and other employments which may be profitable to the commonwealth" which concerned these far-sighted legislators. The church and the ministry are nowhere mentioned. It was upon the selectmen or prudential men of the town that the duty of enforcement was laid. It was to the magistracy or any court that all final authority was assigned. The law primarily concerned "the calling and employment of children" and specified parents and masters as especially concerned. So far it was the English statute of artificers in a New England setting. But one phrase was interpolated which made this a revolutionary enactment—"especially of their ability to read and understand the principles of religion and the capital laws of the country." This is the only provision which is foreign to the laws of apprenticeship as they were enforced in England and in the remaining colonies. But it is the germ of our public school system. During the seventeenth century there were numerous offenses for which the penalty was death. Massachusetts Bay had passed a number of such laws. Under these conditions it was quite necessary, in building up a new and model commonwealth, that the children should understand these capital laws. Such a penalty was decreed by law for the child that should strike its parent in anger. A law passed somewhat later (Quo. 174) forbade the penalty if the education of the child had been neglected by the parent, who thereby violated the Law of 1642.

In the Law of 1642 there is no mention of schools. Schools might and did exist at the time, but the education of the child was possible without schools. Long after the School Law of 1647 was passed, this earlier Law of 1642 was enforced without any relation to the later enactment. Many town records show curious entries dividing up the town for the purpose of such supervision as was necessary and required for the enforcement of the law. The following[1] comes from Cambridge in 1643, and similar entries recur throughout the Colonial period.

"The division of the town for the looking to the well educating (of) children.

"It is ordered that according to an order of court made the last general court for the townesmen to see to the educating children, that John Bridge shall take care of all the families of that side the highway his own house stands on to my brother Winshepes & so all the families from Gouldi More to Mr. Holeman and Carie Lathum's families: and Sergeant Winshepe is to see to the families on the other side the common to Grissall next Brother Bridg (   ) is to see to all the families that the lane going from the meeting house down to the river and so the lane going from the meeting house down to (   ) brother Dunstars house and so water townward (   ) his own house John Russell to see (   ) between that highway and the high (   ) George Cooke to take care of all the families between that way and the highway going from the meeting house into the neck by Tho. Davenport and my brother Shawe all the rest between that and the river and my brother Oakes all on the other side the river."

[1] From Records of the Town and Selectmen of Cambridge, 1630–1703. Page 47.

THE TOWN SCHOOLS OF NEW ENGLAND

More frequently specific action was taken covering particular families or individuals. Such records run as follows: "Ordered that John Edy, Senior, shall go to John Fisk's house and to George Lorance and William Priest houses to inquire about their children, whether they be learned to read the English tongue; in case they be defective, to warn in the said John George and William to the next meeting of the selectmen."

This obligation was assumed and enforced throughout the Colonial period. It was often recognized as a burden and one to be minimized as far as possible. One of the towns puts into its order to its selectmen: "to drive a bargain about it if they can." Especially was this provision burdensome during the eighteenth century when population became scattered and poverty great because of wars and other hardships. At the same time the apprenticing of children under this law became one of the best means for meeting the problems of poverty and threatened pauperism.

The Town the Basis of the Schools System.—Few public documents are more impressive than the simple records of the early New England towns as they testify the faith of the people in the importance of education. Boston's earliest educational entry, "that our brother Philemon Pormont shall be entreated to become schoolmaster for the teaching and nurturing of children with us" is often quoted. In 1642 at Ipswich "the town votes that there shall be a free school."

FIG. 27. School house and block house of Dedham, Mass. (From a drawing in the old records reproduced in the *New England Magazine.*)

The following year Dedham records its resolve to support the three fundamental institutions of society: "Also it is with unanimous consent concluded that some portion of land in this intended division should be set apart for public use, viz., for the town, the church, and a free school."

An understanding of this early growth and of the character of the New England school can be had only through an understanding of the New England town. Most of the early settlers came to New England in groups, usually under the leadership of a minister, often as a church congregation. For some decades the new towns inland were settled in the same way by groups from the older towns. Even when individual settlers joined these groups, they were first carefully scrutinized and then admitted by town consent. The assisted individual emigration of the other colonies hardly existed, and redemptioners or bonded servants were never numerous. To these towns the general court granted the entire land of the community. While there was no fixed standard of allotment, six miles square was an approximate town area. Thus the New England town corresponded to the township of our Central and Western states with this modification—that during the early Colonial period the settlers lived in a central village. In fact a law of 1635 (repealed, however, in 1640) demanded that the settlers live within one-half mile of the church. This town land was allotted among the inhabitants. When additional lands were obtained subsequently or former common lands were divided up, the division was on a basis of equality, or on the basis of previous allotments or of taxable property. The land holdings of any citizen were usually scattered in a number of places of the town, so that no one inhabitant might be unduly favored. Large land or large wealth was not possible except through the trade and commerce of the seaport towns.

These democratic groups were thus held together by like ecclesiastical beliefs, by a tenure of land which at basis differed little from communal property, and by common social beliefs and aspirations secured by scrutinizing each individual settler before admitting him. These towns more nearly approximated a pure democracy than any preceding forms, though the aristocratic social sentiment was yet strong. They exercised many rights of local government. In 1636 the general court sanctioned the exercise of these rights so far as they did not contravene the rights and enactments of the general court, thus giving precedent to one of the essential features of our national constitution. But as a matter of fact, in this case as in most others, the enactment of the general court merely gave legal sanction to what the towns were already doing. Among

THE TOWN SCHOOLS OF NEW ENGLAND

these early forms of town activity was the establishment of schools. We know from extant records that half the towns of Massachusetts had established schools before the law of 1647 required them to do so, and it is a fair presumption that a private school authorized by the town existed in each of the others. Such a school would fulfill the provisions of this first compulsory law.

It is often stated that the towns were not democracies, because freemanship in the colony was limited to members of the authorized Congregational churches. This however is not true: for on most matters of local concern non-freemen or non-church members were allowed to vote. This was particularly the case concerning the school. An act of the general court in 1647 (Quo. 179) confirmed the custom of the towns in allowing non-freemen to vote on matters not concerned with the general government of the colony, including by specific mention the right to vote concerning all school matters. Thus the control of schools was made purely democratic and remained so after the passage of the compulsory law now to be noted.

Previous to this time the support of schools went along with the support of the church. A town charge had been planned on a democratic basis. A law of 1638 declared "that every inhabitant in every town is liable to contribute to all charges, both in church and commonwealth, whereof he doth or may receive benefit."

The Town School System Made Compulsory.—In 1647 the government and general court of Massachusetts Bay Colony enacted a law (Quo. 181) which was the foundation of the American public school system. The voluntary custom of most towns was now made obligatory on all towns of fifty or more families. This compulsory provision was not removed throughout the Colonial period. People moved by as deep religious conviction as were the Puritans were apt to assign great importance to the common deeds of every day. Consequently we have quite full accounts of the life of many of these towns. In all of them the attention given to the schools is close and continuous. During the early century this Law of 1647 needed little enforcement by compulsion. During the eighteenth century conditions of living changed the character of the school; but, while there are numerous instances where the compulsion of the court was necessary for the maintenance of the Latin grammar schools, there are few where disobedience to the law concerning the elementary school called for any exercise of power from the outside.

The motive for this law is clearly expressed in the preambles. Just as the vocational education provided for in the Law of 1642 had a social basis, this requirement of a literary education through schools found its justification in religious beliefs and necessities. The preamble runs:

> "It being one chief point of that old deluder, Satan, to keep men from the knowledge of the Scriptures, as in former times, by keeping them in an unknown tongue, so in these latter times, by persuading from the use of tongues, that so at last the true sense and meaning of the original might be clouded by false glosses of saint-seeming deceivers,—that learning might not be buried in the graves of our fathers in church and commonwealth, the Lord assisting our endeavors, it is therefore ordered," etc.

Personal knowledge of the Scriptures through an ability to read was essential to the eternal welfare of the individual as well as to temporal welfare of the community.

Support of Schools. Development of the Free School.— The Law of 1647 did not prescribe the method of school support. It stated that the master should "be paid either by the parents or masters of such children, or by the inhabitants in general, by way of supply, as the major part of those that order the prudentials of the town shall appoint." This provision indicates that the various customs of the towns in supporting schools by charges for tuition of the pupils, or by salary paid by the town, or by combination of the two were confirmed. The last phrase of the quotation is ambiguous; but practice indicates that it was intended to confirm the general supervision and control exercised by the selectmen or prudential men of the town. From the records of the individual town we can build up the story of the development of its free school. For the free school was the gradual outgrowth of the provision

THE TOWN SCHOOLS OF NEW ENGLAND

that the master might be paid "by the inhabitants in general." Payment of the master through some form of tuition rates was quite common and persisted in many localities well into the eighteenth century. But the school gradually became "free" by the exclusion of such rates to a greater and greater degree and the ultimate complete dependence on general taxation.

Here the experience of the English settlers with the poor law system of England, described in Chapter I, is of significance; for the Colonial development of school support on the public basis passed through the same three stages, as did also that of the ministry. An illustration from the support of the church will be illuminating. In the early years at Salem "there was a voluntary town contribution toward the maintenance of the minister, quarterly to be paid." This evidently went on for many years but finally proved unsatisfactory. In 1657 "it was voted and agreed by the town that they voluntarily yield themselves to be rated; those whom they shall choose for the receiving of the maintenance of the ministry, where need shall require." Two months later "It is ordered that all those persons that will not subscribe nor contribute towards the maintenance of the ministry shall be rated, and the selectmen to rate them." Two years later it was "ordered that those sums for the ministry shall be raised upon the town by way of rate" (i.e. assessed tax). Here the succession of the three steps of voluntary contribution, forced contribution based if necessary on an official assessment by town officials, and finally a general tax levy is clear.

Much earlier than this (1633) it was recorded by the general court that "after much deliberation and serious advice, the Lord directed the teacher, Mr. Cotton, to make it clear by the Scriptures that the minister's maintenance, as well as other charges of the church, should be defrayed out of a stock or treasury which was to be raised out of a weekly contribution." In 1638, however, the general court declared "that every inhabitant in any town is liable to contribute to all charges, both in church and commonwealth, whereof he doth or may receive benefit." Furthermore that if he did not contribute willingly he could be assessed by the selectmen.

This particularly applied to "those who are not freemen or church members" and pertained to both church and school. Here again we find the court confirming the customs of the town.

In 1654 Governor Winthrop in surveying the practices of the towns wrote, "Divers free schools were erected as at Roxbury . . . and at Boston . . . and the charge to be raised yearly by contribution either by voluntary allowance or by rate of such as refused," etc., and this order was confirmed by the general court. Here both the voluntary and the forced contribution are indicated. The Boston Latin school to which the Governor referred was supported primarily by the voluntary contributions of forty-five "of the richer inhabitants," as first recorded in 1636.

The school at Roxbury was wholly supported by voluntary contributions but could not be called a town school (Quo. 236). In Dedham there was first a general voluntary contribution, supplemented later by the levy of a tuition rate upon the inhabitants, graded according to the distance of their homes from the school. This, together with the statement of the general law of 1647 and the statement of Governor Winthrop given above, furnishes illustrations of the forced contributions which were perhaps quite general in the towns. Such action would be administrative and of individual application, and consequently does not appear in the town records.

One of the earliest cases of the use of direct taxation for the support of schools is a striking evidence of the relation of school support to the machinery evolved for the relief of the poor. In Salem in 1644 it was "ordered that a rate be published on next lecture day, that such as have children to be kept at school would bring in their names and what they will give for one whole year, and also, that if any poor body hath children, or a child, to be put to school and not able to pay for their schooling, that the town will pay for it by rate." Quite generally throughout the Colonies and well into the nineteenth century free education was pauper education. While the same origin is indicated in Salem, this soon ceased to be true in the Massachusetts towns in general.

In most of these towns the schools were supported by a combination of rates for tuition paid for each child, funds from common

THE TOWN SCHOOLS OF NEW ENGLAND

lands or from gifts, and an appropriation from the "common stock" or treasury of the town. There was no presupposition or theory in favor of free schools. They grew out of the experience of the town. But the compulsion of the general court of 1647 very shortly led to compulsory support on the part of all inhabitants by the town. In 1648 at Charlestown "it was agreed that a rate of fifteen pounds should be gathered of the town, towards the schools for this year." Five additional pounds' rental from town land made up the customary twenty pounds annual salary of the master. In 1650 in the Boston town meeting "it was agreed that Mr. Woodmansey, the schoolmaster, shall have fifty pounds per annum for teaching the scholars, and his proportion to be made up by rate." In 1652 Dorchester voted "that the school rate be gathered with the town rate."

However, this great principle of support of schools by taxation was not adopted by all so readily. Even the towns mentioned reverted from time to time to the use of a tuition rate levied on the children. While there was a great variety of plans, yet for half a century or more practically all of the towns used some combination of tax rate and tuition rate for school support. Most of them also drew some support from common lands or gift funds. There was no uniformity of plan among the towns and usually no consistent practice in any one town. A later generation worked out under the same law the general plan of public support.

The difficulty of maintaining a school for a scattered population under frontier conditions necessitated more stringent laws. The fine for neglect was successively increased until by the Law of 1701 the penalty in the case of the elementary school became almost as great as the cost of the school. These conditions led to the gradual abandonment of dependence on tuition. This was a slow process, the details of which we cannot follow here, and it was accompanied by other important changes to be noted later. But during the first half of the eighteenth century practically all Massachusetts towns abandoned tuition rates and came to support their schools wholly by funds raised by general taxation. It will be seen that this, though seemingly a tardy development, occurred quite a century earlier than a genuine free school system was built up in any state west of New England.

Control of Schools.—Through these New England town schools also grew up the forms of administration and supervision characteristic of the American public school system. The Law of 1638 confirmed the towns in this right to establish, support, and control schools. The Law of 1647 required that each town should maintain at least one school using such means of support as the selectmen might determine.

The democratic town meeting was the earliest and most general mode of school control in both legislative and administrative affairs. When power over the schools came to be delegated, it was usually placed, with all similar powers, in the hands of the selectmen or prudential men who were agents for the town in all governmental affairs. This was a remarkable innovation, for in England school control was in the hands of special feoffees or trustees, or in the hands of the church; and in Scotland as well as the Netherlands and the other Protestant countries of the Continent it was placed largely in the hands of church officials after the initial acts were taken by the civil authorities. In Massachusetts, however, the school from the first was a civil, not an ecclesiastical institution. Its control, supervision, and support lay wholly with civic officials. Seldom is the minister mentioned in connection with the local school, though no doubt he exerted great influence.

Not only did the town meeting exercise general legislative control over the school but it often had administrative functions as well. Legislative responsibility is shown in the decision to employ a master, and to have a school, in determining the length of session and the date of beginning, in fixing the master's salary, in deciding the method of raising the salary, and in determining tuition rates. But in the early years the town meeting often performed such administrative acts as voting on the employment of a certain master, on locating a schoolhouse, on ordering the collection of rates or the actual payment of salary. Such quaint illustrations are to be found as the vote of the town meeting of Salem in 1640 that "young Mr. Norris choose by this assembly to teach school." In Dorchester

THE TOWN SCHOOLS OF NEW ENGLAND

it was clearly stipulated that "the said schoolmaster was to be chosen from time to time by the freemen." Even such small affairs as the replacing of a broken pane of glass or the purchase of a pair of tongs were not beneath the notice of the entire town.

However, very early, and especially after 1647, the board of selectmen exercised both executive and legislative power. In fact the power conferred by the Law of 1647 was legislative. While the New England government was democratic in form, New England society was still strongly aristocratic. The institution of prudential men conformed to this aristocratic sentiment and to the English traditions of representative government. It is obvious, quite as much from what is not recorded as from what is, that these selectmen exercised the greater part of both legislative and administrative control of the schools. Their functions included all those mentioned above and in a general way extended throughout the Colonial period, though greater during the earlier portion than the later.

It is in the building up of special authorities for school control that educational administrative machinery develops. From the earliest day special committees of one, two, or three men were frequently employed to contract with a teacher, to rent school lands, and for similar purposes. A Dedham record of 1662 reads: "The school being laid down, Peter Woodward and Timothy Dwight are deputed to treat with Arthur Metcalfe for the keeping of the school." Even after the selectmen were given general charge, the special committee was called into being very frequently. In the same town about a century later we find "Assembled the selectmen and desired John Metcalfe to endeavor to procure a schoolmaster as soon as may be, Mr. Marsh having lately laid down the keeping of the school."

The permanent or standing school committee was the next stage of development of school machinery. In the very early years, permanent committees were appointed to look after lands given by the town or by individuals for the use of the school. After the English custom there were often feoffees or trustees holding for life and with self-perpetuating powers. In a few cases these had complete control over the school. In but one case, Roxbury, did this plan persist throughout the Colonial period; and therefore its school cannot be considered a town school.

The period of importance for the permanent school committee was the eighteenth century. With the growth of population and its general dispersion over the town, one school would not suffice; school affairs became complicated and detailed. Many towns appointed a committee to look after the schools for six months or for a year. Soon this became an established custom with most of them. Each year at the annual election of town officers, a committee, varying in numbers, was elected to have complete charge of all the schools of the town for the year. The laws which established the school system of the early National period, 1789 and 1826 (Doc. 187), made such committees obligatory.

A less common type of standing school committee was one of supervision or inspection. While this duty was assigned to special committees on occasions or more frequently to the standing committees when appointed, in a number of towns, notably at Boston, the annual committee of inspection became a permanent feature. It was made up of the ministers and other prominent men. The occasion of its inspection became a notable social function. In time these social features overbalanced any professional value the inspection might have had; for it was required that all schoolmasters be warned of its coming. Reports of these committees show that for a long period at least their work was effective. It was the custom for the committee to entertain all the schoolmasters at dinner at the town expense, as the following record shows: "Agreed with Mr. Waort to dine seventy or eighty persons in the day when the public schools are to be visited, at five shillings per man, and all the liquors that shall be drunk are to be paid for."

The Law of 1789 assigned this supervisory duty, as well as that of licensing teachers, to the standing school committee. The Law of 1826 made such assignment obligatory.

Origin of the District School System.—Eighteenth century New England was a very different society from that of the seventeenth century. The compact unified groups which formerly made up the towns were now broken up. New towns were built up by

THE TOWN SCHOOLS OF NEW ENGLAND

accretion of individuals or single families. The ties which bound the members of such groups together were now much weakened if not dissolved. Exploration was made by hardy adventurers in search of more fertile land and more promising sources of wealth. The frontier was pushed forward by the courageous families, braving the terror of the savages and of wild beasts and the loneliness and hardships of pioneer isolation. Commerce and trade developed. Economic interests, long partially submerged in the semi-communistic scheme of the church town, now began to exert an influence more powerful than the religious and social ideals of the earlier period. The military activity of the Indian wars and later of the struggle with the French and Indians brought in its train the moral and social laxity which always accompanies or follows the relapse of civilized men to the laws of savagery. Each of the wars was followed by a series of legislative enactments which specify the growing laxness in morals and the increase of crime and pauperism. With the changes of government in England came the appointment of successive royal governors, surrounded by counselors, dependent officials, and miniature echo of court life, and entirely out of sympathy with the traditions and aspirations of the people. Developing political problems and increasing trade and commerce brought the legal profession to the front. The lawyer now competed with the minister for the leadership of society. By the Revolutionary War period he may be said to have supplanted the minister as the dominant factor in shaping public opinion. General Gage stated "that all the people in his government are lawyers or smatterers in law." While Burke's opinion was that "in no country perhaps in the world is a law so general a study" and that as a result the American people were able to "augur their government at a distance and snuff the approach of tyranny in every tainted breeze."

The change in religious sentiment had really occurred in the late seventeenth century. The "Half-way Covenant" had been adopted in 1662 and marked the division of the church into conservative and progressive branches. Greater toleration for Baptists, Quakers, and other persecuted sects followed. In 1672 the law of banishment against the first of these was republished; but in 1679 a Baptist church was built and public worship begun. In 1684 an Episcopal church was established in Boston and maintained thereafter, usually having the patronage of the governor and the official group. The new Charter of 1692 granted by the monarchs (William and Mary) who were in no danger of lapsing into apostacy and Catholicism, made the state supreme over the church. The official party at the head of the state was not in sympathy with the state church, and the freemen who composed the state were no longer necessarily in sympathy with the establishment. Dissensions within as well as divergence of views without quite destroyed the unity of belief and policy found in earlier generations.

Dispersion of the Population.—This doubtless was the immediate cause of the modification of the school system. The early law (1635) which required settlers to live within a half mile of the church was repealed five years later. But fear of savages, religious fervor, the strong feeling of social unity, and the method of granting land by the town, as well as the tradition of the mother country, held the people in compact settlements. All these influences gradually lost their strength and by the opening of the eighteenth century ceased to operate to keep the people in village groups. With the increase of population, both by accessions from without and by natural growth, all the town land remote from the village centers was allotted. Subordinate villages grew up to some extent within the town; but for the most part the life on the isolated farm, now so universal in America, was developed. All these forces operated to carry the population into new towns farther west in which the influences which had produced the centralized town settlement were never strong.

The Moving School.—The dispersion of population was followed by a marked change in the school system. The one town school in the central village no longer sufficed. Travel from the farm to the village was very difficult, for roads were poor, in some parts of the year practically impassable. It was a great hardship for children to reach the central school by forest paths or over poor roads in severe winters and in spring floods. Indians remained an occasional danger well into the eighteenth century. Wild animals,

THE TOWN SCHOOLS OF NEW ENGLAND

especially wolves, abounded until the middle of the century. The surface of New England is quite broken; streams and swamps, fresh and salt water meadows are numerous; hills and mountains necessitate long detours. In one Massachusetts county there are over eighty lakes or ponds. The scattered population, taxed for the support of a school, compelled by law to maintain one, but dominated by a democratic sentiment, demanded that it have the service of the school for which it paid. So the school was "put on wheels." The village schoolmaster, still employed for the year, was sent from time to time to different parts of the town. The equitable division of the master's time became a matter of practical difficulty and great concern for the town meeting, the selectmen, or the school committee. Some such records as the following from Lunenburg in 1737 are found yearly for most of these towns—"Voted that . . . be a committe fully empowered to hire a lawful schoolmaster for the town of Lunenburg and to provide four convenient places for the school to be kept in, where it may best convenience the inhabitants, the time of keeping in each place to be proportioned according to the number of scholars for the space of one year next ensuing." Malden in 1710, after employing a master for the town, "voted that the school be removed into three parts of the town, the first half in the center, and one quarter in the southwardly end, and one quarter in the northwardly end of the town." There is still one school, taught by one master, but it is held in three or four different places. These various parts of the town were frequently called squadrons for militia purposes. So the process was frequently called "squadroning out the school." The most serious effect of this scheme appears on the surface. Children who had been receiving a year's schooling, if they could not travel now could attend for but three or four months.

The Divided School.—Other results developed. More mature children, especially the boys, could travel far, braving inclement weather. Hence in the winter such pupils dominated the school. In the summer time the children or youth were needed on the farm, but their younger brothers and sisters could easily attend. So there grew up a difference in the character of the attendance dur-

FOUNDING OF AMERICAN SCHOOL SYSTEM

ing the two seasons. Since each locality was entitled to a school it began to demand it at a time desired. Summer and winter schools needed different types of teacher. For both seasons, instead of one town master there came to be several. For the summer school for little children, women and girls were more and more frequently

FIG. 28. A New England dame school. (From an old book.)

employed. For the short term even in the winter school there was sought a cheaper teacher than the old town schoolmaster on annual salary, teaching all the time. Consequently the character of the teacher declined and naturally his standing in the community was lowered. As the worth of the school decreased, influence was les-

[120]

sened. In many cases existing local schools kept by private masters, often by dames, were incorporated into the town school system. These various aspects of the changes then going on are revealed in one record in 1735—"Voted that the £50 voted for the support of a free school in Manchester, one half of said £50 to be expended to support four school dames to keep a free school, one at that part of our town called Nuport and one in that part of our town called the Plain, and one in that part of our town called Cittal Cove: the other half of said £50 to be expended to support a schoolmaster to keep a free school in the schoolhouse in Manchester in the fall and winter season." It is to be noted that this somewhat complicated system is yet called a school! Moreover its branches are all free, supported by one general appropriation from town funds.

Beginnings of the District System.—With the adjustment of the machinery of school organization and control to these changed conditions, the germs of the district school were planted, though the system itself was not legally established in Massachusetts until 1768, and under the new state constitution of 1789 (Quo. 187). The chief educational factors contributing to these origins were the demands of a scattered

FIG. 29. The woman teacher in the summer school. (From Bolles's *Spelling Book*.)

population to participate in the privileges of a town school for which they were taxed, and which they were compelled by law to support. This led to the division of the town school into several parts, taught by several masters; to the incorporation of existing dame schools as public charges; to the differentiation into summer and winter terms; and above all to the abolition of the rates for tuition. The point previously made (p. 113) that the Massachusetts schools all became free during the first half of the eighteenth century can now be explained. The scattered population could not attend a central school: under these conditions neither the central schools nor small local schools could be supported by tuition rates alone. Children were not numerous enough or the pitifully small tuition rates remunerative enough to secure a teacher. The law demanded a school, penalizing non-compliance with a heavy fine. The school must be supported by a general tax. This would be voted only on condition that the local communities, the scattered population, had reasonable opportunity to use the school, which must be brought within reach. Hence the divided school, or the early form of the district school.

Political evolution favored this evolution of the district school. Seventeenth century New England society was aristocratic; eighteenth century New England society was by comparison democratic. This was true at least in the exercise of governmental powers. Many forces were at work breaking up the centralized aristocratic town government into local units. The division of the town by the selectmen for the enforcement of the Law of 1642 and for the care of the poor laid a basis for later subdivision. Highway surveyors were appointed for the oversight of the roads in small areas, and hog reeves for the oversight of swine; to constables and assessors were assigned certain local areas. Militia duties required a similar division. After the general dispersion of population over the farms or the formation of local villages in addition to the central village of the town, religious services were held in different localities and often churches were established. Later these parishes became the units for schools as well as churches. But the local school centers within the town were more numerous than the church centers. Thus the democratic desire for local self-government permeated and undermined the town government, tending to reduce it to yet smaller units, the parishes, squadrons, or precincts. There was the greatest variety in this development and no uniform process or system can be described. When the prudential men were selected or the members of the school committee chosen, it became customary to represent each part of the town. Thus by the middle eighteenth century the school committee of many if not most of the towns was composed of men representing the local schools or precincts or districts; that is, there were as many members of the committee as

THE TOWN SCHOOLS OF NEW ENGLAND

there were local schools. Naturally it came to be the custom for each member to represent and look after his own school.

The same forces that had built up the town school now became of service in building up the district. Numerous localities supplemented their share of the town funds by voluntary contribution, by additional rates for tuition, or even by local tax rate. Following New England custom, in 1768 the general court authorized this

FIG. 30. A dame school. (From Murray, *History of Education in New Jersey*, p. 136.)

plan where "such precincts may be disposed to expend more for the instruction of children and youth in useful learning, within their own bounds, than as parts of such towns or districts they are, by law, held to do." Apparently the law encouraged educational endeavor. Ultimately, since it led to the transfer of all taxing power and control of schools to the district, it effected a marked deterioration of the entire public school system. This, however, is to be considered under the early National period.

Educational Conditions in Other New England Colonies. —Connecticut and New Haven (colonies) consciously followed

[123]

Massachusetts legislation in most things. It has been previously noted (p. 46) that they adopted the principle of the Law of 1642 concerning literary education under the form of the apprentice system. Connecticut was organized in 1639. In 1650 a code of laws was adopted, including one modeled on the Massachusetts Law of 1642, and the Massachusetts Law of 1647 verbatim. As in the parent colony, local schools existed from the first, but the remainder of the Colonial period was passed under the Law of 1647 without substantial modification. New Haven colony, founded in 1643, also shows local schools from very early days. The code of 1656 (Doc. 189) includes provisions of the Massachusetts Law of 1642 much elaborated. In 1669 New Haven was merged with Connecticut and came under the provisions of the education Law of 1647. The revised code of the united colonies made in 1672 repeated the provisions of the Connecticut code of 1650. A few years later the requirement was made that all town schools should be in session at least nine months out of the twelve, and yet later (1678) that towns of thirty families should come under this law. These ideals proved too difficult of attainment in the pioneer life and so a few years later (1700) the standard was lowered to seventy families in the town and six months' session during the year.

When the Law of 1647 was passed New Hampshire was a part of Massachusetts and it remained so for a generation after. Shortly after, obtaining a separate legislature, New Hampshire (also Quo. 191 and 192) passed a law (1693) incorporating the compulsory school provision of 1647 but with the notable addition that the fund for "building of churches, ministers' houses, schoolhouses, and allowing a salary to a schoolmaster in each town" should be raised "by an equal rate and assessment upon the inhabitants." This, then, is the earliest free school system in the Colonies. One town was exempted "during the war" and from time to time thereafter frontier towns suffering from Indian attacks were exempted. Otherwise the law was re-enacted in slightly different terms from time to time and was valid throughout this period.

Plymouth colony depended upon private schools for quite fifty years. In 1670 (in Plymouth) a town school was erected with the

FIG. 31. A dame school. (From a painting by Webster.)

FOUNDING OF AMERICAN SCHOOL SYSTEM

assistance of colony grants. Almost every plan of supporting the school was tried but in time resort was had to support by public taxation alone and this method was maintained thereafter. In 1692 Plymouth colony was incorporated with Massachusetts Bay and its various towns came under the provision of the Law of 1647.

Maine was a part of Massachusetts throughout the Colonial period. Local records indicate the enforcement of the general educational provisions of the Colonial laws. Vermont was under the jurisdiction of New York. Rhode Island lacked the unity of social and religious sentiment prevailing in the other colonies. Its settlers were largely committed to the belief in complete separation of church and state and therefore had a less definite state policy concerning school. They were strongly individualistic as well as democratic, so we find no effort toward government compulsion regarding schools or educational standards. They added nothing to New England educational experience and lagged behind the other colonies in the general development of schools.

Connecticut was the only one of the colonies except New Hampshire that added any feature of importance to the experience of Massachusetts. This addition was in the earlier and fuller development of the germs of the district system. Connecticut early in the eighteenth century had legalized the ecclesiastical society or the parish organizations within the town for religious and educational purposes. In 1717 the law requiring a school in any town of seventy families was made applicable to every parish or ecclesiastical society of seventy families. These local units

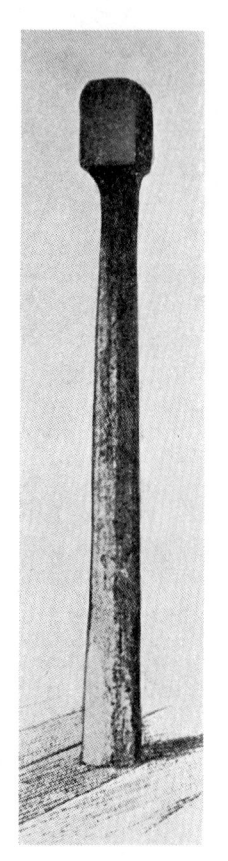

FIG. 32. Whipping post set into the floor of a New England district school. (Preserved in the Deerfield Museum.)

[126]

THE TOWN SCHOOLS OF NEW ENGLAND

were also given power to levy a tax and appoint a collector. In 1766 towns and societies were permitted "to divide themselves into proper and necessary districts for keeping their schools and to alter and regulate the same from time to time." Such districts were to share in the school moneys in proportion to the taxable lists. Thus the district system, with the exception of taxing power, was quite fully developed in Connecticut before the close of the Colonial period.

One other phase of educational development was initiated by Connecticut in 1733. In that year the legislature set aside generous portions of the public lands in the unsettled part of the colony, and provided for the division of the proceeds as a permanent fund in the several towns of the state for the support of schools and of the ministry. Thus the land policy and the common school funds of our nation were foreshadowed.

Other Features of the New England Schools.—*Private and Dame Schools.*—From the first private schools existed in these New England towns. In various localities records reveal the existence of schools long before the town school was established. These were usually reading and writing schools kept by masters. Often such masters were subsidized or "encouraged" by a grant from the town. Such schools enabled the town to comply with the Law of 1647 and were often used for this purpose by the weaker towns far into the eighteenth century. The larger towns frequently had several of these competing with the town school after its establishment. In these instances the selectmen usually required the masters to satisfy them of their qualifications. In Boston and elsewhere this was enforced as a local ordinance. In some places writing was recognized as a distinct art, beyond the scope of the ordinary master's work and therefore taught in a separate school. To this was sometimes added the other art of reckoning or arithmetic.

Some of these private schools were of still higher grade, including the teaching of Latin. In most cases this meant little more than that the village minister taught the classics to a few select boys.

But the commonest form of the private school was the dame school, a popular institution of Old England. Because of local conditions this school was far more common in New England than in the other American colonies. The town life favored it, the town schools usually did not provide for the teaching of the rudiments. The rules of the Roxbury school contained the phrase, "all ABCdarians excepted."

Even the town schools often provided "that no children shall be admitted into such schools who have not perfectly learned the letters of the alphabet," which task was often the work of months. Such were the requirements in many schools. Frequently girls were

Fig. 33. The dame school. (From a contemporary drawing in Bartley, *Industrial Schools for the People*, p. 404.)

not admitted to the town school at all: often they were allowed to come only at times outside of the regular school hours. So to the dame school of most elementary character was added the dame school of more advanced grade. Scattered population and smaller group settlements demanded more and cheaper schools. How common these private ventures were in some towns is indicated by the Concord report of 1680, "in every quarter of the town men and women that teach to write English when parents can spare their children and others to go to them." Thus the laws of 1642 and 1647 were both complied with. At the same time Cambridge reported, "For English, our school dame is Goodwife Healey"; and a neighboring town, that it had "also several school dames." An-

THE TOWN SCHOOLS OF NEW ENGLAND

dover, a town of great educational repute, defends itself when presented to the grand jury in the early eighteenth century by stating, "We do take the best care we can for to bring up our children to reading by school dames."

The work of these schools was exceedingly simple. Perhaps no better description could be found than that of the poet Crabbe speaking of the dame school of Old England:

> "Where a deaf, poor, patient widow sits
> And awes some thirty infants as she knits—
> Infants of humble, busy wives, who pay
> Some trifling price for freedom through the day.
> At this good matron's hut the children meet,
> Who thus becomes the mother of the street;
> Her room is small, they can not widely stray,
> Her threshold high, they can not run away;
> With band of yarn she keeps offenders in,
> And to her gown the sturdiest rogues can pin."

During the early eighteenth century, these private and dame schools tended to be absorbed into the divided town schools or be-

FIG. 34. The "Kitchen school," annexed to a New Jersey farmhouse. (From Murray, *History of Education in New Jersey*, p. 108.)

cause of the competition of these to disappear. The record on page 121 indicates the process, as does the following. In 1731 Worcester "voted that a suitable number of school dames, not exceeding five, be provided by the selectmen at the charge of the town for the

FOUNDING OF AMERICAN SCHOOL SYSTEM

teaching of small children to read, and to be placed in the several parts of the town as the selectmen may think most convenient." The free school placed conveniently, divided now into many small units with teachers correspondingly multiplied, took in small children and girls and left little room for the private master and the dame school. Only in the larger towns or cities did they survive, and here as an institution of the aristocratic class or for specialized needs.

The Organization and Work of the School.—The town school of the seventeenth century held the entire year: the moving, divided, and district school of the eighteenth century reduced this term to a fraction—one half or even one quarter—of the time. The sessions were usually long, seven hours in winter and eight in the summer being the average. In the earlier years school was held in the master's home; here it continued in the case of the dames who taught. With the moving or divided school, farmhouses were frequently called into service; hence the so-called "Kitchen school." Later a small room was added to the home for the same purpose. In time the precincts were provided with schoolhouses as was in earlier days the town. These buildings possessed the most meager equipment. Usually there was an open fireplace; later in some regions a stove furnished heat. Wood was furnished customarily by the patrons; the fire was started early by the teacher and replenished by the pupils in turn. A teacher's desk, rough-hewn log seats, facing a table or shelf attached to the wall around the entire room, completed the equipment. Frequently an hourglass was added.

FIG. 35. Interior of a district school, with benches for pupils facing the wall. (From Johnson, *Old-time Schools and School-books,* p. 105.)

The town schools were primarily for boys. The earliest account of girls' schooling is the Dorchester records of 1639, when it was left "to the discretion of the elders and the seven men whether maids

THE TOWN SCHOOLS OF NEW ENGLAND

should be taught with the men or not." These seven wise men thought not, but it was something for the question to be raised. The more usual attitude is expressed in such action of the towns as follows: "that the girls have liberty to attend the master's school the three summer months"; or "that each sex may attend school at different hours"; or "that the females attend school from the first of May to the end of October"; or "that their hours of instruction be from eleven to one o'clock and from four to six. That they be

FIG. 36. Whipping post and public square at Salem, Mass., with school nearby. (From Johnson, *Old-time Schools and School-books*, p. 30.)

admitted at seven years of age or more." These are all late in the eighteenth century. In many towns a more liberal policy was pursued. As early as 1650 Watertown voted "that if any maiden that have a desire to learn to write, that the said Richard (the schoolmaster) shall attend them for the learning of them."

During the early seventeenth century, the standard salary of the schoolmasters was £20 a year—quite a respectable income, about one-fourth that of the minister who was the highest salaried officer of the town. The grammar school master was paid two or three

[131]

times as much, but often had to employ his own usher or assistant teacher. During the eighteenth century salaries greatly deteriorated in real value as did the character of the teacher. After the early period, especially after the break-up of the central town school, there was no standard; each community paid what it had to; each master or dame bargained for as much as could be obtained.

In general the school dame was paid most meagerly, usually a few pence per week for each child. Two shillings a year for a pupil was generous. When her salary was paid by the town it was not much more liberal—sometimes it was only the cost of mere living, as when she "was to be furnished by the selectmen with what she wants for her subsistence." When the woman teacher was incorporated in the town school system it was on a similar basis—"Twelve months of school taught by a female be reckoned as equivalent to four and four-fifths months of a master's school" was the standard of one. Sometimes the adjustment was on the basis of half pay.

The school dames taught the alphabet, the catechism, and perhaps the simplest forms of reading, as the *New England Primer*. Occasionally they could not even read themselves. As has been said, knowledge of the alphabet, sometimes even an ability to read, was usually required for entrance to the town school. Instruction in the catechism was of fundamental importance and on this the children were frequently examined. After the *New England Primer*, first printed about 1660, and the catechism, the chief reading book was the Bible, especially the Psalter and the Testament. To these writing was added; sometimes spelling appears as a special subject. When arithmetic or reckoning appears, it is usually specified as an extra subject. By the eighteenth century it is common. Writing and arithmetic are frequently taught by special masters. All the more popular towns have special masters of writing and ciphering. Girls added sewing and knitting to the subjects named above. The sampler was the work of the school as often as of the home. A single illustration from the many such found in contracts with schoolmasters or in orders of selectmen will suffice. Selectmen in providing for an orphan girl in 1670 stated "when it shall be capable,

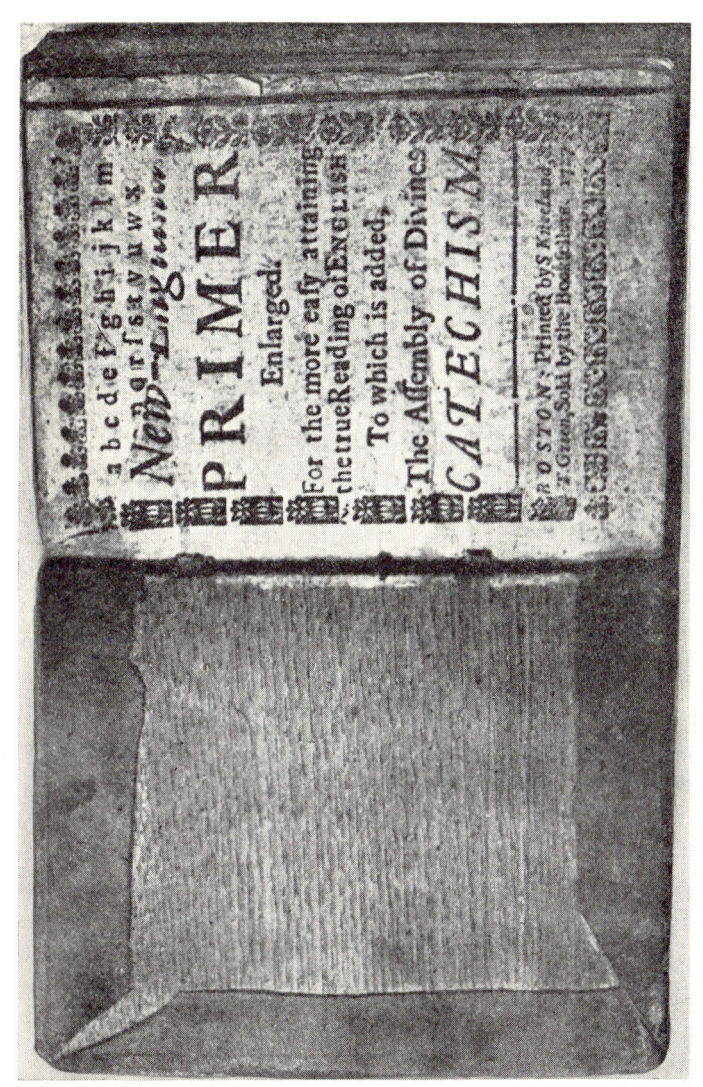

FIG. 37. The *New England Primer*. (Oldest extant copy of the *New England Primer*, printed 1727. In the New York Public Library.)

[133]

FOUNDING OF AMERICAN SCHOOL SYSTEM

to teach or cause it to be taught profitably the English tongue, and also instruct her in the principles of the Christian religion, and in such housewifely employment of spinning, knitting, as she may be capable to learn."

The schoolmaster himself was more nearly a professional man in New England than in the other colonies. His appointment was more permanent, his position more dignified, and his salary more adequate. For long the supply did not meet the demand. Governor Dudley wrote in 1642—"There is a want of schoolmasters hereabouts." This scarcity is evidenced by the difficulties of the town in obtaining masters. Yet some towns maintained high standards. Of the seventy schoolmasters at Dorchester for the century and a half of the Colonial period, fifty-three were graduates of Harvard. Many masters were preparing for the ministry or were assistants to the minister. Occasionally they were physicians. All must be approved by the selectmen or the minister. However, the high repute of the New England schoolmaster is based largely upon the character of the Latin school teacher. Especially in the eighteenth century did the character of the elementary teacher decline in moral and social as well as intellectual qualities.

VERBS.

Active.   Passive.   Neuter.

FIG. 38. A realistic method of instruction. (From *The Little Grammarian.*)

Summary.—Adopting the universal economic or vocational provisions of the apprentice system, New England added to them the requirement of reading, and thus for the first time universalized literary education. The devotion of the local communities to higher educational ends not being proof against the difficulties of frontier life, these colonies within the first generation of their existence universalized schools and literary education through the schools. Through the same laws they universalized the opportunity for secondary or advanced education. By the local development of the eighteenth century, free public education on the basis of universal

[134]

THE TOWN SCHOOLS OF NEW ENGLAND

taxation was established throughout these colonies. At the same time the control as well as the support of education was localized in the smallest community unit, and responsibility in education was universalized. One colony, New Hampshire, early universalized support of education, free to the individual, compulsory to the community. One colony, Connecticut, early did the same for school control. Both sexes were brought within the scope of the school operation; and the eighteenth century saw the teaching profession as well as the pupil's opportunity opened to women and girls. The private school and the dame school, universal features in the early day, were ultimately incorporated in the public schools. Opportunity, attendance, literary acquisition, support, control, responsibility, were thus universalized through school experience of a century and a half in New England.

Chapter VI

THE LATIN GRAMMAR SCHOOL, AND SECONDARY EDUCATION IN THE COLONIES

Cotton Mather wrote of John Eliot, "the Apostle to the Indians," "... A grammar school he would always have upon the place, whatever it cost him; and he importuned all other places to have the like." It was for these schools that Eliot prayed before the synod of the churches, "Lord, for schools everywhere among us! That our schools may flourish! That every member of this assembly go home and procure a good school to be encouraged by the town where he lives! That before we die we may be so happy as to see a good school encouraged by every plantation of the country."

This devotion was not only characteristic of Eliot; it was true of many others. In fact to all of the colonists the Latin grammar school was an essential part of the structure of society. When the question came to be decided what should be done with the first philanthropic gift to the Virginia settlers, the answer was, "Give us a Latin grammar school" (Quos. 65, 66). The colony was then a frontier settlement of less than 2,000 souls, on the verge of extermination by savages.

When Boston was but five years old it was voted that "our brother, Philemon Pormont, be entreated to become schoolmaster." The dignity of the calling, the value of the service, the worthiness of the servant, the compelling force of the group request, all are indicated by this simple entry in the records of the town meeting. The following year a meeting of the "wealthier" (Quo. 125) inhabitants validated this invitation by subscription and laid a foundation for the school which flourishes to this day. At the time of the original vote the community numbered but a few hundred.

In the trading post of New Netherland in 1649 when the colonists had made "great remonstrance" (Quo. 113) concerning the neglect

SECONDARY EDUCATION IN THE COLONIES

of their interests, the reply admitted as one element of this neglect that no Latin school had been established (Quo. 114). Two years later the authorities in Holland informed their representatives on this side that they agreed to establish a Latin school and to pay the salary of a master. The city at this time numbered 700 and the entire colony about 3,000. In the original "frame of government" drawn up for Pennsylvania in advance of its settlement, it was stipulated that the authorities should "erect and order public schools," as the Latin grammar schools were then termed (Quo. 158).

It is not to be doubted that the Colonies looked upon the Latin grammar school as a component part of the institutional organization of any independent community. To these forefathers of ours this was the institution which represented "education" as we think of it now. By some of them, elementary or vernacular schools were deemed necessary as a part of the religious scheme of society. Such schools, however, did not represent a literary education. Education, as concerned with books or literary study and formulated for the training of the leaders of society, was represented by the Latin grammar school. Here prospective members of the learned professions were trained. Here were selected and developed the leaders "in church and in commonwealth" who were to defend the rights, privileges, opportunities, and beliefs for which these people had sacrificed so much at home and for which they were venturing so much in the wilderness. In this day when a "classical education" is so little valued, and when the study of ancient languages is all but disappearing from our schools, it is difficult to appreciate the value then placed on the work of these schools. In a textbook illustration of the period which represents the muse of rhetoric as the Roman Emperor, the muse of geometry as the great merchant, the muse of logic as the great scholar, the muse of grammar is the Deity (see p. 138). Only when we consider school as the instrument by which talent is winnowed from the chaff of mediocrity, and ability developed to leadership in church, in state, and in the business and social affairs of men, can we estimate these schools as did our forefathers.

Such schools were not always known by the same name. The

Latin school or grammar school indicated that they were devoted to the study of the classics, for at that time there was no other recognized grammar than that of Latin or Greek or Hebrew. It has been often said, and with great plausibility, that when they were termed

FIG. 39. The presiding genius of grammar represented as Deity. (From the *Margarita Philosophica* of 1497.)

"free" schools, the adjective indicated the "liberal" education in the classics, not freedom from tuition charges. Upon this interpretation have been based far-reaching judicial decisions in England which restricted these schools for the most part to the well-to-do; whereas if "free" in the pecuniary sense, they would have been for the service

SECONDARY EDUCATION IN THE COLONIES

of the poor. It has now been established that the original meaning of the term, and the one commonly accepted in the seventeenth century, related to money or fees. As such these schools were one of the most democratic institutions in society, guaranteeing the equality of opportunity and the freedom for talent. It is true that the term "free education," as used in the legislature of Virginia and the Southern colonies, may mean a liberal education. However, in

FIG. 40. Determining and defining of terms, method of work, of grammar school. (From a medieval illustration in Schreiber und Heitz, *Die Deutschen Accipies*.)

these cases the term is applied to education, not to schools. Frequently the term "endowed school" is used. By this is indicated a prevalent form of support. In this respect our contemporary colleges are the direct successors of the Latin school of the Colonies. Often the term "public school" is used. Thus is indicated the secure place such schools had in the social philosophy and the social economy of the times. In Great Britain the term English Public School is yet used in this sense and not to indicate the free elementary school as with us. And the gibe that such schools are called "English" because the curriculum consists of Greek and Latin, "public" because intended for and used by the aristocracy and "schools" because the boys spend their time in football and cricket, was applicable, omitting the last count, to the Colonies as well. It is also to be remembered that frequently in England and occasionally in Colonial America such schools were called "colleges." The term "college" originally had a meaning similar to our word "corporation." An endowed school of this character, having a definite organization of the administrative and teaching staff, was a corporation, and as such it was often called a college though the pupils received might be boys of eight or nine. This use of the term was quite infrequent in America. Occasionally the term "trivial school" (Quo. 114) was used to designate the Latin school, from the medieval characterization of the subjects of its curriculum as the *trivium*. The term indicates that the study of Latin included grammar, rhetoric, and logic or dialectic. This term was more frequently used on the Continent. But it is evident that the traditions of the Latin grammar school were brought to the Colonies from a variety of European sources. A survey of these schools in each of the colonies can be made in a brief compass.

The Latin Grammar School in Virginia and the South.— The earliest of this class, the East India School, founded by the friendly interests and fellowship of the antipodes, met the melancholy fate previously recorded (p. 64). It is of interest to note that this school was termed a "free public school" and that a school was decided on in preference to a church "as that whereof both church and commonwealth take their original foundation and happy estate." Another reason assigned was that the planters "have been hitherto constrained to their great cost to send children from thence hither to be taught." A thousand acres of land given by the company, an iron foundry and reducing plant built from the endowment, and proposed "benevolence" from every patron to the master, would seem to offer abundant foundation for the future. But the Indian massacre and the downfall of the London Company brought all plans as well as gifts to naught.

The Symmes, Eaton, Moon, and other endowed schools of the seventeenth century, described on pp. 64–67, were to all intents and purposes elementary schools. The one reference to the teaching of grammar is a very insecure basis for an argument that these schools taught Latin grammar to more than an infrequent student, at least during the seventeenth century. The first actual grammar school was in connection with the College of William and Mary, founded in 1693. In fact for many years the college was really but little more than a Latin grammar school. We will, however, discuss it as named—as a college (p. 67). Earlier and more clearly than in any other of the stronger colonies, did the inappropriateness of the Latin grammar school show itself in Virginia. The Latin grammar school prepared for the church; but there was no bishop of the established church in Virginia or even in America, and consequently no candidate could be inducted into office on this side. It prepared for the service of the state, but the governors of Virginia needed no Latin secretary. The only foreign relations which these colonists had demanded an interpreter of the languages of savages never reduced to pen, not one skilled in the classics of old. "The Latin grammar school of early Virginia was a short ladder with nothing but empty space at the top."

The Latin Grammar School in the Other Southern Colonies.—In North Carolina the absence of any considerable centers of population, the sparsity of population scattered over so great a territory, the variety of social and religious groups represented, all tended to retard the development of interest and action concerning the Latin schools. Not until after the middle of the eighteenth century were definite steps taken toward this end. Several times in the two decades preceding the Revolution, funds were appropriated by the legislature for this purpose, only to be used each time for urgent military or administrative purposes before any school was developed. During this period grammar schools were authorized and assisted by grants of land or funds in the towns of Newburn and Clinton. Representatives of the King's councilors were usually successful in finding sound objections to such proposed laws, delaying any action for some years after the community was ready for it. Such objections did postpone until after the Revolution the proposed founding of Queens College by the Scotch Presbyterian element. Meanwhile several such schools of a somewhat more ele-

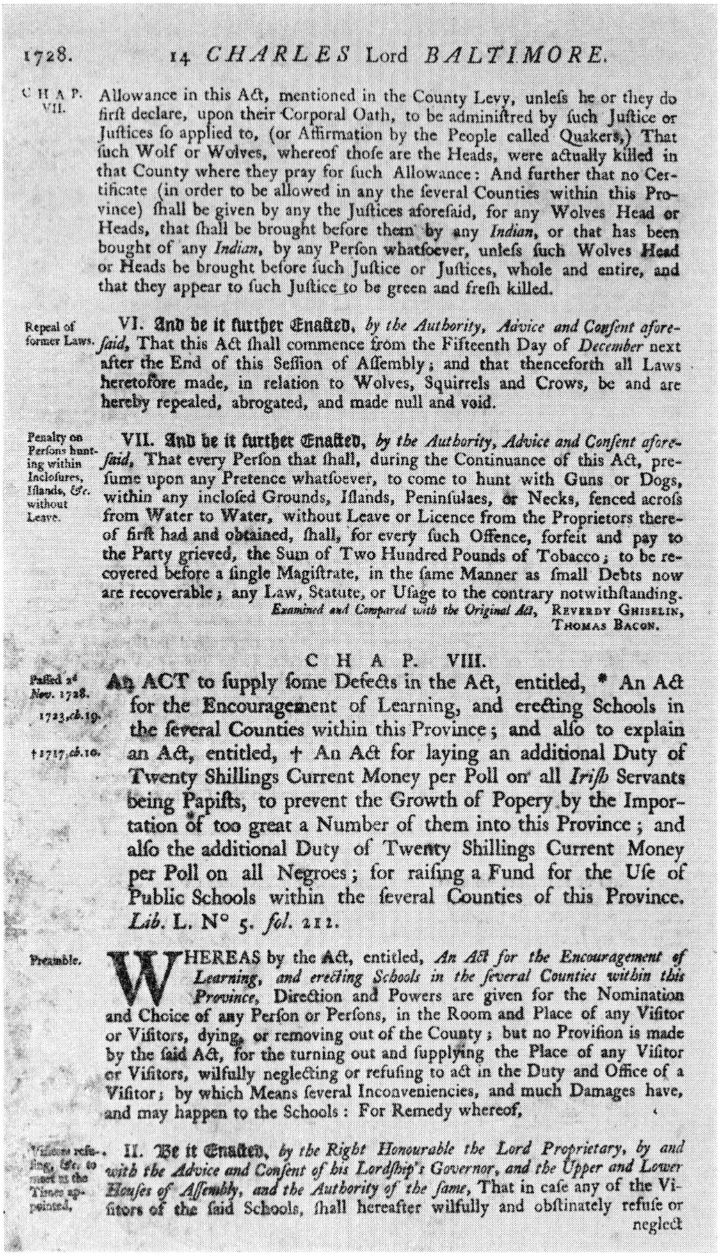

1728.   14 *CHARLES* Lord *BALTIMORE.*

CHAP. VII. Allowance in this Act, mentioned in the County Levy, unless he or they do first declare, upon their Corporal Oath, to be administred by such Justice or Justices so applied to, (or Affirmation by the People called Quakers,) That such Wolf or Wolves, whereof those are the Heads, were actually killed in that County where they pray for such Allowance: And further that no Certificate (in order to be allowed in any the several Counties within this Province) shall be given by any the Justices aforesaid, for any Wolves Head or Heads, that shall be brought before them by any *Indian*, or that has been bought of any *Indian*, by any Person whatsoever, unless such Wolves Head or Heads be brought before such Justice or Justices, whole and entire, and that they appear to such Justice to be green and fresh killed.

Repeal of former Laws. VI. **And be it further Enacted,** *by the Authority, Advice and Consent aforesaid,* That this Act shall commence from the Fifteenth Day of *December* next after the End of this Session of Assembly; and that thenceforth all Laws heretofore made, in relation to Wolves, Squirrels and Crows, be and are hereby repealed, abrogated, and made null and void.

Penalty on Persons hunting within Inclosures, Islands, &c. without Leave. VII. **And be it further Enacted,** *by the Authority, Advice and Consent aforesaid,* That every Person that shall, during the Continuance of this Act, presume upon any Pretence whatsoever, to come to hunt with Guns or Dogs, within any inclosed Grounds, Islands, Peninsulaes, or Necks, fenced across from Water to Water, without Leave or Licence from the Proprietors thereof first had and obtained, shall, for every such Offence, forfeit and pay to the Party grieved, the Sum of Two Hundred Pounds of Tobacco; to be recovered before a single Magistrate, in the same Manner as small Debts now are recoverable; any Law, Statute, or Usage to the contrary notwithstanding.

Examined and Compared with the Original Act, REVERDY GHISELIN, THOMAS BACON.

C H A P. VIII.

Passed 2d *Nov.* 1728.
1723, cb. 19.
† 1717, cb. 10.

An ACT to supply some Defects in the Act, entitled, * An Act for the Encouragement of Learning, and erecting Schools in the several Counties within this Province; and also to explain an Act, entitled, † An Act for laying an additional Duty of Twenty Shillings Current Money per Poll on all *Irish* Servants being Papists, to prevent the Growth of Popery by the Importation of too great a Number of them into this Province; and also the additional Duty of Twenty Shillings Current Money per Poll on all Negroes; for raising a Fund for the Use of Public Schools within the several Counties of this Province. *Lib.* L. N° 5. *fol.* 212.

Preamble. **W**HEREAS by the Act, entitled, *An Act for the Encouragement of Learning, and erecting Schools in the several Counties within this Province,* Direction and Powers are given for the Nomination and Choice of any Person or Persons, in the Room and Place of any Visitor or Visitors, dying, or removing out of the County; but no Provision is made by the said Act, for the turning out and supplying the Place of any Visitor or Visitors, wilfully neglecting or refusing to act in the Duty and Office of a Visitor; by which Means several Inconveniencies, and much Damages have, and may happen to the Schools: For Remedy whereof,

Visitors refusing, &c. to meet at the Times appointed. II. **Be it Enacted,** *by the Right Honourable the Lord Proprietary, by and with the Advice and Consent of his Lordship's Governor, and the Upper and Lower Houses of Assembly, and the Authority of the same,* That in case any of the Visitors of the said Schools, shall hereafter wilfully and obstinately refuse or neglect

FIG. 41. The Maryland statute of 1727.

[142]

BENEDICT LEONARD CALVERT, Esq; Governor. 1728.

neglect to meet, and be present, at any of the Times appointed for the Meeting of the said Visitors, so that the necessary Affairs of the said School or Schools cannot be transacted and directed, that then it shall and may be lawful for the Visitors of each Schools, or the major Part of such Visitors, who shall so meet, are hereby directed and impowered to nominate and choose one or more of the principal and better Sort of the Inhabitants of the County, into the Place and Room of the said Visitor so refusing or neglecting as aforesaid, which Person or Persons so elected and chosen, from Time to Time, are always to be qualified in the same Manner as is directed for the Qualification of Visitors, by the said recited Act.

CHAP. VIII.
Others may be chosen in their Room, who shall qualify as directed by the original Act.

III. **And be it further Enacted,** *by the Authority, Advice and Consent aforesaid,* That the Master of every Public School within this Province, shall, and is hereby required to teach as many poor Children *gratis,* as the Visitors, or the major Part of them, of the respective Schools shall order, or be immediately discharged and removed from his Trust in the said School, and a new Master put in.

What poor Children shall be taught gratis.

IV. **And whereas** some Doubts have arisen on the Explanation and Construction of an Act, entitled, *An Act for laying an additional Duty of Twenty Shillings Current Money per Poll, on all* Irish *Servants, being Papists, to prevent the Growth of Popery, by the Importation of too great a Number of them into this Province:* And also the additional Duty *of Twenty Shillings Current Money per Poll on all Negroes, for raising a Fund for the Use of Public Schools within the several Counties of this Province,* whether the Twenty Shillings Current Money thereby imposed on *Irish* Servants, being Papists, and Negroes imported into this Province, by Land or Water, were intended by the said Act, or shall be construed to be imposed on such *Irish* Servants, being Papists, and Negroes, as have been, or shall be imported in any Ship or Vessel built in this Province, whereof the Owners have been, or shall be actually Residents in this Province, or in any Ship or Vessel, *English* or Plantation built, purchased, enjoyed or held, by Owners Residents within this Province.

Doubts on the Act of 1717, ch. 10, recited.

V. **Be it therefore Declared, and it is hereby Enacted,** *by the Authority aforesaid, by and with the Advice and Consent aforesaid,* That no Ship or Vessel, whereof all the Owners have been (or shall be) actually Residents of this Province; or no Ship or Vessel, *English* or Plantation built, purchased, enjoyed, and held, by Owners Residents within this Province, shall be construed to have been, or shall hereafter be discharged, and not liable to the Payment of the aforesaid Duty of Twenty Shillings Current Money per Poll on all *Irish* Servants, being Papists, and all Negroes imported into this Province, in such Ship or Vessel; any Law or Usage to the contrary thereof in any wise notwithstanding.

The Duty thereby imposed, shall be paid for Irish Servants being Papists, and Negroes, imported in Country Bottoms.

Examined and Compared with the Original Act, REVERDY GHISELIN,
THOMAS BACON.

CHAP. IX.

An Act to appropriate Part of the Land laid out in the City of Annapolis *for the building a Custom-house on, to and for the building a Market-house.* Lib. L. N° 5. fol. 214.

Passed 2d Nov. 1728.

N. B. By this Act, (1.) *Henry Ridgely, Mordecai Hammond,* and *John Welsh,* Gent. or any Two of them, were impowered to survey, lay out, and mark, 60 Feet in Breadth on the Water, 360 Feet in Length, and 25 Feet on the Head of the Land formerly allotted to build a Custom-house on (which is contained by 250 Feet in Breadth on the Water, 360 Feet in Length, and 82 Feet in Breadth on the Head of the said Land) and return a Certificate thereof, to be recorded in the Mayor's Court; and the Corporation to be seized of an Estate in Fee-simple in and to the Land so laid out, &c. Provided the Corporation build a Market-house thereon within Two Years after such Survey, &c. (2.) The Corporation are impowered to sell the Land formerly laid out for a Market-house; and to apply the Money arising from such Sale towards building the Market-house intended by this Act. See 1751, *ch.* 21, which impowered the Corporation to sell the Market-house and Land established by this Act, and to apply the Money arising from such Sale towards the Purchasing some other Piece of Ground within the City, and building thereon a new Market-house.

Y y   CHAP.

(Thos. Bacon, *Laws of Maryland at Large,* Annapolis, 1765.)

mentary as well as broader character had grown up among this people, bearing the new title of seminary or academy. These are to be noted later (p. 160).

In Maryland frequent legislative discussions throughout the Colonial period attest the general recognition of the fact that those charged with public affairs were responsible for the support of Latin schools. After repeated efforts to found such a school, Governor Calvert writes to his father, Lord Baltimore, the proprietor, concerning the master who had been sent over—"No doubt he will not find the people here so desirous of that benefit of educating their children in that nature as he might probably expect, for the remoteness of the habitation of one person from another will be a great obstacle to a school in that way that I perceive your lordship arrives at and that would much conduce to the profit and advantage of the youth of the province." The Latin master remained a private tutor in the governor's family. Nothing further was accomplished during the sixty years of proprietary government. In 1692 the province became a royal colony. Two years later the governor began an agitation for a "free school," which resulted in the issue of a charter by the legislature two years later. Numerous legislative enactments in the course of the next thirty years prove both the feeling of responsibility for this school at Annapolis and the difficulty of maintaining it. In 1723 an act was passed authorizing the establishment of a Latin grammar school in each of the twelve counties of the province and creating a board of trustees for each school. Thus Maryland took a more advanced position regarding the secondary schools than any other Southern or central colony and agreed with the New England colonies in establishing a system of them (Quo. 255). But in this case the ideal was beyond the need. Before the Revolution it was necessary to combine several of these schools and to abandon others.

The Latin Grammar School in the Middle Colonies.—*In New Netherland.*—One of the objections raised in the Great Remonstrance of the citizens of New Amsterdam in 1649 (Quo. 113) was that nothing was done for higher education. In response the Lords Directors in Holland in 1652 (Quo. 114) authorized the

SECONDARY EDUCATION IN THE COLONIES

director-general of the colony to make a beginning of a "trivial school" by appointing one usher or teacher. A French Huguenot was employed and paid for several months. After an agitation led by the local pastor a Latin schoolmaster "late professor in Lithuania" was sent over by the Company in 1659. The petition states that "the burghers and inhabitants are inclined to have their children instructed in the useful languages, chief among which is the Latin tongue." This school under successive masters continued until the downfall of the Dutch rule.

In New York.—The English government showed far less interest than the Dutch in secondary education, as they did in the elementary phase. There was frequent agitation for a grammar school, but little permanent interest. Neither the church nor the people seemed to take the matter to heart as they did under the Dutch rule. This is the more surprising as the English rule was distinctly aristocratic, in strong contrast to the democratic spirit of the Dutch and the Church of England was now the established church. It was not until 1702 that provision was made by the Colonial government for such a school. The Society for the Propagation of the Gospel was requested to send a teacher as no one "proper and duly qualified to take upon him the office of schoolmaster of said city" was to be found in the colony. It is to be noted that this school was recognized as a municipal school, while the existing elementary schools were not. At the same time it was provided that the master be licensed and the school supervised by the authorities of the established church. This school continued but a few months. In 1732 the city Latin school was again established and lasted for six years. From 1741 to 1760 it is probable that Latin and the trivial subjects were taught in New York City by some teacher of the S.P.G. schools, or by private schoolmasters continuing the work of the city school, which ceased in 1738. With the founding of Kings College—now Columbia—in 1754 instruction in the trivial subjects was provided for in a preparatory school established on a distinct foundation in 1763 and flourishing through the remainder of the century. But it is evident that the traditional Latin grammar school had but slight hold upon the English colony, since it survived only as a

FOUNDING OF AMERICAN SCHOOL SYSTEM

preparatory school under the protecting influence of a stronger institution.

In New Jersey.—There are no records of Latin schools in this colony until near the middle of the eighteenth century. Such schools were supported by the religious bodies and were not due to governmental initiative. There being no cities in the colony, an important factor in the support of such schools was wanting. The chief influence in the building up of these schools was the religious revival of the third and fourth decade of the eighteenth century known as the "Great Awakening." The schools which were the outgrowth of this movement followed less conventional lines than the Latin grammar schools and soon developed into institutions known as academies, to be noted later.

In Pennsylvania.—As noted, the Latin grammar school appears as the earliest school in the colony. The school chartered in Philadelphia in 1697 was a Latin as well as an elementary school. Reorganized in 1711 as the Penn Charter School, this institution continues to thrive, retaining many of its traditional features. As seen in the previous chapter, subsequent legislation resigned all authority over schools to the various religious denominations. Latin schools were built up by the Quakers, the German sects, especially the Moravians, the Scotch Presbyterians, and others for the training of ministers. Except the early school of the Quakers and the German schools of very limited influence, these were of the broader type of the middle and late eighteenth century, so soon to replace the Latin grammar school, under the name of academies.

Latin Grammar Schools of Massachusetts.—Here beyond all other sections of the country did these schools find fertile soil. In 1635 the Latin grammar school of Boston was founded. The town meeting called and authorized the master. Presumably he served, though it is not absolutely certain, and presumably he taught Latin. Concerning the school in 1636 there is no doubt, and from that time it has been in continuous existence to the present. There were earlier schools attempted probably in several places, and in other colonies as well. But so far as evidence is available,

SECONDARY EDUCATION IN THE COLONIES

this is the oldest school of continued existence in the English colonies.

Latin grammar schools were established in other towns of Massachusetts Bay. In 1636 the town of Ipswich modestly records "a grammar school is set up, but does not succeed." Charlestown in the same year established a schoolmaster who, later on at least, taught Latin as well as the elementary subjects. Salem's school dates from the following year and Dorchester's from two years later.

FIG. 42. The Latin Grammar School, connected with King's Chapel on School Street, Boston. Early 17th century. (From Barnard's *American Journal of Education*, Vol. I, p. 306.)

Of Dorchester's master it was required that he teach "English, Latin, and other tongues and also writing." Among the stipulations was also "the said schoolmaster to be chosen from time to time by the freemen." Thus a democracy interested in education succeeded where an aristocracy failed; for every little town in Massachusetts supported a Latin school, while the aristocratically constituted and governed colony of New York—almost a century later—could not find a master within the colony competent to teach such a school.

As previously shown (p. 113) this school at Dorchester was probably the first to be supported entirely by public taxation. On the other hand, the school of the neighboring town of Roxbury, founded in 1645, continued its original plan of control by separate trustees and support chiefly by private contributions and special funds until the day of the nineteenth century high schools. Meanwhile Newbury and Cambridge had also established grammar schools.

Thus these early frontier settlements, in the first few years of their existence, proclaimed their belief in a higher education and substantiated their faith by sacrifices sufficient to support with pupils and funds seven such schools. This was before any law requiring schools had been passed and when the settlements had been in existence only from seven to seventeen years.

In 1647 Massachusetts Bay passed its first school law (Quo. 181). The portion of this law which relates to the elementary school has been noted (p. 110). But from the wording of the preamble it is quite evident that the need for Latin grammar schools was uppermost in their minds (Quo. 181). The most effective "wile of that old deluder, Satan," was "persuading men from the use of tongues," that is, from Latin and Greek, "so at last the true sense and meaning of the original might be clouded by false glosses of saint-seeming deceivers." There was no doubt in the minds of those men as to the value of Latin and Greek. But that value was not cumbered with any extraneous purposes nor was it bolstered by any artificial arguments for its disciplinary value. It was to be studied that in this wilderness "learning might not be buried in the graves of our forefathers in church and in commonwealth."

The law provided that every town of one hundred families should support a Latin school. That meant a school for the entire year. The master was a public official, receiving about half the salary of a minister, and thus stood second in importance among the public officials of the community. For the most part after this time, his salary was raised by public taxation. He was employed by the town and could properly leave only by town consent. In a way he belonged to the town, as did the minister, especially in the

SECONDARY EDUCATION IN THE COLONIES

early Colonial period when the town was at much expense in obtaining a master. When Harvard or Yale called the minister of a town to its leadership, the college paid the town liberally for his release. This was in recognition of the town's proprietorship in the minister. Somewhat the same idea prevailed regarding the master.

Subsequent legislation in Massachusetts reveals that it became more and more difficult to support these schools. In 1691 the fine for the failure to support a grammar school was raised from five pounds to ten pounds. In the same decade grammar masters were freed from poll tax and from military service. In 1701 the fine for non-observance of the law was again doubled (Quo. 185). By the same law the master was compelled to obtain a license from the ministers of three towns, including the one where he taught. This same law also indicated one method of evading the requirement that a grammar school should be maintained, or at least of lessening its effectiveness, for it provided that the minister of a town should not act as the grammar master. Yet once more, some seventeen years later, the fine for failure to maintain a Latin school was increased.

At the same time it is obvious from the local records that the law was enforced. Thus for example we find a court record of 1658 that "Newbury upon their presentment for want of a Latin school is to pay five pounds to the Ipswich Latin school, unless they by the next court provide a Latin schoolmaster according to law."

Examples of enforcement appear in the town records throughout both centuries, as is shown by one from Tisbury in 1783—"met to choose an agent to appear at the next court of general sessions of the peace to be held at Tisbury on the last Tuesday of October instant, to appear on behalf of said town to answer to an indictment brought against said town for not having a grammar school kept in said town in the year 1782." The record of even Dedham, where the school sentiment was very strong, reveals the difficulty that the community had to keep up the grammar school and proves that the town did not always escape the judgment of the court (Quo. 234).

During the eighteenth century the sentiment in favor of these schools was greatly weakened. The legislature notes that the observance of this "wholesome and necessary law is shamefully neglected by divers towns." Yet later (Quo. 185) "by sad experience it is found that many towns that not only are obliged by law, but are very able to support a grammar school, yet choose rather to incur and pay the fine or penalty than maintain a grammar school."

This was because the need for these schools was passing, and with it the belief in them. Some of them had been "put on wheels" and "squadroned out" to visit different parts or squadrons of the town. Thus in Gloucester in the middle eighteenth century the three years' term of the grammar school was divided among the seven precincts of the town for nine, seven, five, five and a half, four and a half, three, and one and a half months respectively. This was literally a "moving school." The statement does not mean that the boys of the one precinct had instruction in Latin for one and a half months out of three years; but that for the remainder of the time they must go to other portions of the town to attend the master. But before the Revolution the interest in Latin had greatly declined. The grammar school taught other subjects. Few of its pupils studied Latin—probably none studied Latin alone. In 1770 at the famous Roxbury School, but nine of the eighty-five pupils were studying Latin.

Latin Schools in Other New England Colonies.—Plymouth town remained a small village practically throughout its independent existence. After four years the colony numbered only 180 inhabitants; after six, only 300. In 1643 the eight towns of the colony included 3000 population. This would average less than 400 people or 50 families to each township. The numbers did not greatly increase though the jurisdiction of the colony spread to the west and south until it conflicted with the settlements of the Dutch. The Plymouth grammar school based on public support did not develop until the settlement was fifty years old. It is probable that previously instruction in grammar was given to a few select boys by the ministers. During this period boys from the colony prepared in the grammar school subjects entered Harvard. In 1692 the colony

SECONDARY EDUCATION IN THE COLONIES

was merged with Massachusetts Bay and came under the Law of 1647.

Connecticut and New Haven were even more rigid in adherence to high standards in religion and in education than Massachusetts. Settlements were made as early as 1635, and the colony was founded in 1639 by drawing up a constitution which Fiske pronounces "the first written constitution known to history that created a government." Before this year a grammar school master taught. In 1642 Hartford made an appropriation for the town school. A year earlier it was ordered in the neighboring colony of New Haven "that a free school shall be set up in this town and our pastor, Mr. Davenport, together with the magistrates, shall consider what yearly allowance is meet to be given to it out of the common stock of the town." Other towns in these colonies made similar provision. New Haven in 1661 established a colony grammar school (Quo. 237). In 1658 one of the early settlers, Edward Hopkins, a former London merchant, left most of his large estate for the promotion of higher education. Part of this fund went to Harvard College and part to establish Latin grammar schools in Hartford, New Haven, and Hadley. These schools were maintained throughout the Colonial period. The one at New Haven yet remains as a successful exponent of the high ideals of the Colonial period.

In 1650 Connecticut adopted the Massachusetts Law of 1647 as a part of her legal code. In 1665 New Haven and Connecticut were united under the name of the latter and the educational provision of the Law of 1650 was re-enacted. In 1672 the county instead of the town was adopted as a unit for grammar schools. On this basis four county grammar schools were developed, assisted by the colony and by the Hopkins bequest.

New Hampshire was a part of Massachusetts for much of the Colonial period and so came under her school law. Even when a separate legislature was given to the province the Massachusetts policy was continued. A statute of 1721 (Quo. 191) laid the penalty for the non-observance of the school law upon the selectmen personally, instead of upon the town, thus ensuring its enforcement. Nevertheless frontier conditions made the maintenance of Latin

FIG. 43. The Grammatical Tower. Woodcut by Hans Holbein, 1548. (From Emil Reiche, *Lehrer und Unterrichtswesen in der Deutschen Vergangenheit*.)

SECONDARY EDUCATION IN THE COLONIES

grammar schools not only very difficult of attainment but of little worth to the community. Therefore frequent exemptions were given to localities bearing the burden of defense against the Indians.

Maine continued throughout the Colonial period a part of Massachusetts and thus subject to the Law of 1647. Though the settlements were older and population denser, the conditions there were similar to those of New Hampshire.

While the people of Rhode Island were moved by much the same motives as those which inspired the Massachusetts settlers, they had other ideas also. Most of them were refugees from Massachusetts, for reasons of conscience, of policy, or of economic conditions. They believed in a much less despotic form of government than the Massachusetts commonwealth, in religious toleration, and above all, in separation of church and state. If education was a function of the church, as was then very commonly believed, it was as truly by the same token outside the function of government. If it was to be considered a state concern, as became a pure democracy such as was established in Rhode Island, responsibility for it lay with the town. Presumably some form of classical education was conducted by the ministers, but there is no conclusive evidence of a Colonial Latin school until near the close of the period. In 1764 such a school was established, on private foundation, but with Colonial backing. This became the preparatory school to Rhode Island College, later Brown University, founded the same year.

FIG. 44. The whipping table. From a Latin grammar school. The boy put his head under the table and his arms on top of the table while the master instructed. (From Chambers, *Book of Days*, Vol. I, p. 240.)

Thus all the colonies save Georgia developed the Latin grammar school as an essential part of the structure of society and as one of the three components of the educational system transplanted from Europe—perhaps the most important of the three.

The Grammar School Master.—The masters of the Latin schools were necessarily men of learning, usually men of high character, always men of repute and influence in their community. Their salary was much above that of the vernacular teacher and approached that of the minister. Though in most cases they were under contract for a period of years, their positions were usually permanent, dependent of course on their own choice and good behavior. To their names was prefixed the title Mr., then allowed only to the chosen few in a society where Goodman or Goodwife marked their sober address. Two New England schoolmasters stand out as the greatest representatives of their profession. One was Elijah Corlett, who taught at Cambridge certainly for fifty years; how much longer is not known. *New England's First Fruits* (Quo. 263-4) mentions Corlett as one of the ornaments of the colony, noted for his "abilities, dexterity, and painfulness in teaching" and fitting his scholars for "academical learning." Ezekiel Cheever was the second of these, his life covering almost a century, of which seventy years were spent in teaching. Of this period, twelve years were given to New Haven (from 1638); eleven to Ipswich; nine to Charlestown, and thirty-eight to the Boston Latin Grammar School. Of these two men Cotton Mather wrote:

> " 'Tis Corlett's pains and Cheever's we must own,
> That thou, New England, art not Scythia grown."

The poem on Cheever (Quo. 297) in which the great Puritan divine records his estimate of his early schoolmaster is a better evidence of the high estimate of learning and of the teaching profession in Colonial New England than of literature there.

> "A mighty tribe of well instructed youth
> Tell what they owe to him, and tell with truth.
> All the eight parts of speech he taught to them
> They now employ to trumpet his esteem."

It is in his sermon (Quo. 296) at Cheever's funeral that the eminent divine has paid the highest honor to the memory of the early schoolmaster. This address, despite its turgid rhetoric, is one of the

SECONDARY EDUCATION IN THE COLONIES

greatest tributes of literature to our profession. "Schoolmasters that have used the office well purchase to themselves a good esteem to outlive their death, as well as merit for themselves a good support while they live. 'Tis a justice to them that they should be had in everlasting remembrance; and a place and a name among those just men doth particularly belong to that ancient and honorable man—a master in our Israel."

And the noted divine must even have challenged the dread of the sacrilegious in his auditors as he closed his eulogy with the paraphrase—"My father, my father, the chariots of New England and the horsemen thereof."

A successor to Cheever, John Lovell, served in the same school for forty years during the eighteenth century. It was these masters serving for a generation who left their impress on these centuries and their name to posterity. Outside of New England the teaching profession has had few representatives so notable as these. The second master in New Amsterdam, Curtius, "the learned doctor from Lithuania," was undoubtedly a learned man. He was a practicing physician, raised his own medicinal herbs, and taught with remarkable success for seven years. Greed of gain, so great as to be intolerable even in a commercial settlement, brought about his downfall.

For the most part the Latin schoolmaster was a far less stable character, who belonged to one of two classes. Those of the first class were qualified and reputable, but made the teaching profession merely a stepping stone to the ministry. One reason for the short-lived efforts in New York was the fact that the masters were usually assistants to the minister, waiting "to take orders" and naturally feeling a stronger interest in the more dignified, influential, and lucrative profession. For the middle and Southern colonies, many of these schoolmasters were sent out by the Society for the Propagation of the Gospel and hence were educational missionaries in the modern sense. In New England many such teachers were divinity students from Harvard and Yale. Numerous town meeting committee records show efforts to obtain the services of these. Many such teachers were graduates, indicating their achievement by the use of the proud title "Mr." In smaller communities the minister himself was the grammar master in some instances until this species of economy was forbidden by law.

The second class of Latin teachers comprised the more or less unstable characters, averse to a settled habitation of long duration, and often of questionable morals. Frequently they were the "ne'er-do-wells" of the mother lands. Many were "redemptioners," who sold their services for a term of years for payment of debt or for their ocean passage. Many advertisements in the Colonial newspapers give us information of such in all the colonies. In Franklin's *Pennsylvania Gazette* of 1739 appears a notice: "Stolen on the 15th instant by one William Lloyd out of the house of Benj. Franklin, etc. . . . The said Lloyd pretends to understand Latin and Greek and has been a schoolmaster. He is an Irishman about thirty years." This is an illustration of many similar notices. The "pretense" indicated is probably but the limitation of knowledge common to all teachers. The wandering Irish schoolmaster was a well-known feature of Colonial life. But, as in the case above, the term Irish is probably used to cover all Celts, including the numerous Scots or Scotch-Irish masters. However, many with such roving commissions taught with great power and influence.

Character of the Latin Grammar School.—There are few accounts left to us of the actual curriculum or method or organization of the Latin grammar school, perhaps because the character of the work was so obvious as to need no description. On the other hand, the requirements for admission to the Colonial college, for which these grammar schools prepared, are frequently stated. According to the earliest description of Harvard (Quo. 263), "When any scholar is able to understand Tully, or such like classical author *extempore;* and make and speak true Latin in verse and prose, *suo ut aiunt Marte;* and decline perfectly the paradigms of nouns and verbs in the Greek tongue; let him then, and not before, be capable of admission into the college." These standards were not greatly modified during the Colonial period. Common arithmetic was added by Yale in 1745 and by Princeton in 1760. Greek was not always specified; sometimes two years' study of this language was required as at William and Mary in 1727; sometimes certain

SECONDARY EDUCATION IN THE COLONIES

FIG. 45. The alphabet from Comenius, *Orbis Pictus* or *Visible World*, London edition of 1777.

Greek texts, such as Isocrates and the New Testament, were mentioned, as at Harvard in 1734.

In general the work of the grammar school was directed to a mastery of Latin. Ability to read Cicero and Virgil *extempore*,

[157]

considerable ability in Latin composition, both prose and verse, a knowledge of Greek grammar, together with ability to read simple Greek,—these were the aims and the accomplishments of the secondary schools. How far the ability "to make and speak true Latin in verse and prose" was attained it is impossible to say. A rule of Harvard of this period compelled students to use the Latin language in conversation on the campus. Doubtless the ideal was attained by a few, was attempted with mediocre success by the many; and in time became the formal accomplishment of a few phrases acquired by all. Throughout the Colonial period, occasional scholars were to be found who attained the accomplishment of Latin speech. Many of them were the products of the Colonial grammar schools. The rule of the grammar school of William and Mary College specified: "And because nothing contributes so much to the learning of languages as daily dialogues and familiar speaking together in the languages they are learning, let the master therefore take care that out of the *Colloquies* of Corderius and Erasmus and others who have employed their labors this way, the scholars may learn aptly to express their meaning to each other."

A knowledge of classical literature, an aspiration to imitate classical standards and customs, was far more prevalent than in modern times. This was largely the work of the grammar school. How great an influence this knowledge of life and ideals of the Greeks and Romans exerted on the political beliefs and activities of the Revolutionary and early period can be readily imagined if not demonstrated. Manners, customs, taste, architecture, vocabulary, oratory or public address, literature, were all profoundly influenced by the classics as learned in the grammar school.

One college required testimony of "blameless and inoffensive life," another that "no blockhead or lazy fellow in his studies" be admitted. The grammar school saw to the development of character and habits of work. Herein lay the influence of the great masters.

The pupil entered the school at eight or nine if this was possible, and remained until a sufficient mastery of Latin and Greek was acquired to meet the standards fixed by the college. He might then

SECONDARY EDUCATION IN THE COLONIES

be from fourteen to eighteen years of age. School was in continuous session throughout the year except for the church or established holidays, rather few in number. Hours of sessions were long. Corporal punishment was severe and frequent; it was used as an incentive to study, a penalty for failure in acquisition, a means of discipline for "training the will," as well as a punishment for bad conduct or for breaches of rule.

Methods were the traditional ones of Latin study. But as these were most tested and based on broad experience and had stood the test for generations, they were probably better, especially in the hands of a good teacher, than the methods of any other subject even of recent times when empirically determined alone. The pupils recited singly or in pairs as in the European schools. The classical languages were studied for use—use not only in reading but in all forms of composition and in speaking. Some of the work to be done in college was still done in Latin; addresses were made, letters written, notebooks kept, even lectures heard, in the language. Its use in writing and speech made of it a much more virile and comprehensive subject for teaching than it has been in more recent times. In the middle seventeenth century (Quo. 240) the Boston town meeting appointed a committee to consider the introduction of Comenian inductive methods into the Latin school. The books of this great teacher were used at least to some extent.

As to organization, little was needed. The school consisted of the master and one or two ushers or assistants. Support came primarily from the local government, since the Latin school was generally recognized as a public institution. In addition pupils were frequently charged for tuition, but these rates were definitely fixed by law or custom. Supervision or inspection, where it existed, was in the hands of the church, or in New England of a school committee. Teachers were licensed by the church or by the governor as representing the church as well as the state. In Massachusetts the ministers of the church, as being the only persons having the requisite knowledge to test the attainment of the prospective teacher, issued the license.

Most of the very voluminous notices of the Latin grammar school found in the Colonial records relate to organization; that is, to questions of establishment, support, control. Few of them directly concern the actual procedure of the school. For the school, once established, worked according to traditional methods towards universally recognized ends. All that was necessary in the way of initiative was the supply and the support of the master. The rest followed as a matter of custom.

Rise of the Academies: A New Type of Secondary School.—During the eighteenth century the Latin grammar school declined, partly because Latin was ceasing to be of value except for the specialist—the minister. Among the other factors causing this change was the need in a new country for men trained in practical subjects such as surveying, navigation, bookkeeping, all of which demanded mathematics. A new society with its new needs and ideals developed new leaders. The lawyer now came to share with the minister the primacy in society. His training demanded a knowledge of history, of geography, of government. The new thought of the eighteenth century was largely expressed in the French language, and all the leaders of thought and action needed this rather than the Latin. The natural sciences offered a message and became of interest not only to the developing professors of medicine, but to the minister, and indeed to all intelligent people.

Beginning in the third decade of the century a mighty religious movement, termed the Great Awakening, swept over the Colonies. The great interest in evangelical religion continued until after the Revolutionary War; in fact it was this interest that fixed the dominant religious attitude during the nineteenth century as well. This interpretation of religion emphasized the emotional origin of religion, and laid less stress on the intellectual formulation and acceptance of creeds and more on worship and on conduct. Consequently the education desired was a broader one than that of the Latin grammar school. This linguistic training was still valued but much was added in the way of newer subjects and newer interests. The formal education as well as the formal religion of the established Episcopal church of New York and the South and of the established Calvinistic or Congregational church of New England

SECONDARY EDUCATION IN THE COLONIES

alike fell under popular disfavor. The newer religious influences favored the building up of a new type of secondary school—the academy—usually of denominational origin and support.

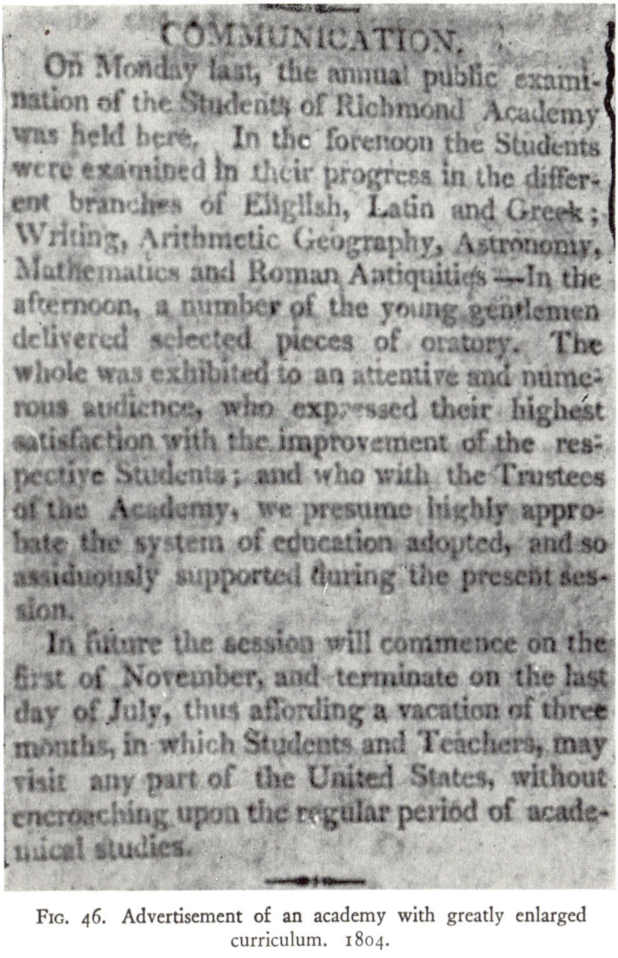

> **COMMUNICATION.**
>
> On Monday last, the annual public examination of the Students of Richmond Academy was held here. In the forenoon the Students were examined in their progress in the different branches of English, Latin and Greek; Writing, Arithmetic, Geography, Astronomy, Mathematics and Roman Antiquities.—In the afternoon, a number of the young gentlemen delivered selected pieces of oratory. The whole was exhibited to an attentive and numerous audience, who expressed their highest satisfaction with the improvement of the respective Students; and who with the Trustees of the Academy, we presume highly approbate the system of education adopted, and so assiduously supported during the present session.
>
> In future the session will commence on the first of November, and terminate on the last day of July, thus affording a vacation of three months, in which Students and Teachers, may visit any part of the United States, without encroaching upon the regular period of academical studies.

Fig. 46. Advertisement of an academy with greatly enlarged curriculum. 1804.

There was no fixed program of studies, but the classics formed the dominant element. Methods were those of the individual teacher. In fact such schools in the earlier period centered around a teacher of striking personality, usually a minister.

One factor of great importance in building up these institutions was the influx of Scots or, since many of these were settlers from Ireland, the Scotch-Irish. These were mostly Presbyterian; they opposed an established church, whether Episcopal or Calvinist, and because of harsh experience were antagonistic to the English government, even as exercised throughout the Colonies. They sought the interior and the highlands regions of the middle and Southern states. They were a particularly hardy, independent, fearless, pioneer class; yet their ministry was probably better educated than that of any other Colonial church. Hence they were not only peculiarly inclined but also peculiarly equipped to build up these new schools. Since the academies are especially the secondary schools of the early National period, a full description of them must be deferred. But their origins lie in this period. In Pennsylvania, New Jersey, Virginia, and the Carolinas, numerous centers of learning of this type grew up. Few of them attained sufficient size or stability to demand legal organization. Most of them avoided it. Some few asked and received Colonial charters near the Revolutionary period. Some never received the name of academy but flourished nameless, to develop later into permanent institutions. Of these the famous "Log College" of the Tennant family—father and sons, Scotch Presbyterian ministers, fired with the new evangelical zeal, was the most important since it was the germ of Princeton College (Quo. 261).

Of all the Colonial academies, the most important and probably the earliest to receive the name was "The Academy and Charitable School in the Province of Pennsylvania" (Quo. 258) founded through the efforts of Benjamin Franklin. Dissatisfied with the formal and undemocratic educational conditions of the time, as he was with similar religious and political conditions, Franklin had proposed this school in 1743. "As to their studies, it would be well if they would be taught everything that is useful and everything that is ornamental. But art is long and their time is short. It is therefore proposed that they learn those things that are likely to be most useful and most ornamental, regard being had to the several professions for which they are intended."

Penmanship, drawing, arithmetic, accounts, geometry, astron-

SECONDARY EDUCATION IN THE COLONIES

omy, English grammar and composition, history, geography, chronology, logic, languages, civil government, natural history, agriculture, horticulture, commerce, mechanics, morality, and religion, all found place in this ample curriculum. Sports and physical training were included. Training in the professional or practical subjects was provided for. The school opened in 1751 in a building provided for Whitefield, the great evangelical revivalist, when none of the Philadelphia churches would permit his preaching.

FIG. 47. Academy and Charitable School of Philadelphia, in the Province of Pennsylvania. 1751. (From Wood, *History of University of Pennsylvania,* p. 10.)

Thus was freedom in education combined with freedom in religion. The academy was organized in three schools, Latin, English, and Mathematical. The Latin school soon grew into a college (1755), out of which developed the University of Pennsylvania.

The English and the Mathematical schools were dwarfed by the growing college but, united, they continued throughout the century as a preparatory school. That they were thus subordinated and attained only a moderate success merely indicates that the time was not quite ripe for the new ideas in education. But no other man so left his impress on the early educational ideas of the coming nation as did Franklin. These practical ideas are nowhere more clearly expressed than in his concept of an academy (Quo. 258). Their manifold though fragmentary realization is to be found in the history of the academies during the century which followed (see Ch. 12).

Summary.—The Latin grammar schools were the most commonly accepted educational institutions among the colonists. Every colony except Georgia had such schools. Where the population was scattered, no cities existed, and where the university was supplied from England by the established church, these Latin schools did not flourish. South of Maryland they were supported chiefly by private endowment, though Virginia maintained one in connection with the college. Maryland finally developed a system of one in each county. This was more than the population demanded or could support. When the population belonged to a variety of religious sects, as in all the middle colonies, such schools were left to the various religious denominations. Here for the most part they were tardily developed when they took the new form of the academy. New York made repeated efforts to maintain such a school but did not succeed until the college was founded near the Revolutionary period. Each of the New England colonies, except Rhode Island, developed a great number of such schools and at first required one for each town of 100 families. Even here, however, the demand for these schools declined during the latter eighteenth century, as they failed to meet the new needs of an independent and growing society. Hence they disappear before a new institution—the academy, more democratic in its organization and ideals, more practical in its curriculum and method, and more efficient in its effort to contribute to the social welfare. In general, however, there was no plan of the universal scheme of education of the seventeenth and eighteenth centuries in which all colonists more nearly reached agreement than that of the Latin grammar school.

Chapter VII

THE COLONIAL COLLEGE

Universality of Belief in the College or University.—The belief of the colonists that educational institutions form an essential part of the universal structure of society is nowhere more clearly shown than in their attitude towards the college or university. When the Massachusetts Bay settlement was but seven years old, it established such an institution and voted for its erection a sum which Palfreys says was equal to the entire Colonial tax for a year. Though New Haven contributed to the support of Harvard and sent her students thither, this colony had been in existence but a dozen years when it initiated a plan for a college of its own and raised a generous subscription. The Dutch of New Amsterdam, though only commercial adventurers and not considering themselves a self-sufficient society or a political unit, yet debated in their public proposals the establishment of an "academy" or university. The English had been in control of this colony for less than a generation when in 1701 they initiated a plan for a similar institution. Large gifts of land were offered by the church but, as in the Dutch period, the time was not yet ripe.

New Jersey, divided between New York and Pennsylvania, felt no consciousness of community need in this respect until her independent colonial entity was recognized. It was not until 1738 that the final separation of the colony from New York was effected and within the next decade the educational aspirations of the various religious sects, especially of the Scotch Presbyterians, resulted in the founding of the College of New Jersey. General provision for the care of higher education was made in the "frame of government" which laid the very foundation of the colony of Pennsylvania. As in most of the other colonies, two generations or more elapsed before such an institution materialized. In Virginia while yet the colony was little more than a military garrison, at least in its government, the home company made appropriations for a university. For the same end private gifts were made and local contributions of land voted. The Indian massacre of 1622 put an end to these visions. Undismayed, two years later the legislative assembly voted land for an "Academia Virgeniensis et Oxoniensis." However, this Oxford in the wilderness did not materialize. The Restoration of 1661 was signalized by a new plan for a Colonial college, backed by appropriations of the grand assembly, and subscriptions by the governor and notables. Again no institution materialized. But after a generation, supported by the church and under the leadership of a persevering and able man, the goal was reached. For this college (William and Mary) Maryland as well as Virginia taxed itself, the two colonies sharing in the advantages of the institution as well as in its support.

The scattered population of the more southern colonies never attained sufficient consciousness of independent social or political existence to develop a higher institution of learning. The aspiration for a college, as well as the realization of the need of one, developed most strongly in the religious bodies of each colony. As a result several schools of secondary grade and of the new type came into existence (see pp. 141-44). Several of these were to rise to the rank of college early in the National period. At the same time the political feeling of the colony demanded higher institutions of learning for the social group as a whole—so the early state universities were provided for (Ch. XIII). The demand of the religious sects for institutions of collegiate grade for the training of their ministry was very definite. But the Church of England was provided with such a college near at hand in William and Mary. The Presbyterians and the Baptists, though strong in this section, located their institutions in the North, nearer the center of population.

Founding of the Early Colleges.—There are no accounts of the steps preliminary to the founding of Harvard. In 1636 the general court voted "to give four hundred pounds towards a school or college, whereof two hundred pounds shall be paid the next year

THE COLONIAL COLLEGE

and two hundred pounds when the work is finished; and the next court to appoint where and what building." The next court did appoint a governing board of twelve men, six of whom were magistrates and six ministers. The following year John Harvard, a minister who had been in the colony but one year, dying, left to the college his library and one half his estate. His gift established the college, and in his honor it was named. Opened the next year under a single teacher, Nathaniel Eaton, it graduated its first class in 1642. In the same year it was given a corporate organization and a president (Quo. 265).

The second Colonial college was William and Mary in Virginia, founded in 1693. The numerous vain attempts to found a college earlier in this colony have been mentioned. Social leadership here was in the hands of the large land-holders. The ministry, while an essential profession, was quite weak. Few clergymen had come over from England and these were mostly of inferior character and qualification. In 1685 there came one James Blair, a Scotchman, commissioner to the Bishop of London, of great ability, force of character, and zeal for education. General sentiment favored a college, but needed such a leader to attain realization. Six years after reaching America, Blair returned as agent of the colony to petition the new monarchs (William and Mary) for a charter and assistance. Both were given, though the objection of the Attorney-General Seymour has made a greater impression on history than did the king's kindly interest. To the royal official's objection, Blair replied that Virginians as well as Englishmen had souls to save. Seymour replied somewhat more frankly than politicians are accustomed to express their sentiments, "Damn your souls; make tobacco!"

The third college was founded in 1701 as the "Collegiate School of Connecticut" by a group of Congregational clergymen, graduates of Harvard, alarmed at the growing heterodoxy and tolerance of their Alma Mater. At this period one eighth of all Harvard students came from Connecticut. The new college had its being where its president and tutors lived. These for the most part being ministers with charges, the institution consisted of small disunited groups or classes of students. After six years of migratory life, the college took up a settled habitation at New Haven, and received its present name because of the generous gifts of a London merchant. No other of the Colonial colleges had so rapid a growth in student body as did Yale.

The fourth college, unlike its predecessors, was the outgrowth of a very scattered group, held together by religious bonds but having no ties of contiguity or political loyalty. The College of New Jersey, or Princeton as it was popularly known, was really the outgrowth of the determination of the Presbyterians, chiefly Scotch and Scotch-Irish, to have an institution for the training of their ministers. The newly attained independence of the colony of New Jersey intensified the desire of its inhabitants to become independent of the two New England colleges, while the religious feeling of the day, which looked with little favor on the conservatism of Yale and the threatened apostasy of Harvard, also contributed. So the College of New Jersey came into existence in 1746, the first college to be created by authority of a colonial government alone. For some years the college work was carried on in the studies of the pastors of various towns, but after ten years it came to rest at Princeton, anchored by a gift from the community.

The fifth college was established in New York City as the outcome of a long series of efforts on the part of leading citizens, of the church, and of the colonial government. The local Church of England, Trinity, made the most liberal contributions, on condition that the president should be a communicant of that church, and that religious (see p. 171) service be read each day. As at Princeton, various religious bodies were represented on the board of trustees, which included *ex officio* several representatives of the colonial government. The college was chartered by George II, and in his honor was termed King's, a title which the patriots of the Revolution changed to Columbia.

The sixth college was more largely the work of one man than any of its predecessors; but Benjamin Franklin came nearer to determining the public spirit of his colony, Pennsylvania, than did any other Colonial leader. The novel academy which Franklin

THE COLONIAL COLLEGE

founded in 1740 did not persist; but out of its classical and its philosophical school developed in 1751 the "College, Academy, and Charitable School of Philadelphia." During the Revolution this became the University of the State of Pennsylvania, though still a privately controlled institution.

The next two colleges, now known as Brown and Rutgers, were outgrowths of denominational needs and efforts. The Great Awakening which through its evangelical stimulus had contributed to the founding of Princeton, contributed also to the founding of these two institutions. The Baptist denomination, greatly stimulated in its growth by this movement, deliberated on the founding of a college for the training of its ministry. As a result the College of Rhode Island was chartered in 1764 by the colonial legislature, as that of New Jersey had been. It was not until the early nineteenth century that it changed its colonial name to Brown, honoring a generous patron.

In 1766 the colony of New Jersey repeated its earlier usurpation of royal power and granted to the Dutch Reformed Church the charter for Queen's College in New Jersey. Through the remaining years of that century and for a decade of the next, the condition of the college was precarious, owing largely to the division of its supporting church into conservative and progressive branches. As with Rhode Island, the change to a personal name, Rutgers, came through later benefaction (Brown in 1804, Rutgers in 1825).

The ninth and last of the Colonial colleges was also an outgrowth of the religious spirit, now turned toward work for the Indians. More truly even than Pennsylvania was Dartmouth "the lengthened shadow of a man." Eleazar Wheelock, pastor of a village church in Connecticut, was accustomed to take some Indian youths into his family to train. After some years, assistance was given to the work by other benevolent persons, and "Moore's Indian Charity School" flourished from about 1754 to 1770. A charter being refused by Connecticut, New Hampshire granted one, together with a tract of land. The appeal for the conversion of the savages met with generous response in England and in 1770 Dartmouth College was established, named after its most liberal benefactor, the

[169]

Earl of Dartmouth. Located on the frontier, it expected to come into intimate contact with the Indians. During the Revolution the powerful tribes of that region sided with the British; and it proved more feasible for the institution to train the youthful ministers and missionaries who were attracted by the low fees from the more settled regions of New England and New York than to carry on the work originally planned.

Motive in Founding the Colonial Colleges.—The dominant motive was the religious one. The need for a trained ministry was uppermost in every case except that of Pennsylvania and of Dartmouth. It is to be remembered that there was an established church in every colony which was the seat of a college, with the exception of Rhode Island, New Jersey, and Pennsylvania. Calvinistic theory subordinated church to state: but on the other hand, all magistrates were to be faithful adherents of the church and carry out her behests. In New York the governor was the official head of the church in the colony; this was true also in Virginia until the sending of Blair. From the founding of William and Mary until the Revolution, the head of this college was the head of the colonial church.

Yet the social or community motive was also strong. It was so obvious in early Massachusetts that no official motive was stated. The general law providing for education gave as its reason that "learning might not be buried in the graves of our forefathers in church and commonwealth." The Virginia assembly in 1660 stated as its motive "the advance of learning, education of youth, supply of ministry and promotion of piety." The actual grant of 1692, expressing the purposes of the home government, said "to the end that the church of Virginia may be furnished with a seminary of ministers of the gospel, and that the youth may be piously educated in good letters and good manners." The Connecticut formulation of purpose was broader and distinctly stated that an institution was desired "wherein youth may be instructed in the arts and sciences, who through the blessing of Almighty God may be fitted for public employment both in church and civil state."

The New Jersey charter was broader yet. The college was erected

THE COLONIAL COLLEGE

"for the education of youth in the learned languages and in the liberal arts and sciences," and it was provided by charter "that those of every religious denomination may have free and equal liberty and advantages of education in the said college, any different sentiment in religion notwithstanding." One important influence in the founding of Princeton was the very narrow attitude of Yale in respect to the religious beliefs of its students.

The educational consciousness of the colonists was now rapidly widening. The first public statement of the purpose of King's College, now Columbia, was as follows:

> "The chief thing that is aimed at in this college is to teach and engage the children to know God in Jesus Christ, and to love and serve him in all sobriety, godliness, and righteousness of life, with a perfect heart and a willing mind; and to train them up in all virtuous habits and all such useful knowledge as may render them creditable to their families and friends, ornaments to their country, and useful to the public weal in their generations."

It was also provided

> "that as to religion, there is no intention to impose on the scholars the peculiar tenets of any particular sect of Christians; but to inculcate upon their tender minds the great principles of Christianity and morality, in which true Christians of each denomination are generally agreed. And as to the daily worship in the college morning and evening, it is proposed that it should, ordinarily, consist of such a collection of lessons, prayers and praises of the liturgy of the church as are, for the most part, taken out of the Holy Scriptures, and such as are agreed on by the trustees to be in the best manner expressive of our common Christianity: and as to any peculiar tenets everyone is left to judge freely for himself, and to be required to attend constantly at such places of worship, on the Lord's day, as their parents or guardians shall think fit to order or permit."

In the charter of the College of Pennsylvania it was hoped "that the institution prove a nursery of virtue and wisdom and that it will produce men of dispositions and capacities beneficial to mankind in the various occupations of life." The trustees in requesting aid from the city and community urged that the purposes of the institution were (1) that the youth of Pennsylvania might have the opportunity of a good education at home, (2) that "a number of the poorer sort be hereby qualified to act as schoolmasters," and (4) that it might draw a number of students from the neighboring provinces.

The charter of Rhode Island College (Brown) averred that

> "institutions for liberal education are highly beneficial to society by forming the coming generation to virtue, knowledge, and useful literature, and thus preserving in the community a succession of men duly qualified for discharging the offices of life with usefulness and reputation."

Of far greater influence than would be imagined at the present was the desire to educate the Indians. This motive was greatly emphasized in all the early colleges. The charter of William and Mary specified among its purposes "that the Christian faith may be propagated amongst the Western Indians." An Indian school was built up here, as also at Harvard. Even on the eve of the Revolution Dartmouth was able to draw large funds from England chiefly because of the great interest in the Christianizing and civilizing of the Indian. Though some of these children of the wilderness survived the college course, none of them could withstand in addition the ravages of the diseases of civilization.

A somewhat detailed analysis of the purposes of the founders of the colleges will be found worth while, for it gives the conception of formal literary education held by the colonists.

Support of the Colleges.—To most of the colleges the Colonial legislatures made direct contribution. These appropriations continued for many years at Harvard and Yale, and throughout the period in Virginia, though they were never regular and never large. The meager support which could be given to the early presidents and tutors of Harvard forms one of the tragic elements of the early Colonial life. During the eighteenth century government contributions ceased altogether. The union of church and state was greatly weakened in all the colonies, and along with it the obliga-

THE COLONIAL COLLEGE

tion of government to an institution which was recognized chiefly as an instrument of the church. For many years in the New England colonies annual collections for the college were made in the various towns. In some towns a corn tax was levied for this purpose. In far-off Connecticut this was continued for at least twenty years. In a similar way both Virginia and Maryland levied a tobacco tax.

That generosity of business and public men which has ever been conspicuous in the history of American colleges was early in evidence, as is proved by the names borne by five of the nine Colonial institutions. Gifts from monarchs give names to two; from a locality to two. Yet even these contributions, with one exception, were inadequate at best: the early records of presents of silver buttons, spoons, and salt cellars tell a pathetic story of poverty as well as of devotion. The general tax on tobacco for William and Mary and that on rum for Yale tell a different tale; while the very common use of the lottery, by which most of the Colonial institutions profited, reveals the morality of a different age. When a bill to prohibit lotteries was introduced into the Pennsylvania legislature, it was defeated on the ground that its object was to injure "our college."

Timely gifts from England were made to at least eight of the nine. Early in the eighteenth century the oldest of the colleges began to profit by substantial endowment gifts, supporting professorships and fellows. For the most part the income thus derived was insignificant. Harvard was given control of the first printing press, and William and Mary of the surveying of all public lands. This latter provision gave the Virginia college a close connection with public affairs, as well as a considerable income, and brought to the service of the college two of its most influential friends, Washington and Jefferson. Of all the Colonial institutions, William and Mary alone had an income adequate to its needs.

Administration and Control.—The most characteristic features of higher educational institutions in the United States today, in comparison with those of other countries, are the freedom of so many of them from the state and the responsiveness of all to the public needs and ideals. The basis of these qualities was laid in the Colonial period.

The characteristic feature of the universities of Continental Europe was their control by the government; and of those of England the power lodged in the teaching body and the graduates of the institution. The colleges of Oxford and Cambridge were controlled by the teaching staff, that is, by the head of the college and the "fellows," who gave the most of what little instruction was given. The universities were under the general control of two bodies, one called "the greater congregation" or known by some similar title, made up of all who held the degree; the other, "the lesser congregation," comprising those graduates who did the actual work of teaching and administration in the university or its colleges. This structure had made these bodies unresponsive to ideas and forces outside the immediate university circle.

In the two earliest Colonial institutions this principle of bicameral control was perpetuated, but there were no graduates to constitute the governing bodies. Hence at Harvard the "board of overseers" and at William and Mary the "board of visitors" were made up of the most prominent of the clergy and the laity of the respective colonies. In each case the actual governing body was "the president and fellows." These constituted the "corporation" as well as the faculty. This plan of organization continued at William and Mary until after the Revolution. At Harvard it was not until 1721 that after a long controversy it was decided that the tutors, or faculty members, did not have an *ex officio* claim on the fellowships. In time the control was shifted entirely to representatives of society at large.

In all the later colleges, the control was placed by the original charter in the hands of a group of trustees, usually enumerated in the charter itself, to whom was given the power of selecting their successors. Some, however, like the college of Rhode Island, had also a board of fellows. At Yale this body was limited to representatives of the Colonial government and to Congregational ministers. The original board of control of Princeton contained *ex officio* representatives of the colony, with members of the Society of

THE COLONIAL COLLEGE

Friends and of the Episcopal as well as of the Presbyterian church. The trustees of King's College were mostly selected *ex officio:* in addition to numerous representatives of province and city, the chief

FIG. 48. A scientific disputation in a medieval university. (From John de Cuba, *Hortus Samitatis* of 1491.)

ministers of the English, the Dutch Reformed, the Lutheran, the French, and the Presbyterian churches were included. The College of Pennsylvania had no connection with any church. The College of Rhode Island carried this ecclesiastical representation further

[175]

than King's and stipulated the number of its thirty-six trustees that should belong to the Baptist, to the Congregational, to the Episcopal church, and to the Friends. Thus in these various ways, the control of American institutions of higher learning was placed, as it has always remained, in a body representative of the interests of society in a large way.

Curriculum and Method.—The narrow scholasticism of the late medieval university persisted in the early Colonial colleges. About half the time was given to philosophy, including logic, ethics, and metaphysics, and probably some theology; the greater part of the remainder was devoted to rhetoric, the Greek tongue, and Oriental languages, especially Hebrew. Mathematics, the catechism, history, and botany appeared as minor or subordinate subjects, perhaps one seventh of the time covering all. Latin was not taught, because a mastery of it was demanded for entrance, since students were required to use it for conversation within college walls and for purposes of recitation or lectures. How thoroughly and how long this rule was carried out cannot be determined. The Yale curriculum was similar. William and Mary taught much Latin, since adequate preparatory schools did not exist.

No great change in the curriculum came until the middle of the eighteenth century. Even then the change was in ideals and in recognition of needs rather than in actual accomplishment. As in all periods and in all stages of education, a long time passed after the recognition of a need before it was embodied in a working curriculum.

The curriculum proposed by Franklin was very broad (Quo. 257).

The visions of the founders of King's College were quite as broad and met with the same inadequate realization. The first president announced his curriculum as follows:

> "To instruct and perfect the youth in the learned languages, and in the arts of reasoning exactly, of writing correctly, and speaking eloquently; and in the arts of numbering and measuring, of surveying and navigation, of geography and history, of husbandry, commerce and government; and in the knowledge of all nature in the heavens above us, and in the air, water, and earth around us, and the various kinds of meteors, stones, mines and minerals, plants and animals, and

THE COLONIAL COLLEGE

of every thing useful for the comfort, the convenience and elegance of life; in the chief manufactures relating to any of these things; and, finally, to lead them from the study of nature to the knowledge of themselves and of the God of nature, and their duty to him, themselves, and one another, and everything that can contribute to their true happiness, both here and hereafter."

When it is remembered that the president taught this curriculum himself with the aid of one tutor and that the student body in these first few years numbered no more than thirty or forty, it will be seen that anticipation must have far outrun realization. The second president of King's College was an Oxford graduate, scholarly and able but holding the traditional view of a college education. Before the Revolution both Pennsylvania and Columbia had relapsed into the conventional groove where they remained throughout the early National period.

Some very definite gains were made during the eighteenth century. Both mathematics and the sciences received a definite recognition and a more generous time-allotment. Arithmetic came to be required for admission by two institutions and geography by one. Harvard founded a professorship of mathematics and natural philosophy in 1726; Kings a similar one in 1757; and Yale in 1771. The professions, aside from theology, were scarcely recognized by the Colonial college. Theology had been included in the scheme at William and Mary from the first; a separate professorship was established at Harvard in 1721. Kings provided for theology in its scheme, and more or less formal instruction in this subject was given in all the colleges. Medicine was organized in a school at Pennsylvania in 1765 and at Kings in 1767. Law was nowhere so organized until after the Revolution, though in 1773 instruction in the subject was begun at Kings.

The period of the Revolution and the time immediately following it witnessed some radical attempts to broaden the curriculum. Not until that period did the modern languages or the sciences, other than astronomy and physics, appear.

The methods of the Colonial colleges were chiefly those of formal verbal instruction, but with this merit—subjects were studied to be used. Latin was used to a large extent in the classroom; it was prescribed—probably an ideal inadequately reached—as a means of communication between students; notebooks—especially the popular "common-place book"—were written in it; collegiate addresses were so given. Greek and Hebrew were used for the study of Biblical texts. No public address, civic or ecclesiastical, was acceptable without abundant adornment of quotations from these languages. The literature of the period is a learned and, to our age, a pedantic one.

Extensive training in logic and metaphysics found expression in the extensive use of the disputation. This in turn prepared for preaching and polemic discussion. Professors and students alike were called upon, as in the medieval university, to demonstrate their command of knowledge by frequent participation in such public debates or presentations. The wide applicability of this method is shown by the lists of disputation topics preserved to us from these early days (Quo. 285). Harvard seniors "disputed" whether a monarchical government is best and whether civil government is founded on the consent of the people; whether doubt is the beginning of all philosophy and whether the act of creation is eternal; whether there was a rainbow before the deluge and whether a comet, which reappears after many years, is more of a foreboding of divine wrath than a planet, which rises daily; whether cold water is the most efficacious of all means for removing fever. Similar questions of controversy were: Is there a circulation of the blood? Did Adam have an umbilical cord? Is a lawyer justified in accepting a reward from the opposite party? Is it right for an advocate to defend even a good cause by twisting the law? Does a mistaken conscience compel one to sin? And, are the virtues of the heathen genuine virtues? Is it lawful for anyone to do good works, with a view to a reward in Heaven? And, whether it is right for a physician to pray for the health of the people.

A study of the very wide range of subjects considered by these students gives one a far greater respect for the scope of Colonial studies than one derives from an examination of the course of study. Perhaps we are too prone to undervalue this past training, as

THE COLONIAL COLLEGE

we are now to argue the satisfactory education of the modern youth from an examination of the elective curriculum.

The obligation of the student was an individual one; methods of recitation were also individual. Most of the instruction during the period was given by tutors to small groups of students. The president usually took the senior class, while a tutor took each of

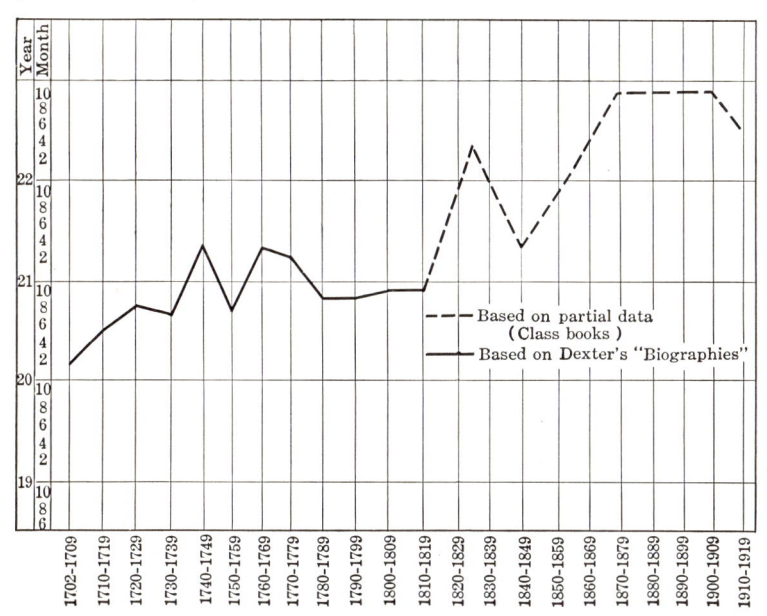

CHART IV. Age of graduation at Yale University. (From Burritt, *Age of College Graduation*, published by U. S. Bureau of Education.)

the lower classes, in all subjects. With the growth of the student body the number of these tutors increased. After about 1720 at Harvard and a little later elsewhere, instructors in certain subjects were added rather than instructors for classes. William and Mary was the one institution which from the first had the scheme of professors of subjects.

Demonstration by the instructor in the sciences was added during the eighteenth century. Orreries, globes, and a few physical instruments were supplied. Until near the Revolution science played no great part.

Student Life (Quos. 282-285).—A study of the manners and customs of the students reveals the conception of the college as more nearly that of the late Middle Ages than that of the present. The term college, then as now, was given to the building as often as to the institution. But with these differences: that it then implied dormitories only, and that the essential part of collegiate discipline was the community life in a college building under semi-monastic regulations, supervised by an official. All students were obliged to live in college buildings. Many of the earlier gifts were avowedly for the purpose of erecting such buildings. In the early period instruction was given in the residences of president and tutors, not in the college buildings. Students were compelled to keep a rigid schedule of hours within the buildings and yards. The lower classmen acted as servants for the upper classmen and were compelled to remove their caps to them.

Meals were furnished by the college authorities, and much of the trouble with students throughout the period was due to disagreements concerning quality or quantity of food. The first head of Harvard lost his position and his standing in the colony over such troubles, and the first president of Dartmouth met his greatest personal difficulties in the same field. The governor of the province writes to the president of the college long epistles of which the burden is, "your provision for the students is extremely bad, their entertainment neither clean, plentiful, nor wholesome."

The conception of a corporate life as an essential of college life was not limited to the students. For the most part tutors as well were required to live in commons. Even after the middle of the eighteenth century an instructor at William and Mary was dismissed from college for preferring the matrimonial state to that of single blessedness in commons (Quo. 272).

Religious regulations were strict; Yale attempted to compel even secret devotions. But it must be chronicled that moral lapses were not infrequent. Especially during the eighteenth century are accounts of the misbehavior of the students numerous. Moral standards, however, were quite different from those of the present. Nearly all of the colleges depended upon lotteries, though the early

THE COLONIAL COLLEGE

ones all had stringent regulations forbidding the students to indulge in bear baiting, cock fighting, horse racing, or card playing. Most of them served beer or ale on the official bill of fare; and it is certain that neither students nor staff confined themselves to the malt category. Yale had the benefit of a tax on rum, but expelled students for petitioning to use Locke's *Toleration in Religion* or for

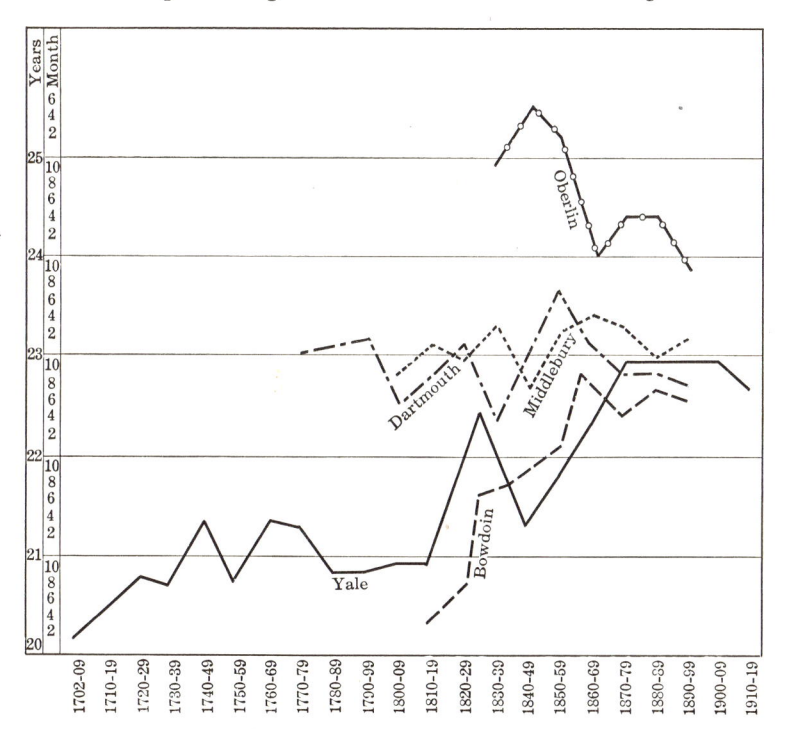

CHART V. Age of graduation at various colonial colleges. (From Burritt, *Age of College Graduation*, published by U. S. Bureau of Education.)

attending a Methodist meeting even when at home. The general court of Massachusetts granted a lottery for the benefit of Harvard but reprimanded the college for printing Thomas à Kempis' *Imitation of Christ*. All of these, however, show merely that the college was a normal part of the social structure, revealing the same ideals with much the same degree of realization as obtained among the less favored classes.

Summary.—The belief that a university or college is essential to the welfare of society and even to the existence of every independent or self-sufficient group was held by all the colonists. Nine Colonial colleges were developed in eight different colonies. While their immediate purpose was the training of a ministry, which was a universal need, their general purpose was the advancement of social welfare, in state as well as church. The obligation to support these institutions was acknowledged to be a universal one; hence the Colonial and the local government contributed. Whereas in Europe the control of such institutions was limited to the government, to the church, or to a closed corporation of teachers, in America it was universalized and placed in the hands of those who would emphasize the general interests of society. While the curriculum in its origin was the narrow traditional course, common to the English universities, by the middle of the eighteenth century it had become in principle, though not in fact, as broad as the universal needs of man. Methods embodied a training in the use of knowledge and forms of public address then most influential in all phases of public life. Student and college life revealed the moral ideals and moral delinquencies common to society at large.

PART II

THE EARLY NATIONAL PERIOD TO THE CLOSE
OF THE CIVIL WAR

EDUCATION NATIONALIZED, DEMOCRATIZED,
AND MADE FREE

Chapter VIII

EDUCATION NATIONALIZED

The Factors and the Development to 1830. Combination of Tendencies towards Universality.—In the analysis of our educational growth, certain great features are assigned to specific periods: thus, education is said to have been universalized in the Colonial period, nationalized and democratized in the early National period. This does not mean that the evolution along any one of these lines was confined within the limits of any one period. Even now education is neither completely universalized nor completely democratized; but the chief stress and the chief achievement of this period are best indicated by the titles of the chapters.

During the Colonial period the idea that a certain type of education was necessary for each class in society became generally accepted. So also did the belief that every self-sufficient social group or colony should have an educational system. Such a system included a university for the professional leaders, Latin grammar schools to afford opportunity for the talented, some form of apprentice education for vocations, and catechetical or literary instruction for the welfare of the soul of every member of society. These ideas were realized in various forms in different colonies and with different people.

Many aspects of universality remained to be worked out in periods subsequent to the Colonial. For instance, a scheme of education which would include girls and women was one of the achievements of the early National period. The universalizing of the support and the form of control, which had been achieved by the New England Colonies, was yet to be tested by experience in the communities of these Colonies as well as to be initiated in all the others. Universal secondary education was not thought of during the Colonial period. The secondary curriculum was of the most restricted character.

Nor had it yet been shown how general education for a large group of people, state-wide or even city-wide, could be supported.

Almost all of the features to be considered under the democratization of education might be included under its universalization. Yet democracy involves the factor of individualizing as well as universalizing. The conceptions of the Colonial period were aristocratic; the middle nineteenth century interpretations of universality were democratic. While the forces working throughout the Colonial period and characterizing it continued to operate during the next, it is this novel aspect of them which will give us insight and interpretation.

Scope of the Period.—Educational development in the early National period falls into two well-defined stages: one, lasting until about 1830, during which American leaders and educators were groping for some feasible scheme which would realize their theories concerning the necessity of universal education in a democracy. The second stage extended from about 1830 to the close of the Civil War. By the decade of the sixties a definite scheme of education, at least in outline, had been agreed upon: by means of vigorous agitation the people had been persuaded into support of the system; a regular teaching profession was being built up, and a definite school procedure organized. During the first stage (1760–1830) the structure of American society and the control of government remained essentially aristocratic. After this time they became essentially democratic. Similarly the control of education, which during the first stage was left in the hands of the leaders, the masses evincing little interest, came during the second stage to be exercised by the people.

In a very general way it might be said that during the first stage of this period the idea was established that education is actually essential to national development and stability. While during the second education became democratic in its organization, its content, its method, and its support (the free school). However, the American states represent such a variety of types and stages of social development that uniform development in any one social feature cannot take place all over the country at a given time. Consequently, these processes of the nationalization, the democratization,

EDUCATION NATIONALIZED

and the freeing of education went on throughout the earlier period, now one factor, now another, receiving chief emphasis,—now one region, now another, forming the chief center of educational activity and development.

In general, however, there was such preponderance of interest and emphasis that the first half period (1780-1830) saw the establishment of education on a national basis—the acceptance of the belief that national welfare and perpetuity are dependent upon the dissemination of intelligence and that the nation itself is responsible for the education thus necessitated. In the decades from 1830 to 1870 the interest in education was concerned chiefly in giving it interpretation in terms of democracy. This effort touched all phases of education—organization, subject matter, schoolroom work, and support. Democracy of support—a system absolutely free—was the last to be achieved. While the conflicts over this question occurred in most of the states before the Civil War, contrary to the general impression now held, the free school system became an actual realization in most cases only after that time.

The status of education and its slow development during the period from the end of the Revolution to about 1830 can better be understood in the light of certain facts concerning the population, means of communication, the economic conditions, and the political situation.

Population.—In 1789, when the Constitution was adopted, none of the original states had definite boundaries. The settled area was about 240,000 square miles, or less than 30% of the area claimed by the new government. The frontier of settlement included most of the New England states, only the Hudson and Mohawk valleys of New York, the southern half of Pennsylvania, that of the southern Atlantic coast including the shore plains, or the seaboard portion of the states in the valleys of the Alleghenies, and a small part of Georgia. The First Census of the United States, made in 1790 and recorded in a small volume of 56 pages, showed a population of little over 3,000,000 plus about 700,000 slaves. This gave an average density for the regions enumerated of 9.4 persons per square mile, whereas in 1900 it was over 80 per square mile. That is, the population was

FOUNDING OF AMERICAN SCHOOL SYSTEM

nowhere as dense then as it now is in the state of Texas or in the sparsely settled Western states. In 1800 the population had become five millions, in 1810 seven millions, in 1820 nine millions. By 1820, while the density of the population as a whole had not increased because of the large addition of territory, that of the original area had doubled. Even in 1820 the population of the original area, if evenly distributed, would not have brought this region under the original Massachusetts law of 1647 requiring a school for each town of fifty families.

Of the population of 1790 a small proportion, only 3.3%, lived in cities of over 8,000, of which there were only five. In 1900 41% of the population in the same area was urban dwelling. Even if the standard of an urban community be set at 6,000, about the size of a county seat of the present day, there were in 1790 only seven communities that could qualify. Several communities that before the Revolution were thriving cities had lost much of their population through economic changes and the unfavorable commercial conditions and regulations.

Of greater importance to education than the density of population is its composition. The most striking fact concerning the nationality of our population in 1790 was the preponderance of the English element and its uniform distribution. This factor constituted over 83% of the entire population. In only two states did it fall below this percentage. These were New York, where the English element formed 78% of the population, and Pennsylvania, where it comprised only 59%. The next largest element was the Scotch, also generally though not uniformly distributed. These people, however, formed less than 7% of the total population. In Massachusetts and Virginia they were 15% of the whole, and in New York and Pennsylvania 10%. The Dutch element, constituting only 2% of the whole, was confined almost wholly to New York. The colonists of German descent, making up 5.6%, were settled chiefly in Pennsylvania. The Irish, who formed 1.6%, were distributed throughout the colonies. Other national groups, such as the French, the Jews, and all others combined, represented less than 1%.

The facts of greatest educational significance regarding the

EDUCATION NATIONALIZED

population in this period are the very general distribution of the Scots and the gradual diffusion of the English population of the seaboard colonies on parallel lines to the west. The latter meant that New England ideas of education were transmitted into New York, Michigan, the northern part of Pennsylvania, and of the states of the Northwest Territory; while the educational ideas of Virginia and the Carolinas were passed on to the states to the southwest. The effect of this we shall see later (p. 216).

While the composition of the original population is of significance, the addition of new elements through immigration, now so important a factor in the educational situation, had but little influence in the early National period. During the first thirty years under the new constitution, foreign immigration amounted to only about 250,000 persons; while the original population increased almost threefold, or to nearly 10,000,000. Foreign immigration did not begin to have any particular significance until after 1830.

Means of Communication.—This probably constituted a more important factor in building up a system of schools than density of population, not only as regards the actual facilities of transportation, but also in respect to unifying the ideas of the people and giving them common purposes. In 1790 the postal system of the United States included 75 post offices, only one of which was in the great state of New York. Roads suitable for travel were very rare and for the most part of recent development. Stage lines carrying the mail had been developed between the chief centers of population, but there were then only 2000 miles of post roads all told. It meant a week's journey for the clerk of Congress to notify Washington in Virginia of his election to the Presidency; and the notice of the first President's death, forwarded with the greatest possible dispatch, took ten days to reach Boston. To travel by post from New York to Philadelphia required two days, and from New York to Boston four days. This schedule time was generally doubled in actual experience. In the South travel by water had always been and yet remained the chief means of communication. Postal rates were high and the mails were not widely used.

According to the First Census there were 103 newspapers published, eight of which had daily issues. But of these dailies, three were in New York and four in Pennsylvania. No paper had a circulation of over 1000. There were few means outside of political and religious discussion for arousing the interest of the people or for conveying general information.

The territory of the early nation was so vast, its population so sparse, and the means of communication so poor, that Jefferson predicted that it would be a thousand years before the country would be thickly populated as far west as the Mississippi. More than a generation later, when the Oregon country was under discussion, Webster held it impossible to incorporate this region under the Constitution, since a Congressman's term would expire before he could reach the capital.

Economic Conditions.—In 1790 nine out of every ten persons engaged in gainful occupations were concerned with agriculture. In all the states south of Pennsylvania the proportion was even larger. In 1900 only about one third of the labor population was so engaged. Except in the case of the large landed estates of the South, most of those interested in agriculture tilled their own land. In all sections life on the isolated farm instead of in the village was the normal—almost the exclusive—custom.

These conditions did not greatly change until after 1830. Manufacturing had been discouraged if not forbidden during the Colonial period. The protective policy of the new government greatly stimulated industry, but the influence of the Napoleonic struggle in Europe as well as the policy of the home government during this period retarded manufactures as well as commerce. With the exception that iron was mined and manufactured to some extent in each of the original states, mining hardly existed. Some manufactures of various products had begun to develop, mostly on the handicraft or local industry basis. There was no minute specialization of industry as yet. Each workman, for example, made a pair of shoes entire.

Commerce flourished, except as restricted by the European wars and at times by our own national policy; and along with commerce went ship-building. Commerce and trade were the chief outlets

EDUCATION NATIONALIZED

of capital and were about the only occupations in which large wealth could be accumulated. After the Revolution the country was greatly impoverished. The national system of money, the National Bank (1791-1811), the opening of Western lands, a patent system, gave greater security and inducement to economic endeavor and to individual initiative and enterprise.

The opening up of the Western lands was probably the most important single factor in the development of the country, both economically and politically. Much of the Northwest Territory was granted in large tracts to companies, or to individuals preparing settlements on a large scale, or to veterans of the Revolution. To these latter the price was 60 cents an acre payable in continental currency, a nominal price only. In a short time, after a variety of experiences, the policy which has since been followed was adopted: this gave to the bona fide settler or homesteader land at $1.25 an acre with a period of time for payment. Lines of communication were opened up. Besides the already established water routes of the Ohio and the Great Lakes, the national road from southern Pennsylvania to St. Louis was authorized in 1802.

This policy settled all this region with sturdy pioneers who from the first adopted the isolated life on the farm, and reproduced the life of the original Colonial frontier in many respects. In their resourcefulness, in their sturdy independence, in their impatience of any government interference, in their democratic ideals and practices, in their indifference to the traditions and even to the customs of a cultured society, these settlers surpassed the Colonial generations and soon established a new type of American citizenship of pure if somewhat crude democracy. They were interested in education as a means of bettering one's individual lot and of giving every individual a chance. The old ideals of education were not of general compelling force nor were the older types of educational institutions appropriate.

However, the streams of population from New England, from the Middle States, and from the South here met and each attempted to establish the general policies of education which they had inherited. Here in the course of a half or three quarters of a century these old policies were molded into the educational system substantially as we know it now.

In the territory of the Southwest or of Mississippi the Ordinance of 1787 was adopted with one change. The provision forbidding human slavery was omitted. The economic development of this region was much affected by this fact and it had a determining influence on the formation of society and the accompanying education. The rich lowlands of all these regions were available for cotton, rice, indigo, and such crops, which could be profitably cultivated only in large areas and with an abundance of cheap labor. This was relatively true even of the tobacco and hemp crops of Kentucky and Tennessee. Consequently in this Southern territory the policy of sale in large area was adopted by the government and the land fell into the hands of wealthy land-holders.

Thus the aristocratic structure of society of Virginia and the Carolinas was perpetuated in the Southwest and the large class of small land-holders and the landless were crowded upon the poor soil of the uplands or mountains, where the profitable crops would not grow. Hence the democratic elements and forces of society were stifled in one section by wealth, in the other by poverty. The Virginian class system of education was reproduced and the democratic theory of education which grew up elsewhere in the frontier territory and was struggling for expression in the older commonwealths of the South, found no realization.

Political Conditions.—While these economic conditions unfavorable to democracy prevailed in all the new territory to the south of Ohio, it should be noted that the political situation throughout the country was far from democratic. The Ordinance of 1787 restricted suffrage in the Northwest Territory to those possessed of a freehold of fifty acres. The national Constitution was adopted in 1789 by delegates elected by the state legislatures. In all the states there were property qualifications for members of these bodies which varied from a freehold of $10,000 (or $35,000 for a non-resident of the parish) in South Carolina to a freehold of $500 in New Hampshire.

Not only was eligibility to the legislature conditioned on property

EDUCATION NATIONALIZED

(practically always property in land) but the suffrage itself had some property qualifications in all the colonies. In several, the requirement was simply the payment of taxes; in New Hampshire the payment even of poll tax would suffice. In Massachusetts the minimum qualification was a freehold furnishing an annual income of $15 or any estate of $300 value. Some states were more liberal, others less so. This property qualification for the suffrage was allowed to remain in New York until 1821 and in Connecticut and Rhode Island until after 1840. Though craftsmen who had served their apprenticeship and had, after the Colonial custom, been admitted as freemen of the various states or towns, were exempted from these provisions, yet the records show that in New York, for example, fully one third of the adult males were excluded from the suffrage.

Similar property qualifications were placed on practically all important offices, administrative and judicial as well as legislative. In other words the states were far from realizing democracy even in its primary essential—manhood suffrage. Property interests actually controlled. The official class was drawn from a social aristocracy. Hence the Constitution left to the states the determination of the qualifications of voters for members of the houses of Congress, and made the qualification of suffrage for the President the same as that established by each state for its own legislators.

Many other illustrations could be cited to show how far from an actual democracy, both in sentiment and in reality, our forefathers were. Imprisonment for debt was still all but universal. Several states had a council of appointment to pass on all appointees to office. Distrust of democracy was shown by the general custom of appointing judicial officers, by long tenures of office, and by a variety of the political features of the times.

This want of democratic sentiment and of democratic trust in the people will explain the very tardy development of the free school sentiment and of universal popular education during this long period. In a country where in theory all men were "free and equal" and where the government was supposedly founded on the consent of the governed, the actual working out of the sentiment for national education and of a scheme of popular and free education waited on the actual development of democracy.

Education Nationalized through the Commonwealths or States.—We speak of having a national system of education in the United States and of the national belief in, devotion to, and liberal support of education. And yet the national government exercises practically no authority over education, has done little for it except to make liberal donations of land as subsidies, and has no administrative department that does much more than collect and disseminate information. Nevertheless we can speak accurately and truly of a national system of education. The situation is similar to that in the former German Empire, Switzerland, and other federated states, where educational initiative and authority are centered in the constituent states.

In reviewing this historic period, then, we mean by "nationalization" that general growth of public sentiment accepting education as one of the essential functions of government, and the education of the masses of the people as an essential condition of the preservation of the state. But both of these were the achievements of the respective states; the national government played but a slight part in this development. This general situation remains true to the present day. We have a national system of education and national aspirations in and through education; but the respective commonwealths remain the chief organs of the nation in achieving these ends.

In the national Constitution there is no mention of education. In the deliberations which led to the formulation of this document there was little consideration of education. In fact in few of the original constitutions of the early states does it find any place. These facts are evidences that education was not a national affair at that time. Such educational discussions as did occur in the Constitutional Convention and such educational efforts as were put forth at that time by the political leaders of the nation related to a national university. In accordance with the views common throughout the Colonial period, they conceived such an institution to be essential. And though the country was provided with private

EDUCATION NATIONALIZED

colleges or universities endowed by individuals, they believed that the national organization could not be complete without a university of its own. This view was advocated chiefly by Washington (Quo. 357). How far from essential such an institution is in our scheme of national education is evidenced by the fact that after a century and a half none has been founded.

The popular views concerning education began to shape themselves and were worked out through the state governments. Our problem is to trace out the development of these national ideas and the national system in the various states and to analyze the factors which contributed to this growth. However, two or three factors of general significance demand brief notice first.

The Ordinances of 1785 and 1787.—Steps of far greater importance for education were taken under the weak and ineffective government of the Confederacy (1777-1789) than the national government took for many years. These actions are usually referred to as the provisions of the Ordinance of 1787—though as a matter of fact this document contained but one sentence relating to education, and that of a most general character (Quo. 348). The significant action was included in the Land Ordinance of 1785 and the land laws subsequent to the Ordinance of 1787 (Quo. 349).

The Revolutionary War really included two struggles, one which secured independence, the other which freed the vast empire between the Alleghenies and the Mississippi from savage control and British claim. This second struggle, though usually overlooked in our conception of the Revolution, was no less fierce, was cause for no less patriotism, and gave a reward scarcely less valuable than the first. As its result this great territory was ultimately given to the United States as a national possession. Probably no one factor was of greater importance in strengthening the national government, for by these lands the national government attained substantial power and control. They enabled it to discharge much of its obligation to the unpaid Revolutionary soldiers and to give some shadow of validity to its promises by redeeming, though at a low rate, much of the currency which "was not worth a continental." Moreover, this great territory, with its tempting possibilities, drew to itself many malcontents who might otherwise have been a source of agitation and rebellion at home.

A series of ordinances dealing with this vast territory were proposed, and several of them were adopted. The great problem was to weld this territory and its new settlers to the national government. Not only threats but actual attempts to achieve local independence were made, more than once, some after the adoption of the Constitution. Many prominent statesmen were interested in the search for some organized form of settlement and government which would bind this region to the national government.

In 1785 an "ordinance for ascertaining the mode of disposing of lands in the western territory" was adopted. This ordinance laid the foundation of our public land system and its survey (Quo. 347). Though the plan of survey was soon changed, the ordinance included one provision which has been of incalculable value. This read, "There shall be reserved the lot No. 16 of every township, for the maintenance of public schools within the said township." Under this provision and its subsequent elaboration, more than 80,000,000 acres of land have been granted to the public schools, through steps that will be shown subsequently. This is an empire in itself, one-third larger than the New England States combined.

In 1787 the famous ordinance for the government of this territory was passed. This document has often been spoken of as one of the most famous instruments of government ever issued. "I doubt," said Daniel Webster, "whether one single law of any law-giver, ancient or modern, has produced more distinct, marked and lasting character than the Ordinance of 1787." Yet this ordinance violated the terms of the Articles of Confederacy, then the basis of government. But so also did the new national Constitution, adopted two years later. The Ordinance of 1787 has only one sentence concerning education, but that is a notable one, for it states a social theory and initiates a policy. Article 3 of the Ordinance reads: "Religion, morality, and knowledge being necessary to good government and the happiness of mankind, schools and the means of education shall be encouraged." This is the charter of the public school system of the great Middle and Far West.

EDUCATION NATIONALIZED

This ideal did not remain a mere aspiration, nor did the general government limit its interest and activity to the statement of a high ideal. By subsequent land grants, now to be followed, the nation did much to bring to realization this far-sighted policy, which then was but a vision of a few.

National Grants in Aid of Education.—More by the gift of land than through any other activity or policy has the national government lent its aid to education. The use of these lands and of the funds obtained from their sale has been far from judicious; at times and in some respects it is one of the most unhappy features of our record, a record marred, frequently by inefficiency, at times by irregularity or dishonesty. We can realize that these lands would now afford a princely income or the funds which were realized from their sale would furnish an endowment of untold value; but it is to be remembered that at the time of the gift, land was the cheapest of commodities, that the settlement and development of the country was the primary necessity; that land would be valueless and education of no purpose if settlement and development were blocked by the holding back of important land tracts. Schools were in great need of help from outside sources where the settlements were newest, and there the population was least able to stand taxation. Here also land was of least value. Each generation is naturally inclined to look after its own needs first, if not exclusively, and this is peculiarly true in a democracy.

So the wisdom and efficiency of the use made of this vast domain must be judged by the standards of the generation to which it was given and which made disposition of it. It is sufficient to say that almost all of the domains granted before the Civil War were quickly disposed of and that the funds resulting have been largely dissipated. Their disappearance was due in part to the use of the funds for temporary purposes, in part to the exigencies of war, in part to the unsettled conditions of a new region where government loans were considered government gifts; in part to poor investment and management, in part to defalcation and the easy public morality acceptable to democratic conscience if the evil is not too obtrusive.

Even the original Ordinance of 1785 has been represented as the work of land speculators, for the same group of people that put through the two ordinances of 1785 and 1787 was instrumental in forming the Ohio Company which obtained from the general government a vast tract of the public lands at a nominal price. But these same parties formulated the terms of the ordinances as well as the constitution of the Ohio Company, and it is demonstrable that their great aim was the settlement of the region in the interest of the new nation.

By a later Ordinance of 1787, for contract of sale of land in the "Western Territory" (Quo. 349) provision was made for the disposition of the land voted in 1785. In addition to the grant of lot 16 in each township for public schools, lot 29 was set apart for the promotion of religion, and two complete townships were given "perpetually for the purposes of a university."

A provision of the Constitution (Art. IV, Sec. 3, Par. 2) confirmed Congress in the control of the public lands and thus indirectly sanctioned this policy of endowing public schools. The Act of Congress providing for the admission of Ohio in 1802 and a subsequent one of 1803 confirmed these earlier provisions and established a national policy for the disposal of public lands and incidentally for the endowment of public education. (See Cubberley and Elliott, *Source Book*, p. 23.) The control of this land reserved for public education, including a variety of other grants in addition to the general one of lot 16 in every township, was vested in the state legislature, in trust for the people.

Among these grants were the salt springs—saline lands—and one twentieth of the proceeds of the sale of all public lands. These several provisions were extended to the Mississippi territories. Specific acts followed for each of the new states, Tennessee in 1806, Indiana 1816, Illinois 1818, and other states later. For Illinois the share in public land proceeds was increased to one fifteenth, three fifths of which should be devoted to the encouragement of learning, and one sixth of this portion exclusively bestowed on a college or university.

With the Michigan Ordinance of 1835, the land policy was further changed, complete control of its school lands and funds now being

EDUCATION NATIONALIZED

given to the state. Out of this control grew up the general or common school fund to be noted later (pp. 210-11). With the Oregon Act of 1848, the grant of land for school purposes was doubled, Congress now reserving sections 16 and 36 out of each township. All states admitted after this time received these two sections. In 1896, with the admission of Utah, the school lands were increased to four sections. Oklahoma, Arizona, and New Mexico have received this amount.

Eleven states were admitted to the Union previous to 1830. Three of them,—Maine, Vermont, and Kentucky,—came in before 1802, the year when this land policy was settled, and received no land grants. The remaining eight states received about six and one-half million acres of land for school purposes, a territory larger than Massachusetts and Rhode Island combined and almost as large as Belgium or the Netherlands or Denmark.

Until the period of the Civil War the national government did nothing more for the encouragement or support of education.

Attempts to Found a National University.—Aside from the land endowment for a public school system, the national government through all of this early period showed interest in only one other aspect of education, that of a national university. Though recommendations and proposals concerning this institution were made to the government from time to time, no definite step to this end was taken nor indeed has been to this day. President Washington's interest in national education or in public education was also limited to the scheme of a national university (Quos. 351-358). Jefferson's advocacy of a general scheme of popular education (Quos. 381-382) did not seem to influence other national leaders from the South. The idea of a national university was discussed in the Constitutional Convention, in which it was proposed that the power to establish such a university be conferred upon the general government. However it was decided by vote of six colonies to four to exclude this power. The subject was again taken up for popular discussion and the mention of articles upon the subject appeared in magazines.

Washington's correspondence furnishes the fullest record we have of this project (Quo. 351). In his first message to Congress he recommends government aid to education, leaving open the question whether this would be best afforded by subsidizing institutions already established or by the founding of a new national university. Again (in 1795) (Quo. 352) he recommended to the commissioners of the District of Columbia the founding of such an institution and offered to give liberally toward its endowment. Later in the same year, as the plan for a national university did not seem to materialize, he wrote to the Governor of Virginia of his regret at "the youth of the United States migrating to foreign countries in order to acquire the higher branches of their erudition" and agreed to give toward an endowment for an institution within the limits of Virginia. Again in his message to Congress in 1796 he "proposed to the consideration of Congress the expediency of establishing a national university and also a military academy" (Quo. 355). This was repeated in the next Congress but the legislative body still was unwilling to act.

In his will, dated 1799, there is a long paragraph expressing his desire that the national government take action (Quo. 356), and he bequeathed to this end the fifty shares in the Potomac Company which he had previously offered. Still no action was taken. Washington's idea was still much like that of the Old World, that the university is an essential part of the structure of a government and adds greatly to its prestige and actual power. In his will he again cites the fact that the youth of the states are sent to foreign countries for education, where they contract principles unfriendly to a republican government and to liberty. "For these reasons," he says, "it has been my ardent wish to see a plan devised on a liberal scale which would have a tendency to spread systematic ideas through all the parts of this rising empire, thereby to do away with local attachments and state prejudices . . . from our national councils." It was not until 1816 that a definite bill to this end was actually presented to Congress. This bill, however, failed of passage and though from time to time recommendations were made that the project be again taken up, it was not until after the Civil War that Congress once more gave it serious consideration.

EDUCATION NATIONALIZED

Educational Views of Great Leaders.—With the exception of Franklin in the Colonial, and Jefferson in the early National period, none of our early political leaders had any vision of education. Most of them saw that intelligence was the absolute condition of success for the new experiment in government, and many of them saw in a general way that education was the means essential to secure that common intelligence. But few realized that organized education is the only effective means to such an end and that the only way to have this organized education is through public support. None of them saw what is now commonplace—that organized public education must be the chief means for effecting any desired public end and where education was to become the corner stone of government as well as the fundamental means to progress.

Washington accepted the ordinary views of a Virginian or an English country gentleman, that education of the leaders is essential, and that individual and class incentive would be sufficient to secure this. The one feature of public or state-supported education in which he had great personal interest was a national university. This belief, however, was more largely political than educational.

The views of John Adams are expressed in the Massachusetts Constitution of 1780 previously referred to. John Adams is also given credit for the principles involved in the Massachusetts School Law of 1789. This law in outline, however, is but a continuation of the Colonial law with adaptations of the high standards of that time to meet the somewhat chaotic conditions of society following the Revolution. The constitutional provision for education comes under the section on the encouragement of literature wherein knowledge and wisdom are recognized as the basis of political liberties and the social virtues. Since the general diffusion of knowledge and wisdom depended in turn on the opportunities for education among all orders of the people, the obligation for the maintenance of schools of all grades was laid upon the legislature and magistrates. Even with Adams, the common schools played a comparatively insignificant part in this scheme, more stress being laid on the university, the grammar schools, and those private societies and public institutions which usually encourage improvements in agriculture, arts, science, commerce, trades, and manufactures.

James Madison was one of the few public leaders of the times who held a broad conception of education and took a great interest in promoting educational endeavor. With the exception of one or two addresses his views are expressed almost wholly in his private correspondence. But after all, private correspondence was one of the chief means in that period of disseminating public views. Especially is this true since many of these letters found their way into the local channels of publication. On one occasion he writes: "A popuar government without popular information or the means of acquiring it is but a prologue to a farce or a tragedy or perhaps both." He held with Adams that liberty depended on the general diffusion of knowledge. "The best service that can be rendered to a country," he writes, "next to that of giving it liberty, is in diffusing the mental improvement equally essential to the preservation and enjoyment of that blessing." He argued also for the support of education by general taxation. He realized, however, that this view was far in advance of the sentiment of the times but pleaded that the value of an educational system could be tested only by experience and that a beginning to such experimentation should be made. Madison was probably the most widely informed man of his times and gave suggestions to Jefferson on some of the points which the latter made a part of his creed. Madison, however, was neither a leader nor a molder of public thought while Jefferson was, and it is from the latter that we get the fullest and the most advanced expression of the importance of education in the newly organized experiment of a nation controlled by the masses of the people.

As early as 1779, Jefferson had presented a bill to the legislature of Virginia for the more general diffusion of knowledge. While this bill never received approval, it contained probably a more detailed statement of Jefferson's ideals than any of his other writings (Quo. 381). It proceeds on the assumption that the only guarantee against the reversion of a popular form of government into some form of tyranny by those entrusted with its power is to be found in the general intelligence of the people. Particularly should they be

EDUCATION NATIONALIZED

informed concerning the source of history, of the conditions under which they have gained the existing stage of freedom of intelligence. He also saw, however, that the conduct of a government must after all be placed in the hands of those strong enough and intellectual enough to maintain it successfully. Therefore he aimed to establish a common school system which would reach the masses of the people in every community, and a secondary school system which would provide for the education of the ablest of those selected through the operation of the common school system. The ideal was of a common school that was quite similar to that of New England. A secondary school was to be established in each county to be attended by at least one scholar selected from each elementary school, whose entire support and education were to be provided by the state. The pick of these were then to be placed in the university which was to be made a state institution. One essential feature of this scheme was to do away with the sharp class division existing then as an inheritance from the Colonial age, which clearly marked off those children who were going on with the secondary and higher education on the basis of wealth or social position of their family. His was to be a vertical scheme of education, much as we have it now, wherein secondary education is superposed on elementary and the ablest in each group are to be drawn into the higher stage on the basis of their merit and ability alone. The influence of the church was to be eliminated and in the scheme itself the operation of the system was to be placed beyond the control of local political influences. Along the lines of these ideals Jefferson worked for a full half century before he was able to bring about any material embodiment of them. His final accomplishment related to the establishment of a university only. His vision of an educational scheme in theory as broad as the political theory and in fact the basis of the new social and political structure was doomed to remain unrealized.

Of political leaders of the lesser rank, there were a number in the various commonwealths who attained a better apprehension of these truths than did the national leaders. Chief among these were the two Clintons, governors of New York. The work of such local leaders, however, is better interpreted in connection with the development of the state systems.

Influence of Foreign Ideals and Experience.—When the real educational development of America began in the thirties, foreign ideals and experience formed an important factor in its progress. During the early period the people of the United States were extremely conscious of their provincialism as well as of their new nationalism. Limited experience, great self-confidence, unbounded ambition and aspiration, led them to be far more self-dependent, as well as more assertive, than the facts justified them in being. There was little inclination to inquire what the experience of Europe had been and what lessons it had for America, especially on social subjects. On the one important social subject, politics, America was itself the source of information. Consequently, Europe exerted but slight influence before 1830 except in regard to ideas concerning higher education. Our first creditable educational magazine appeared in 1826.

This early foreign influence relating to the universities was chiefly of French origin and is evident in the organization of the University of the State of New York (1787) and that of Virginia (authorized in 1818), and in the early provisions for state universities in general (p. 202). Perhaps Locke's *Treatise* was still the most potent of all foreign influences. Rousseau's views, though not particularly his treatise on education, were well known. These bespoke the ideas of the eighteenth century, stressed tutorial education, affected the views and the practices chiefly of the ruling and literary classes, and had nothing to urge for public or governmental education. In this country they acted as a deterrent on any inclination to foster public interest or governmental activity in education.

Survey of School Conditions during the Opening Decades of the National Period.—The Revolutionary War and the formation of the new nation did not bring in a great educational revival. Rather was the reverse true. The emphasis on individualism was too strong, the interest in new political and economic developments appealed too powerfully to the efforts of a newly

EDUCATION NATIONALIZED

liberated people. A historian of the period writes of a typical Massachusetts town:[1]

> "In point of fact, the children were neither taught much, nor were they taught well; for through life the mass of them, while they could do little more in the way of writing than rudely scrawl their names, could never read with real ease or rapidity, and could keep accounts only of the simplest kind. As for arithmetical problems, the knowledge of them was limited to the elementary multiplication, division, addition, and subtraction. None the less, after a fashion and to a limited extent, the Braintree school child, like the school children of all other Massachusetts towns, could read, could write, and could cipher; and for those days, as the world then went, that was much."

The standards in other communities were not nearly so high as in those which had educational ideals and school traditions developed through nearly two centuries of experience and endeavor.

The conception of education as a national process and a national force was a slow development of this early National period. This fact finds its best evidence in the conditions of education at that time. That it was not considered of sufficient importance to justify any elaborate account of it is significant. Yet a few statements are available. The most extended survey of this period is one made by an English traveler, Rev. W. Winterbotham, in 1795. The educational conditions in the thirteen original states, along with Maine and Kentucky, are summarized with considerable detail (Quo. 359) in his four-volume *View of the United States*. Most space is given to the colleges, each having an elaborate description, and to the academies, more than fifty of which are mentioned by name. It is the brief descriptions of the public school system which are of most interest.

Of Maine the author writes: "Town schools are very generally maintained in most of the towns *that are able to defray the expense.*" Speaking of New Hampshire, he cites the town school law and notes that the grammar schools had degenerated into schools for teaching reading, writing, and arithmetic. Concerning Massachu-

---

[1] Charles Francis Adams, Jr.'s *Three Episodes in Massachusetts History*, p. 781.

setts the author cites the provisions of the Law of 1789 (p. 116) modified from that of 1647, and then adds: "These laws respecting schools are not so well regarded in many parts of the state as the wise purposes which they were intended to answer and the happiness of the people require." Of Rhode Island he says that "the literature of this state is confined principally to the towns of Newport and Providence." Of Vermont—"much could not be said of the 'present state,' so the sketch is a mere prophecy." Of the remaining New England states he writes: "in no part of the world is the education of all ranks of the people more attended to than in Connecticut; almost every town in the state is divided into districts, and each district has a public school kept in it a quarter or less part of the year."

New York had no school system, so one sentence suffices, in addition to the account of the college and the academies. "Besides these," he says "there are schools established and maintained by the voluntary contribution of the parents." For New Jersey three sentences out of five pages suffice for education: "There are no regular establishments for common schools in the state. The usual mode of education is for the inhabitants of a village or neighborhood to join in affording a temporary support for a school master, upon such terms as are mutually agreeable. But the encouragement which these occasional teachers meet with is generally such that no person of abilities will undertake it; and of course little advantage is derived from these schools." The account of Pennsylvania is much the same, this item being added: "and to promote the education of poor children, the state has appropriated a large tract of land for the establishment of free schools."

The account of Maryland is similar, though it is stated that "provision is made for free schools in most of the counties, though some are entirely neglected and very few carried on with any success." This no doubt refers to the old state system of free or Latin grammar schools. The account of Virginia is confined to an outline of Jefferson's plan (p. 202) which was never realized. No mention whatever of elementary schools is made in the account of North and South Carolina. Of the latter he remarks: "Gentlemen

EDUCATION NATIONALIZED

of fortune before the late war sent their sons to Europe for education." Of Georgia "yet in its infancy" a flattering sketch of prospects is drawn; of Kentucky a similar prophecy is made.

Thus it will be seen that there was no public school system at all outside of New England. In these four large volumes, of which perhaps fifty pages are given to education, one page would contain all the description thought necessary of the elementary or public schools.

Eleven years later Noah Webster, editor of the *Speller* and the *Dictionary,* issued his *Historical and Geographical Account of the United States.* In this a description of education in each state is given, much briefer than that given by Winterbotham. He cites the laws of the New England states and adds in the case of Massachusetts, "Although the laws are not rigidly obeyed, still most of the children of the state have access to a school," and of New Hampshire, "This law is not well directed." Of Rhode Island he writes: "In the large towns and in some others, there are private schools for teaching the common branches of learning"; and of Vermont, "Learning receives from the people of Vermont all the encouragement that can be expected from an agricultural people in a new settlement." As in Winterbotham's book, Connecticut has the best record. Such gazetteers as Webster's were usually marked by a patriotic tolerance and the fervor of a new and growing country. Giving us so modest an account of the educational conditions of that region of the country where alone elementary school systems had developed, the conditions in the rest of the country can be imagined.

The new state law of New York, where Webster taught, receives scant praise, since it had lapsed, though its beneficial effects were still "visible." The elementary schools of the remaining states are dismissed with the statement as of Maryland that "there are private schools in many places." It is noted that North Carolina had planned a law for public schools, which came to naught, and that Pennsylvania appropriated public land to this end.

Since elementary education was left to the communities, with little state compulsion except in New England, and no aid, one would expect the wealthier and more populous communities to have reached a higher standard than the others. And this is true, so far as private schools are concerned; but the conception of a state or national education had scarcely dawned outside of New England. The most populous city, Philadelphia, then the national capital, undoubtedly had achieved the most. The *Directory of 1791* gives the following account of its schools:

> "Almost every religious society has one or more schools under its immediate direction, for the education of its own youth of both sexes, as well of the rich, who are able to pay, as of the poor, who are taught and provided with books and stationery gratis; besides which, there are a number of private schools under the direction of masters and mistresses, independent of any public body; and there are several private academies for the instruction of young ladies in all the branches of polite literature suitable to the sex. A particular description of these would be too lengthy for the present publication; let it suffice that there is no individual whose parents or guardians, masters or mistresses, will take the trouble to apply, but will be admitted into some one of these schools, and if they are unable to pay, will be taught gratis."

The schools of New York City were on the same plan, though not so adequately developed.

Boston had attained quite the highest degree of school efficiency of all the communities in the country, partly because of its unified population, more largely because of its century and a half of tradition and experience. In 1789 the town adopted a reorganized system of education (Quo. 366). This consisted of a grammar school for the teaching of Latin and Greek; three writing schools, open to both sexes, for writing and arithmetic "including vulgar and decimal fractions"; three reading schools, one in each part of the town, for both sexes, for reading, spelling, English grammar, and composition. Children were admitted at the age of seven "having previously received the instruction usual at women's schools." Schools for elementary teaching were not supported by the town until 1819 and were not combined with the city system until 1855. Control was in the hands of a school committee, which was also a committee on inspection. This committee gave specific direction concerning subjects to be studied, texts to be used, method to be adopted, hours of attendance and recitation, and even all the details of schoolroom management. However, as late as 1819 it was found that more than 500 of the 2800 children of elementary grade age did not attend schools of any character.

This brief survey gives the best that can be stated of school conditions during the first thirty or forty years of our national existence.

Charity Schools and Apprentices.—The patronage of most of the great number of schools maintained by the various churches in the cities was made up of the very poor. Such schools were often called charity schools, and as such were a continuation of those founded in the Colonies by the Church of England. Some denominations, such as the Quakers and the German sects of Pennsylvania, supported systems for all the children of their communicants. Of this character also were some of the schools of other churches. In the main, however, the well-to-do in the few cities and larger towns sent their children to private schools and supported most meagerly a few charity schools through the churches.

The system of apprentice indenture now began to lose its little remaining power. Industry did not thrive in the early decades and when it did begin to prosper with the close of the Napoleonic wars, the factory system began to develop. The prevailing political and social sentiments were not favorable to that relic of the medieval system found in apprenticeship. The unlimited opportunities on the frontier for new lands and easy wealth, or at least independence, gave the remaining blow. In isolated places and in certain industries, apprenticeship survived but shorn of its social and most of its educational features. The apprentice ceased to be an inmate of his master's household; his labor became of value and his master ceased to own it. With this change of condition disappeared the remaining aspects of the educational significance of this system except as a means of limited vocational training. Like the charity schools, apprenticeship persisted in regions away from the centers of industry as a feature in the care of the poor.

FOUNDING OF AMERICAN SCHOOL SYSTEM

Educational Provisions in the Early State Constitution.
—One excellent indication of the conception of education held during this period is found in the provisions concerning education in the early state constitutions (Quos. 370–373).

As has been mentioned, our forefathers, not thinking of education as a national force, problem, or obligation, made no mention of it in the national Constitution. The educational authority of the general government has generally been considered to be based upon the Tenth Amendment adopted as a clarifying provision almost immediately after the original articles. This amendment provides that all rights not delegated to the general government are reserved to the states or to the people.

Among the original states Connecticut, until 1818, and Rhode Island, until 1842, continued under their Colonial charter. Between 1776 and 1800 the remaining eleven, together with the three new states admitted, Vermont, Kentucky, and Tennessee, adopted new constitutions. Of the entire sixteen only five made mention of education in the first constitutions adopted after 1776. However, since several of them made early revision or amendment, eight of the sixteen had formulated some constitutional provision on this subject. Of these, Massachusetts and Vermont required a school in each town; Pennsylvania and Georgia one in each county. The New Hampshire constitution made it incumbent on the legislature "to cherish" public schools, and that of Delaware to establish schools "as soon as convenient." North Carolina provided for the establishment "of a school or schools." The Massachusetts provisions, the only ones of any length, referred most elaborately to the university and then in general terms to "the encouragement of literature," mentioning for that end the need "to cherish" . . . the University at Cambridge, public schools, and grammar schools in the town. Of the entire sixteen, Vermont alone made specific provisions requiring a school or schools for each town, a grammar school for each county, a university for the state. This was in 1777. In the second constitution ten years later the statement was made more general, namely that "a competent number of schools ought to be maintained in each town for the convenient instruction of youth."

EDUCATION NATIONALIZED

Thus it is seen that even our forefathers of this period, outside of New England, scarcely considered elementary education to be a function of the state but would leave it to private initiative or local interest. This view is borne out by a closer examination of these early constitutional provisions, in that their chief interest is in the higher institutions of learning. The common or elementary school is included only in the general provision for the promotion of virtue and of general intelligence. John Adams' statement in the Massachusetts document is the most typical and comprehensive. It reads:

> "Wisdom and knowledge, as well as virtue, diffused generally among the body of the people, being necessary for the preservation of their rights and liberties; and as these depend on spreading the opportunities and advantages of education in the various parts of the country, and among the different orders of the people, it shall be the duty of the legislatures and magistrates, in all future periods of this Commonwealth, to cherish the interests of literature and the sciences, and all seminaries of them."

Provisions in the Later Constitutions (1800–1860).— From the opening of the century and the admission of Ohio in 1802, the large gifts of land made by the general government for the promotion of education necessitated attention to this subject.

Development of State Systems of Education up to 1830. —Popular education awaited the growth of democratic sentiment and principles, and public support of education could not be established until national power and authority had been placed on a firm basis. These fundamental changes were taking place during the first half century of the independent existence of the American nation. Democracy was not fully conscious of itself and of its power until the decade of the thirties; and nationalism was threatened throughout this period, not only by foreign wars, but by party strife, by sectional prejudices, by the strong sentiment of state autonomy, and by aristocratic or class bias. Consequently little attention was given to problems of education and the state systems developed but slowly.

In New England the old systems were modified to meet the

lower standards and the more general needs of the new period; so that educational changes were chiefly retrogressive though the basis of a new system was being laid. In the Middle States, particularly in New York, some definite steps towards a new system of public schools were taken. In the South any new activity was chiefly in the form of announcement of ideals or formulation of plans which alike proved Utopian.

Development of Schools in New England up to 1830.— As has been seen, in the states of this section alone had a system of public elementary schools been developed previous to the Revolution. The first half century of the National period added little in principle except in the perfecting of the district school system which will be discussed later (Ch. IX). In Massachusetts the two important laws of the period, in 1789 and in 1827, fixed the outline of the system as it remained, with brief periods of exception, until after 1880. The Law of 1789 legalized the district system and lowered the standards for both elementary and secondary schools. Towns of fifty families were compelled to support one elementary school for six months only, those of one hundred families for twelve months. In either case the schools could be divided into districts. Ministers and selectmen and school officials were to "use their best endeavor" to secure attendance. In 1800 the districts were given power to tax and in 1817 full corporate powers. In 1827 the division into districts was made compulsory. Under the Law of 1789 the old grammar schools practically disappeared (p. 160); by that of 1827 the modern high school took its place (p. 410). These laws secured the full application of democratic local control to schools, and at the same time reduced their efficiency to the lowest terms. Horace Mann termed the Law of 1827 the most unfortunate school law ever enacted for Massachusetts.

The two important features of Connecticut experience from 1780 to 1830 were the perfecting of the district system (p. 274) and the development of a common school fund (p. 307) until it replaced all state taxation for school support. The district system was practically established in 1766 (p. 277) under the auspices of ecclesiastical societies. In 1798 the societies, now definitely made school societies,

EDUCATION NATIONALIZED

were substituted for the towns as units of school control and support. In 1799 the school laws were codified and the district system, thus unified, remained without any substantial change till 1856.

In 1795 the Connecticut common school fund was established (p. 308) out of funds received for Western lands, and in 1800 the first distribution was made. In 1820 it was provided that when the revenue from the fund reached $60,000 per annum, as it did the following year, compulsory taxes for education should cease. From 1821 to 1854 no state taxes for education were levied and town taxes were not compulsory. For a time many of the school societies or districts did levy taxes, but this gradually became less common. In effect this resulted in a system of schools which were run for a short period as free schools and then continued as rate or tuition fee schools for the well-to-do. There followed a period of rapid decline in the efficiency of these schools which can best be considered under the effects of the district system and of the common school funds (p. 311).

The experience of New Hampshire was similar as regards the district features, but the common school or "literary fund" established in 1821 never produced sufficient income to be of much effect. In 1805 the district system was authorized. By a law of 1807 schoolmistresses were allowed to dispense with the teaching of arithmetic and geography as being beyond their qualification.

In Vermont the district system was established by the first school law enacted, that of 1782, which left to the towns and the districts the option of a school tax. In 1821 the county grand juries were directed to inquire whether the school law was enforced by the towns and to impose a fine in towns where schools were not maintained. A series of laws throughout this period were directed chiefly to the details of school support by a combination of taxes and rate bills. In 1826 a common school fund was established, which, however, was used some years later to pay the state debt.

Maine was admitted as a state in 1820, and continued the district school law of Massachusetts, except that a few years later its three leading towns were given permission to organize town or graded schools.

FOUNDING OF AMERICAN SCHOOL SYSTEM

Development of the State System in New York, 1780–1830.—Of all the states which had not established free schools in the Colonial period, New York made the most progress during this early National period. Borrowing to some extent from the experience of New England, this state took several steps in advance of any other region, among them the establishment of a common school fund, the creation of the office of state superintendent of schools (1812), and the organization of a centralized state system.

The schools existing in New York during the last quarter of the eighteenth century were private schools, or church schools, or charity schools. The church schools were for the children of the regular communicants and were sometimes free schools. This was particularly true of the schools maintained by the Friends and by the Church of England. In these schools the church might pay the fees of poor pupils or it might support a distinct school for them. Such was frequently the custom in New York City and the other larger centers of population. The early state constitutions made no mention of education.

New York, however, possessed a number of far-sighted political leaders, several of whom realized the importance of education. Chief among these were the two governors, George Clinton (1777–95) and DeWitt Clinton (1817–22 and 1824–28). Twice during the period of the Confederation and afterwards under the Constitution, Governor Clinton called the attention of the legislature to the importance of this problem. In 1784 he wrote to the legislature: "The neglect of the education of the youth is among the evils consequent on war. Perhaps there is scarce anything more worthy of your attention than the revival and encouragement of learning."

The University of the State of New York was first organized in 1784 and reorganized three years later (p. 432). At first many thought that, after the French model, this institution might include elementary as well as secondary and higher education. In 1793 the regents of the State University called the attention of the legislature to the neglect of elementary education and of its importance.

Two years later the legislature established a school system on the basis of a $50,000 appropriation annually for five years. It is

EDUCATION NATIONALIZED

notable that the result was termed a common school system, not a free school system. This law required each county to duplicate the state's contribution, gave to town school commissioners the right to apportion the moneys, and to district trustees the immediate control of the schools. But one report was made for this embryo system, which showed 1352 schools in sixteen out of the twenty-three counties, with nearly 60,000 children under instruction. The population at this time was about 550,000. The system lapsed in 1800 and, despite the efforts of the governor and other leaders, was not renewed.

In 1805 two other attempts of significance were made. One was the founding of a common school fund (p. 307) out of the proceeds of public lands; the other was the chartering of a private organization to conduct free or charity schools for New York City, out of which the city school system ultimately grew. These actions show that the people were not yet ready to tax themselves for the support of schools, but were interested in experimenting with means of providing for this expense.

After prolonged agitation and repeated efforts on the part of a few leaders, a law was passed in 1812 which proved the foundation of a permanent system. This again employed the county, town, and district in the administration of schools, but gave more power to the districts. State and town contributions were to be used exclusively for teachers' salaries. The district erected the schoolhouse and the parents contributed to the support of the teachers through rates for tuition. One important feature of this system was the creation of the office of state superintendent, the first of such offices.

The marked centralization of this system was the beginning of that feature which has since characterized the administration of education in New York beyond that of any other state. Reports of this system, by Gideon Hawley, the first superintendent, indicate a considerable degree of efficiency. Within ten years every county reported the system at work; 649 towns and wards reported, and 6255 out of 7051 districts. More than 350,000 children out of 371,000 of school age were reported enrolled. It is quite obvious, however, that the early anticipations were accepted as evidences of realization;

and that attendance was a very different thing from enrollment.

This early system of New York was really the work of a few determined leaders. The legislation was formulated and advocated by Gideon Peck, an itinerant minister from New England. A few political leaders, including the governors, were favorable. The first state superintendent was an able leader as well as administrator. But the system was not the result of the beliefs or the desires of the people. In politics as well as social structure, New York was aristocratic; the suffrage was still limited. In 1821 the suffrage was extended on a democratic basis, but—whether in spite of this change or because of it—from this time on there was in reality a decline of the system for a decade or so. In 1820 the state superintendency was abolished and the administration of the schools remained in the hands of the secretary of state. The propositions advocated by the governor during the twenties, that the county high schools be established and that training for teachers be provided in the various academies which the state subsidized, were rejected. For fifteen or twenty years there was little or no progress, but rather a state of lethargy, until the spirit of revival seen elseswhere in the "thirties" affected New York.

Schools in the Other Middle States.—In Pennsylvania all accomplishment for elementary education during this half-century (1776–1830) was in the form of assisting poor children to attend existing private or church schools. This type of solution will be discussed later under charity schools (p. 296). In 1818 Philadelphia and in 1822 Lancaster were organized as the first and the second districts of Pennsylvania for the purpose of supporting Lancasterian schools for poor children. There was much discussion in the legislature and in the public press, but the people were not yet prepared for any form of free education.

In New Jersey the same policy was followed. A state school fund was established in 1816 and in 1820 the towns were authorized to tax themselves, the proceeds in both cases to be used to pay for the tuition of poor children.

Delaware's experience was very similar. While a school fund was established in 1797, out of marriage fees and tavern licenses, which in 1817 began to give a meager dividend, it was used for the assistance of poor children in private schools. The "free school law" of 1829 authorized a district organization which could depend on a voluntary contribution or subscription and this would entitle the district to share in a distribution from the state fund. This was not a "free school" but a form of the charity school modified with state aid.

Educational Proposals in Virginia and the South.—The aristocratic character of society prevailing throughout the early United States was more influential in the South because of large land holdings, the dominance of the landed aristocracy in politics, and the system of slavery. The popular democratic theories of the leaders, backed by the views of the Scotch population of the uplands, bore fruit in the formulation of many educational proposals which, however, accomplished little. Those of Virginia, advanced chiefly by Jefferson, are the most important.

The actual steps taken by the state related, as did those of the Middle States, to the establishment of a school fund and the use of the revenue from this to assist poor children. The early constitutions of Virginia (1776 and 1830) do not mention education. In 1779 an important measure (Quo. 381), framed by Jefferson, for the "General Diffusion of Knowledge" was offered to the legislature, but was rejected. Seventeen years later "An act to establish public schools," furthered by the same leaders and interests, was actually passed. Under this system the county was the unit of administration and was given power to levy a local tax as well as to erect houses, to select and examine as well as to pay teachers, and in general to supervise the schools. However, enforcement of the law was made optional, and as neither the local leaders nor the people were ready for a free school, it does not appear that anything at all was accomplished by the law.

In 1810 Virginia adopted the common experiment of a school fund, which in 1815 was made an effective instrument through the incorporation with it of a sum due from the national government. This fund produced a considerable income and in 1818 a law for free schools was proposed. However, this law was changed before enactment to refer to the common charity school of the period. The major part of this "Literary Fund" was directed to the support of academies and colleges, the type of schools in which the ruling class actually believed.

Jefferson's interest in education during all this period is responsible for some of the most interesting contributions to educational literature; but their value lies in indicating the dawning conception of education and the views of wise statesmen, not in recording actual accomplishments. His disappointment in the outcome appears in a letter of 1820 to Jos. Cabell, one of his most effective co-laborers, when he wrote: "Six thousand common schools in New York, fifty pupils in each, 300,000 in all; 1,600,000 dollars paid to the masters annually for forty academies. The whole appropriation for education is estimated at $2,500,000. What pigmy is Virginia to this, and with a population equal to that of New York! And whence this difference? From the difference their rulers set on the value of knowledge and the prosperity it produces." It is significant to note that not even Jefferson attributes the status of education to the lack of interest on the part of the people, but of their rulers.

As a matter of fact even the charity school provisions did not work to any adequate or satisfactory end, either in this period or up to the Civil War. Practically, parents were compelled to admit their pauperism before their children could have the benefit of free tuition paid for out of state funds. The system was hated by those whom it was designed to benefit, and despised or ignored or manipulated to personal or partisan ends by those responsible for its administration.

Attitude and accomplishment in the other Southern states was similar to that in Virginia. Maryland established a school fund in 1812, and in 1816 a charity school scheme, for which counties might tax themselves if desired. This was elaborated in 1826 but valid only when adopted by local vote. No effective use of this law for public schools was made before the Civil War, except in and around Baltimore.

In North Carolina, though provision for charity schools was made by the county and repeated proposals for state free schools

EDUCATION NATIONALIZED

were made in the legislature, nothing was actually accomplished for elementary education until 1825 when a state school fund was established. However, it was not until 1839 that a law was passed providing for the establishment of common schools assisted by the fund.

South Carolina provided a system in 1811 which was superior to that of the other Southern states in its implication. It provided for free schools open to all white children, these schools to be assisted from state funds. However, provision was made that in case funds were insufficient for all they were to be applied for the benefit of poor children. As nowhere outside of New England were people at this time educated to the point of taxing themselves for schools, these funds never were sufficient and the schools remained, as in all neighboring states, merely charity schools.

The Georgia law of 1785 placed the control of all moneys for public education in the hands of a university. Under this rule all such funds were devoted to colleges and academies until 1817, when a sum was set aside for free schools. To this were added the proceeds of certain public lands. From 1822 on, the income from this fund went for the support of children in charity schools.

New States to the West.—In most of these states constitutional provisions were made; but the actual achievements previous to 1830 were slight and can be more briefly stated under the organization of the district school system (Ch. XVI) and the scheme of support of the charity schools (p. 296). In these states, because of the land grants of the ordinance providing for the Northwest and the Southwest territory, school funds actually existed from the first. Because of the problems of isolated frontier life—the scattered population, and above all the intense individualism—little beyond provision for the district school system was accomplished.

Summary.—The idea of universal education, affecting in some form every class of society and relating to every region of the country and every stage of the educational process, was established during the Colonial period. But certain aspects of the realization of this ideal remained to be worked out during the National period. These aspects are more significant, however, if viewed as problems

FOUNDING OF AMERICAN SCHOOL SYSTEM

of formulating education as a national force, organizing it under democratic forms of government, and establishing it on the basis of public support. In the attainment of these latter ideals, the early National period falls into two subperiods; one until 1830, during which time society was essentially aristocratic; the other from 1830 to the close of the Civil War, during which time American social and political structure became essentially democratic.

Certain factors must be taken into account in order to understand the problem of the first subperiod. Population was diffused over a large area of virgin territory. Economic conditions represented most serious hardships and the growth of prosperity was very slow. In political sentiment and practice, aristocratic ideals still controlled. The government under the Continental Congress established the policy of extensive land grants for the support of education, but little aid was realized from this source for generations. The new Federal government continued this policy but did nothing further. National leaders were interested in a national university, which has never materialized, and in the general theory of the necessity of general intelligence as support of popular government. But they saw no practical way of realizing this ideal. The summaries of school conditions during this period indicate that colleges and academies were flourishing, but that little advance was made beyond the Colonial achievement in working out a school system. In the New England States the town school system gave way to a district system. In length of school period and quality and breadth of instruction, standards of attainment were below those of the Colonial period. The New England States completed the details of the district school system. Connecticut, in addition, established a common school fund which was adequate to support its district schools for a minimum period each year without resort to taxation. This, while affording relief from public taxation, in reality operated to lower the standards of her schools. Of all the states, New York alone made marked progress during this period, establishing a state system, developing public taxation, establishing a common school fund and a centralized administration under a state superintendent. The other Middle States and the Southern States all experimented

EDUCATION NATIONALIZED

with charity schools for poor children, expecting that such schools could be supported by the revenue from a common school fund. In the new states of the West and South, population was too sparse, wealth too meager, individualism too strong, to permit much progress to be made toward the establishment of effective schools.

Chapter IX

EDUCATION NATIONALIZED. DEVELOPMENT OF SCHOOL SYSTEMS FROM 1830 TO THE CIVIL WAR

Characteristics of the Period.—This period extending substantially from 1830 to 1870 includes the "educational revival." Outside of New England and New York, however, it was a time of origins rather than of revivals. General public interest in education now first developed throughout the country. Most of the states east of the Mississippi established working systems of education; they formulated by constitutional or statutory enactment the principle of the free school and made some progress toward the practical realization of a system of such schools. This was also the period of growing democratic sentiment and of the earliest control of government by extreme democratic elements of the population.

During this time the economic expansion of the country was very great, immigration on a large scale began, means of communication multiplied, wealth increased; both increase and movement of population were marked. The development in education was related to and conditioned upon all of these changes. The democracy developed was possessed of an intensely individual initiative. So education partook of the same characteristics. Some further analysis of these other factors will aid an appreciation of the nature of the educational advance.

Population and Area.—The population of 1830 was nearly thirteen million, four times what it had been in 1790. The original area contained less than one sixth of this population. By 1860 the population had increased to nearly thirty-two million, less than half of which was in the original area. Compared with 1790 the United States had become literally a new country and a new people.

A factor equally important, at least for the future, was the change

SCHOOL SYSTEMS FROM 1830

in composition of the population. Even in 1790 a considerable portion of the population was not of English origin. Little of this, however, was of foreign parentage, for the German element was of at least one generation in America, the Dutch of several. Most of the foreign born were of British origin. Up to 1830 there had not been sufficient immigration to attract public attention or to form an item of interest in legislation. In 1860 there were in the

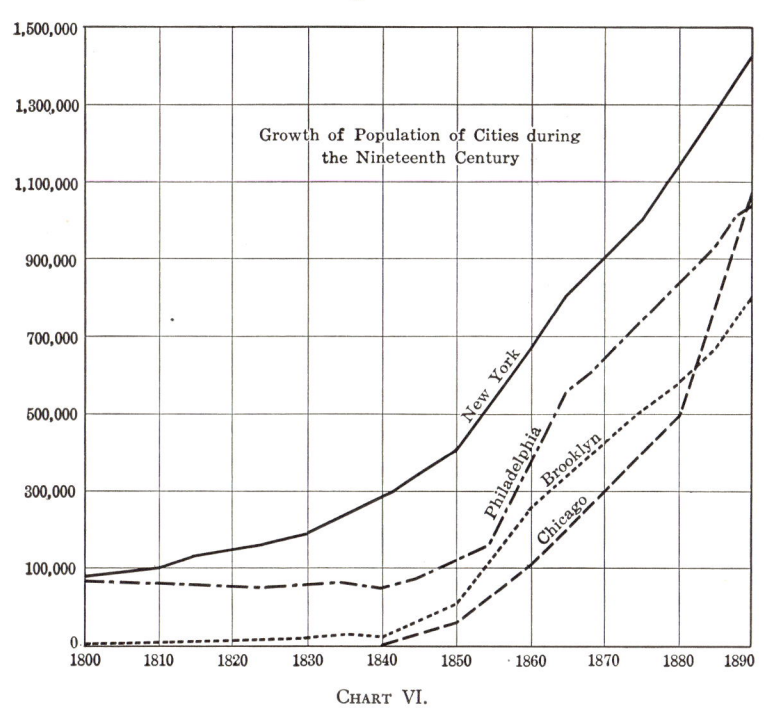

Growth of Population of Cities during the Nineteenth Century

CHART VI.

United States more than four million people of foreign birth. This large growth of immigration was popularly supposed to have resulted in an increase of lawlessness and mob violence, which had, however, not been absent in the earlier days. The newly won freedom which led men to object to all form of governmental restraint caused such excesses that the success of self government was seriously questioned. Much of the responsibility for this condition approaching anarchy was popularly attributed to the untrained and unbridled foreign element, unfamiliar with American conditions and amenable only to force, much as illiteracy, ignorance, and civic instability are attributed to it today. Many of the immigrants were employed on the great public work of the times, the building of railroads and canals. Fear of industrial outbreaks and of the political influence of these workmen led to a strong anti-foreign sentiment which expressed itself in a variety of ways. Wise and broadminded statesmen turned to education rather than to exclusion of immigrants or restriction of the franchise as the effectual means of meeting this new problem of democracy.

During this period more than a million and a half of Irish and a similar number of Germans were added to the population. Great numbers of English and Welsh had also come, but the two former nationalities were sufficiently concentrated in location to cause their different racial temperaments and social customs to become new factors in our political, social, and economic life. The Germans of the migration of the late forties added a progressive influence to education. The immigrant elements as a whole made the educational problem more distinct, and by accentuating the tests to which our political and social structure must be subjected directed the attention of the native population to the significance of education.

One other "foreign" element had increased enormously during this period—the negro slaves. In 1790 these numbered less than 700,000, and made less than 5% of the population. In 1860 they totaled nearly 4,000,000, forming 12½% of the population. In 1790 there were nearly 4,000 slaves in New England, mostly in Connecticut, and 45,000 in the Middle States. In 1860 there were none in New England and only 18 in the Middle States outside of Delaware. Slavery had been concentrated in the Southern states, where it formed an insurmountable barrier to the establishment of an effective free school system.

One other change in population had educational as well as other social consequences. While the total population was increasing from 32 to 36% for each decade, the urban population increased from 5% of the total in the second decade to 19% in the fifth decade. In 1790 there were but 5 cities of over 8,000 population—New York,

Philadelphia, Boston, Baltimore, and Charleston. In 1840 the number of cities having 8,000 population or over was 44; in 1860 it was 141. Four out of every five of these were in the North; for,

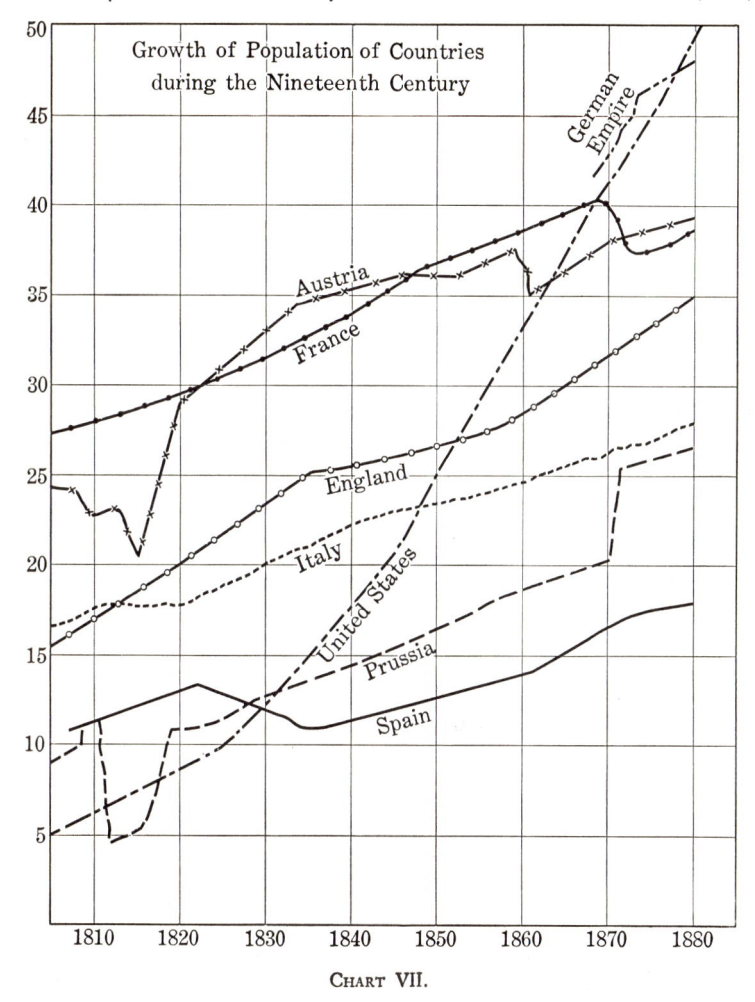

Chart VII.

owing to greater ease of transportation, manufacturing had now come to be a dominant factor in the growth of the cities, whereas before this concentration of population had been chiefly determined by commerce.

FOUNDING OF AMERICAN SCHOOL SYSTEM

Economic Changes.—Economic expansion had been quite slow until 1830. From the Panic of 1837 to that of 1857 the national wealth quadrupled. During this period the per capita wealth doubled. The North became a great manufacturing as well as an agricultural region, while the South remained agricultural. Cotton had come to be a product of greatest international importance. This gave increased value to the system of slavery. The field hand that brought $200 in 1790 and $500 in 1840 was worth $2000 in 1860; and the number of slaves had increased to nearly four million.

Much of the increase in wealth during this period was due to vast enterprises, especially in the way of "internal improvements" hitherto unknown—roads, canals, railroads, etc. This demanded large capital, so banks were multiplied, the currency increased, great public debts were incurred. The loose standards of financial and commercial integrity, fostered by great chances for speculative wealth and government loans, were largely accountable for the indifferent care of the large public endowment for education and for the unwillingness of people to tax themselves further for schools. Numerous inventions mark the period. Patents were granted at a rate of 646 per year from 1840 to 1850, at a rate of 2225 per year from 1850 to 1860. While the inventions underlying the preparation of cotton and the manufacture of cotton and woolen goods had been made during the previous period (1790–1830) their general application came during the period from 1830 to 1860. The sewing machine was invented in 1846 and was soon applied to the shoe industry. The grain reaper was invented in 1833, and while in 1840 but 3 of these machines were manufactured, 20,000 per year were being sold by 1860.

These numerous inventions not only tremendously stimulated manufacture and commerce, multiplied wealth through the saving of labor, and gave liberal rewards to ingenuity and enterprise; they also placed great emphasis on individual initiative and on that attitude towards education which placed much of the responsibility upon the individual and left little to society.

This was the period of America's greatest prosperity in the ocean carrying trade. Though the first steamship to cross the Atlantic had been built in America in 1819, the sea was ruled by the fast sailing vessel in the building of which America predominated. Foreign commerce reached unprecedented heights, the tonnage in 1865 being five times that of 1830. Notwithstanding the two panics of 1837 and 1857 the period as a whole was one of great prosperity, expansion, and enterprise.

Means of Communication.—An economic change of peculiar importance to social conditions and educational improvement was the growth of means of communication. First there were the roads which were needed everywhere. The greatest of the government undertakings in this line was the national road (p. 191) stretching one thousand miles from the Potomac to the Mississippi, begun in 1806 and completed in 1838. While a system of such roads was a feature of the great plan of internal improvements projected at this time, government attention was centered on the more novel and spectacular means of rapid transit just then brought into prominence. The feature of national improvement which attracted the greatest attention during the first half of the century was canal building. From the close of the War of 1812 great public interest and general activity were concentrated on these. From 1817 to 1825 was built the Erie Canal from Albany to Buffalo, probably the most profitable and useful of them all. To protect the trade of Philadelphia a canal was put through to Pittsburgh, thus connecting with the great West by the Ohio and Mississippi rivers. The Ohio was connected with Lake Erie, the Hudson with Lake Champlain and the Delaware; Chesapeake Bay with the Ohio River and with Delaware Bay; Delaware Bay with the waters adjoining New York. A series of canals near the sea coast was constructed giving an inland water way to the South. Many of the rivers of Pennsylvania, of New England and other regions were paralleled with canals, affording means for developing the coal and iron industries of Pennsylvania, the factories of New England, and the agriculture of the West. Many of these canals had been projected by Washington but it was the third and fourth decade of the century which saw their construction.

To obviate the greatest difficulties of surmounting water sheds

FOUNDING OF AMERICAN SCHOOL SYSTEM

the canals had developed short rail lines, upon some of which steam was tried as a motive force. Very shortly, as in the fable the camel became sole occupant of the tent, the canals decreased in popular favor and economic worth. In 1831 the Baltimore and Ohio placed a locomotive in operation and thereafter railroads developed rapidly. While it was not until 1853 that the Baltimore line crossed the Alleghenies, yet before 1850 a series of lines connected Portland, Maine, with Wilmington, North Carolina. Before 1860 a network of railways crossed the states of the old Northwest.

With the railroad came the telegraph. Though Morse's invention was made in 1835, it was nine years later that Congress made appropriation for the first line between Washington and Baltimore. By 1850 all the large cities from Milwaukee and New Orleans to Portland, Maine, were connected. By 1861 the Pacific coast was reached and a cable was laid from the Atlantic seaboard to Europe, though the cable was successful for a brief time only. Thus the means for fostering a common intelligence and developing genuine public opinion were provided. These had marked effect on the growth of a desire for public schools as they had on other phases of the social order.

Political Changes.—The fourth decade of the century ushered in the control of democracy. Some property qualification for suffrage remained in six of the original states as late as 1844. Property qualifications for the governorship were abolished in seven of them between 1837 and 1845, and for membership in the state senate even somewhat later. Imprisonment for debt was yet legal in most states and was not abolished in some until the eve of the Civil War. The judiciary had been the stronghold of the old aristocracy in its protection against democracy, but during this period a change of policy is clearly marked in the new or revised state constitutions, most of which favor an elective judiciary, short terms, and a full bench rather than a small judiciary appointed for a long period.

Perhaps no one process so clearly illustrates the growing confidence in democracy as that of adopting the fundamental law. In the thirty years from 1770 to 1800 there were 43 cases of voting on constitutions by various states. In 35 of these the final action was taken by a representative body; in the remaining 8, though the suffrage was direct, it was much restricted. In the three decades between 1830 and 1860 5 state constitutions were passed upon by representatives in assembly and 32 by popular and now almost unrestricted manhood suffrage. The system of rotation in office, "the spoils system," was introduced as a feature if not as an essential condition of democracy. The principle involved was the same that worked against special training in education—namely that in a democracy one man is as good as another and therefore competent to fill any position.

This generation also fought a great Civil War. This war was more destructive of human life than any fought previously and also caused a greater destruction of the accumulated wealth of existing civilization. The same generation also witnessed the destruction of a social system of great economic and social significance, namely, human slavery. The effect of the two-fold destruction was of enormous indirect significance to education but of little direct influence. The indirect influence is to be seen in the development of democratic institutions produced by the great sacrifice for human liberty, and the general influence of an economic and social character produced by the sectional struggle. Besides the very general influence, which can be overlooked in this account, there was little direct result of the conflict on education. It is significant that the history of education of the period can be written with little or practically no reference to the great struggle which undoubtedly was the outstanding feature, and which was the event of the greatest human interest to the entire generation. Though the effect on the life of every individual and on every institution was profound, such effects were immediately realized through political, economic, and social influence and not directly through education. No doubt many laws establishing free public school systems which were passed in the United States immediately following the close of the Civil War, owed much to the clarification of sentiment and of ideas due to that conflict, but this cannot be proven by citation of evidence.

Consequently this volume has little to say of the influence of that great conflict on education. The fact that certain changes occurred during the period could be cited, but that does not indicate the existence of causal relationship.

This account is limited to the presentation of demonstrable facts.

Factors in the Establishment of State Systems, 1830–1860.—The economic, political, and domestic conditions which have been discussed influenced education indirectly and in a general way as they influenced all other social activities. There were, however, a number of social forces which had direct and specific effect on education in general and on the development of a system of free schools and popular education. These are now to be considered.

Influence of the Working Class and of Organized Labor (Quo. 413-420).—A factor of importance in the development of the free school system was the influence exerted by the working class. Just growing into self-consciousness during this period, the laboring classes began to organize and to formulate their views on political and social subjects as well as on labor. One of the causes leading to this development was the establishment of the factory system previously mentioned (p. 226). Another was the general decline of the apprenticeship system and the consequent need of some form of organization through which labor might be related to society. Consequent upon the industrial changes had come the segregation of the manufacturing population in cities. Thus groups of workmen in particular industries were brought together and made conscious of their common conditions, needs, and ideals. From early in the nineteenth century organizations had been formed in a few industries, particularly those of shipwrights and carpenters. In 1817 the printer's trade was similarly organized and because of the intelligence and position of its members this union came to have considerable political influence. Such organization took place in New York, Boston, and Philadelphia. By 1825, or at least by 1830, a very considerable number of such unions existed. It was not until 1852, however, that the first national organization, that of typographers, was effected.

Meanwhile, however, the laboring groups began to find a voice. In 1825 issue began in New York of *The Working Man's Advocate,* which was probably the first representative of the labor press.

SCHOOL SYSTEMS FROM 1830

This continued for five years and was succeeded by the *Daily Sentinel* and *The Young American*. Such labor papers were issued from time to time in Philadelphia, Boston, Baltimore, and Cincinnati. In 1830 the first workingman's convention was held and made a nominaton for the governorship of New York. For a number of years the labor element either organized an independent political party or exerted considerable influence on the other parties. Especially was this element a considerable factor in the Jacksonian democracy.

Through their publications workmen impressed their views and exerted their greatest influence. In the programs issued during this period were demands for the freedom of public land, the abolition of monopolies, the abolition of imprisonment for debt, even of all laws for the collection of debts, a general bankruptcy law, a labor lien law, removal of property qualifications for voting, equal rights for women with men in all respects, the abolition of slavery, operation of the United States mails on Sunday, and a general demand for public education. Among the friends of this labor movement were many of the men prominent in the educational agitation of the day, such as James G. Carter, Horace Mann, William Ellery Channing. Both educational reform and the improvement of the conditions of labor were recognized as a part of a general social program. One other practical aspect of the labor demand was the reduction of factory hours to twelve hours a day. Later on, in the forties and fifties, the agitation was for ten hours a day. In 1840 this reform movement received a great impetus from the approval by President Van Buren of a general order introducing the ten-hour system into government employment.

A brief examination of the expressions of labor will throw light not only upon their own attitude but upon the developing conception of education itself. The most effective and succinct of these statements is found in the series of six *Essays on Public Education* (Quo. 413), published first in 1830 and republished in a great number of periodicals during the following years. The first essay raises the question: "What sort of education is befitting a republic?" and answers: "One that is open and equal to all." The particular objection to the prevailing interest in collegiate or higher education was on the grounds that to shut the book of knowledge to one and open it to another, was thoroughly undemocratic, and that if this could not be remedied it was farcical to talk about republican education. Such an education as would give the poor the benefit of that which had previously been restricted to the rich was considered entirely just and was demanded by the political organizations and aspirations of the times. The next essay raised the question of the source of the funds for such a school system. The answer was "from the government, because education is in reality a form of legislation and if wisely cared for might to a great extent supersede the necessity and save the expense of criminal laws, jails and almshouses." In a somewhat surprising way, however, the pamphlet argues for the continuation of the tuition charges or "the children's tax" as the source of at least half the funds, but asserts that the government should contribute the other half. The greater part of the pamphlet is devoted to a justification of this demand for support from the government on the grounds that the tax of ignorance was very much heavier than any money levy which might be approved for education. When one considers the radical character of some of the laboring men's propositions, or even of some of their beliefs concerning education, it is surprising to find that they did not even then take the stand that education should be supported wholly by the state.

The third essay raises the question: "What sort of education should the common people have?" The answer was: "Whatever is good enough for human beings." It rejected the idea that reading, writing, and accounts "and by way of a finish, a little grammar and geography" were sufficient. Such education was available at that time for a small fee. On the other hand the dominant aristocratic education of the times was rejected "not because Hebrew and velvet painting are only good for the rich and the privileged; but only because we think them useless for anyone." Few specific directions are given, aside from the argument that agriculture and the trades should be taught. It was urged that in common practice we still followed Europe in thinking that the idle and privileged class should be educated in the subjects which produced such a class. What we had yet to learn, it was argued, was that the same man may labor and may think, may be both a producer and a consumer, a mechanic and a legislator, a practical farmer and the president of the United States. The problem was how to amalgamate these classes, how to make men "not fractions of human beings, sometimes mere producing machines, sometimes mere consuming drones, but an integral republic, at once the creators and employers of industry, at once master and servant, governor and governed." This was to be done by combining agriculture with literature and scientific instruction. Such a condition would be reached if all children were taught agriculture or gardening and some useful trade or occupation. The Fellenberg system (p. 439) was cited as a realization of this ideal.

One important recommendation of essay four indicates how Utopian the entire scheme may have seemed to many practical or conservative men of the times. The question is discussed whether the public education of all children should be conducted in day schools or in boarding schools, and the verdict is unequivocally for boarding schools. The theory of education upon which this demand was based was sound enough, but the practical application of it seems to us even now quite far fetched. The author states:

"For our own parts, we understand education to mean everything which influences, directly or indirectly, the child's character. To see his companions smoke cigars is a part of his education; to hear oaths is a part of his education; to see and laugh at drunken men in the street is a part of his education; to witness vulgar merriment or coarse brawls is a part of his education. And if anyone thinks that an education like this (which is daily obtained in the streets of our city) will be counteracted and neutralized by half a dozen hours daily schooling, we are not of his opinion. We had almost as soon have a child of ours brought up among the Indians as have him frequent a common day school one half the day, and wander about our streets the other half."

In these modern days when all of these influences are also considered a part of education the child comes in contact with all of them through the cinema, the radio, or the music hall, which are now considered a part of this education.

In the platforms drawn up by the various mass meetings or conventions of the laboring men of the times the subject of public education frequently received attention. Perhaps in no other form so brief can be shown the advanced views and the great influence on education of this element of the population than by the quotation of some of their resolutions. The following among others were passed at a meeting held in Philadelphia in 1830 and were published in *The Working Man's Advocate* (Quo. 414):

> Resolved, that knowledge is favorable to the moral and political conditions of man, and to the well being of society.
>
> Resolved, that the time has arrived when it becomes the paramount duty of every friend to the happiness and freedom of man to exert himself in every honest way to promote a *system of education that shall equally embrace all the children of the state, of every rank and condition.*
>
> Resolved, that we hereby pledge ourselves to each other, and to all the other citizens of the state, that we will never cease to make common cause for the promotion of a system of public education until all the sources of general instruction are open to every child within this commonwealth.
>
> Resolved, that the legislature be memorialized to enact a law for the establishment of public schools throughout this state, by which the object of the foregoing resolutions shall be effectually secured.
>
> Resolved, that a committee of correspondence be appointed whose duty it shall be to promote and uphold the cause of general education, by correspondence with such persons and bodies of men as are friendly to the cause of universal instruction.

Before the middle of the century the interest in education seems to have disappeared among the workingmen's groups, or at least to have greatly decreased. A number of factors contributed to this. Among these were the growing importance of the slavery problem and the greater significance of the immediate needs of the working man, such as reasonable hours of labor and just rate of wage. The deciding factor, however, was the establishment during this period of popular systems of education in all of those states where the labor element was strong.

Influence of European Educational Ideals (Quos. 427-429).—During the early National period provincial prejudice was strong. The fact that European society had reached certain conclusions concerning education or had attained certain results afforded no reason why America should modify her own individualistic attitude of indifference toward collective educational efforts. Nevertheless a series of influences of European origin began quite early in the century to act on the ideas and purposes of educational leaders. During the thirties and forties these influences, resulting from actual practices, became very pronounced. However, even near the middle of the century some of Horace Mann's reforms were defeated in the most intellectual community in the country, largely on the grounds that they were European ideas.

While many of these influences are best traced in the efforts to establish particular educational institutions, such as monitorial schools, infant schools, manual labor institutions, yet it is instructive to trace their operation through a series of publications or reports which give us the most tangible evidence of the nature of these influences and how they became operative upon American conditions.

The earliest of these specific influences was that exerted by William McClure, a Scotchman from Pennsylvania, who was sent as a member of the Commission to France. In 1806 upon his return to this country, Mr. McClure published the earliest account of the Pestalozzian experiment, which he had observed in Europe. McClure was a philanthropist as well as a student, and went to Europe again in 1819 for the purpose of studying the social experiments then being made by Robert Owen, Pestalozzi, and Fellenberg. In 1824 he returned to the United States and devoted himself to the work of social reform in which the methods of Pestalozzi and of Robert Owen were fundamental (see p. 251).

The most popular of these earlier accounts of European educational endeavor was that written by John Griscom, a Quaker philanthropist of New York City, who after retiring from a very successful and remunerative teaching career made a trip to Europe. The results of this investigation were published in 1819, under the title *A Year in Europe*. The two volumes of this report contain an extensive description of the various types of monitorial, infant, and industrial schools, as well as the numerous social, agricultural, and industrial reforms, which were then in progress through Europe. This book was very widely circulated and probably did more to popularize the idea of educational reform than any other one force.

About the time of Griscom's visit a young New England teacher, William Channing Woodbridge, spent some years in Europe devoting himself to the study of geography. Upon his return in 1824 he collaborated in the preparation of some texts in geography embodying the Pestalozzian principles of teaching. Returning to Europe he spent some years as a teacher in the Fellenberg institution in Switzerland and as a student of the methods of Pestalozzi as well as those of other educational reformers of the time. Upon his return to the United States he undertook the publication of an educational magazine, the *Annals of Education* (1830–37), in which appeared many descriptive articles on these European endeavors. The seven annual volumes of this magazine contain the fullest account we have of the Fellenberg system and of Pestalozzi. This magazine was one of the great factors in the reform movement of the thirties in New England.

Associated with Mr. Woodbridge in his work on geography was Mrs. Emma Hart Willard, the leader of the movement for the higher education of women in this early period. Among Mrs. Willard's many activities was a journey to Europe in 1830–31 for the study of educational institutions for girls. The fruit of this study appeared in 1833 in a volume of *Journals and Letters from Europe*. This work was extensively circulated and netted a very considerable sum which was devoted by Mrs. Willard to a fund for establishing a college in Greece for the women of the Near East.

More important than any of these investigations by Americans were the reports of the French philosopher, Victor Cousin (1792–1867), who was a member of the Council for Public Instruction under Guizot when the public school system of France was founded, and who later was himself minister of public instruction and head of the University. He was virtually the leader in educational affairs in France from 1830 to 1848 and one of the most popular and influential statesmen of the time. In 1831 he published his famous report on *The Study of Public Instruction in Germany, particularly in Prussia,* which, with his other reports, the *Edinburgh Review* stated "mark an epoch in the progress of national education and are conducive to results not only important to France but to Europe." The reviewer need not have limited his statement to Europe because Cousin's report on Prussia was reprinted as a legislative document by Massachusetts, New Jersey, New York, and other states. This report had more influence than any other one thing in the shaping of the state system of Michigan, just then being formulated, and in some others of the newer states. The work was published in England in 1834 and ran through a number of later editions in America. In 1837 M. Cousin made a similar report on the school system of Holland, which also had a wide circulation in this country.

Professor Calvin Stowe, husband of Harriet Beecher Stowe, was authorized in 1836 by the legislature of Ohio to investigate the educational system of the German states and to make a report with recommendations for Ohio. This report (Quo. 428) was published in 1837 and was reprinted and distributed as a legislative document by Michigan, Massachusetts, and a number of other states. It is very brief and the recommendations are forceful. The substance of these is as follows: (1) Teachers must be skilful and must be trained for their work; (2) there must be institutions for the training of teachers; (3) the financial support of teachers must be adequate; (4) children must be made comfortable in their schools, and their punctual attendance throughout the course must be compulsory; (5) children must be given up implicitly to the discipline of the school; (6) modest beginnings should be attempted and a general and continual advance made until the entire system is reorganized along these principles. These first five recommendations contain the essence of the Prussian system. Argument was backed with great skill of presentation, breadth of argument, clearness of illustration, and brevity of statement. The chief effect of this report no doubt was the introduction of the Pestalozzian methods of teaching and the training of teachers, though it had some influence also on the organization of state systems.

In 1836 Alexander Bache, the first President of Girard College for Orphans, then recently founded in Philadelphia, was sent to Europe by the trustees to spend some years in investigating education. His report issued in 1839 included not only the forms of education peculiarly appropriate for orphans but was devoted largely to a discussion of the methods and organization of the public school system of the European countries. This voluminous work was on the whole exceedingly valuable. The discussion was confined to the presentation of essential facts, but these facts were very illuminating to those interested in the current problems of American education.

Of the same general character as the Stowe report but far more detailed was Horace Mann's *Seventh Annual Report* (Quo. 429), published in 1844. The previous year had been devoted to a study of educational conditions in Europe and this volume proved to be one of the most influential documents Mann ever wrote. His recommendations in substance were: (1) that religious teaching should be substituted for the dominant theological type; or if people preferred to call the existing instruction religious it should be replaced by moral instruction and training; (2) that corporal punishment should be abolished; (3) that ample provision should be made for the training of teachers; (4) that oral methods should be used in preference to relying entirely on textbooks. He advocated teaching reading by the word method instead of beginning with the alphabet and commended the object lesson in geography and nature study, and the substitution of analytical arithmetic, the so-called "mental" arithmetic, for the blind following of rules. A fifth recommendation concerned the appeal to emulation or competition which then prevailed in the American school. For this motive Mann would substitute some of the more modern conceptions of interest which developed from the psychological theories of German teachers. His sixth point called for an enrichment of the curriculum especially

SCHOOL SYSTEMS FROM 1830

through the introduction of music, drawing, and the study of natural objects. Out of this report grew some of the reforms which are still connected with the name of Horace Mann, and also that final controversy with the Boston schoolmasters which, while it may have assisted in bringing to an end his service to the schools in Massachusetts, yet greatly aided in the dissemination of his views throughout the country.

The last of these great means of spreading European ideas were the various reports and publications of Henry Barnard. Dr. Barnard had made an extensive study of European conditions in 1835-36. As the Secretary of the Board of School Commissioners of Connecticut he published an account of these observations in the *First Annual Report* in 1839. In 1850 Dr. Barnard was authorized by the legislature of Connecticut to prepare two works for general circulation among the teachers of the state. The first of these volumes was on school architecture; the second on the institutions, agencies, and methods for the professional education of teachers. The earlier book was practically the first general treatise on the subject and long remained a standard. The second brought together the essence of all that had been previously published in America on the training of teachers, surveyed conditions here and brought to bear on the problem the most complete summary of European experience that we have had even to this date.

Subsequent visits to Europe gave Dr. Barnard a vast mass of information which appeared in 1854 under the title *National Education in Europe*. This was the fullest account of national education which had yet been published and is still the largest single work in English on this subject. It covers all European countries and gives a wealth of detail concerning methods, types of teaching, subjects of study, nature of school buildings, and in fact practically every topic concerning education which could be of either professional or general interest. Following this Dr. Barnard launched in 1856 his great plan of publishing the *American Journal of Education,* in which appeared a continued survey of these foreign conditions.

It is very difficult indeed to appreciate the extent of the influence of such publications as these, since it is usually as hard to determine the source of an idea as to estimate truly its value as a cause of action. But undoubtedly these investigations and publications, along with those next to be mentioned, constituted one of the fundamental forces in establishing the belief in public education and directing its practice during this period.

Educational Magazines and Literature.—During this period the press became a great factor in American life. Daily, weekly, and other periodicals increased, pamphlets and books abounded. Education claimed its share of such publications. These were continuous from 1825. Previous to that time there had been one or two brief attempts, chief among which was the *Academician,* published in New York in 1818–19. From 1826 to 1830 the *American Journal of Education* appeared, and was continued for seven years thereafter as the *Annals of Education.* For the breadth of their interest, the quality of their contents, the scope of their influence, these two magazines have not been excelled by any subsequent publications on education. They furnished a very thorough record of facts, they diffused liberal views of education, they presented reforms and emphasized new aspects of education. Physical education, moral education, woman's education, domestic education, public or free education—all received marked attention. These publications disseminated a knowledge of manual labor education, of the Pestalozzian principles or method, of the Lancasterian and infant school organization; they advocated the education of the blind and the deaf and practically all the educational reforms of the times. They were followed by a number of periodicals of a somewhat different type and more familiar to us of the present day. These were the various state magazines, the chief interest of which was in the details of methods of teaching. These made their appeal primarily to the schoolroom teacher, not to the public educator and administrator as did the earlier magazines mentioned.

The first of these teachers' magazines was the *Common School Journal of Massachusetts,* which ran from 1838 to 1848. This was initiated by Horace Mann, Secretary of the Massachusetts Board of Education, and used by him as the chief means of reaching teachers and making his ideas of reform effective. Henry Barnard issued a similar magazine in Connecticut from 1840 and in the same year the *Common School Journal of New York* came into existence. These were all fostered by the state and issued with the assistance of the State Department and Commissioner of Education. A little later appeared the privately owned magazines appealing to the teacher, such as the *Massachusetts Teacher* (1845) and the *New York Teacher* (1850). Similar periodicals followed in quick succession in Pennsylvania, Ohio, Michigan, Illinois, Rhode Island, Indiana; in fact during the period of the fifties practically every state then organized had its school magazine. Several of these earlier publications were circulated by order of the state legislature. Some had merely a nominal price; the aim of all was to be of very practical service to the teacher and to bring to each schoolroom in a usable form the ideas which were uppermost in the minds of the leaders of the times.

Similar to these serial publications were the annual reports of a number of associations, notably those of the *American Institute of Instruction,* which have been issued in annual volumes from 1829 to the present time. The influence of these was limited very largely to New England. In the Middle West the *Western Literary Magazine,* issued in Cincinnati from 1835 to 1839, was of peculiar worth and prominence.

The earlier magazines appealed generally to those interested in education, the leaders of public life—clergymen, public men, legislators, educators—and resulted in a recognition of the need of public education and the establishment of a general belief in its efficiency. The later group of the forties and fifties appealed to the rank and file of the teachers and effected the creation of a professional sentiment and standards.

Period of Educational Reform (Quos. 383-400).—The fourth and fifth decades of the nineteenth century have commonly been recognized as a period of great progress in American education. Frequently they are referred to as the period of educational reform or of revival. Not infrequently, through undue emphasis on the importance of the work of one great leader, they have been termed "the

Horace Mann revival period." Unquestionably this period marked the rise of general public interest in education. It was characterized by definite persistent attempts on the part of the New England and the Middle States to improve their educational system, and on the part of the states to the west and south to establish public school systems. In many of them this period included agitation for schools absolutely free and supported by public charge. In a few of them it witnessed the success of this movement. This period was particularly conspicuous for its great variety of social experiments. The rise of democracy to power was followed by many political experiments which modified the form of our political institutions. Economic unrest showed itself in different types of communistic experiment, in the organization of labor and in much labor legislation. Many of the contemporary comments on the educational features of the times sound strikingly familiar now. An address before the American Institute of Instruction in 1834 is in the following vein:

> "But the precipitous movement of the present age seems to have multiplied them (the difficulties of education) to an extraordinary degree insomuch that we rest not upon one point long enough to make a fair experiment before we fly to another. Indeed innovation seems to be the prevailing support of education. It is not restricted to this country or to the subject of education. A large portion of the political, civil and religious world is partaking of it. . . . There is danger lest in our zeal to cast away what is bad we cast away the good with it. On no subject does this danger press more heavily than on that of education. . . . By innovating upon doctrines and professions tested by long and wide experience and by pushing out supposed principles to the extremes of ultraism instead of conducting the mind steadily toward the goal, they will only send it round in a circle of revolutions. . . . The present is not an age of deep, strong, thorough thinking. Of profound study there is great impatience. Calm and solemn inquiry is rare. The mind of this generation is restive, fevered, impassioned, and consequently prone to reckless radicalism."

A study of the evils of the existing school system was made by the Secretary of the Connecticut School Board in 1846 and remedial

SCHOOL SYSTEMS FROM 1830

measures were proposed (Quo. 397). In substance the analysis is as follows: The first defect noted was the apathy of parents and of the general public as shown by their failure to visit schools and to attend school meetings. As remedies he proposed: (1) a regular system of reports on the condition of schools, to be printed and widely circulated among parents and school officials, (2) lectures and discussions on methods of instruction and discipline, qualifications of teachers, schoolhouses, books, apparatus, (3) the circulation of educational tracts, (4) the publication of the *Common School Journal*.

The second defect indicated was the employment of cheap and unqualified teachers. The remedies proposed were: (1) the establishment of normal schools, (2) the holding of teachers' institutes and conventions, (3) the organization of schools and teachers in towns and counties for practical discussion, (4) a system of examination of teachers by county boards of examiners, (5) a system of visitation by supervisors, (6) higher wages.

For the third defect, the constant change of teachers due chiefly to the double system of summer and winter sessions, he advocated: (1) higher compensation and permanent employment of teachers, (2) a classification and grading of schools.

To meet the fourth evil, insufficient and unfit schoolrooms and playgrounds, the remedies proposed were: (1) the examination of every school and the publication of its actual conditions, (2) the erection of a few model schoolhouses in each county.

The means suggested for overcoming the lack of uniformity of textbooks were: (1) appointment of a state commissioner to examine and select textbooks, (2) prescription of books by such a committee, (3) a system of school visitors who should establish uniform requirements for the schools of the local administrative unit.

The sixth defect was the irregular attendance of pupils. This might be obviated by: (1) distributing state moneys on the basis of actual attendance, (2) securing the co-operation of parents.

The seventh fault found was the unwillingness of communities to contribute to the support of schools by local taxation. The remedies proposed were: (1) a discussion of the subject by public lecture and report, (2) the conditioning of participation in state funds on local contribution.

The eighth failing was the short term of school in small districts, to be overcome by: (1) a partial distribution of the general fund on the basis of local need, (2) the abolition of small districts, (3) the more extensive employment of women teachers.

To remedy the lack of supervision the report proposed: (1) the appointment of a state commissioner, (2) the establishment of a state board of education with a permanent secretary, (3) the appointment of a school visitor or supervisor for each county, (4) local supervisory officers in place of a school board for each town.

The tenth defect was the existence of numerous private schools. These might be diminished in number (1) by making the common better than the private schools, (2) by establishing graded schools.

Finally the lack of suitable apparatus might be supplied by (1) a small state appropriation to each district, conditioned upon local contribution of the same amount, (2) public lectures on the value of illustrative material or apparatus in education.

It is obvious from an examination of this and similar analyses that the educational leaders of the time were quite well informed both as to actual conditions and as to the necessary remedial measures. It will be recognized that this prescription of means for improving the public schools included to a remarkable degree the actual means employed in the subsequent development of the public school system. The great difference between that period and more recent ones was not so much in educational ideas as in the realization of those ideals through adequate concrete measures.

The Educational Reforms of the '30's and '40's.—Preceding the reforms of Horace Mann, Henry Barnard, and their colaborers, the great work of educational improvement had been begun. The work of these leaders was not to lay the foundations; this had already been done. Lancasterianism, with its mechanical settlement of all educational problems, had almost run its course. The infant schools had reduced the little children to the common school denominator, and had broken them to the lock-step. The followers of Fellenberg had sought to unite labor and learning, hand and head, in education. The ideas of the manual labor institutions were still popular, especially when institutions were new and capital was scarce. Even Pestalozzian ideas were not unknown, though scarcely practicable. The district school system was fairly well established throughout the country, at least in the East, North, and Northwest. Educational magazines had familiarized the professional classes with educational conditions, needs, and ideals. The general public had been aroused to an interest in and a casual belief in education.

Consequently the great movement of the late thirties and the forties, led by Mann (Quos. 393, 395, 396, 400) and Barnard, was literally a reform movement. It was reconstruction rather than construction. What the earlier period had witnessed was partly a great social movement towards public education, partly a great philanthropic accomplishment in a widespread system of academies and colleges, and of public education on a quasi-public basis. The movement which Mann and Barnard headed was primarily a technical reform. It related chiefly to organization of the principles or details of the school system, to methods of teaching, to subjects of study, to the selection of a teaching staff,—in brief, to the building up of a profession. Though it was a technical or professional reform it had to be carried with the masses of the people rather than with the teachers and officials of schools. For the latter hardly yet existed as a definite class and the people now had fairly definite ideas on the more or less technical questions in education as well as the power to realize their will. To educate the public to an appreciation of adequate educational standards and a demand for more efficient technique was the task of these leaders.

Seldom has there been a better demonstration of the truth that one sows and another reaps than in the work of Mann. A number of devoted men had worked with great zeal for the betterment of education in New England. Chief among them was James G. Carter. In 1824 he published an essay outlining a plan for the training of teachers and advocating the reforms which led to the laws of 1824 and 1826. These laws attempted to improve the district school system by means of a more adequate system of control and supervision through the school committees, but they also fixed the system by making it mandatory and its support obligatory. This latter provision was an achievement, though the general effects of the laws might have been detrimental. For the first time the public school became by law a completely free school.

For ten years Mr. Carter continued unremittingly to advocate several great measures for the improvement of schools. The first was the establishment of a free school fund, which was done in 1834. This has never been of the importance in Massachusetts, however, that similar funds have been in many other states. The second of these measures, which proved to be revolutionary, was the establishment of a State Board of Education to have oversight of the schools of the state. This was accomplished in 1837. The third was the establishment of professional schools for the training of teachers, achieved in 1839.

Meanwhile the cause of education had received a great recruit, for Horace Mann had been selected as the first secretary of the new Board. This choice was a great surprise and disappointment to the many friends of Carter. Mann was a lawyer and a member of the legislature, with no previous experience in public school work. But he brought to the task a keen intellect, a familiarity with men and with legal and political methods, and also the high purpose and the moral fervor of a reformer. He soon became the protagonist of education reform throughout the country. When reproached for relinquishing his brilliant prospects as a lawyer and public man, Mann replied, "The interests of a client are small compared with the interests of the next generation; let the next generation, then, be my client."

For twelve years (1837–1848) Mann labored to bring the schools of Massachusetts up to the standard of excellence requisite in an institution selected as the chief instrument, as well as the chief bulwark, of democracy, to infuse a spirit of enthusiasm concerning education into the public mind, to give technical efficiency to a body of untrained teachers, and in a large way to arouse an interest in education throughout the nation. This work of educating public opinion was no small part of the work of Mann. The district school, with all of its limitations, had become firmly entrenched in the sympathies of the people, and they were extremely hostile to any attempt to interfere with their "rights," supposedly bound up with democracy, even if such interference were in the interest of a greater intelligence and definite progress. As Mann himself wrote:

> "The education of the whole people, in a republican government, can never be attained without the consent of the whole people. Compulsion, even if it were desirable, is not an available instrument. Enlightenment, not coercion, is our resource. The nature of education must be explained. The whole mass of men must be instructed in regard to its comprehension and enduring interests. We can not drive our people up a dark avenue, even though it be the right one; but we must hang the starry lights of knowledge about it, and show them not only the directness of its course to the goal of prosperity and honor, but the beauty of the way that leads to it."

Speaking of his own work and the hard problems which confronted him, he said:

> "In some districts there will be but a single man or woman, in some towns scarcely half a dozen men or women, who have espoused this noble enterprise. But whether there be half a dozen or but one, they must be like the little leaven which a woman took and hid in three measures of meal. Let the intelligent visit the ignorant day by day, as the oculist visits the blind man and detaches the scales from his eyes, until the living sense leaps to the living light. Let the zealous seek contact and communion with those who are frozen up in indifference, and thaw off the icebergs wherein they lie imbedded. Let the love of beautiful childhood, the love of country, the dictates of reason, the admonitions of conscience, the sense of religious responsibility be plied, in mingled tenderness and earnestness, until the obdurate and dark mass of avarice, ignorance and prejudice shall be dissipated by their blended light and heat."

Results of the Reform Efforts of Mann.—These were foreshadowed in Mann's survey of the task when confronted by his own lack of experience as a schoolman. He wrote to his sister:

> "If I can be the means of ascertaining what is the best construction of houses, what are the best books, what is the best arrangement of studies, what are the best modes of instruction; if I can discover

by what appliance of means a non-thinking, non-reflecting, non-speaking child can most surely be trained into a noble citizen ready to contend for the right and to die for the right—if I can only obtain and diffuse throughout this state a few good ideas on these and similar objects, may I not flatter myself that my ministry has not been wholly in vain?"

The enormity, not to say hopelessness, of the task before him is indicated by the analysis which Mann himself gave:

"(1) In two-thirds of all the towns in the State teachers were allowed to commence school without being previously examined and approved by the committee as required by law. (2) In many cases teachers obtained their wages from the treasurer without lodging any duplicate certificate with him, as the law required. (3) The law required committees to prescribe text-books. In one hundred towns —a third part in the Commonwealth—this duty was neglected, and all the evils incident to a confusion of books suffered. (4) The law required committees to furnish books to scholars whose parents were unable or had neglected to provide them. In forty towns this was omitted, and poor children went to school without books. (5) The law required committees to visit the schools a certain number of times. From their own statements it appeared that out of three hundred towns about two hundred and fifty did not comply with the law. (6) On an average one-third of all the children of the State between the ages of four and sixteen were absent from school in the winter, and two-fifths of them in the summer."

What the reform movement led by Mann accomplished (Quo. 400), even in the state of Massachusetts, is difficult to measure. What it accomplished outside of that state cannot be given tangible estimate. Certain significant quantitative results can be cited. First among these was the actual physical extension of schooling. Schools had been democratized in control before Mann's day, but the people were indifferent to them. More than 40,000 children of the state were receiving no schooling, while the others averaged an opportunity for only four months schooling a year. Though compulsory as well as free schooling of all children was not obtained during his administration yet by 1848 a full month was added to the school terms and not long after it (1856) the first effective Massachusetts law for compulsory attendance was passed.

The great hindrance to the development of the public school system was the private school, supported by the aristocratic sentiments of the better-to-do in culture and social standing. One sixth of the children of the state were in private schools, for the support of which there was paid nearly four times as much as was expended for the children in the public schools. As a result of Mann's twelve years of service conditions were reversed and only one third as much was spent on private schools as on public. The appropriation for public schools had more than doubled.

Material conditions had been greatly improved. The condition of schoolhouses, especially as to sanitation, was almost unbelievably bad. Reform of these conditions was one of Mann's first efforts. A special report on schoolhouses was issued, great numbers of buildings were closed, many new ones were erected. More than $2,000,000—a large sum for those days—was spent on new buildings. The material rewards of the teacher were greatly increased. The average wage of men teachers ($25.44) was increased 62%; that of women ($11.38) increased 54% during this twelve-year period.

At the beginning of the period less than 200 teachers in the public schools of the state really made teaching a definite or permanent calling. Through the creation of normal schools, three of which were founded as a result of Mann's efforts, a definite teaching body with the technique and spirit of a profession had been built up. There had been no supervision under the district system, though the machinery for it existed. In one town of 40 districts the town committee had not examined a teacher or visited a school in eight years. The committee to whom the selection of teachers and the care of the school were given received no pay, had no definite legal obligation except to render an annual report, and consequently gave little attention to the schools. Now remuneration of the committee was made compulsory and the supervision of the schools obligatory. The work of building up the normal schools and a professionally trained body of teachers is recorded in another place (Chapter XV). But even more important than this was the training of the rank and file of teachers in new and better ideas of organization of the school, management of the pupils, and method of teaching. Through numberless personal addresses, through annual reports and the bi-monthly *Common School Journal,* through teachers' institutes and public conventions, and through twelve years of continuous visitation of the schools of the state, this was achieved.

The change was so great that it may be termed the creation of a profession. The remaining phase of Mann's work, more intangible, yet even more important, was the creation of a public sentiment not only favorably inclined toward but willing to support a public system of common schools. The philanthropic or sectarian quasi-public system of education, built up in the previous decades, had great hold and was strongly entrenched. It was fostered and fortified by the aristocratic, cultural, and social feeling of the times, which was not dissociated from the conservative religious interests. It must be remembered that at that time there was still a general belief that social classes were essential; that while it was necessary to perpetuate a cultivated and refined class it was unavoidable that the masses of the common people should live under hard conditions, without refinement of manners or any great need of education. It was the great work of this period to replace this narrow view with the idea of a broader and more sympathetic democracy. So far as this change related to education it was Mann's great work to accomplish it.

Such results were not obtained without great opposition, an opposition which came from various sources, political, religious, and professional. Of this it is said, "The most serious came from the legislature; the most contemptible from the religious press; the most humiliating to the friends of education, from the schoolmasters." The first found its basis in the resentment on the part of local districts toward all supervisory or executive power exercised by central state authority or even by town authority. Democracy, especially rural democracy, was willing to stay in its ignorance and its restricted environment, provided it was let alone. Part of the opposition was due to partisan politics, the emotions of which were then running very high after the early triumphs of Jacksonian democracy. This political reaction, however, was soon overcome, as is indicated by the various educational reforms put through by the legislature during and after Mann's incumbency, and by the election of Mann after his retirement from the secretaryship to succeed Daniel Webster in the national Congress there to further a yet greater political reform, the destruction of human slavery.

The sectarian opposition continued throughout his term of service and was determined and acrimonious until the last. It was the natural feeling of a conservative orthodoxy in the losing fight against an intelligent liberalism, which in its extreme form was violently heterodox. Its fundamental opposition was to the theory of human nature which rejected belief in the total depravity of human nature and favored the more tolerant educational view then coming in under the guise of Pestalozzianism. A few sentences from a review of a book by Pestalozzi will illustrate:

> "If there be a people between the Alps, in the bosom of whose offspring there is an innate principle of faith and love, that needs only to be cultivated and cherished by the sacred power of innocence, to produce pure morality and exalted devotion, this book belongs to them. It need not have been put into English, or any language into which the word of God has been translated; for it belies it utterly. We have no such children to educate, and therefore the book is useless to us."

Mann also opposed personal religious instruction in the schools, and disbelieved in the efficacy of corporal punishment. These views aroused intense opposition among those who were unwilling to examine the educational side of the question. He endeavored to build up common school libraries, which were condemned as "Godless." The new normal schools were considered by many as a means of introducing unorthodox views into the schools by eliminating the influence of the local ministers in the selection of teachers, and as a means of indoctrinating the prospective teachers with liberal or positively evil views in religious matters.

The antagonism of the schoolmasters, centered in though by no means wholly confined to Boston, was founded upon opposition to new methods, particularly to Mann's condemnation of corporal punishment, to his advocacy of new and foreign ideas, chiefly Pestalozzianism, to the building up of training schools for teachers, destroying the aristocracy of the old profession, and in general to conservative personal and aristocratic forces hostile to all that Mann stood for. While this controversy embittered the last years of Mann's great service it nevertheless served to bring into national consciousness the reforms for which he labored. The dispute became a subject of attention in publications of national circulation.

Meanwhile Mann had become a dominant figure in various educational meetings in New York, Ohio, and other states where educational forces were struggling against the inertia of conservative public opinion. Through participation in this opposition he exerted a national force making for progress. Through his participation as well as through other factors the educational reform movement was felt all over the country and is recognizable in the advance made during this period in practically all of the states of the Union, though particularly great in New England and the new West. An illustration of its character and of its early existence in the Middle West, preceding the work of Mann, is found in the following list of special committees appointed by the Western Literary Institute of Cincinnati in 1835 (Quo. 394):

1. On infant schools.
2. On the most efficient modes of conducting examinations in common schools, high schools and academies.
3. On the introduction of the study of criminal and constitutional law into literary institutions.
4. On the utility of cabinets of natural science as a means of education.
5. On the causes of the idle habits of pupils in the classroom, and a remedy for the same.
6. On the expediency of employing a traveling agent and lecturer for the college, and the means of defraying his expenses.
7. On the most efficient means of exercising and educating the moral sense of students.
8. On vocal music as a branch of education.

SCHOOL SYSTEMS FROM 1830

9. To enquire into the causes and report on the fluctuation of schools and the evils and remedy thereof.

10. Ought the principles of agriculture to be a regular branch of common school education, and how shall it be introduced?

11. On elocution and extemporaneous speaking.

12. To what extent may manual labor be employed as a means of reducing the expenses of a collegiate education, and should the engaging in manual labor be optional or should it extend to all the students?

13. What is the best method of prosecuting the study of the Bible in common schools?

14. On the establishment of agricultural lyceums.

15. On the expediency of employing superintending agents for the common schools.

16. On bookkeeping.

17. To devise the best method of reaching and animating the community on the subject of education.

18. What branches of elementary education are appropriate to the two sexes?

19. On physical education.

20. On stenography.

21. On the best method of introducing and prosecuting the study of anatomy and physiology in the schools.

22. To what extent is it expedient and desirable that the chartered institutions of learning in each state form themselves into a university for the purpose of examining candidates for degrees and conferring the same according to proficiency and not according to the period of residence at any school, college, or other institution of learning whatever.

23. To what extent may the reading of fictitious composition be rendered beneficial to students?

24. What is the best method of employing the principle of emulation as a means of instruction?

Grading and Classification of Pupils.—This was one of the important achievements of this period. Previous to this time such classification of pupils as had been attained was by schools. The A–B–C–darian or dame school taught the alphabet, syllabic combinations, and the catechism. The reading school and the writing school followed as separate institutions; arithmetic was usually taught in the writing school; spelling, perhaps grammar, and later geography, in the reading school. During the late eighteenth and early nineteenth centuries the English grammar school absorbed the teaching of grammar and often included geography and elementary history in its work. The Latin school and the French school were always separate institutions, as were also a variety of private schools giving instruction in special subjects. As seen elsewhere (p. 19) the English grammar school developed into the English high school, beginning with the third decade of the nineteenth century. A child usually attended the reading school and the writing school at different times on the same day and fortunate children might attend one or two other schools in special subjects. Outside the Latin grammar school and later the English classical or high school there was little grading, and indeed this was not always found even in these schools. Recitation was by individuals or by pairs of pupils. Even when grading in the modern sense was substantially achieved it was still considered by the schoolmen of the day as a grading by schools.

The Boston Report of 1863 states: "There are in this city 250 primary schools which are grouped in buildings containing six or more separate schools. When 'graded' each school is a single class. The child at first is *educated* to the sixth class. After six months he is promoted to the next higher school, or class, and so passing from one school to another he reaches the highest where he is prepared for admission to the grammar school."

The Lancasterian monitorial plan introduced grading into the elementary school (p. 360). But this division was based on steps so minute, as for example the ability to spell words of one syllable, of two syllables, of three syllables, that the grades did not correspond to the present notion of classifying pupils. But at least the idea was made familiar. The Public School Society of New York divided its schools into three departments, infant, grammar department for girls, and grammar department for boys. By 1840–50 there were nine classes graded on the basis of reading and arithmetic. The Board of Education, founded in 1843, adopted this division of the school. When the two organizations were amalgamated in 1853 the scope of classification was as follows:

SCHOOL SYSTEMS FROM 1830

Primary Department.
  1st class. Alphabet cards.

* * *

  6th class. Webb's *Reader No. 3*, Pearson's *Speller and Tables*, Monteith's *Geography*, ciphering through division.

Upper Department, Male.
  Class 1. Reviews simple rules; becomes thoroughly acquainted with tables of weights and measures. Geography.

* * *

  Class 5. Square and cube roots. Historical and grammatical recitation. Begins algebra.
  Class 6. Prepares for full academy.

Upper Department, Female.
  1st class. Sanders' *Speller*, Underhill's *Table Book*, Parley's *Geography*, Sanders' *Third Reader*, Davies' *Arithmetic*—numeration, addition and subtraction.

* * *

  7th class. Thomas' *Etymology*, Collins' *Mental Arithmetic*, Haynes' *Second Grammar*, Scott's *United States*, Burr's *Chronology*, Smith's *Astronomy*, Mitchell's *Geography*, Pinnes' *Reader*, Davies' *University Arithmetic*, Greenleaf's *Arithmetic*, from decimal fractions.

This was the most elaborate system of grading to be found in the country and represents in the thirteen grades the inclusion of the secondary school program, which persisted until the establishment of public high schools in 1897.

Outside of New England most of the cities or large towns which had developed previous to the middle of the century established the graded school idea on the Lancasterian monitorial basis. Of these schools New York had far the most elaborate.

Another source of influence in the establishment of the graded system of schools was that exerted by visitors to European schools, particularly to those of Germany (pp. 235-41). Recently, as a result of war psychology, this has been interpreted as a most pernicious influence on the development of American education. The argument is as follows: The hard and fast eight-grade system of American schools is one of our great educational limitations; it results in an undemocratic division of the favored few who may go on to a secondary school course from the common mass of children; it leads to an undue expansion of the elementary curriculum, to the spending of an unnecessary amount of time on the details of these subjects, especially grammar and arithmetic, and to the justification of this state of affairs on the false basis of mental discipline. In general it is argued that "the elementary schools of the United States borrowed their plan of organization and the general definition of their course of study from Prussia. . . . That (now) we must get rid of the eight-year *rudimentary* vernacular school. . . . In this way we shall get what the district school and the academy started to give us before we were allured from the path of democracy by the enticements of Prussian organization." The objections to this interpretation are several. In the first place, the German schools of that period were divided into three departments somewhat similar to those prevailing in American cities at that time. Within these departments there was a very flexible classification of pupils on the basis of similarity of subjects studied. There was no eight-grade system; there was no hard and fast classification. In the second pace, there did not exist in the American schools at this period (1835 to 1850) or for long afterward any fixed system of grading; there were few if any towns where an eight-grade system had been attained; and there was no agreement or conformity as to number of grades. In the third place, none of the contemporary students of the German system, Stowe, Mann, Gricom, Bach, Ryerson, reported or advocated any fixed number of grades or any fixed system, or gave any great attention to it.

The most influential of all these reports was that of Mann. Of the 200 pages of this report just one page is given to the subject of "classification," but no mention is made of any number of grades or of a fixed system. The substance of Mann's statement is "the first element of superiority of the Prussian schools is the proper classification of scholars. In all places where the numbers are sufficiently large to allow it the children are divided according to ages and attainments;

and a single teacher has the charge only of a single class, or of as small number of classes as is practicable." Other reports of this period have even less to say.

Of the 309 towns of Massachusetts of which records appear in the State reports of 1842-3 and 1843-4 only eight mention the subject of classification and gradation, and these usually refer to it as a classification of schools rather than of pupils. The New Bedford report reads: "There are now four grades or classes of our schools: the primary schools, for children between four and seven years of age; the intermediate schools for those between seven and ten years; the grammar or commerce schools for those over ten years of age; and the high schools." Pawtucket reported: "The scholars were classed agreeable to their respective attainments, thus forming three distinct schools in each house."

Evidently the graded school system had not arrived at that period in the most progressive school state in the Union. From this time the subject of grading assumes a constantly growing importance. In 1850 the successor of Horace Mann devotes practically his entire report to this subject. His conclusions, however, show how remote from our present custom were the results achieved. They were: (1) That in cities and more populous towns grading was already achieved. "When there are no obstacles in the way it is better to have four grades than three. In small cities it may be more economical to bring all the grades of schools into one building than to bear the expense of purchasing several sites and erecting as many houses." Thus it appears that grading by schools seems yet to be more feasible than grading within schools. (2) Compact towns or large villages "will admit of two or three grades, several primary schools, two grammar schools and a high school." (3) Towns having one or more small villages should have a grammar school in the center and primary schools in the various neighborhoods. (4) In towns of extensive territory with sparse population "it will be very difficult and often quite impossible to grade schools."

Barnard and other authorities give the Quincy school of Boston in 1848 as the first school with modern grading. Barnard makes the following statement:

"When the organization is complete the school will be divided into four classes, each class containing 168 children, and each class into three divisions. At present the three lower classes contain two divisions each, and the first class three. On the third floor are the first divisions of the first class under the instruction of the principal, and the several divisions of the second class instructed by assistants. On the second floor is the second division of the first class instructed by the sub-master with the usual divisions of the third class under assistants; the usher takes the third division of the first class with the several divisions of the fourth class on the first floor. . . . The whole school is brought together in the hall for devotional services and other general exercises."

While Mann had urged the importance of grading in practically all of his reports, from this time on it receives increasing emphasis in each report. The Report of 1852 first clearly states the ideal long since achieved—"Our schools should be so graded that the child, when he enters the lowest class in the primary school, sees an unbroken series of promotions before him till he finishes his education in the higher school." The Report of 1854 shows great enthusiasm for this innovation on the part of many cities and towns. From now on the various towns consider the subject in their annual reports with greater and greater fullness until it becomes the topic of greatest attention. In other states this development was similar and from 1855 to 1865 and later the subject is one of first importance in the reports of the various state superintendents.

It is impossible to state where true grading within the school first took place. The New York Report of 1840 says of one of the counties: "Each school is divided into five or six classes; very few are learning the alphabet." Here evidently is the division of the school into classes, probably of very few children each, but grouped irrespective of scholastic attainments. Grading within the school was of slow growth. It was an achievement of the fifth, sixth, and seventh decades of the century. By the close of the Civil War grading was achieved but there was no uniformity in any one region, in any type of school, or in any state. In 1863 the schools of

Cincinnati were the only ones in the state of Ohio that had as many as 6 grades. In 1867 less than 6% of the graded schools of the state had reached that standard. The actual number of grades in Ohio at that time varied from 2 to 9, with the great majority of communities favoring 4 or 5.

Union vs. District Schools (Ch. XVI, Pts. I and V).—The chief factor in developing the graded system was the "union" school. It is to be remembered that the independent ungraded school not only was the school of the rural region and of the village, but that the same organization was carried over into the larger towns, where the Lancasterian or public school system did not exist. In some New England cities this district control lasted until the twentieth century, though the ungraded feature had long been eliminated. In some states the extremely decentralized system was modified for the growing centers of population by special acts of the legislature. For example, in New York such acts were passed in 1837 for Buffalo, in 1841 for Rochester and Hudson, in 1842 for New York City, in 1843 for Poughkeepsie, in 1850 for Brooklyn, and still later for other cities. In each of these cases Lancasterian or public school societies had previously controlled the schools. In smaller cities special acts effected the union of districts.

The union school laws were enactments authorizing two or more of the local units of government to form a legal unit for control of schools, thus doing away with the more minute subdivisions of school population, in which any great improvement in the character of schools was impossible. While there were many advantages in these union schools—improved organization, lower cost, better teachers, enriched curriculum—the most immediate and obvious gain was in grading and classification. Massachusetts passed a law permitting the formation of union districts in 1838, Connecticut in 1841, and New York in 1853. In the latter state 200 such union schools had been established by the close of the Civil War period. In 1848 Massachusetts passed a Union High School Act permitting towns to combine to form secondary schools.

While the union of schools was favored at this time chiefly for financial advantage or because it permitted the establishment of free schools, yet the establishment of such schools was closely connected with the development of grading.

The Massachusetts Report of 1854 states: "The gradual abandonment of the district system results from its connection with another measure regarded by the people with great favor, namely, the gradation of schools."

This struggle was long drawn out. In a later period the district system was modified by a state-adopted graded curriculum which forced a classification of pupils even if they were under one teacher. But in this earlier period gradation could be accomplished only by the abolition of the district system.

Religious vs. Secular Control of Education.—The establishment of a free public school system not only conflicted with the political beliefs and prejudices of many people, aroused their antagonism to taxation and increased public charges, and interfered with vested interests; it also challenged the fundamental religious beliefs of many and aroused religious prejudice. The conflict with religious beliefs revealed itself rather subtly in regard to the content of school textbooks (p. 357) where the developing political and economic interests of the people demanded materials in reading and history, geography, etc., appropriate to those interests. Occasionally, as in New York City, there was a violent controversy over the selection of texts. Here it was charged by some that the textbooks used by the Lancasterian schools were non-religious and particularly by the Roman Catholics that they were controversially Protestant in character. The elimination of materials of a religious nature soon followed. A more difficult problem appeared when the question of financial support was involved in the case of the division of public subsidies. Objections arose that such funds were to be assigned only to institutions under public control. Finally such problems arose when the effort to make public support sufficient to permit such superiority of the public school in length of term, character of teachers and equipment, school buildings and curriculum, that the private schools would be unable to compete with them. Yet more profound hostility was aroused when it was believed by many that the whole atmosphere and purpose of the public schools and of their philosophy, both political and psychological, was "godless." Many worthy people persuaded themselves of the truth of this accusation. There was no portion of the country that was not involved in some form of this controversy. But so far as it affected the public common schools it was fought out to a conclusion during this period.

This dispute is to be seen in its most elemental, aggravated, and unattractive form in the history of the New York City schools. The School Law of 1812 provided that that portion of the state funds allotted to the city should be divided between the Public School Society, several similar charitable organizations and the charity schools supported by the several religious denominations. These included the Baptist, Dutch Reformed, Episcopal, Methodist Episcopal, Presbyterian, and Roman Catholic. Modification of the law soon extended to sectarian schools the privilege, first accorded to the Free School Society, of expending appropriations in excess of needs for teachers' salaries on the erection of buildings and on material aids. The funds were distributed on the basis of number enrolled. An unseemly rivalry developed, which resulted in efforts to attract children from rival schools, in the padding of school enrollment, in the lowering of teachers' salaries, in miserable instruction under the inefficient monitorial plan, and in charges at least of actual misappropriation of funds. After a long controversy, involving city council and state legislature, decision was reached in 1824 that funds should be allotted only to the Public School Society and to a few similar non-sectarian societies. In 1831 the city was authorized to levy a tax for the support of education, and the conflict broke out anew over the distribution of these funds, chiefly on the grounds that the Protestant Orphan Asylum had been designated in 1824 as a recipient of the state funds. It was finally decided that such funds should be given to sectarian organizations only when they were founded for the care of orphan children and, after another acrimonious dispute, only when such children were wholly under the care of the institution and not merely attending its schools. The provisions of this agreement, extended to include delinquent and defective as well as dependent children, is still a feature of the New York system. In 1841 the controversy again broke out, this time initiated by the Roman Catholic church, and on the claim that the education given by the Free School Society was in fact sectarian because Protestant in character. Prolonged public discussion followed, in mass meeting, in the public press, in the legislature and the current political campaign. It was obvious, or at least it now is, that the Free School Society was out of harmony with our political structure, and had outlived its usefulness. The problem was solved by the formation of a board of education to take charge of public schools, by the refusal to grant any further aid to the Free School Society for erection of buildings or the expansion of its system, and by the reaffirmation of the principle that public funds, state or local, should be used only for non-sectarian state supervised education, and for such philanthropic institutions as relieved the state of the care as well as of education of their inmates. This principle has remained a feature of the state policy ever since.

In all parts of the country such controversies were waged though these were perhaps less distinctly focused than in New York. In Pennsylvania the entire educational system of the eighteenth and early nineteenth centuries was that of church schools, plus a considerable number of ephemeral private schools. During the early nineteenth century, as it became obvious that large numbers of poor children were not being educated by either of these agencies, charity schools were established in various localities by those philanthropically inclined. The opposition to the establishment of free schools, by the incorporation of these charity schools into a public school system supported by tax, came to a certain extent from private school interests. But these schools when purely private were unorganized and uninfluential. The chief opposition came from those who still firmly believed in the church control of education. This conflict was particularly intense in Pennsylvania, since religious control there was not by the nation-wide denominations, but by sects representing a culture and a language foreign to the great bulk of the population, or so distinctive in their views that these could be preserved only by isolation and decisive educational influences. The very existence of some of these sects depended upon an exclusive educational scheme. Hence since the application of the free school law was optional, every effort to increase its efficiency through any centralized control was bitterly opposed on religious and political as well as educational principles, and the final adoption of the law by the last county was delayed until near the close of the century.

In New England the question concerning the public control of schools, and the state subsidy of denominational educational endeavor, had long been settled, both in principle and in fact,—the former in the affirmative, the latter in the negative. But here were first fought the battles still agitating many parts of our country as to whether the public schools should inculcate sectarian doctrine, even when the dominant elements in society demand it, whether even the Bible should be read if persons objected to it on principle, whether the custom of giving religious instruction or information of a sectarian character should be allowed, even for supplementary or library reading, and whether the dominant theological interpretation of child and adult human nature should control the shaping of educational methods and principles.

The educational controversy was closely connected with the one concerning religious ideas and ecclesiastical institutions; for at this time the more liberal Unitarian views had become very influential throughout New England, to the alarm and dismay of the adherents of the traditional conservative views. Again the controversy centered in Horace Mann, for he was not only the representative of novel or dangerous educational doctrines: he was also a Unitarian.

It was charged that Mann, or the State Board of Education, or the upholders of the new education were responsible for the elimination of the shorter catechism and of direct religious and theological instruction from the schools. But it was shown that most towns had taken this action of their own volition and that the Law of 1827 forbade sectarian instruction. It was charged that the liberal forces would even forbid the use of the Bible in the schools; and this charge was admitted if the use of the Bible involved sectarian interpretation or exposition, but that the authorities advised a daily reading from the Scriptures, without comment. The assertion that the state authorities refused to admit the volumes of the American Sunday School Library was met by a disclaimer by the State Board of any exercise of authority. The abolition of corporal punishment was also opposed on religious grounds, and because such abolition would permit moral laxity and indifference, for it would nullify all efforts at correction except "talk."

The most fundamental objection, however, to the new educational theories was that they constituted a force which negated both in theory and in practice any attempt at religious education in home and church. The conflict here was real, for the orthodox religious views held human nature to be essentially evil and asserted as the purpose of religion and education to eradicate the tendencies of human nature and to "break the will" of the child: while the new education asserted that human nature is essentially good, that its interests should be followed, and that the child's will should be strengthened and developed. This divergence could not be compromised; the conflict was a long and acrimonious one. And if our own generation has come to hold with certainty the new views in education, perhaps even in religion, that human nature is to be shaped either for good or for ill by nurture—that is by education—it is because of these early conflicts.

The controversy had many ramifications; it affected every part of the country. It involved not only the question of compulsory religious education, but also that of state control of religion. As Mr. Mann stated: "This year the everlasting fires of hell will burn to terrify the unrepentant; next year, and without any repentance, its eternal flames will be extinguished, to be rekindled forever or to be quenched forever as it may be decided at the annual town meeting." These controversies are interesting, for the questions are still raised; they are hardly edifying, certainly not complimentary to human nature as nurtured by such discussions. Their real effect can best be given by another sentence from Mann: "Can aught be conceived more deplorable, more fatal to the interests of the young? Such strifes and persecutions on the question of total depravity as to make all men depraved at any rate; and such contests about the nature and the number of Persons in the Godhead in heaven, as to make little children atheists on earth." Out of this came finally the fundamental democratic principle of American education; that to be free and public, education must be secular in character, leaving religious education to be cared for by other institutions.

During the Colonial period the association between education and religion in aim, content, method, and control had been quite close, both in public mind and official act. During the early portion of the National period the consciousness of the need and appropriateness of public education developed more rapidly than did the means for its effective realization. Consequently this was a period in which public authority leaned heavily on the institution under religious control for effecting the purposes of public education. Such institutions, of all grades but particularly of the secondary grade, were quite generally subsidized by public funds. In many regions even large systems of elementary schools were so supported. This led to acrimonious public discussion over the sectarian control of schools throughout the country. The result was the demonstration to the satisfaction of the public that public control and support was the only solution in a free democratic society, that state and church should have no connection even through education. Consequently from about the middle of the century, through both fundamental law and statutory enactment, the Commonwealths of the Union quite generally forbade any religious control of the public schools or any state support of religious schools. From 1850 on, such legislation may be found in practically every state. It is usually negative in character and effective through the following prohibitions: (1) That no religious tests shall be made of either pupil or teacher for any public educational institution; (2) That no public support shall be given to sectarian institutions,—though this provision is not universally found; (3) That no sectarian instruction shall be given; (4) That the use of the Bible in the public schools shall not be compelled or allowed. This last question is left to the decision of the courts except in one state, Mississippi, where the use of the Bible is guaranteed by the Constitution. These decisions have been numerous and conflicting, some upholding and some prohibiting the reading of the Bible in the schools. The most common ruling is that parents objecting to the reading of the Bible may withdraw their children from participation in such exercises but may not legally demand the exclusion of the Bible. If parents object to the use of any particular version of the Scriptures,—as the Roman Catholics to the King James or other Protestant translation—they have the same privilege and are subject to the same restriction. A recent decision in California excludes the King James version as sectarian. This question then becomes one of guaranteed religious freedom rather than one of education.

The outcome of these controversies and of the resultant legislation is the establishment of the American principle of complete freedom of religious belief and practice, implying the separation of state and church, the elimination of religious influences and instruction from public schools, and the general if not universal prohibition of state aid to sectarian institutions and of restrictions on the use of the Bible in school exercises.

Adult Education.—During the mid-century period this phase of education attracted much attention, to fall into abeyance later and to be revived only in recent times. The reasons for the interest in adult education from 1825 to 1860 were peculiar to the times. With the growing interest in public democratic education it was realized that large portions of the population were illiterate and were ignorant of more than letters. This large democratic element had now come into control in political life. During this period, foreign immigration having begun on a large scale, it was recognized that these newcomers were ignorant of American ideals and political institutions. Moreover, a great change was occurring in the industrial organization; the factory system was replacing the traditional handicraft system, and apprenticeship, with its training of the youth in industry and in reading and writing and with the responsibility of the master for the apprentice, was rapidly dying out,—in fact it was practically gone long before the Civil War. Efforts to supply adult education took the form of mechanics' institutes, evening schools, public lyceums, and libraries.

Mechanics' institutes (Quo. 434) were founded in most of the large cities for the education of apprentices under the growing factory system. These were supported by philanthropic contributions, by fees, and by endowments. Instruction was by public lectures, by evening classes—some of them technical ·but most of them in the common branches, and by libraries. Most of these disappeared in time, but where endowments had accumulated they have developed into valuable modern technical or trade schools as in New York, Rochester, and Cincinnati.

Evening schools, both private and public or semi-public in character, also flourished. These were but a continuation of the old custom under the apprentice system (Ch. II) and met the needs of the neglected native industrial population rather than, as in recent times, of the immigrant population. The newspapers of the period contain very numerous advertisements of such schools. A survey of educational conditions in Boston in 1817 revealed that there were 162 private schools in the city. While most of these were for children, a number were evening schools for adults. The Public School Society of New York in 1823 passed a resolution permitting its teachers to hold private evening schools. In 1833 the evening schools "for apprentices and others who had left school without the advantages now offered" were made a part of the system; but as the teachers were required to serve without extra compensation, the plan was abandoned after four or five years of indifferent success, though the use of the Societies' buildings for private evening schools was continued. In 1847 the Board of Education recently established opened six evening schools for men and boys. These schools were under the direct control of the Board, not as in the case of the day schools, under ward committees; consequently they became an important factor in building up a centralized school system. In 1848 similar schools for women and girls were opened. By 1849 fifteen such schools of both types were in successful operation.

In the Middle Western cities such as Cincinnati and Louisville such schools under public control opened some years earlier. In general evening schools became a recognized part of city school systems during this period. But with the expansion of the school curriculum to include upper grades or secondary schools and the more general diffusion of public education, so that a substantial part of the population shared in its benefits, such schools ceased to be of immediate importance until recalled a few decades later to meet the problem of educating the immigrant citizen.

The Lyceum (Quos. 430-434) was an organization of public spirited citizens providing a series of public lectures on all sorts of subjects of practical or intellectual interest, financial support being secured by small admission charges. Many were mere debating clubs; many bore pretentious names, the Ciceronian Association being popular. The movement spread all over the country. As early as 1829 a national organization of lyceums was formed, with state and local branches. A national convention in 1831 represented more than a thousand organizations. The strength of the system, however, lay in local interest and support and the general organizations did not flourish long.

The most prominent men of the times in every walk of life devoted much time to the lyceum platform, which became a powerful factor in political discussion, in social improvement, and in intellectual advance. During this period the lecture or public address was the dominant form of expressing thought, as was the epistolary form in an earlier period. Reformers such as De Witt Clinton, Edward Everett, Ralph Waldo Emerson, William Lloyd Garrison, Edward Everett Hale; political leaders, as Sumner, Douglas, Greeley; women leaders, as Julia Ward Howe, Susan B. Anthony, Emma Willard; foreign visitors such as Dickens, Thackeray, George Combe, Miss Martineau; and every man of literary prominence took part in this form of education. The most important contributor to the lyceum type of education and its chief adornment was Emerson (1809-1882). Emerson was an essayist, as we think of him now, because he was a platform lecturer, rather than a lecturer because he was an essayist. His essays were mostly delivered on the lyceum platform. Such lectures must be gauged to a mixed audience and limited to an hour's time: they must be varied and stimulating, and conform to certain literary and technical forms. Of the lyceum

Emerson says: "I preach in the lecture room, and there it tells, for there is no prescription. You may laugh, weep, reason, sing, sneer, or pray according to your genius." The stimulating and illuminating idealism of Emerson's essays is an indication of the high purpose, if not an index of the normal attainment of the adult education of this generation. Another sign of the times may be found in the usual remuneration received for these lectures, when compared with the huge sums frequently demanded now. The usual price received by Emerson for the evening lecture was $10 and traveling expenses. He expressed grave doubt of the morality of accepting the fee of $50 each for a series on the one occasion when this maximum was reached.

After the Civil War, interest in adult education declined until the modern immigration problem and the Chautauqua movements forced themselves on the public attention.

State System.—Throughout the experience in all the states ran common influences, common development, and reaction. Beginning with Massachusetts in 1789 and New York in 1795, state support or subsidy of public schools, with some form of state supervision, was established during this period in practically all states of the union. In the early stages state supervision and control was of the most general character and usually connected with the distribution of state funds. Its usual and most effective form was the requirement of some proportionate support, either equal or greater, upon the part of the local unit, assisted by the state contribution. State supervision seldom went beyond this financial aspect until after long experience, when it began to determine the length of the school term, the preparation of the teacher, the content of the curriculum, and the physical condition of the school plant.

The earliest form of this state supervision was usually the designation of the incumbent of some existing office, usually the State Treasurer or State Auditor, as Superintendent of Common Schools, or of Public Instruction, was in time created in all the states. In the New England states and some others a State Board of Education with an Executive Secretary was the form chosen. Many of these were able and influential leaders to whom the early educational developments were due. Among these were Hawley of New York, Mann of Massachusetts, Barnard of Connecticut and Rhode Island, Lewis of Ohio, Pierce of Michigan, Wiley of North Carolina, Mills of Indiana,—all outstanding personalities of their time.

A third step in the building up of the state system was the establishment of supervising authorities over larger local areas than the individual school. The office of county superintendent was established in New York in 1841, in Ohio in 1847, and in Pennsylvania in 1854. The primary function of this office related to the assessment of taxes and distribution of funds, but it usually had also some supervising powers, particularly over the qualification of teachers. Town or township superintendents were also created in several of the states, some with supervisory powers over instruction, but concerned chiefly with the distribution of funds.

With the creation of county superintendents, teachers' institutes were introduced into New York (1842). In a less systematic form such meetings had been previously organized by Horace Mann in Massachusetts. From this time on they came to be one of the chief instruments in improving the qualifications and professional knowledge of the teacher as well as of developing the morale of the profession.

Popular educational conventions proved to be very effective means, particularly in New York and Pennsylvania, of developing public support for education and for improving conditions within the school and the teaching profession. In New England this service was performed on the largest scale by the American Institute of Instruction, our oldest existing educational organization. After the establishment of free schools such conventions soon ceased to be of interest to the general public.

In a similar way the establishment of normal schools or teachers' training classes in academies, of libraries in school districts, of a state school journal, were means of improving public education adopted by most of the states.

City School Systems.—The early city school systems grew out of either the district or the town system or out of the quasi-public school societies. In general the former development oc-

SCHOOL SYSTEMS FROM 1830

curred in New England, the latter in the Central states and in the few cities of the South. In the Middle Western states both modes of development were found.

In 1840 Mrs. Emma Hart Willard was made superintendent of schools in the town of Kensington in Connecticut. The duties here were purely supervisory, and her authority circumscribed. In 1841 Springfield, Mass., elected a town superintendent of schools. Here again the authority was merely supervisory and marked a step in the developing of grading. Permissive provision for the office of superintendent was made in the state Law of 1854. Boston established this office in 1851 and gave it a permanently recognized place in the Massachusetts system.

Meanwhile in 1839 Providence, Rhode Island, had appointed Nathan Bishop as "Superintendent of Public Schools." This is claimed to have been the first city superintendency. It has often been stated that this office was created in imitation of the superintendents of factories then becoming numerous in this region. No doubt there was an influence by way of suggestion from this source. A better explanation, however, is found in the fact that the public schools had been rapidly growing, that several primary schools and grammar schools had been created out of the old system of reading and writing and advanced schools, that numerous new buildings were being erected, that the teachers there numbered "six males and twenty-eight females," the pupils 1670, and that the committee serving without remuneration was unable to attend to the details of management. Further explanation may be found in the fact that at the same time the school committee petitioned the legislature for a law "to prevent the disturbance of schools by intruders interfering with the same, or by riotous persons from without." Mr. Bishop became superintendent of the Boston schools in 1851 and was succeeded in Providence by Samuel S. Greene, who had served as superintendent at Springfield, thus establishing that custom of progressive advancement through actual service rather than through professional training which yet prevails. Mr. Greene also set another precedent, occasionally repeated thereafter, for at the same time he served as Professor of Didactics at Brown University. Both of these men were educational leaders of national influence in their generation.

In New York early city schools were all founded by public school societies, and were supported by philanthropic contributions and subsidies from the state fund. The members of these societies elected a president, a board of directors, and a secretary. This secretary, in looking after the business affairs of the society, came to perform many of the administrative functions of a superintendent of schools. At times he even assumed some of the supervisory functions also. Beginning with Buffalo in 1837 and extended by 1850 to practically all the cities of the state, special acts were passed creating a board of education, giving to it powers of taxation, making it the recipient of funds, and creating the office of superintendent of schools. In Buffalo members of the city council were made *ex officio* the school board, the superintendent being at first appointed by it, and later elected by popular vote. In New York the board of education was created in 1842, the county superintendent of schools serving as the administrative officer over the independent ward school system until 1852, when a city superintendent of schools was created. At first the functions of this officer were largely those of superintendent of school buildings. Elsewhere the office included the ordering, the administrative, and the supervisory functions. General provision for unification of schools in cities and towns of New York was made by the Law of 1853.

In Pennsylvania the development was more tardy. Out of the Law of 1843 providing for district superintendents, six cities in turn developed an office corresponding to city superintendent, though it remained with one exception under the jurisdiction of the county superintendent. When in 1856 the office of district superintendent was abolished, special permission was given to some of these cities to continue the office. Out of these permissive acts grew the Law of 1867 permitting the adoption of this type of organization in any city. By 1870 fourteen cities had availed themselves of this privilege.

In Southern and Western states city school systems with a city superintendent were usually created by special acts for cities when

SCHOOL SYSTEMS FROM 1830

the rural regions were not yet ready for such a step. This occurred in 1841 in New Orleans. In Cincinnati the public school system had been authorized as early as 1825 and free schools were opened three years later. The city superintendency, however, was not created until 1850. From 1839 on special laws were enacted

FIG. 49. A district schoolmaster. (From Johnson, *Old-time Schools and School-books*.)

for several cities. These provided for free schools, for grading, and for supervision, out of which last point shortly grew the city superintendency. The Law of 1847 for Akron provided for a high school and this permission was soon extended by general law to all the cities of the state.

Thus the establishment of the city system of schools is seen to be closely connected with the development of free schools, of grading, of supervision, and of centralized administration through a superintendent. This occurred first through voluntary agents, later through permissive acts applying to individual cities and then through general permissive laws. These latter steps were not taken until after the middle of the century.

The District School System (Quos. Ch. XVI, Pt. I).—If the development of a nationalized school system depended upon the willingness to support it wholly or in part by public tax, the condition upon which this support was given was the transfer of the control of the school to the smallest unit which bore the tax. Whatever the limitations of the district school were, it satisfied conditions which had to be met to secure the public school system at all. The district school is government by pure democracy applied to education. We might also add the words of Mr. Martin that it was "the high water mark of modern democracy and the low water mark of the Massachusetts school system," and might generalize from the commonwealth of Massachusetts to the entire Union.

FIG. 50. Interior of a district school. (From Johnson, *Old-time Schools and School-books*.)

During this period of three decades the district school system was established in practically all of the commonwealths where there was any attempt to work out a public school system. Though in some it was speedily modified, as it later was modified in all, yet most states formed subsequent to this period have also had a more or less extended experience with the district system. Its highest, or one might say its lowest, development in the legal form occurred in Indiana, where, by Law of 1836, upon the failure to elect a district trustee, any householder might employ a teacher and demand his share of the common school funds. In working perfection the local ideal is facetiously reported to have been reached in a state some-

SCHOOL SYSTEMS FROM 1830

what further west, where a farmer elected himself district trustee, employed his daughter as teacher and his wife as janitor, sent his own children (the only ones in the district) to school—and the Transcontinental railroad paid the bills.

The system itself had many aspects and many modifications. But the essential feature was always the same, namely that the

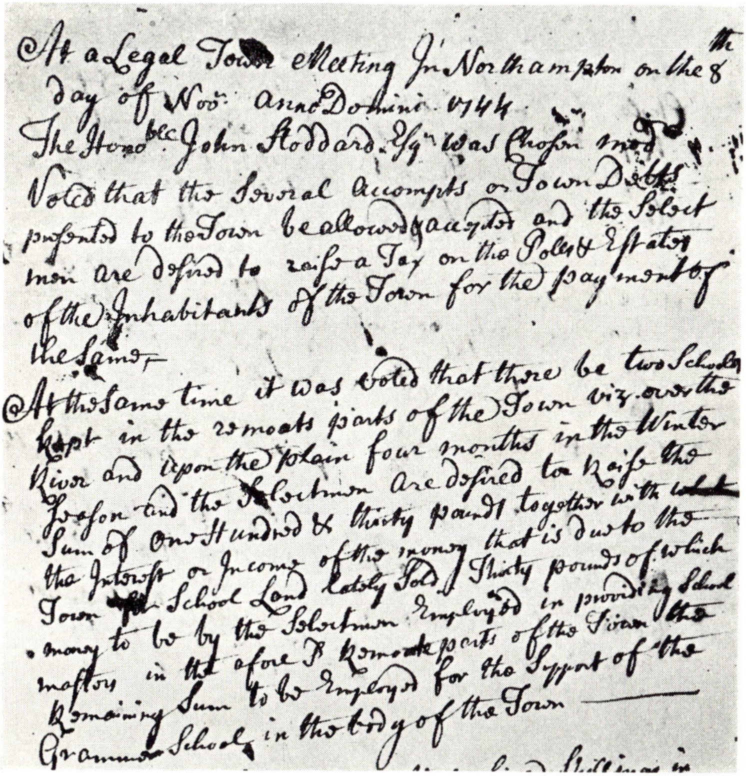

FIG. 51. Record of a town meeting, Northampton, Mass. 1744.

immediate control of schools was reduced to the lowest existing political unit. If none such existed conforming to the area readily served by a single school, a school district was created as such a unit.

The Development and Spread of the System.—As has been seen, the system was evolved in the New England states in the late Colonial period. The Massachusetts Law of 1769 authorized the

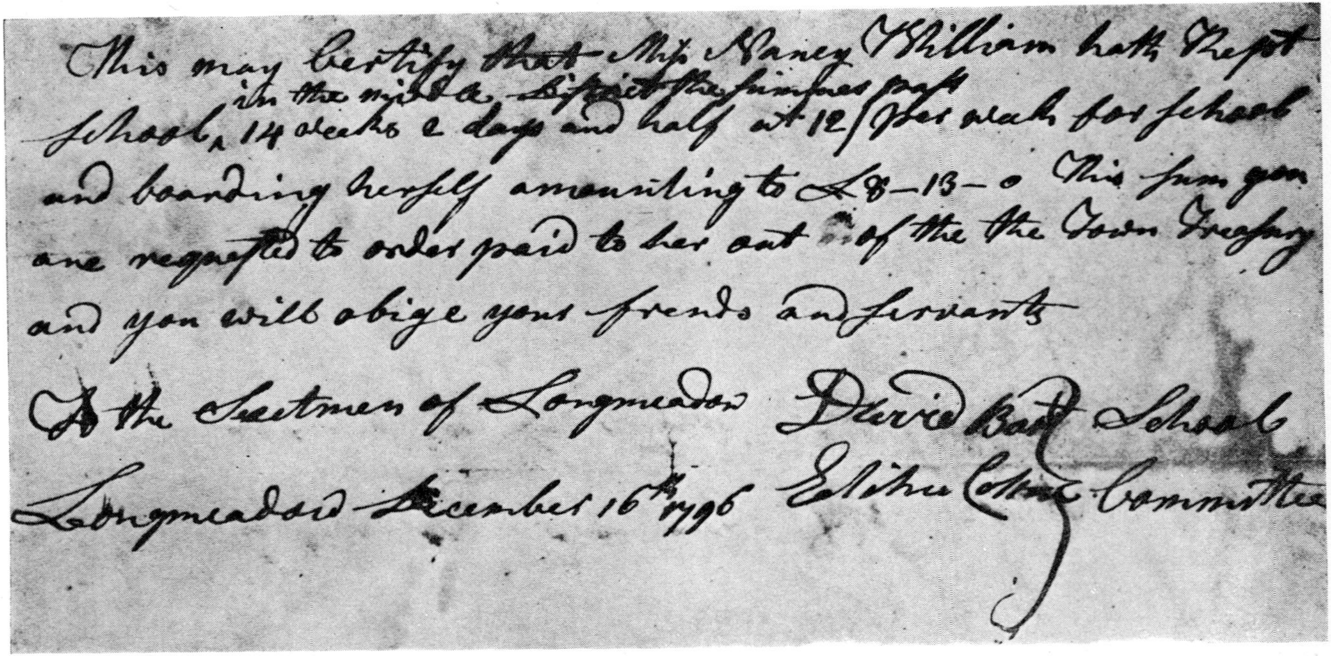

This may Certify that Mrs Nancy William hath kept
school in the middle District the summer past 14 weeks 2 days and half at 12/ per week for school
and boarding herself amounting to £8-13-0 This sum you
are requested to order paid to her out of the the Town Treasury
and you will obige your frends and servants

To the Selectmen of Longmeadow David Burt School
Longmeadow December 16th 1796 Elihu Colton Committee

FIG. 52. Certification to selectmen of amount due a schoolteacher at $3 per week. Longmeadow, Mass. 1796.

SCHOOL SYSTEMS FROM 1830

system; the Law of 1800 conferred the power to tax—the chief evidence of sovereignty; the Law of 1817 made the districts corporations with power to sue and be sued; the Law of 1827 required that all towns should be so districted. There yet remained some minor restrictions upon the Massachusetts district, for the town determined the amount of tax and the qualifications of the teacher, but the district had full control in employing and supervising the teacher, and expending such school funds as were raised. Such was the system to accomplish the modification or abolition of which Horace Mann expended most of his energy. It was not until his term of service ended, after the middle of the century, that a temporary modification of the system was effected. Not until 1882 was it definitely abolished.

In Connecticut, the preliminary stage having been passed in the successive steps which developed the parish or ecclesiastical societies, the system was established in full force by a law of 1799. This remained without essential modification until 1856, when the town control was made optional. But it was not until well into the twentieth century (1909) that the district system was abolished. The first school law of Vermont in 1782 and the first one of Maine in 1820 established the district system. The first school law of New York established in 1795 a system which was essentially that of town control. This was never popular and was effective only five years. When a state system was re-established in 1812 it was on a district basis. Pennsylvania and New Jersey had been familiarized with the experimental form of local control under the ecclesiastical system in vogue at the opening of the National period, so that when an optional public system was effected it was almost of necessity on the district plan. For the states to the west the ordinance of 1785 had paved the way for the district system. Though the early laws of Indiana and Michigan, because of sparse population, provided a township system, this was soon modified in each case to the district form. Similarly the district system came to prevail in the other states of the Northwest Territory.

In some of these states, notably in Indiana about 1859, the township system was superposed on the district system. In fact with

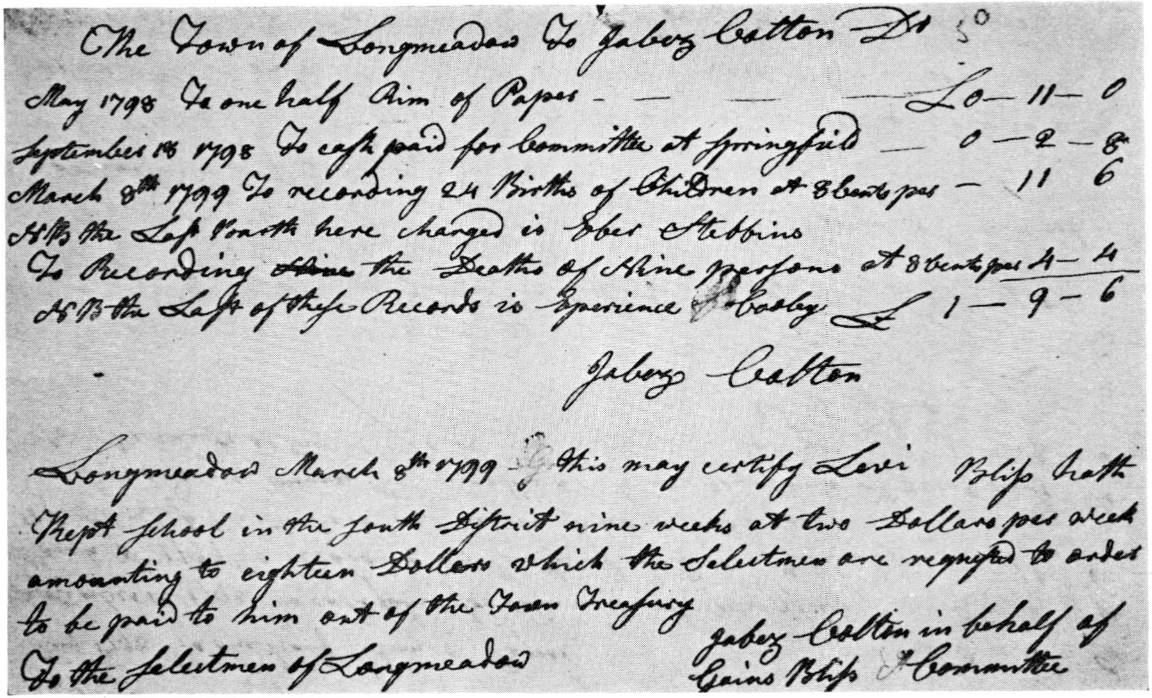

The Town of Longmeadow To Jabez Colton Dr 5°

May 1798 To one half Rim of Paper — — — £0—11—0

September 18 1798 To cash paid for Committee at Springfield — 0—2—8

March 8th 1799 To recording 24 Births of Children at 8 cents per — 11 6

N B the Last Birth here charged is Eber Stebbins

To Recording ~~Nine~~ the Deaths of Nine persons at 8 cents per 4—4

N B the Last of these Records is Experience Woolley £ 1—9—6

Jabez Colton

Longmeadow March 8th 1799 — This may certify Levi Bliss hath Kept School in the South District nine weeks at two Dollars per week amounting to eighteen Dollars which the Selectmen are requested to order to be paid to him out of the Town Treasury

To the Selectmen of Longmeadow

Jabez Colton in behalf of
Gains Bliss & Committee

FIG. 53. MSS records of a Connecticut town including certification for a schoolmaster at $2 per week.

SCHOOL SYSTEMS FROM 1830

the rise of the county superintendency throughout the West and the South the extreme form of the district system was modified. But for this early period the district system was a form all but universal until the Civil War. The characteristics of this system we have now to see.

Limitations and Defects of the District School System.—On the part of the public these were the loss of interest in the schools, the destruction of general standards, and the multiplication of petty local quarrels. On the part of the school official the system developed

FIG. 54. A district schoolhouse, commonly known as the "Little Red Schoolhouse," although usually without any paint. (From Johnson, *Old-time Schools and School-books*, p. 103.)

an indifference except to the most routine performance of mechanical duties. So far as the teaching was concerned the system reduced salaries to the lowest possible point, the competition always being toward the minimum; it failed to maintain any adequate standards of preparation or of attainment; it furnished little opportunity for improving school conditions; it made the lowest paid and hence the most poorly equipped teacher most sought after; it fostered frequent changes and short tenure of office and rendered desirable the earliest possible escape from the profession. As to the pupil, it gave him the shortest term consistent with general law; it frequently put a premium upon irregular attendance (Quo. 489); it stimulated bad conduct; it led to the frequent breaking up of the school by rowdy pupils (Quo. 492); it exalted force in the form of corporal punishment as the sole means of control; it prevented grading and rapid advancement; it gave to him a minimum of the teacher's time and of instruction; it made possible the use of every variety of books in the same class (Quo. 493).

In general this system produced the most general indifference to education on the part of all concerned; it prevented the establishment of any general standards; it fostered a pernicious and mean

FIG. 55. A kitchen school, attached to a New England farmhouse; an old form of the district school. Still River, Mass., built about 1690. (From *Journal of American History*, Vol. III, p. 404.)

spirit; and it proved the greatest obstacle to technical educational advance.

Educational Advance from 1830 to the Close of the Civil War Period.—While the main features of this advance are treated in detail in this and related chapters, an outline summary of the essential legislative enactments is desirable.

In New England.—The essential achievement was the establishment of a central educational authority. The function of this authority was limited, it is true, to the collection and dissemination of information. Such information, however, became the basis for legislation and for advocated reform; its dissemination became the

SCHOOL SYSTEMS FROM 1830

means of enlightening public opinion and of improving the morale and the technical knowledge of the teaching profession. The State Board of Education, with its Secretary, was established in Massachusetts in 1837; in Connecticut in 1839, revoked in 1842, re-established in 1849, in each case under Dr. Barnard; in Rhode Island in 1843 with Dr. Barnard as secretary; in Vermont in 1843; in New Hampshire and Maine in 1846.

The establishment of normal schools for the professional training of the teachers of the common schools began with Massachusetts

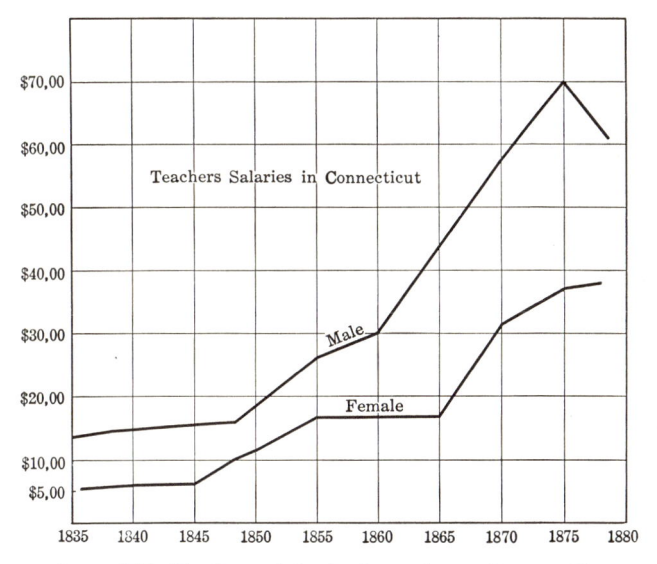

CHART VIII. Teachers salaries in Connecticut. 1835 to 1880.

in 1839; Connecticut followed in 1849 and other states within the period (Quos. Ch. XVII).

The chief efforts of these central authorities and the aim of the most important legislation was to modify the evils of the district system. The actual elimination of this system by the substitution of a town basis of organization was not achieved within the period. The experience of Massachusetts was typical. In 1838 union of districts was authorized (Quos. Ch. XVI, Pt. II); in 1848 union of districts or towns for a high school was authorized; by the laws of 1853 the district system was to be discontinued unless the town voted triennially in favor of it; in 1859 the district system was abolished but the same legislature in its autumn session rescinded the law; in 1861 a law was again enacted requiring every town with the district system to vote triennially on its continuance. The final abolition of the system did not occur until 1882.

Another leading feature of this period was the effort to establish free schools on the basis of public taxation. While this was accomplished by law as early as 1827 in Massachusetts (Quo. 375) and later in the period in other states, the value of this achievement was greatly limited by the unwillingness of the local communities to tax themselves to any great extent for this purpose, and by the fact that private schools had a powerful following and a great influence. The establishment of the free public school was so important an achievement of this period that a full presentation of the entire subject is given in Chapter XIII following.

The material accomplishments of the early portion of this period are indicated in the paragraph on the Horace Mann Reforms; later achievements were along the same lines.

In the Middle States.—As noted in the previous chapter New York made in the early National period a greater advance than New England. A central authority and a public school system, based on public tax and private rate bills, had been established in 1812. The office of Superintendent of Common Schools created in 1812 was abolished in 1821, and its duties transferred to the Secretary of State. It was not re-established as a separate office until 1854. The outstanding feature of the period was the agitation for the establishment of a free school system through the abolition of the rate bills, extending from 1845 to 1867; this is dealt with in the chapter (XIII) on *The Free School System*. The entire period is marked by a steady increase in the public support of the schools both from state and local sources.

Greater centralization of educational control than in New England has always been a feature of the New York system. This resulted partly from the fact that the state has contributed to the support of local schools through funds accruing from the common school fund ever since 1816, as well as by state tax. This tax was in 1851 a lump sum of $800,000; in 1856 it was made ¾ of a mill on each dollar of taxable property and it increased to 1¼ mills when the rate bills were abolished in 1867. Such state aid was conditional upon the raising of similar or greater amounts by local taxation.

Further centralization of control and supervision was secured through the establishment of the office of county superintendent

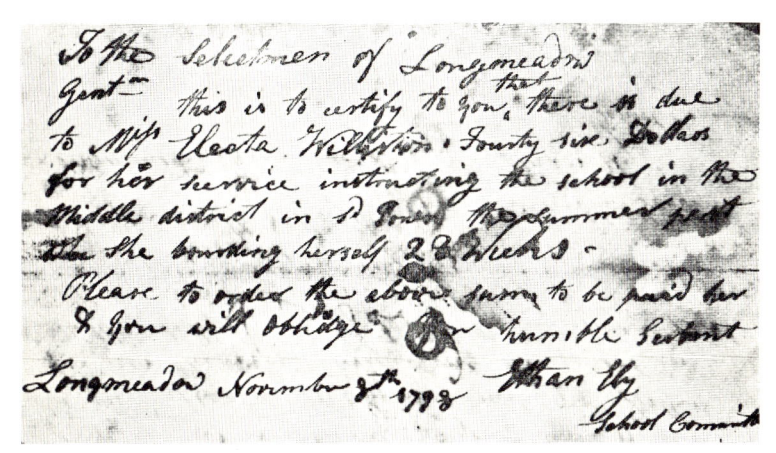

FIG. 56. Certification for a schoolmistress including amount for board. Longmeadow, Mass., 1798. (From MSS records.)

in 1841, which was abolished in 1847, but re-established in 1862. In a similar way the creation of the office of town superintendent in 1842 and the substitution of town supervisors and commissioners in 1856 indicates another phase of the conflict between centralized authority and local control. State conventions of these superintendents, beginning in 1845, exercised great influence in improving educational conditions.

New York was the first state to make provision for the training of its teachers by the subsidizing of a teachers' training course in various academies in 1833 (Quos. Ch. XVII) and the formation of special departments in 1839. The first normal school was established at Albany in 1844. District school libraries were established in 1835, teachers' institutes in 1843. The creation of

FOUNDING OF AMERICAN SCHOOL SYSTEM

city school systems controlled by local board from 1837, and the Union School Law of 1853 were similar steps in the centralization of authority.

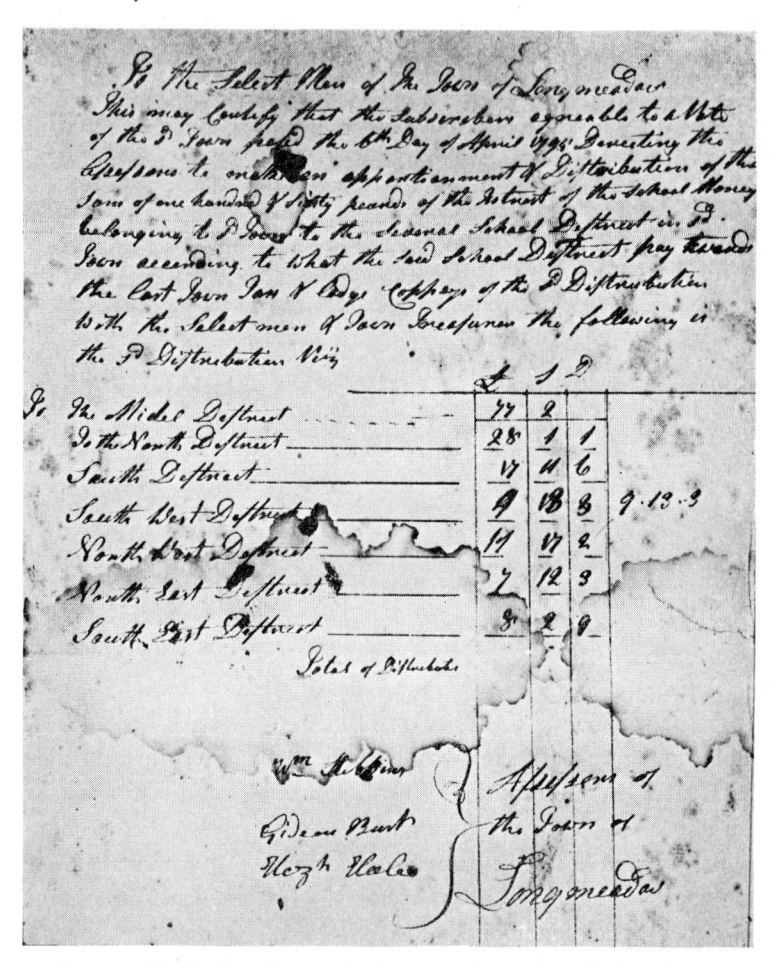

FIG. 57. Distribution of town funds among the various district schools. Longmeadow, Mass., 1795. (From MSS records.)

None of these changes were accomplished without extended public agitation and great efforts by the advocates of improved educational conditions. The entire period was one of controversy;

of repeated triumphs of the reactionary parties; and of the general education of public opinion in the support of free and efficient public education.

Development in the other Middle States followed a similar course but was much more retarded. Pennsylvania established a school fund in 1831, and a free school system based on the district organization in 1834 and 1836. These state schools were free but their establishment was a matter of local option. Where the free school was not established poor children were to be educated on the basis of the charity school provision. Half the districts of the state accepted the Law of 1834. Adoption of the system by all the counties was not achieved until 1886. This law made the Secretary of State the Superintendent of Common Schools. Consequently the office was filled by politicians until 1852, and no great educational advance was made. The educational revival in Pennsylvania occurred during the sixth decade of the century. County superintendents were established in 1854; normal schools were authorized in 1857; the office of State Superintendent was separated from that of Secretary of State in the same year. The Law of 1854 made the township instead of the district the administrative unit. From this time on there was rapid increase in the number of townships adopting the free school system, in the length of the school term, in the wages of the teacher; a curriculum adding geography and grammar to the three fundamental processes was required, and a system of county supervision was established. Local opposition to such advance in state control of education continued chiefly against this office of county superintendent; its virulence may be judged by the fact that at times mobs interfered with the attempted performance of the duties assigned. During this period also occurred the establishment of the graded school. In 1857 about 900 schools out of over 10,000 in the state were reported as having adopted the graded system.

Virginia and the Southern States.—In a previous chapter (p. 217) it was seen that the long conflict between the aristocratic and the democratic forces in Virginia resulted in 1818 in a system of elementary schools of the charity or pauper type similar to that of

Pennsylvania. These were dependent upon local interest for their continuance and a meager contribution from the Library Fund, as the state school fund was called, for their support. It was noted also that in 1829, in response to prolonged agitation on the part of the western and more democratic counties, a law was passed providing for the permissive adoption of a district system supported partially by local taxation. However, Virginia had no experience in this form of local government and no political machinery for it. Before the Civil War portions of four counties organized under this law. The greater part of the state—nineteen twentieths at least—preferred the freedom and the moderate expense of the old charity system. Sparse population, bad roads, inadequate teaching staff, lack of a system of local government, the sharp class organization of society, concentration of wealth in the eastern lowlands where large estates prevailed, the slavery system, political traditions hostile to all centralization and to an unrestricted electorate which would give voice to the poorer classes of people, all shared the responsibility for this condition.

During the decade of the forties Virginia was touched by common school revival of the country, due particularly in this case to the revelation by the Census of 1841 of the high degree of illiteracy in the state. Prolonged and widespread agitation, at least three popular conventions on education, much public discussion, many bills in the legislature, and finally the Law of 1846 resulted. This but slightly amended the existing laws of 1818 and 1829. A permissive county system was established; taxation was left to the counties, voting being permitted only on petition of one third of the electorate. Where the permissive system was adopted a county superintendency was established, the incumbent to be elected by the county board of education and to supervise the old voluntary system still made up chiefly of charity schools. The superintendent was to license teachers, the commissioners to supervise the schools and report to the State Auditor.

The Law of 1849 granted the widest option to counties and cities, but established no compulsion. As a result conditions varied widely. However, by the time of the Civil War approximately one

SCHOOL SYSTEMS FROM 1830

fourth of the state had adopted the principle of common schools, but only in a few instances was there that provision for local taxation that was essential to make the system effective. For the most part there remained tuition schools, with charity funds for the poor.

In North Carolina a literary fund had been established in 1825. Prolonged agitation, the consideration of many bills by the legislature, and finally the realization that one third of the white population of the state was illiterate led to a permissive free school law in 1839. Counties were permitted to establish a free school system under a board of superintendents, with the district as a unit. Each district was to receive $20 by tax and twice that amount from the library fund. Such a sum was far in excess of that raised or received by many of the poorer districts of New England. But because of the hostile social sentiment, fostered particularly by the friends of the private or old field schools, the stigma of pauperism adhered to those using free schools, and the system never flourished. Lack of supervision, financial as well as educational, was also detrimental. In 1853 a State Superintendent with supervisory powers was created. The incumbent until 1865 was Caleb H. Wiley, who performed a service for his state similar to that of Mann in Massachusetts. Increased attendance, lengthened school term, better qualifications for teachers, an extended curriculum, a state school journal, subsidized normal study, a quickened public opinion, and a better qualified teaching body were some of the results. In 1860 the length of the school term, the rate of stipend to teachers, and the proportion of school population in attendance were all greater than at any other time during the next forty years.

In Georgia a school fund was created in 1817, and in 1822 a charity school system, similar to that of Pennsylvania and Virginia, was established on this support. In 1837 after a study of the New England schools this system was replaced by a free school system for all white children. But three years later the state reestablished charity schools. The system was more accurately named here than in the North, for it was called "the poor school fund plan." While this plan was improved from time to time and free or common school experiments were permitted in various localities,

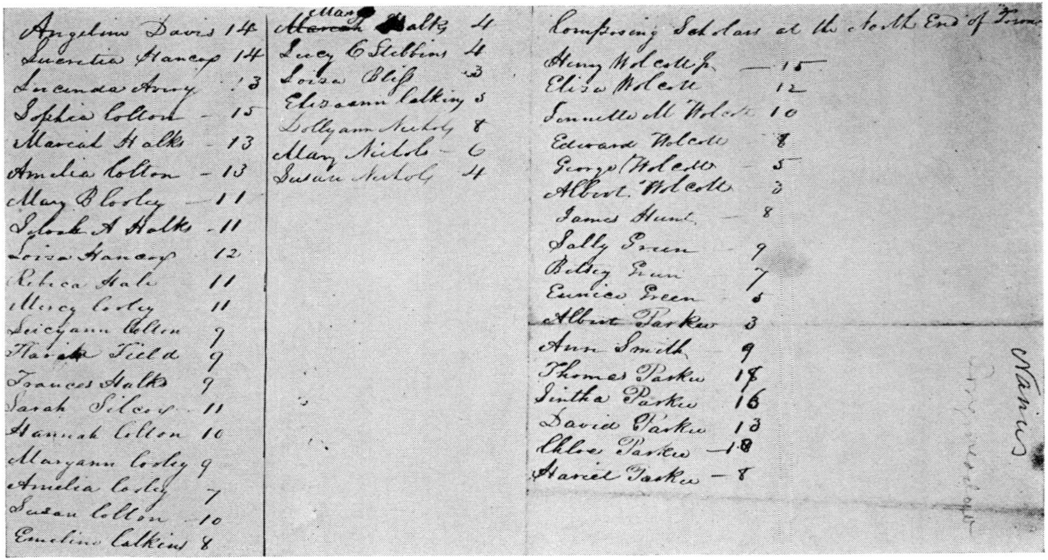

FIG. 58. Roster of children attending district schools, showing diversity in age. Longmeadow, Mass. (From MSS records.)

SCHOOL SYSTEMS FROM 1830

the system remained essentially unchanged until after the Civil War.

Other Southern states had similar experiences, though the development was more retarded than in the commonwealths mentioned. In them all, the lack of a middle class of any extent and influence prevented large developments of the free school system projected by the law.

The Middle West.—It was in the new region of the Middle West, untrammeled by tradition, strong in initiative, and able to profit

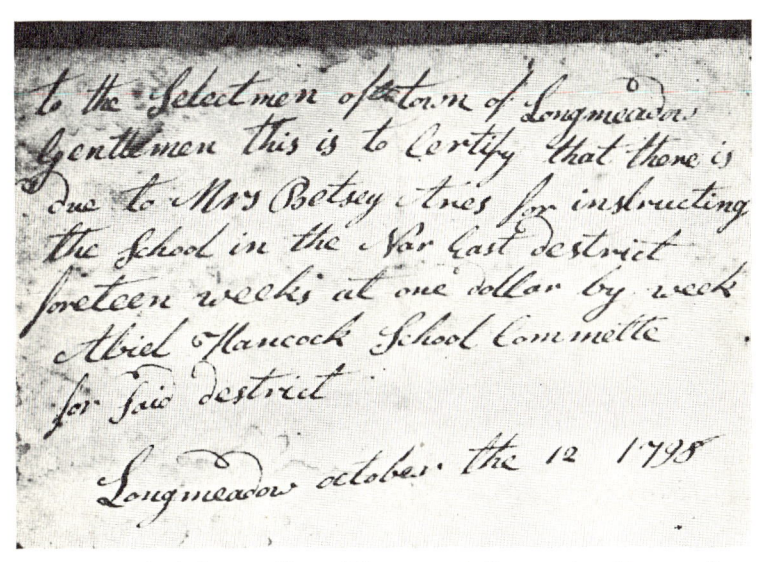

FIG. 59. Schoolmistress paid one dollar per week. Longmeadow, Mass., 1798. (From MSS records.)

by the experience of the East and South, that the chief progress was made during this period. In Ohio early settlers from New England were influential. It was the first state to profit by the common school fund founded by the Ordinance of 1785 (p. 195). Several educational organizations were formed and conventions were held during the early thirties. A Superintendent of Common Schools was created in 1837 and a General School Law passed in 1838. A state tax, a county tax, and a permissive district tax were levied; township superintendents as well as district trustees were created; towns and cities were made separate districts. The inevitable reaction followed during the next few years and all of these advanced provisions were modified, the state superintendency being abolished. Later special legislative privileges for the cities provided for continuous advance. In 1847 county superintendencies were created, to be annulled six years later. In 1847 also teachers' county institutes were established, school reports were required in 1848, separate schools for negroes were established during the same year, and in 1849 the curriculum was enlarged to include grammar and geography.

Ohio and practically all the Middle Western States adopted new constitutions during the early fifties (Quos. 384, 385). These made more liberal provision for public schools and laid the basis for free schools as well. The rate bills were abolished in 1853, though all schools were not free until considerably later. Graded schools were established and the powers of the district school were again limited by the creation of township and county officers.

In Indiana the early population, drawn largely from the Southern states, resented centralized government control of education and favored private institutions, subsidies by the state, and a highly decentralized district system. Indiana was the first state to make constitutional provision (in 1816) (Quo. 317) for a general system of education, ascending in regular gradation from township schools to a state university "wherein tuition shall be gratis and equally open to all." The state university or seminary was early realized; permission for township schools was given in 1816, though with no provision for their support; and in practice the schools were not free until after the Civil War. In 1833 the township system was replaced by the district system, each district having the power to determine whether it was to have a school or not, and only those patronizing the school being obligated for taxes. This was but another form of a tuition-supported school. By a law of 1836 a householder might employ his own teacher, drawing his share of state funds. Still later the requirement of a teacher's certificate was made optional with each district, and private and

SCHOOL SYSTEMS FROM 1830

church schools were permitted to share in the public moneys. Decentralization could go no further, and from this time the steps in the opposite direction were continuous though slow. General taxation of all property for schools was established and county supervision begun. Free schools appeared in 1848, by referendum in 1851, and by legislation in 1852. Legal enactment, however, was negated for almost twenty years by court decision.

Fig. 60. The district school in New York. (From an illustration in Washington Irving's *The Legend of Sleepy Hollow*.)

The development in Illinois was similar to that in Indiana with the interesting addition of a law (in 1827) which forbade that any citizen should be taxed for school purposes without having previously given his consent in writing. The chief interest of the early Illinois history lies in the conflict between the southern part of the state, populated from Southern states, and the northern, settled somewhat more tardily from the East. The former adhered to private and church schools, to decentralized control, to rate bills rather than to school tax, the latter to more centralized author-

FOUNDING OF AMERICAN SCHOOL SYSTEM

ity and community standards. In 1837 a modified township control was introduced, and the joint district and township system has persisted to the present day.

Fig. 61. The district school. (From a painting by W. L. Taylor.)

Michigan furnishes the best illustration of the influence of experiments other than those from the East and South for both French and Prussian ideals shaped her early laws. In 1817 control over education in connecting towns and cities was given to a central body. Little came of this scheme. In 1827 a system of common schools independent of the university and modeled after

SCHOOL SYSTEMS FROM 1830

the provisions of the early Massachusetts law was adopted. This was a township system with support by public tax, but was soon changed to a rate bill system which persisted until 1869. The first effective state law (1837) combined state and local taxes with rate bills, gave local control with centralized supervision, and created an appointed state superintendent and board. Little real progress was made toward a free public school system until after the Law of 1850.

Summary.—During this period population increased nearly 150 per cent; foreign immigration on a large scale began; negro slavery greatly increased but became confined to the Southern states. The number of cities multiplied. Economic changes were great, per capital wealth doubled, the Northeast became a great manufacturing region; internal improvements in roads, canals, and railroads took place on a large scale; numerous inventions were made; the ocean carrying trade flourished. Means of communication were multiplied; national roads were built; the telegraph was invented; the postal system expanded; railroads were built; newspapers sprang up everywhere; the political system became more democratic; and the influence of the masses of the people especially through the expression of views of the laboring classes became marked in education. Their influence in the establishment of a free school system was great. European educational ideas and practices were popularized and a number of influential reports on education in Europe were published. Educational magazines were established and educational literature of all types multiplied. Numerous professional leaders aroused great public interest in education and initiated popular movements of reform. The changes advocated include most of the essential features of the present day educational system. Many of these reforms came in through educational ideas imported from Europe, such as the monitorial system, the infant school system, the Fellenberg plan, and Pestalozzianism, most of which have long since lost their significance. The reform movement, as it centered in New England through the efforts of Horace Mann, was most conspicuous. Grading and classification of pupils were introduced. The district system of schools dominated; union school laws were adopted to eliminate the evils of the district system. State machinery of school administration was elaborated; centralized control in various forms was developed out of the district system or out of the quasi-public societies. These permitted centralized administration through superintendents of schools, and introduced grading and supervision. Controversies concerning the religious and secular character of public education occurred throughout the period. The American principle of the non-religious character of public education was established in its extreme form. Efforts at adult education were general. The outcome of the period was the general establishment throughout the country of the free public school system.

Chapter X

EDUCATION MADE FREE

The Problem of the Support of Education.—No other single problem connected with education presented greater difficulties to our forefathers than that of its support. To begin with, most of them agreed with Jefferson that that government is best which governs least. Certainly they believed that government to be best which taxes least. But they quite generally disagreed with Jefferson when he held that the support of education is one of the undoubted responsibilities of government. Even in populous communities, the protection of property against fire and against marauders was left largely to private care. The cleaning and lighting of the streets was still a private obligation. Benjamin Franklin had been the first even to organize private groups of citizens for better fire protection and street lighting. Outside of the more thickly settled regions, government had given but little attention to the building of roads and the fostering of means of communication. However, after the troubles with Europe at the close of the Napoleonic wars had been settled, and the opening of the great Western territory had resulted in the addition to the Union of new commonwealths unhampered by traditions of limited governmental functions, there came a period of great internal improvement fostered by government.

In addition to indifference to education and disbelief in governmental activity in this field, the actual poverty of the times precluded any great assistance to education. So it happened that a variety of plans for the support of education were tried before the people could be brought, by dint of hard experience, to pay for schools out of their own pockets.

Yet the theoretic belief in the necessity of universal education in a democracy was very general. Thus various attempts were made to support some scheme of universal education without actually depending upon complete support through taxation. To us now some of these appear quite puerile, many of them woefully inadequate, all of them futile. Yet some have left an indelible impression on our public school scheme. A number of these plans representing important stages in our educational development are worthy of attention. The first of these plans was characteristic of the Central and Southern states and will be illustrated by the experience of Pennsylvania and Virginia.

Charity or Pauper Schools (Quos. 439-445).—The Pennsylvania Constitution of 1790 contains this section: "The legislature shall as soon as conveniently may be provide by law for the establishment of schools throughout the state in such manner that the poor may be taught *gratis.*" This was the only provision concerning schools. It had been adopted after a prolonged controversy in which the representative of some of the communities settled by New Englanders had advocated a scheme of public support with which they were familiar. That they were far ahead of the times, however, is indicated by the fact that the next constitution of Pennsylvania, adopted in 1838, contained this same provision concerning the schools as that of 1790. In fact, there was no other constitutional provision on the subject of education until 1874. When the support of free schools became acceptable to certain communities and was made optional by law, its constitutional basis was found in the fact that the provision quoted above did not actually forbid the establishment of schools in which all children, rich as well as poor, should be taught free.

Laws of 1802 and 1804 actually established a system of charity schools. These laws obliged all schoolmasters or mistresses who taught reading and writing in either the English or the German language to receive and teach all such poor children as should be recommended to them by the poor authorities. Payment for the instruction of these children, at the usual rates, was to be made by the poor authorities. Thus the system of private schools or church schools in vogue at the time was made to serve the purpose of a public school system by taking in all poor children. This is the

EDUCATION MADE FREE

simplest and at the same time the most comprehensive scheme of the charity schools. A few years later it was made obligatory upon the assessors of the county to take the census of all school children and to report those that were entitled to receive free instruction. The teachers were compelled to keep a record for each child of each day of attendance, the subjects taught, the amount of books and materials furnished. The parent, on the other hand, had to make public acknowledgment of his poverty in order to receive this assistance.

Not a single school was established by these laws, but the private school became a thriving institution. Nevertheless the system was disliked by the teacher, it was offensive to those in smaller communities who had to send their children to schools attended by paupers, and it was hated by the beneficiaries of the system themselves. However, it was not opposed to the general social scheme which was yet dominant, and was a very fair expression of the political and social ideas of public men. It received the support of the private and the church school societies, which profited by it both in the receipt of fees and in the number of children thus brought under their influence. Even in 1818 when the schools of Philadelphia were organized into a system and the city instituted the first district of Pennsylvania for free schools, the benefit of the system was limited "to indigent orphan children or children of indigent parents." These schools were not open to all children until after 1836 and then were still considered charity schools.

About this time two means of escape began to be advocated. In the cities the organization of public school societies using the monitorial method permitted the teaching of large numbers of children at a small cost. The contributions of philanthropists, together with subsidies from state or city, enabled such societies to provide a free education for large numbers without making this discrimination between the rich and the poor.

The second means of escape advocated was through the establishment by the state of a general school fund (Quos. 450, 455) whose income, it was hoped, would in time suffice for the support of schools. In succeeding years a variety of modifications of this scheme were adopted. One, in force for a few years, set three years as the limit of time during which the child might receive free (pauper) education. Another gave to two or more contiguous townships the right to establish a joint school and receive their share of county funds for the education of poor children. In time many of the defects of the system became obvious. There was no actual establishment of schools to meet local needs; there was no supervision or control of these schools whatever. The number of children attending school was only a small part of the children of the community. It was recognized, even in official reports, that the scheme in many regions was wholly inoperative and in many others was much abused. In 1829 it was estimated that there were 350,000 children in the commonwealth between the ages of five and sixteen, though at this time there were less than 5000 being instructed on state support and less than 5000 in the monitorial schools of the chief cities. The private schools probably did not reach half of the children. Thus the system was recognized as utterly inadequate to meet actual conditions. At the same time it became evident, with the growth of the spirit of democracy, that the system was out of harmony with the actual political structure and the social ideals of the time. Public memorials began to reach the legislature calling for a school system more in harmony with these ideals. A Society for the Promotion of Public Schools was formed to foster public agitation to this end. The public schools became a matter of discussion in the newspapers and of continuous consideration by the legislature. Finally, in 1834, a law was enacted giving permission to each locality or county to maintain a free school.

The educational experience of Virginia is typical of that of most of the Southern states. In 1811 the permanent school fund was established under the title of the Literary Fund for the purpose of "providing schools for the poor in any county of the state." When the income from this fund amounted to $45,000 per year it was to be distributed on the basis of the white population and used for the education of indigent white children. From that

EDUCATION MADE FREE

time until the Civil War this fund was ostensibly devoted to this purpose. In reality so great was the indifference to free or charity education that, notwithstanding the provisions of the law, most of the fund was used for other purposes. A few excerpts from the reports of the various county commissioners from the period just preceding the Civil War indicate very clearly the character and the defects of the system. The Commissioners of Clark County report: "Many prejudices exist against the system owing to false pride, and children grow up in ignorance rather than be educated from public funds." Those of Augusta County wrote: "The main defects of the system are lack of funds and a prejudice among the people against poor schools." The general inadequacy of the system to provide schools is indicated by the report of the Commissioners from Fluvana County who wrote: "There are no schools especially established by the government but several are confined to indigent children and there does not appear to be any difference in the progress of indigent and other children." The report of the commissioners from Matthew County is typical of the attitude of school officials: "Commissioners do not visit the schools; teachers are not selected by them; they have to send the poor children to schools already established." The indifference of the parents, almost universal, was recognized by the Commissioners of Rappahannock County who submitted that "the parents of many indigent children cannot be prevailed upon to send their children to the schools."

Thus the charity school borrowed from England of the eighteenth century became a part of the general scheme for the support of public education in the early National period of the United States, and the feeling which it engendered against free popular education became a part of the public opinion of a large element of the population and of one large section of the country.

Support of Schools by Public School Societies.—Experience had familiarized the public in almost every colony with the support of schools through private organizations. The churches had been the chief means of such support and the Society for the Propagation of the Gospel had also operated in almost every colony. Un-

FOUNDING OF AMERICAN SCHOOL SYSTEM

der the influence of this society or in imitation of it, many local societies had also been founded, such as the South Carolina Society for the Free Education of the Indigent; Library Societies, even

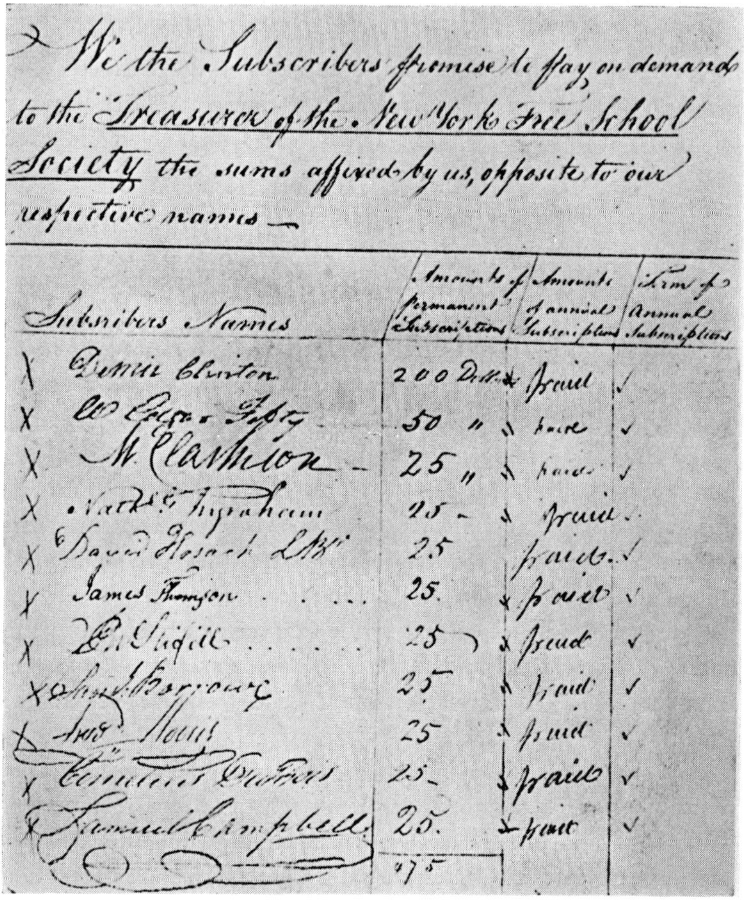

FIG. 62. First page of subscription book for support of the New York Public School Society. The first entry on the next page is for $5. Subsequent entries are for that amount or less. Governor Clinton heads the list with a $200 subscription. (From Palmer, *The New York Public School,* p. 22.)

societies for the advancement of learning, had been formed during this period. After the Revolution the English societies withdrew, leaving many communities hitherto but inadequately supplied

EDUCATION MADE FREE

with schools now with almost none. Private enterprise and philanthropy came to the rescue, though with very inadequate results. The cities were the homes of these organizations, for here the want of education and the need of assistance for the education of the poorer classes was most obvious.

New York City (Quos. 454–458) probably furnished the best example of support by societies, as well as the one which endured longest, since public education was thus maintained wholly until 1842 and largely for ten years longer. Private schools were multiplied after the Revolution. In 1798 associations of private school teachers existed. In 1805 there were estimated to be 141 teachers of private schools in the city. But a great majority of the poor children were still unprovided for. After the close of the Revolution the charity schools of a few of the churches were reopened. In 1785 the Manumission Society was founded, the first president of which was Governor Jay. In 1787 this society opened a school for the negroes which it maintained until amalgamated with the Free School Society almost half a century later. In 1802 a Friends Association for the Relief of the Poor opened a school for girls.

In 1805, stimulated by this example, a number of philanthropic citizens received a charter from the legislature for a "Society for Establishing a Free School in the City of New York for the education of such poor children as do not belong to or are not provided for by any religious society." This association included representatives of the best people of the city, both English and Dutch. Funds were collected amounting to about $6000 for the first year. In 1806 the first school was opened with sixty-seven pupils taught on the Lancasterian monitorial plan. The following year the city granted a schoolroom in the almshouse, together with funds, and the society took over the education of the children of the almshouse. A year later the state legislature granted a subsidy of $4000 for building and $1000 a year from the state educational funds, while the city gave an additional building. This year the title of the association was changed to the Free School Society. In 1809 the first building was erected, planned after the Lancasterian monitorial school, the one room accommodating 500 children.

FOUNDING OF AMERICAN SCHOOL SYSTEM

From time to time hereafter the state and the city made additional appropriations, the latter continuously, while legislature permitted it to participate in the state school funds after 1816. Trinity Church and other bodies also contributed. Additional buildings were erected and schools opened, and in 1819 girls as well as boys were accepted, special schools being provided for them.

In 1826 the society was reorganized on a tuition basis as the Public School Society. It opened the schools to those paying rates for tuition, but still admitted a large number of pupils on the charity basis. This plan continued for five or six years, with the result of developing a caste spirit and an opposition between the fee-paying scholars and the pauper scholars which injured the discipline of the school, aroused the bitter antagonism of the church schools, caused dissension in the board and threatened the very existence of the society's work. After six years the fee system was abolished and notice was given that admission was free to all. The schools had now been graded; primary departments and advanced grammar grades were included, as well as a course for the training of teachers which practically amounted to a rudimentary high school. Meanwhile the society had taken over the work of the Infant School Society together with that of other associations formed earlier. The state and city contributions had greatly increased with the growth of the number of students.

However, as early as 1822 a controversy with the various religious associations had broken out. A similar controversy arose under the free system because of the competition of the church schools. Again a few years later a controversy arose, particularly with the Roman Catholic Church, over the character of the religious matter in the textbooks. Various factions now demanded that these schools should become city schools. Consequently in 1842 a Board of Education was formed and the city funds for schools put at the disposal of this board. Competition with the city schools necessitated the employment of a number of teachers instead of the old monitorial scheme. This greatly increased the expense while at the same time the income became much less. Finally the state legislature approved the attitude of the city government and refused to grant further funds to the school society. Consequently this organization was merged with the Board of Education in 1852. Having the record of educating more than 600,000 children and 1200 teachers, it turned over 115 schools and property valued at more than half a million dollars.

In Philadelphia (Quo. 456) a Society for the Establishment and Support of Charity Schools was organized in 1799. This society maintained a day and an evening school, and in 1811 established an industrial school where girls were taught sewing, cutting, and the making and mending of garments. A few years later the "Association of Friends for the Instruction of Poor Children" established schools, again on the monitorial plan. In 1830 Matthew Carey, a noted political economist, wrote an essay entitled "Public Charities of Philadelphia," in which he enumerated twelve different societies interested in the support of public schools, listing the number of pupils under instruction, the amount of each society's contributions, and the value of its property. Of the most important of these, somewhat similar to the Public School Society of New York City, he says:

"Although the Institution for the Support of Public Lancasterian Schools does not, strictly speaking, fall within my plan, I think it may not be amiss to devote a few lines to its details. It was organized in 1816. There are at present nineteen schools, ten in the city and nine in adjacent districts. About 30,000 children have been educated in them. The average number at one time is 4000. The cost to the city and county averages about six dollars each per annum. The boys are received between the ages of six and fourteen; the girls between five and thirteen."

Among these associations was the "Society for the Promotion of Public Schools" founded in 1827, typical of many such organizations all over the country. This society was not directly concerned in the support of schools, but was particularly interested in the agitation for the establishment of the public school system (p. 208).

The $6000 contribution with which the New York Society began its work does not seem a large sum for the school system of the second city in the land, with 18,000 children to be educated. Yet it is to be borne in mind that the chief income throughout its history came after all not from private parties, but from the city and the state. The usefulness of these societies lay not only in their persuading the philanthropists to contribute but also in their educating the populace through local and state governments into a willingness to assume the entire expense of an adequate public school system.

Though the record of the Public School Society in New York is by far the most conspicuous and spectacular, it is not at all unique. In very many towns as well as in the larger cities the public schools were founded in this manner. By no other means did it seem possible at this time to secure funds adequate for the education of all poor children.

Lotteries as a Means of School Support (Quos. 459-463).— The call of the highest ideals being inadequate to secure sufficient support, appeal was also made to the lower instincts of gain. It will be recalled that there was scarcely a Colonial college that did not resort to the lottery as a means of income. While there was growing recognition of the incongruity of supporting religious education in this way, the general moral condemnation of the lottery had not yet become common. Consequently it was frequently adopted or at least projected as a means for supporting schools. Advertisements in the earlier newspapers reveal this as an expedient frequently used for the community school. Moreover, the lottery played quite a prominent part in the origin of a number of our school systems.

The most conspicuous of these cases was that of the state of New York. In 1801 when a law subsidizing district schools had expired, an act was passed authorizing lotteries for the raising in four successive years of $100,000, seven eighths of which was to be distributed for the assistance of schools. When the Common School Fund was established in 1805, the portion of these lottery proceeds appropriated to the common schools was merged with it. The constitution of 1821 forbade all lotteries and brought an end to this educational scheme, which worked for evil as well as for good.

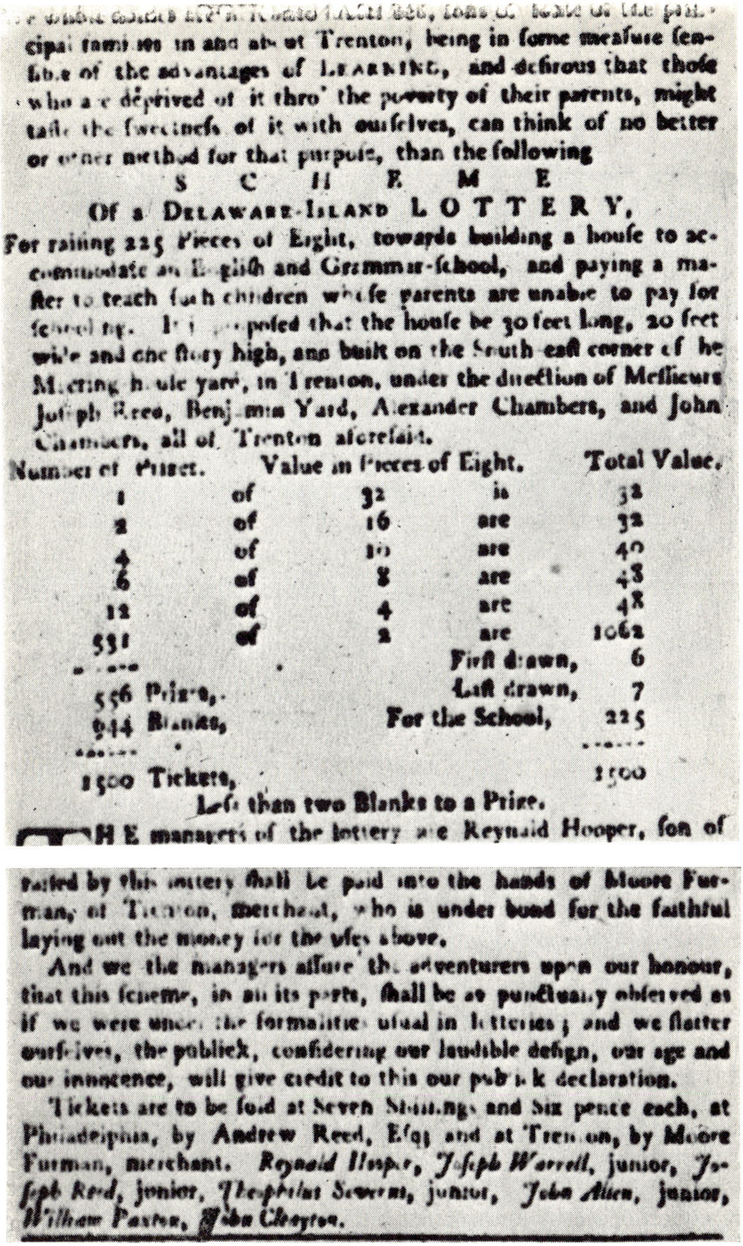

...which consists of a Board and Faculty, some of some of the principal families in and about Trenton, being in some measure sen-
sible of the advantages of LEARNING, and desirous that those
who are deprived of it thro' the poverty of their parents, might
taste the sweetness of it with ourselves, can think of no better
or other method for that purpose, than the following

SCHEME
Of a DELAWARE-ISLAND LOTTERY,

For raising 225 Pieces of Eight, towards building a house to accommodate an English and Grammar-school, and paying a master to teach such children whose parents are unable to pay for
schooling. It is proposed that the house be 30 feet long, 20 feet
wide and one story high, and built on the South-east corner of the
Meeting-house yard, in Trenton, under the direction of Messieurs
Joseph Reed, Benjamin Yard, Alexander Chambers, and John
Chambers, all of Trenton aforesaid.

Number of Prizes.	Value in Pieces of Eight.		Total Value.
1	of 32	is	32
2	of 16	are	32
4	of 10	are	40
6	of 8	are	48
12	of 4	are	48
531	of 2	are	1062
		First drawn,	6
556 Prizes,		Last drawn,	7
944 Blanks,		For the School,	225
1500 Tickets,			1500

Less than two Blanks to a Prize.

THE managers of the lottery are Reynold Hooper, son of
...raised by this lottery shall be paid into the hands of Moore Furman, of Trenton, merchant, who is under bond for the faithful
laying out the money for the uses above.

And we the managers assure the adventurers upon our honour,
that this scheme, in all its parts, shall be as punctually observed as
if we were under the formalities usual in lotteries; and we flatter
ourselves, the publick, considering our laudable design, our age and
our innocence, will give credit to this our publick declaration.

Tickets are to be sold at Seven Shillings and Six pence each, at
Philadelphia, by Andrew Reed, Esq; and at Trenton, by Moore
Furman, merchant. *Reynold Hooper, Joseph Worrell, junior, Jo-
seph Reed, junior, Theophilus Severns, junior, John Allen, junior,
William Paxton, John Clayton.*

FIG. 63. Advertisement for the support of schools by a lottery. (From *Pennsylvania Gazette,* April 26, 1753.)

Rhode Island adopted the lottery as a means of adding to its permanent school fund when this was created in 1828, and continued its use for fifteen years.

In the Southern states lotteries had been quite commonly authorized by the trustees of various academies and colleges for the support of these institutions. In 1825 North Carolina provided that the state should share in all funds so raised, its portion going into the common school funds. Shortly after this, however, the morality of the use of lotteries, especially for the support of education, was attacked in the legislature, and this source of income was prohibited (Quo. 460).

In Georgia, the use of the lottery was combined with the disposal of public lands, perhaps in recognition of the fact that there is a common element in the two schemes. Not only did most of the states give their sanction to this form of school support, but the national government itself set an example. The first two public schools established in the District of Columbia were paid for by lotteries. Congress passed as many as fourteen joint resolutions from time to time authorizing lotteries in the District of Columbia for educational purposes.

It is interesting to note the arguments set forth for and against the use of lotteries. Not only are such arguments an index of the public morality of the time but they indicate the great change which public sentiment was undergoing concerning the entire scope and meaning of education as well as the obligation of public support. "What other way is left," asked one legislator, "but by lotteries to obtain this assistance (for education)? We could not expect a donation from the public treasury. What do we come here for? Is it not for the purpose of adopting measures to advance the character of the state and to improve the conditions of the people? And what measures are so sure of these results as those which foster and establish schools? Do not let us manifest by the rejection of this bill that we place but little value on the benefit of education. It is known that our laws license the lottery system and that in every part of the state individuals are engaged in vending tickets created for the benefit of their state. I can see no reason for withholding from the friends of literature the privilege of raising funds for purposes connected with the best interests of our citizens. It is certainly good policy to keep our money at home, for persons will venture and if no opportunity exists at home they will seek it elsewhere. . . . From the first establishment of our government acts have been passed authorizing lotteries. The practice was not confined to our own state but has been sanctioned by other members of the Union. Is it possible that they would have been countenanced so long if they were productive of the great evils which have been attributed to them?"

While individual schools were assisted by this means, no great results were accomplished, and lotteries for schools died with the clearer perception of public morality and the growth of general intelligence.

Permanent School Funds (Quos. 450-455).—Even when the political leaders were converted to the policy of state subsidized or supported schools, the masses of the people showed little interest in them. The New York subsidy from 1795 to 1800, which required each township to contribute a sum equal to that received from the state, did not induce half the towns to apply for the state aid. There is no indication that a single county of Virginia accepted the idealistic scheme of Jefferson in 1786. The aversion to state support for schools, indeed to taxation of any kind, was too great. Consequently it was necessary to work out some method for the support of schools which would avoid arousing the antagonism of the people. The most generally approved scheme was that of a permanent fund, to be gradually built up, the income from which would eventually afford sufficient aid to induce the local communities to maintain schools. At first many believed that such funds would be adequate for the entire support of education.

The colonists had been familiar with the permanent endowment of the individual schools or of the schools of a town. These endowments usually consisted of land and occasionally were granted by the general Colonial government. By laws of 1726 and 1733 Connecticut adopted a policy which reserved a portion of the common land of the unsettled towns as the source of a school fund for all the towns of the colony. The plan was consummated by the sale of lands in 1783. The Connecticut settlers of Wyoming Valley in Pennsylvania adopted the same policy in 1768. In 1783 Georgia decided to subsidize a school in each township with 1000 acres of public land, though few allotments were called for. But it was the adoption of the Connecticut plan by the National Government in 1785 and 1787 which encouraged the individual states to follow this policy.

In 1795 Connecticut established a permanent school fund and made provision for the sale of her public lands in the Western Reserve in Ohio, which netted $1,200,000 and became the original principal of this fund. In 1805 New York, after the lapse in 1800 of the attempt to establish a state system of schools and the wholly inadequate and unsatisfactory measure of the state lottery, appropriated 500,000 acres of state land as a permanent fund for the support of common schools. The interest on this fund was to be distributed among the towns as soon as the annual proceeds amounted to $50,000, which came to pass after eleven years. Few of the original thirteen states had sufficient unappropriated lands to attain adequate support or even encouragement. Connecticut had her "Western Reserve"; Massachusetts possessed public lands in Maine, which were used for the school funds of both states after Maine was admitted in 1820. Some of the states, as New Jersey and North Carolina, used all swamp and saline lands for this purpose. Eight of the original states, together with Maine, and later Texas, used in this way unappropriated public lands. Those having no land for this purpose were Rhode Island, Delaware, Virginia, Maryland, and South Carolina. For practically all the states admitted after 1800, the vast public lands granted by the Ordinance of 1785 afforded a princely endowment—which in most cases was dissipated with princely prodigality.

Extension of the Plan to Every State.—Some of the states, not having land, established general funds for the purpose. The first of these was Delaware, which in 1796 provided that all moneys accruing from marriage and tavern licenses should be set apart as a fund whose interest should be distributed to support elementary

EDUCATION MADE FREE

schools. Later a bank tax was added. The Virginia fund, established in 1810, was so constituted, and included all escheats, confiscations, fines, penalties, forfeitures, and all rights on properties accruing to the state. South Carolina established a fund in 1811 from some of the sources used by Virginia. The Maryland fund was constituted in 1812, out of the tax on banks. The Rhode Island fund was established in 1828 upon a direct appropriation from the legislature and the revenue from a lottery.

Of the states admitted between 1789 and 1802, Vermont established a fund in 1825 out of funds already existing, arising from taxes on banks and licenses to peddlers. Tennessee, admitted in 1796, was granted the public lands in her domain by Congress in 1806, and at once devoted a portion of them to the establishment of a school fund. Kentucky established a "literary fund" in 1821 from the net profits of a state bank.

Thus it is seen that every state at one time or another established such a fund; at present all except Pennsylvania and Georgia possess one. Every territory except Alaska and the District of Columbia is also provided with one.

Other Sources of Revenue.—Though public land was the commonest and the most extensive form of endowment, yet in the early days public land was worth little and school lands received little care. Consequently, especially in all of the older states, it was necessary to find other sources of revenue. Fines, escheats, and licenses of various kinds were used in many states. None of these sources afforded much revenue except the excise license, which was granted in but one state. Fully half the states have appropriated all estates without legal heirs to this end. While in time it became quite common to use the sums accruing from the license of the liquor trade, in almost every instance this was reserved as a source of local revenue, to which the states had no right. One popular source which appealed to the financial vision of the time was the revenue from banks, for many still believed that the state could manufacture money or create wealth. So portions of the revenue from state banks and taxes on other banks were quite commonly used. Four states, New York, Rhode Island, North Carolina, Georgia, used lotteries. Florida employed funds derived from the sale of slaves.

In most of the original states direct appropriations of state funds have been made at some time to increase this fund. New Jersey in 1817 and Texas in 1845 provided that one tenth of all funds raised by state taxation should go into such a fund. Most of the states have provided from time to time that the funds returned to them by the National Government should be devoted to the increase of the common school fund. Thus the revenue of the United States deposit fund, ten million dollars, distributed among the state banks in 1833, was so used by some. Various war claims granted by Congress to several states from 1828 to the present time have been so used. Thus in 1891 a Federal war tax of twenty millions levied in 1861 was returned, and several states appropriated their quota to the fund. The most important of all these grants from the general Government was the Surplus Revenue Fund of 1837 amounting to about twenty-eight millions. A portion or all of this fund was devoted to the common school fund by every state except four.

The sources employed by the states to provide a fund for the support of schools are thus seen to be varied. Just how these funds have been used, their value and influence, remain to be noted.

Management of These Funds.—These funds were established when, outside of New England, the American people had had little experience with public support of schools and held little belief in it. When the funds were established by the states under the direction of leaders who probably believed in the necessity of building up a public system of education, the administration of the funds was usually put into competent hands and considered a part of the state government. When the funds were viewed as belonging to certain local areas, as towns or counties, there was no such oversight and the use of the funds was not nearly so effective.

The Ohio Act of 1802 provided that "section number sixteen in every township ... shall be granted to the inhabitants of such township for the use of schools." An act of the following year gave the legislature right of control in trust for all these lands. The policy of the general government was not always clear or consistent; that of individual states varied. In some states the township had

EDUCATION MADE FREE

control; in others, the county for the towns; in still others the state managed the entire funds. In some states different policies were pursued at different times; in some different policies for different portions of the fund at a given time.

The defects of the local management were many. The funds were apt to be manipulated in the interest of the local community. As the early settlers were concerned chiefly with the increase of population, with the clearing of land and the economic prosperity of the locality, and had little belief in public schools, gross carelessness and incompetence, even dishonesty, were tolerated in the administration of the funds. There was no responsibility to higher authority, so these evils went unchecked. There was little continuity of management, so the actions and plans of one official were not carried over to the next. Public officials, state as well as local, connived at the actual use of school lands or funds for other purposes. This was done by legislation for years in succession in some states, as in Virginia. In few states was there any adequate legislative protection for these funds.

When mismanagement became gross and conspicuous, the movement for the transfer of authority to the state government grew strong. Coinciding with the development of a belief in the common schools and with the tendency to greater centralization of governmental power, a more centralized form of control came to prevail. This evolution was greatly assisted by the recognized inequality and injustice of the plan of local distribution. One of the state superintendents recently has said: "the sections set aside for schools in Colorado represent land of every class from the highest grade of mineral and agricultural lands to the comparatively worthless arid lands fit for grazing purposes only and in many instances too barren and desolate even for this purpose." In older states where arid lands did not exist, Section 16 might fall "on barren highlands or in the swamp." Consequently the use of all the lands as a common fund for all the states proved both more just and more effective.

Wasteful Neglect and Loss of the Funds.—When belief in public schools was weak or even non-existent, but that in individual rights and the necessity for the sturdy economic development of the local community strong, little care could be taken to preserve and develop a fund for the benefit of posterity. Especially would this be true when the fund existed in land, the holding of which might block local development, and which originally belonged to the people anyway, and where land was to be had for the taking. There seems to be something peculiarly harmful to individual as well as to public morality in the opportunity for profit out of public or common land. Certain it is that the mismanagement—to use no more harsh or correct a term—of these public funds and lands is one of the most humiliating features of our history, certainly of our educational history. Hardly a state but has experienced a shameful misuse of public property and shameful betrayal of public trust. In all a conservative estimate gives $27,500,000 as the sum thus dissipated. This does not include the sale for fifty cents an acre of land which with a little judicious management might have been worth several times as much. For thirty-three years the school fund of Connecticut practically maintained the schools of that state with a revenue of from $72,000 to $135,000 per year. As the Connecticut schools were frequently spoken of during this period as the best in all the states, it seems probable that the sums dissipated would have been sufficient for the support of a similar system for the entire country up to the Civil War. A superintendent of a Midwestern state where the system of county control existed thus described the system:

"Had the funds been properly taken care of, the income from this source (the permanent school fund) would be sufficient to sustain the schools for at least six months in the year. . . . To say that these funds have been grossly and shamefully diverted from their original purpose is putting the case in a mild form. Many of the county courts in utter disregard of the trust imposed upon them, have not only allowed the funds and lands to be used for purposes foreign to their original purpose, but in many instances have entered into combinations with corporations and individuals to so manage these moneys and lands that they have fallen into the hands of private parties. An act was passed last winter (1869) to recover these lands. The provision of the act itself defeats the very object for which it was enacted. In nearly every instance where lands have been disposed of not in accordance with law, the blame rests with the county court. By provision of the act above referred to, where lands are recovered by suits instituted by attorneys appointed under the act, they shall be allowed such sums for their services as may be deemed reasonable by the county courts of the county in which the lands recovered are situated.

"The county court is not going to stultify itself by first making an unauthorized sale of lands, and then pay counsel to show that the contract they have made is void. . . . They will employ counsel to defend their action. . . . There is a criminal responsibility resting somewhere for the gradual wasting away of the public school fund."

The first superintendent of another state wrote: "School land in Ohio has been taken at six dollars per acre, worth at the time fifty dollars." A national historian writes: "There is no more melancholy chapter in American history, than the record of the amazing waste of this great national gift to the people. . . ."

Some states have appropriated practically all of the funds. Sequestration by the state in time of war when the debt is afterward assumed as a permanent obligation is not here considered a misappropriation. But in few states was the offense so venial. In eight states —all but one in the older portion of the country—the common school fund is wholly or in large part a credit fund, which exists only as an obligation of the state the income of which in reality comes direct from the people by taxation. In fifteen states this is true for a considerable portion of the fund.

Use and Significance of the Permanent School Fund.—The originators of these funds had expected them eventually to furnish adequate support for a free school system. Hostility or indifference of the people to such schools defeated this purpose and caused a great diminution of the endowment. It is stated that only one county in Florida attempted to make the intended use of the original county endowments. Some counties of other states never even claimed their share of the surplus revenue distribution of 1837. Nevertheless such funds were a great factor in educating the people to the need of and a belief in public schools, and since then have become a means of assisting poorer communities and attracting all to a higher standard of efficiency. A brief experience was sufficient to demonstrate that these endowment funds were not adequate to support a school system. This end was never accomplished except in one state, Connecticut. Following the loss of this hope, educational leaders believed that the proceeds of these funds would be sufficient to relieve local communities of the rate bills, or charges for tuition, levied on the children attending. This was accomplished to a considerable extent, notably when the income was distributed on condition of a local tax of equal or greater amount. This restriction could be imposed only when the state had complete control. In such cases the use of the state money was frequently limited to the payment of teachers' salaries, thus warranting more nearly adequate payment for teachers, and forcing the community to furnish houses and equipment. In other cases it was used for teachers' institutes or for other means of securing the professional training of teachers.

Where this fund was distributed to local communities only on compliance with certain conditions, it performed its greatest service. In New York and most of the New England states it was given only when local communities raised by tax a similar sum. In twenty states it has been distributed only where schools are maintained for a minimum period varying from three to nine months. The most common and one of the most useful requirements is that of reports to a central authority describing local school conditions and work. In a few states it was given only when a specified course of study is followed; in others only when school accommodations and equipment reach a certain standard. In some it has been used to furnish free textbooks, in others to maintain attendance or enforce truancy laws. In some, the school attendance must reach a minimum figure; in others the school must be under supervision of a legal official. Thus it will be seen that while the device of the permanent school fund did not fulfill the original expectations of its founders, it did become a factor in bringing about the establishment of such schools and an instrument for increasing their efficiency when established.

Passing notice at least must be given to the one state where the fund did accomplish its original purpose. In Connecticut from 1821 to 1854 the proceeds of funds were used to support a system of free schools, and all state and compulsory local taxation for schools disappeared. Connecticut, the first state to establish such a fund (1795) had preserved a large land endowment which was speedily turned into cash. Though at first this fund was badly mismanaged here as elsewhere, in 1810 the money was placed in the hands of a competent official. This commissioner of the state fund served as the only state supervisory officer of education until a state board was established in 1839. The laws of the early National period had removed the Colonial requirement that the district or town should maintain schools for any minimum period of time. The law of 1801 permitted the closing of the schools whenever the funds distributed by the state were exhausted. With the gradual increase of the funds from the state the inclination to raise funds by local taxation declined, and practically disappeared. In 1821 the state tax was discontinued and for thirty-three years the schools of the state were maintained solely by the revenue of the permanent fund. In 1854 President Porter of Yale wrote, "It is not known that a single town or school society in the state raised a tax for school purposes by voluntary taxation." From 1821 the amount distributed to each district was about $30. As the average salary for teachers as late as 1838 was less than $15 per month for men and less than $6 per month for women, it will be seen that some sort of school could be maintained for two or three months. The report for the same year showed 1018 men teachers and 1109 women teachers, which at the average salary would give a monthly salary list of $21,000. As the distribution from the school fund for the year was almost $96,000, a school session of four and a half months was possible. The general effects, however, were deplorable and the character of the teacher, the quality of the school, the length of the term, all tended toward the lowest level. This was on the eve of the educational reform movement, and for the succeeding years we have complete reports on the system, revealing the indifference of the general public to school conditions, the neglect of local officials to perform their duties respecting schools, the low character and qualifications of the teaching staff, the indifferent attendance of pupils, the unhygienic and poverty-stricken character of the schoolhouses, the growth of illiteracy, and the development of a caste system. This last condition resulted from the general development of private schools supported by the well-to-do through the system of rate bills now to be described. Both within and without Connecticut it was generally recognized that the total support of public schools by the state fund had worked disaster. Though the schools were supposed to be publicly supported, they were really not free; for the rate bills persisted until 1868.

The Rate Bill System (Quos. 446–449).—This was merely the reverse of the charity school system. In Pennsylvania, and in general in the states to the south of it, public school funds were used to pay the tuition fees of poor children to enable them to attend the private schools which flourished in great numbers. Such children became charity scholars, and where they dominated the schools became charity schools. In New England and New York and in general in the states to the west of them, including the states of the Northwest Territory, schools were maintained as public and the teacher was paid primarily out of these funds. However, his salary was materially increased by the rate bill or tuition tax levied upon every child attending whose parent was able to pay. Here the tuition rate was fixed by legal authority and usually collected by such. The rate bill system might operate in either of two ways. The rate bill might be assessed throughout the school term and collected as the local tax was collected. This was the New York plan. Or the school might be maintained as a free public school as long as the public funds would last and then continued for all the scholars paying these rates. The latter was the plan more commonly used, as in Connecticut, Michigan, Illinois, and elsewhere. In many states it was left to the community to choose the plan of operation.

In general the states which had the charity schools boasted the absence of "the odious rate bill system"; while those which adopted the rate bill system congratulated themselves that they did not have "the odious charity school system." To their beneficiaries the systems were equally odious.

It will be recalled that this method of school support was common throughout Colonial New England. This was the form which grew up under the sanction of the Law of 1647, which also authorized a town tax "by way of supply." Under the stress of a high standard maintained by state compulsion the schools gradually became free (p. 110). But during the early National period the standards of length of term and character of studies were greatly lowered or wiped out altogether. Consequently rate bills again came into quite general use. Maine boasted that they were never used in its territory. But elsewhere, even in New England, they were a common resort and did not disappear until a free school law was passed. This was usually after prolonged agitation. The principle at stake was not whether there should be a public school system, but whether the obligation of support rested primarily upon the parent, upon the local community, or upon the state. Colonial experience had not been able to establish the last named principle permanently, and it had never been announced by law as obligatory. During the early National period, the policy was not sufficiently developed to demonstrate the principle. The sentiments of individualism, of aversion to a strong government interfering with personal rights, of dislike of taxation for any purpose, were yet too powerful to permit the overthrow of the old schemes for placing the burden of the cost of education upon the parent or guardian of all save pauper children.

If the charity school system was offensive because it placed a stigma on all the children who benefited by the public school fund, the rate bill system was equally so because it kept such children out of school. School laws in those states where the rate bill system prevailed usually made provision for the payment of the rates of poor children by local authorities. In New York the law required the district trustees to make such provision. Yet in 1851 the official reports showed that a large majority of the 11,000 districts made no such provision and that nearly 50,000 children were prevented from attending school because of inability to pay the rates. In 1866, the year before the abolition of the system, the state report showed that 2327 districts made provision for poor children, while 7764 districts did not. At this time nearly one and one-half million dollars of public money went to the support of public schools in that state. Yet they were free "only in the sense that good dinners at our best hotels are free dinners. They are free to all those who will pay the price for them." So wrote the State Superintendent.

Another serious objection to the rate bill system was that it placed a premium on short or irregular attendance. The law in New York and in most states made the amount to be paid for each child depend upon the number of days he was in attendance. Consequently the oftener the child was out of school, the less burden there was on the parents. In a similar way the system tended toward the employment of a teacher having the least possible qualification and consequently willing to accept the lowest salary. When a well-qualified and "high-salaried" teacher was employed or when the term was long, the tendency was for many to keep their children out of school and thus to increase the burden for those who remained. Poorer people who really believed in schooling often resorted to the expedient of sending one child at a time. Thus was established the too prevalent American attitude towards school attendance as a right or privilege, not an obligation.

In 1839 Henry Barnard reported to the legislature of Connecticut on this system, combined with dependence on the Common School Fund as follows:

"It is difficult to frame a law to operate more unfavorably, unequally, and in many instances more oppressively than this. Owing to the reliance now placed on the public funds—to the almost entire abandonment of property taxation—for the support of schools, it leaves the question of the continuance of a school beyond what the public moneys will pay for, to be decided under the most unfavorable circumstances. There is not only the ordinary pecuniary interest to decide against it, but it is increased from the fact that all the abatements for poor children must come upon them who send to the

EDUCATION MADE FREE

schools. This, in many instances, if the school is continued a suitable period as far as the good of the children is concerned, makes the school-bills nearly equal to what they would be if their children were in private schools. Again, many of them who are thus required to pay the bills of their poorer neighbors are just able to pay their own, and the addition of a single penny beyond that is oppressive, so long as its burden is not shared by the whole community. . . . As to this portion of our school law, I have found but one opinion prevailing among the most intelligent men practically acquainted with the working of it—that it is radically defective. Instead of having within itself a principle of interest which, by its ever-recurring pressure, keeps the sensibility of every individual alive to the subject without oppressing any, it now operates not for the benefit of the poor, for they remain unaffected by it anyway, but to encourage men of property to withdraw children from school and throw the burden of supporting the schools upon those least able to bear it."

Such reports were made year after year by school officials and yet it was not until 1868 that the rate bill system was abolished in Connecticut and the schools made free.

In some states the rate bill system was made compulsory, that is, parents were compelled to pay the rates for their children of school age, or to take oath to their financial inability. This was the rate bill system in its most offensive form, arousing the opposition of those who were opposed to public education in principle and of all who objected to paying taxes. The form of legal warrant used in Michigan (1859) (Quos. 448-449) which follows will indicate the operation of the system.

(Warrant)
To the Assessor of School District No. . . . , in the Township of . . . ;

You are hereby commanded to collect from each of the persons in the annexed rate-bill named the several sums set opposite their respective names in the last column thereof, and within sixty days after receiving this warrant, to pay over the amount so collected by you (retaining — per cent for your fees) to the order of the Director of said District, countersigned by the Moderator; and in case any persons therein named shall neglect or refuse, on demand, to pay the amount set opposite his name as aforesaid, you are to collect the same by distress and sale of goods and chattels of such persons wherever found, within the county or counties in which said District is situated, having first published said sale at least ten days, by posting up notices thereof in three public places in the township where such property shall be sold.

At the expiration of this warrant you will make a return thereof in writing, with the rate bill attached, to the Director; stating the amount collected on said rate bill, the amount uncollected, and the names of the persons from whom collections have not been made.

The decline of the rate bill system was very gradual—that is, it followed a prolonged struggle in each state; for its disappearance meant the establishment of the free school system. The establishment of the free school, however, depended not merely on the negative change—the abolition of the rate bill system—but also on the positive factor—the development of local taxation for school purposes.

Local Taxation.—It is now a commonplace that an effective school system must rely for support chiefly upon local taxation. The actual establishment of the free school system depended upon the development of the willingness and the ability of local communities to tax themselves for school purposes of all kinds. While Massachusetts and to a lesser extent other portions of New England had arrived at the complete support of schools by local taxation during the Colonial period, most of this ground had to be rewon during the early nineteenth century. It must be borne in mind that much of the spirit of revolution and rebellion in the latter eighteenth century was against the exercise of any strong governmental power, and especially against the power of taxation. The rebellions in Massachusetts, Pennsylvania, Rhode Island, and elsewhere following the Revolution revealed this attitude. There was no great accumulation of wealth in the country until after 1830, when commerce and manufacturing gave added value to national resources.

The Massachusetts Law of 1789 removed the requirement of a minimum length of term, following which the standard of attainment as well as the amount of support were greatly reduced. Re-

EDUCATION MADE FREE

sort was had here as elsewhere to the rate bill system. The Law of 1827, however, abolished these and for the first time Massachusetts required each town to support its schools by taxation. Permissive local taxation was of little effect in many states and the response was unsatisfactory even under the best conditions. Mandatory constitutional provisions were of little effect. The first constitution of Indiana in 1816 provided for a free school system from primary school

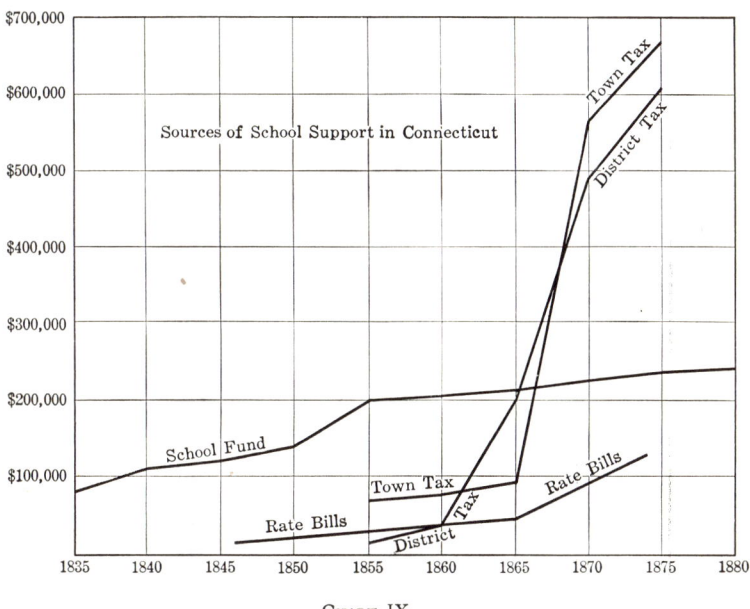

CHART IX. Sources of School Support in Connecticut

through the university. But as late as 1855 a local tax for payment of teachers' wages was declared unconstitutional. As the teacher's wage was the essential expense to be met by local taxation, a free school system under these conditions was impossible. The rate bill system took its place.

New York furnishes one of the best illustrations of the relation between the development of local taxation for school purposes and the establishment of a free school system. The law of 1795, which for five years maintained a state system, required that each county raise by town tax at least one half of the sum contributed to it by the state. Towns in sixteen out of the twenty-three counties took advantage of this law, but not half the children of school age were shown to be in the schools even for a short period. The next law, of 1812,

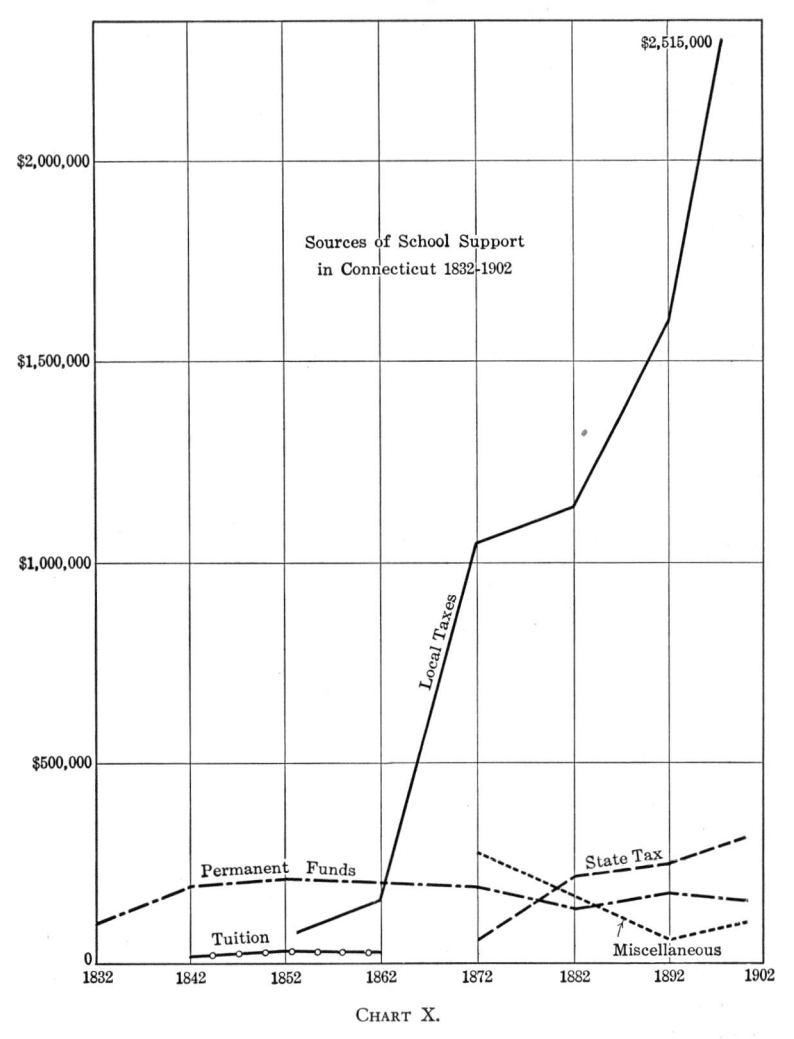

Chart X. Sources of School Support in Connecticut 1832-1902 — showing Local Taxes rising to $2,515,000 by 1902, with Permanent Funds, Tuition, State Tax, and Miscellaneous as additional sources.

required each town participating in the state funds to raise a sum equal to that contributed by the state. However, the towns were so unwilling to assume this obligation that in 1814 participation and

[322]

EDUCATION MADE FREE

local taxation were made obligatory. As seen long afterwards such obligatory laws were frequently not enforced. On the other hand the state appropriation was small and could meet only a small part of the actual cost of schools. Consequently many communities raised from the first much more than an equivalent sum. The chart subjoined gives in a visual form the actual relation of the state contribution to local funds. From 1815, when the local funds were some fifteen per cent greater than the state contributions, the difference increased rapidly until 1835, when the local communities were contributing five times as much as the state. Yet these sums were so inadequate that dependence upon the rate bills became greater. This is shown by Chart 3. In the hope of making the schools entirely free, and in the face of the opposition of the people to schools supported by local taxes, the contributions from the state were greatly increased. Finally, by act of 1851, the legislature made possible a state tax of almost a million dollars. The result of this is shown by the two diagrams (pp. 321–322). As seen in Diagram I, the local contribution fell off and by 1855 amounted to scarcely half the state contributions. On the other hand, as shown by Chart 12, rate bills greatly increased proportionately until they amounted to more than the local taxes. In absolute sums, the local tax fell about one half, the rate bills a slight amount, and the state tax made amends for both. Taught by this, the friends of free education attacked the old system intrenched in the rate bills. By 1865 local taxes had been increased until they were six times what the state contributed and four times the amount of the rate bills. The final extinction of the rate bill system in 1867 aroused hardly any opposition. Experience in other states was similar.

The Indiana case previously cited is of peculiar interest, because of the principle involved. After varying experience with inadequate school support the constitution of 1851 had provided for "a general and uniform system of common schools, where tuition shall be without charge, and equally open to all." Three years later the supreme court decided that if localities were permitted to improve their schools by local taxation, "the uniformity of the common school system would be at once destroyed." On the ground that

FOUNDING OF AMERICAN SCHOOL SYSTEM

the public system must be both general and uniform, local taxes for payment of teachers were forbidden and even those for school buildings were questioned. The court held that "when the state had raised a common school fund by uniform assessment and taxation she has attained the contemplated uniformity in that respect. When she had distributed the fund equally to all entitled to it she has attained uniformity in that respect." So in the name of equality and

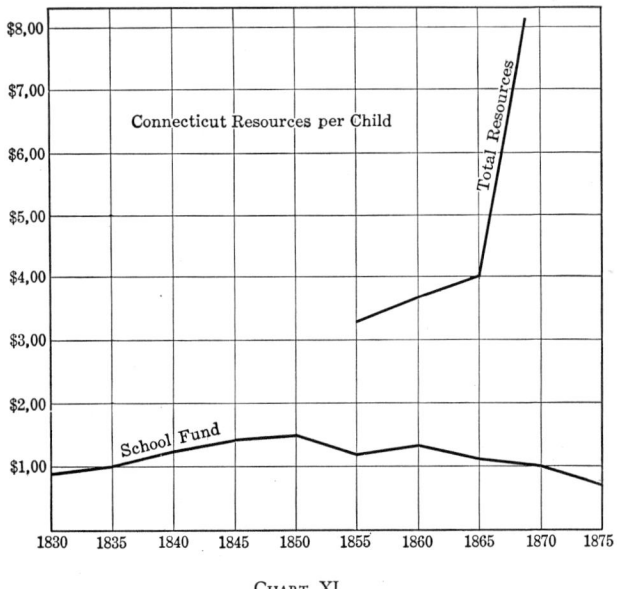

CHART XI.

democracy, the one force that could build up a nation based on these principles was destroyed. The funds provided would maintain schools for less than two months and pay salaries of not quite $55 per year. Not until fifteen years later did the legislature pass a law sustained by the court which permitted local taxation. On this the public school system was built up.

The history of any of the states during this period will furnish illustrations of the importance of local taxation as a factor in establishing the free school.

The Final Establishment of the Free School System.—This, as we have seen, was accomplished through the elimination

EDUCATION MADE FREE

of rate bills and of payment of fees for charity pupils, accompanied by the development of the willingness and ability of local communities to tax themselves sufficiently to support schools. The final transfer from the old system to the free school system was consummated in most states without disturbance, even without exciting attention. But the agitation preparatory to this change was often prolonged and bitter. To us now it is surprising to see the tentative manner in which the leading educators of the day approached the problem. The School Superintendent of New York in 1845, addressing the leading educative officials and teachers of the state, said: "I do not hesitate to say that it is my opinion that in the end we shall find free schools in all respects the best adapted to our wants and condition; and I am persuaded that as a matter of economy they are preferable to any other system." Even so great and far-sighted an educational leader as Henry Barnard, who in his early career had fought for free schools, came to the defense of the rate bill system in Connecticut in the sixties and held it preferable to free schools because it developed local interest.

In New York this controversy was prolonged from about 1840 to 1867 and was the dominant problem of educational interest during that period. The public agitation for free schools was begun by the State Association of County Superintendents in 1845 and continued with the aid of teachers' institutes and state superintendents. In 1849 a free school bill was passed, but it met with very general local opposition which revealed itself in the following legislative session. The question was the main issue in the election of 1851. Forty-two of the fifty-nine counties voted for repeal. The majority in favor of the free school was 25,000, but unfortunately the members of the legislature were chosen through the counties. It is of interest to note that the counties in favor of the free schools were those containing cities. The outcome was the great increase of the state appropriation for education noted in the previous paragraph (p. 323) and the retention of the rate bills. Following this the system was attacked piecemeal and by methods of popular education. In 1853 a law was secured which permitted two or more districts to organize into a union district and to make the schools entirely

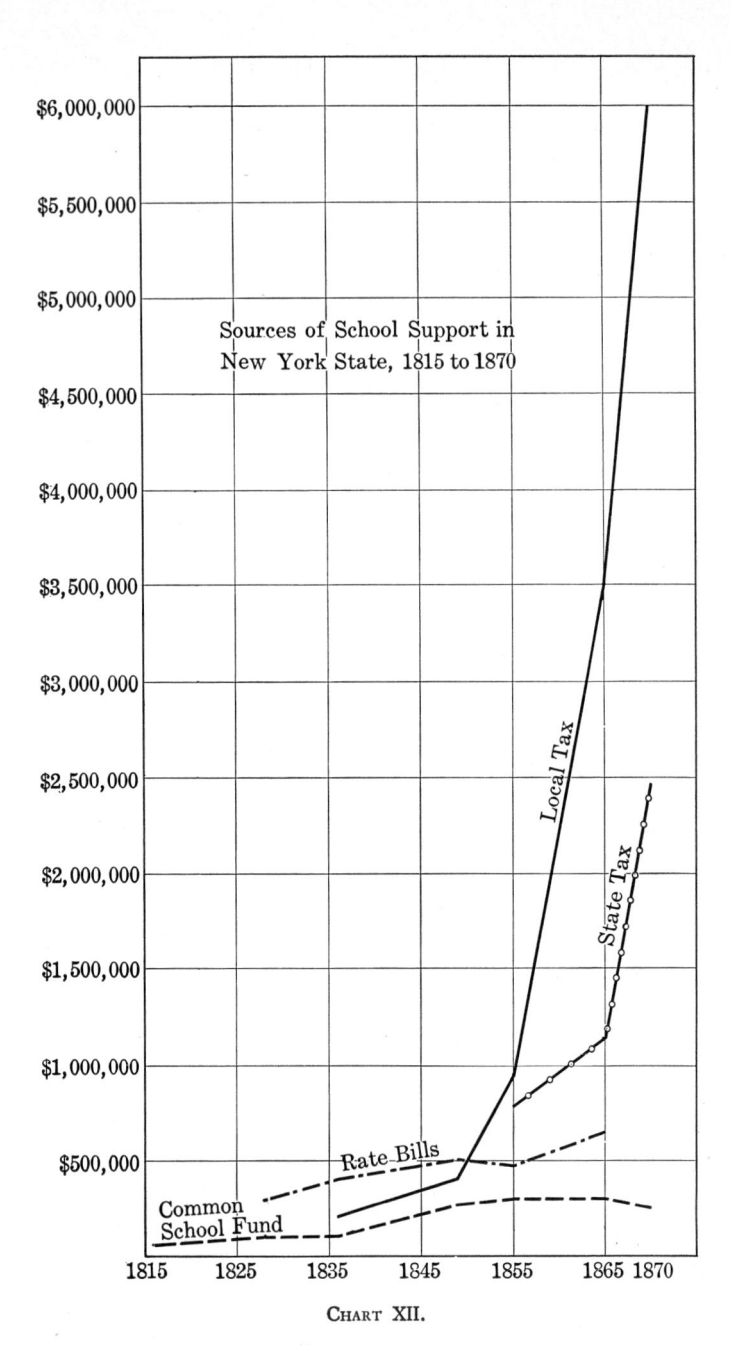

Sources of School Support in
New York State, 1815 to 1870

CHART XII.

EDUCATION MADE FREE

free. This many cities, towns, and villages did. In 1864 a law required that the schools of all such union schools should be free. As all the populous centers were now possessed of free schools which were manifestly superior to the rate-supported schools of the rural regions, little opposition was made to the passage of the law in 1867 abolishing the rate bill. Thereafter all schools participating in the state funds were to be maintained free of tuition charges.

In Pennsylvania the principle of the free school was established by law in 1834. But here as elsewhere a clear distinction must be made between a constitutional provision or a permissive law and an actual system in operation. The Indiana Constitution of 1816 made a clear announcement of the free school principle. It was 1871 before the system was an accomplished fact. The historian of education in Pennsylvania states: "Public schools in Pennsylvania have always been entirely free. Pupils were never required to pay tuition fees." This may be true if a public school is defined as one supported wholly by public tax, not otherwise. The Law of 1834 establishing the free school system was permissive. In 1836 it was amended to allow any district to vote every third year on the question of "school" or "no school." This is a free school by local option, but not what we now understand as a free school system. In 1848 this privilege of a triennial vote was taken away. But as late as 1874, after having connected to the free school a district which had always rejected it, the superintendent of that state wrote: "This ends the work in this direction. For the first time in our history the door of the public schoolhouse stands open to receive every child of proper age within the limits of the state."

In 1868 the Secretary of the State Board of Connecticut wrote (Quo. 473) to the executive officers of the education department of various states to get evidence which might influence his state to establish the free school system. A sentence or two from several of these letters will reveal the situation at that time.

From Michigan: "The public schools of Michigan have never been free.... The rate bill leads many parents to take their children from the schools as soon as public money is expended. I should be pleased to see the schools made free, and an obligation imposed upon all parents and guardians to send the children to the schools. I am aware that compulsory attendance upon the public

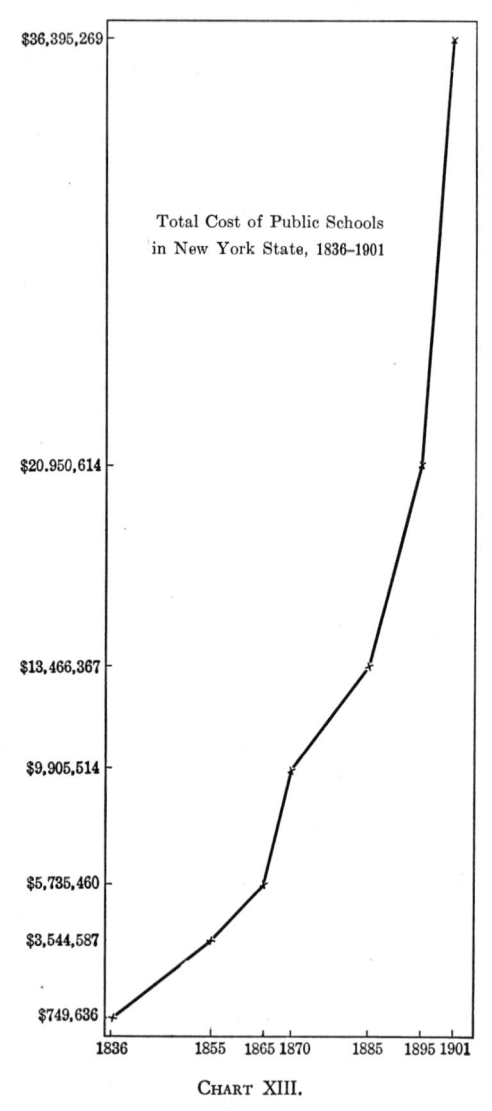

Total Cost of Public Schools in New York State, 1836–1901

CHART XIII.

schools is deemed by many contrary to the genius of our government. But if the safety of our institutions depends upon the intelli-

EDUCATION MADE FREE

gence of the people, where is the oppression in the requisition? That cannot be deemed oppressive which furnished a stable foundation for the government."

From Ohio: "The rate-bill system once prevailed in this state, but since 1853 our schools have been *free*. The change from the old system (which we borrowed from Connecticut) to the new was marked with decided progress. The attendance was greatly increased; school terms were lengthened; better schoolhouses were erected; and a new public interest in the schools manifested. Indeed so satisfied are our people with the *free* feature of their schools, that you would have to search 'with a lighted candle' to find an advocate of a return to rate-bills."

From New York: "For many years before the 'odious rate-bill' was abolished in this state, it had been gaining a very bad reputation. It kept thousands of children out of school; it was, substantially, a tax upon parental affection and solicitude, and a stumbling-block in the way of knowledge. Its operation could not be defended, and its abolition met with no objection. Its existence had been infamous.

"The Law of 1867, providing free instruction to all the children of the state, though it did not go into operation till October, has already resulted in an average daily attendance at the schools of the country districts 20 to 35 per cent greater than during the same period in the previous year. It has already been found necessary from this cause to increase the accommodations for the children in many districts. A state tax for support of schools is more equitable than taxation of counties and smaller localities."

From New Jersey: "Yours containing inquiries relating to the effects of making our schools entirely free, is received, and I regret to say that as our schools, like your own, are also partly supported by rate-bill, I cannot give you the information you desire. From your letter I judge you are striving to make your schools free; I too am striving for the same object. We, as American citizens, fail in providing for the greatest safeguard to our Republic, just so far as we fail in providing free schools for our children. May the time soon come when 'tuition fees,' that great barrier between poverty and intelligence, may not be known in our land. We have no right to ask the poor man to pay for the education of his children. It is capital that is made more productive and more valuable by intelligence in the community, and it is capital that should make education free."

From Illinois: "I have just had the honor to receive your favor of the 6th inst. Under our system, the schools are absolutely *free* for six months in the year, and have always been so. This is a condition precedent to receiving any portion of the public school fund. The local boards of school directors are empowered, by law, to levy any amount of tax necessary, with the public funds, to maintain the six months' free school; no vote of tax-payers is required.

"Our school also encourages the extension of the terms of free schools beyond six months. This may be done by the local boards, ad libitum, without a vote, if the public funds are sufficient for the purpose. But no tax can be levied for the purpose of such extension without a vote of the people (legal voters) of the district.

"Thus a six months' free school in every district of the state satisfies the letter of the law, and entitles to a full participation in the benefits of the public funds. During this period no rate-bills are allowed, or ever have been. Beyond this, it is optional with the people of each district, either to vote a tax to extend or not. If they vote against an extension, the directors may close the schools for the year, or permit private, 'subscription' schools to be taught."[1]

From Indiana: "1. Our schools are free. The constitution, in originating these schools, provided that they should be free; declaring it to be the duty of the general assembly to 'provide by law for a general and uniform system of common schools, wherein tuition shall be without charge, and equally open to all.' So long as these schools are open, they are absolutely free to all white children between the ages of six and twenty-one years. 2. These schools have been free since their origin, which was in 1852. 3. The effect of free schools upon attendance, interest of parents and public at large: (a) Attendance: When the free term closes and the school changes to a subscription school, a very heavy per cent of pupils

---

[1] The last clause of the second sentence in this letter may be questioned as to its exactness.

EDUCATION MADE FREE

withdraw, sometimes 25% and sometimes 40%, and even 60 and 70. In many cases no effort is made to continue the school as a pay school, there being no encouragement for such."

From Iowa: "The rate-bill system of schools was abolished in Iowa ten years ago. During the decade which has since passed, while the number of persons of school age has increased 91%, the number of schools has increased 130%; the attendance in the schools, 223%; and the number of teachers, 245%. During the same period, the compensation of male teachers has advanced 47%; that of female teachers, 90%; while the aggregate amount paid teachers annually has increased 486%. For the support of the common schools alone, Iowa annually expends upward of $2,000,000—more than nine-tenths of which is raised by voluntary taxation."

From Missouri: "I really apprehend the difficulties you encounter in your efforts to enlarge the system of public schools in your state with such a dead-weight upon it as the 'rate-bill' statute. We tried, in Missouri, to establish our system of common schools, engrafting the same idea upon it, in imitation of the practice of the free states, and especially that of Connecticut. Suffice it to say, it was proven by sad experience a failure; and, second to slavery, the prolific source of the inefficiency of the laws affecting public schools, and the consequent disgust and dissatisfaction of the people."

From Pennsylvania: "I have had no experience under the plan of the rate-bill public schools. Since 1834, the public schools of Pennsylvania have been wholly free."

From Rhode Island: "I answer your first and second questions by saying that our general assembly, at its present session, has abolished rate-bills, agreeably to my recommendation. 3rd question—my own experience is that the whole system of rate-bills is a mistake."

This is an official record which reveals how recently the free school system was established. The facts stated earlier in the chapter also reveal how these highest educational officers of several of these states illustrate a too common American habit of covering their own ignorance by substituting for an accurate knowledge of educational conditions laudatory buncombe which is far from the truth.

In the Southern states in general, the establishment of the free school system was subsequent to the Civil War. The general framework of the educational system of these states did not differ from those of the North, but the free school idea developed more slowly. It was incompatible with the system of slavery. The "charity school" plan prevailed and offered a free school only on that basis. In all the states, a development of a mandatory free system, in which tuition rates were debarred, was the product of the Reconstruction period and subsequent to 1868.

The dates for the abolition of the rate bills in a number of Northern states, when brought together, give a vivid reminder of the fact that the establishment of the free school system is of quite recent date: Massachusetts, 1827; Delaware, 1829; Pennsylvania, 1834 (optional, not complete until 1874); Vermont, 1850; Indiana, 1851 (by constitution; in reality, by permissive law, 1867); Ohio, 1853; Iowa, 1858; New York, 1867; Rhode Island, 1868; Connecticut, 1868; Michigan, 1869; New Jersey, 1870.

The Private School.—This institution accorded with the intense individualism of the American not only in allowing each citizen to follow his own choice in the education or the neglect of his own children but also in permitting anyone who wished to do so to adopt teaching as a means of livelihood. Undoubtedly both were important influences opposing the establishment of free schools.

As such private schools were without any supervision or control, it is impossible to give any definite idea of their number, the quality or grade of teaching, or the character of teachers. In fact the number varied from year to year or month to month, every grade of school existed and every subject was taught; the teachers were of every character.

The Pennsylvania Society for the Promotion of Free Schools stated in 1830 that there were 400,000 children of school age (five to sixteen years) in the state, and that there were not over 150,000 who attended schools of any kind. The society made a careful study of the state and found "that the average proportion of children educated in any one year, compared with the entire number of children between the above specified ages, is but one out of three." "Multitudes are living and continue to live in ignorance and multitudes more receive but the most superficial instruction." This, then, was the first effect of dependence on private schools.

If this was the situation where the charity school idea flourished, the conditions under the rate-bill system were no better. Private schools were recognized by both Horace Mann and Henry Barnard to be the most important factors in retarding the development of the public schools of Massachusetts and Connecticut. In the Fifth Annual Report to the Connecticut Board of Education in 1850, the latter wrote: "The extent to which this class of private schools are patronized by the wealthy and educated families of the state is at once the evidence of the low condition of the public schools and the most formidable hindrance to their rapid and permanent improvement. It draws off the means and the parental and public interest which are requisite to make good public schools, and converts them, in some places avowedly, into schools for the poor—as though, in a state which justly boasts of its equal privileges, there was one kind of education or one class of schools for the rich and another for the poor. It classifies society at the root by assorting children according to the wealth, education, or outward circumstances of their parents into different schools; and educates children of the same neighborhood differently and unequally. These differences of culture, as to manners, morals, and intellectual tastes and habits, begun in childhood and strengthened by differences in occupation, which are determined mainly by early education, open a real chasm between members of the same society, broad and deep, which equal laws and political theories cannot close."

While it is impossible to give an exact statement of the numbers of such schools as compared with the public schools, it is estimated that in general they were as numerous in either state as were the public schools, and that they drew for their support a greater amount of funds from their patrons than was devoted to the public schools themselves. In 1818 a school census of Boston was taken which found that there were 154 private schools in the city, eight charity free schools, and eight schools supported by the city. In the city schools there were 2365 pupils, in the charity schools 365, and in the private schools 3767. Samuel Adams, Governor of Massachusetts, in 1795, wrote in his message to the legislature on the private schools throughout Massachusetts: "Should these institutions detach the attention and influence of the wealthy from the generous support of the town schools, is it not to be feared that learning in the early parts of life may cease to be so universally disseminated as it has been hitherto?" Horace Mann was quite as insistent, as was Henry Barnard, in his opposition to the private schools.

Throughout the country the inadequate system of common schools was supplemented by a multitude of private schools. Over these there was neither supervision nor control. They taught what they wished in the manner they wished, collected such funds as they could, and were responsible to no authority except the public demand. Many indeed were of the higher type and were helpful in the development of the common schools in that they set standards of attainment. The historian of education in Indiana says of them: "It is not too much to say that for a generation private schools of high rank furnished a standard by which the efficiency of public schools was estimated"—a distinction which emphasizes Indiana's kinship with the ante-bellum South. But the private schools were no less a factor in those regions of the West which drew their educational traditions direct from New York and New England.

With the substitution of a free public school for all, without distinction of tuition rates or charity support, the private schools quickly disappeared. But throughout the period previous to the close of the Civil War they remained an important part of the accepted educational system, and at the same time constituted a formidable obstacle to the development of a public free school system.

Enumeration of Forces Working for and against the Free School System.—The influences working for (Quos. 435–438, 473–482) and against (Quos. 464–472) the establishment of the free school system may be summarized as follows: (1) Chief among the forces in opposition must be considered the political attitude of the people, which looked with great suspicion upon any increase of power or in fact any exercise of authority by the government, either local or central. The aversion to the exercise or to the authority of government in the collection of taxes was still very strong.

EDUCATION MADE FREE

These two forces were more fully operative and were influential for a longer time in the rural regions than in the urban, for in general the rural population made slower progress along political and social as well as along economic lines; (2) among minor forces were the aversion of large property holders or of the wealthy class to free schools, not only because of the objections mentioned above but because there was still no general belief that property of the rich was under any obligation to support the education of the poor; (3) the belief, still very general, that free schools exist for the poor only; (4) the fact that the small local area was the only condition of government under which free schools could be introduced at all; this made it difficult or impossible to distribute the income in an equitable manner, or at least in a manner satisfactory to the community, and resulted in neighborhood quarrels; (5) the too great dependence upon the common school fund or the rate bill; (6) the influence of the private school both as a vested interest of those who taught and as a class institution for those who patronized; (7) the indifference of the public officials, politicians, and of leading men; (8) in some localities the opposition of religious denominations, particularly the Roman Catholic; this, however, was not of great significance and often resulted in a movement toward the public schools rather than away from them; (9) the indifference of the teachers hardly yet organized as a professional body and largely controlled even yet by those interested in private schools.

The factors working toward the development of the free school system might be summarized as follows: (1) The growing perception by the people of the true nature of democracy was undoubtedly the determining factor; connected with this was (2) their belief in the necessity of universal education as the sole condition upon which our republican government could succeed; (3) a demonstration that the school funds, public school societies, and similar means could not afford sufficient support; (4) the realization that neither the charity school nor the rate bill was either satisfactory in its working or sufficient to the end in view; (5) the fact that the population was still very homogeneous and that immigration had not greatly developed; in Pennsylvania, where there was still a large element alien in language and to a considerable extent in custom as well as in religious belief, this element was a retarding factor; (6) the influence of great leaders such as Mann and Barnard and of wise statesmen such as Clintons; (7) the development of professional ideals which expressed themselves through teachers' organizations, conventions, and institutes, and the resulting formation of a teaching profession; (8) the creation in many states of educational officers having some centralized authority and thus becoming the mouth-piece for educational opinion, and the teaching profession; certain groups of people, such as the laboring class and the ministry, exercised very definite influence as did (9) the public press, together with public discussion.

The actual development of the free school, therefore, cannot be separated from the general political and social development of the fourth, fifth, and sixth decades of the nineteenth century. It was but a part of the growing democracy, the growing nationalism, and the economic expansion of this period.

Summary.—By the Ordinance of 1785 the National Government initiated a great endowment derived from public land grants, which was divided among the new states to form a permanent school fund. In time all the original thirteen states also created such funds by land grants or by funds from a variety of sources. The proceeds of these permanent funds were used to support common schools and to stimulate local taxation to this end.

In large centers of population, where such funds as well as those from local taxation were non-existing or wholly inadequate, voluntary societies, called either generically or specifically public school societies, were organized to furnish school facilities to the poor. With the formation of public schools these were gradually absorbed into the public system, though this did not happen in New York City until 1852.

The establishment of a free school system depended upon securing adequate means of support. At the opening of the National period the masses of the people were not committed in principle to the free school and had not been trained to tax themselves for it. One group of states, including Pennsylvania and those to the

EDUCATION MADE FREE

south of it, depended on the charity or pauper school; that is, the use of state or local government funds to pay for the tuition of poor children in private schools. As all the well-to-do believed in and patronized such private schools, they existed in great numbers. In New England, New York, and states to the west of these the rate-bill system was commonly adopted. By this the funds provided by the government for schools were used to support a teacher for as long a term as possible and the school was then continued by the assessment upon the patrons of rates for tuition. In some cases rates for tuition were assessed throughout, and those unable to pay remained without any schooling or had recourse to poor relief.

The rate bill continued as the normal system of supporting schools in most states until after 1850, in many until after the Civil War. Meanwhile ability and willingness to submit to local taxation increased. During this growth, the returns from rate bills gradually became of less significance, and with their abolition the schools were made free. This change excited prolonged controversy lasting in many Northern states from a quarter to half a century. In the South until after the Civil War there was little effort beyond the statement of theoretical principles to establish free school systems. In the decade following all these states did establish such systems legally; but economic as well as social conditions caused the adequate development of these systems to be slow. In general we may say that the free school was established in principle by the Civil War period and in reality shortly afterward.

Chapter XI

EDUCATION DEMOCRATIZED THROUGH ORGAN-IZATION, METHOD, AND CURRICULUM

Democratization through Organization, Method, and Curriculum. As these factors are but different aspects of the general education process it is not always possible to consider method apart from curriculum or from school organization.

In general it may be stated that democratization was accomplished for the rural and village population through the district system; and for the urban regions through the Pestalozzian system and through quasi-public school societies which adopted the Lancasterian monitorial (Quos. Ch. XVI, Pt. II) or the infant school (Quos. Ch. XVI, Pt. III) plan. While each of these means involved method, curriculum, and organization, yet the district system and Lancasterianism were primarily forms of organization, while the essence of Pestalozzianism lay in method.

Education Democratized (Quos. 510-517).—*Curriculum, Method, and Schoolroom Organization.*—There is no one feature of the public school system of America which has been so influenced by the democratic sentiment as that of method. Conversely, there is no feature of our school work, even to the present time, which is so influential in perpetuating the individualistic conception of democracy which we hold, as the methods in vogue in our public schools. In addition, the common method, as well as schoolroom organization, emphasizes and perpetuates a sense of equality. The one element of democracy which is not provided for through method, and which particularly needs emphasis in American life is fraternity or the community feeling, that is, the realization that each is contributing to a common product, which product when generalized becomes the welfare of the community as a whole. These characteristic features of our schools—individual-

EDUCATION DEMOCRATIZED

ism, equality, and fraternity—were fixed in this early period and have remained without very great modification.

In some respects these methods are in very marked contrast with those of the older countries. In the Continental European schools the teacher is the determining factor in method. Textbooks as a rule consist of outline or summary while the teacher furnishes most of the material. From these two the body of the subject is built up, while the pupils master or absorb. Recitation is usually the co-operative act of the entire class, each contributing materials gained from text or teacher until a satisfactory common product is obtained. For illustration, even in mathematics an example or proposition is seldom presented in recitation by an individual. The recitation is a group procedure, individual pupils contributing steps in the solution of a common problem.

In the American school the individualistic method of mastering material and of recitation has had profound influence on the character of society and on the development of the individual units which make it up.

Organization and classroom management at this time were simple matters, based on the ability of the master to control the conduct of his pupils by the use of corporal punishment. The universality of this harsh discipline, applied to young and old, boys and girls, is referred to by almost every witness. Horace Greeley speaks of one of his masters, in 1815, who rarely struck a blow. Such occasional evidence but confirms the custom. Horace Mann reports that when he began service between 300 and 400 schools were broken up each year in Massachusetts alone by the bad conduct of the pupils. In 1843 he congratulates the state that "last year according to the committee's reports only about forty schools were broken up from both causes of insubordination of pupils and incompetence of teachers." Evidently corporal punishment was not always effective. The custom of "testing out the master," thus challenging his ability to control through physical prowess, was a common one. Except in rare instances, no higher conception of interest than that of fear of corporal punishment prevailed until Lancasterianism or Pestalozzianism modified professional and public opinion. That

Mann should have met his greatest opposition on this point, in the most enlightened center, at the middle of the nineteenth century, is indicative of common opinion and of professional custom.

The schoolroom itself was usually a rude and uncomfortable place, intermittently cold in winter and hot in summer, overcrowded, unventilated except when broken windows or defective

FIG. 64. Barring-out day at school. (From a painting by Ralph Hedley.)

roof or floor afforded too little shelter. With insufficient light and air, no playgrounds, frequently no sanitary provisions, the "little red schoolhouse" and the district school have entered more into our literary and cultural traditions than has the school in any other country. Perhaps this is because our cities and our national culture have been largely built up by the youth from rural regions; perhaps because until very recent times we were as predominantly a rural dwelling people as we now are urban.

EDUCATION DEMOCRATIZED

There was a conventional arrangement of the schoolroom largely carried over from Europe. The master had his desk and high stool at one end of the room; the pupils sat on benches facing the wall, the latter furnishing support for a desk upon which to write. With the increase of pupils the smaller ones were given seats in the central space. Occasionally raised tiers of seats were used. Towards the middle of the century the Lancasterian plan of seats across the center of the room, or even desks for two pupils, came to supplement the older form. The earlier arrangement, however, persisted long in many regions.

Recitation and instruction were for the most part individual. Even where classes or small groups were found, this would still be true because of the dependence on the textbook, the particular text being wholly a matter of individual choice or chance possession. The "simultaneous" or class method of recitation was introduced by the Lancasterian system. This simultaneous method, however, implied concert recitation rather than the present meaning of the term "class recitation." The old district school achieved one of the chief results of the simultaneous method by the custom of "loud" study, in which each pupil studying at his desk vied with his neighbor in shouting the words of his lesson. At such times the simultaneousness resided in all *except* the one reciting.

Instruction was chiefly a method of having the pupil repeat *memoriter* the lesson learned (Quo. 514). Consequently much of the material was organized in question and answer or other forms which would assist memorizing. Only the teacher possessing sure insight and native ability developed a real teaching process. Successful teaching was rather a matter of schoolroom management than of skill in instruction. Consequently skill in management, whether through device, through fear, or through the frequent recourse to the authority of the rod, was the chief asset of the master. Successful teachers were jealous of their reputations, usually refused admission of teachers or others than the "committee" who wished to visit their work, and were hostile to teachers' organizations, meetings, and discussions. Even Joseph Lancaster, who was devoted to the propaganda of his method, refused to admit to his own classroom teachers who had come from long distances to see his work.

The conversion of the teaching profession, if such it may be called, from a belief in this conception of school management as the teacher's function to that of instruction based on interest and knowledge of the child's mind, was the chief accomplishment of the reform movement of the middle third of the nineteenth century. In this conversion, the practice of European and particularly German schools, the establishment of normal schools and the efforts of reformers such as Mann, Stowe, and Barnard were the chief factors.

The Earlier Aspects of Method.—The elementary school of Colonial and early National periods had few books to depend upon. Its purpose was not wide. To develop the ability to read the Scriptures, to write, and to master the simple processes of calculation satisfied ambition. Methods in the early National period, so far as these simple processes were concerned, did not vary greatly. The descriptions of them which we possess show little or no variation and, we may also add, little or no insight into the actual problems of teaching. An idea of current method can be pieced together from this anonymous account dating near the beginning of the century:

"The alphabetical page of the spelling book is presented, and he is asked 'What's that?' But he cannot tell. He is but two years and a half old, and has been sent to school to relieve his mother from trouble, rather than to learn. No one at home has as yet shown or named a letter to him. He has never had even that celebrated, round O, pointed out to his notice. It was an older beginner, most probably, who, being asked a similar question about the first letter of the alphabet, replied, 'I know him by sight, but can't tell him by name.' . . . At length [he] has said A, B, C, for the first time in his life. He has *read,* 'That's a nice boy; make another bow, and go to your seat.' He gives another jerk of the head, and whirls on his heel, and trots back to his seat, meeting the congratulatory smile of his sisters with a satisfied grin, which, put into language, would be, 'There, I've read, ha'n't I?'

"The little chit, at first so timid and almost inaudible in enuncia-

EDUCATION DEMOCRATIZED

tion, in a few days becomes accustomed to the place and the exercise; and, in obedience to the 'Speak up loud, that's a good boy,' he soon pipes off 'A-er, B-er, C-er,' &c., with a far-ringing shrillness that vies even with the chanticleer himself. Solomon went all the pleasant days of the first summer and nearly every day of the next, before he knew all the letters by sight, or could call them by name. Strange that it should take so long to become acquainted with these twenty-six characters, when, in a month's time, the same child becomes familiar with the forms and the names of hundreds of objects in nature around, or in use about his father's house, shop, or farm! Not so very strange either, if we only reflect a moment. Take a child into a party of twenty-six persons, all strangers, and lead him from one to the other as fast as his little feet can patter, telling him their respective names, all in less than ten minutes; do this four times a day even, and you would not be surprised if he should be weeks at least, if not months, in learning to designate them all by their names. Is it any matter of surprise, then, that the child should be so long in becoming acquainted with the alphabetical party, when he is introduced to them precisely in the manner above described? Then, these are not of different heights, complexions, dresses, motions, and tones of voice, as a living company have. But here they stand in an unalterable line, all in the same complexions and dress; all just so tall, just so motionless and mute and uninteresting, and, of course, the most unrememberable figures in the world. No wonder that some should go to school, and 'sit on a bench, and say A B C,' as a little girl said, for a whole year, and still find themselves strangers to some of the sable company, even then. Our little reader is permitted at length to turn a leaf, and he finds himself in the region of the Abs, —an expanse of little syllables, making me, who am given to comparisons, think of an extensive plain whereon there is no tree or shrub or plant, or anything else inviting to the eye, and nothing but little stones, stones, stones, all about the same size. And what must the poor little learner do here? Why, he must hop from cobble to cobble, if I may so call *ab, eb, ib,* as fast as he possibly can, naming each one, after the voice of the teacher, as he hurries along. And this must be kept up until he can denominate each lifeless and uninteresting object on the face of the desert.

"After more or less months, the weary novice ceases to be an Ab-ite. He is next put into whole words of one syllable, arranged in columns. The first word we read in Perry that conveyed anything like an idea, was the first one in the first column,—the word *ache:* ay, we did not easily forget what this meant, when once informed; the corresponding idea, or rather feeling, was so often in our consciousness. *Ache,*—a very appropriate term with which to begin a course of education so abounding in pains of body and of mind.

"After five pages of this perpendicular reading, if I may so call it, we entered on the horizontal, that is, on words arranged in sentences and paragraphs. This was reading in good earnest, as grown-up folks did, and something with which tiny childhood would be very naturally puffed up."

The methods of the early period had been in general that of simple imitation of the teacher. The good dame knew the alphabet, the Lord's Prayer, the catechism, and usually but not always knew how to put the alphabet together to make the latter. Whether she carried the little beginner into actual reading or merely aided him to memorize letter and text, he by dint of repetition and imitation acquired the simple knowledge which enabled him to continue with the reading of the biblical text or such literature as Wigglesworth's *Day of Doom* or other pious selections which the orthodoxy of the time would permit. As one reports, "I was then four and a half years old and had learned *by heart* nearly all the reading lessons in the Primer and much of the Westminster Catechism."

Development of the Textbook Method.—In the early National period came a considerable elaboration of the work of the schoolroom due chiefly to the multiplication of textbooks and their very general introduction into the schoolroom. This brought greater freedom both to the teacher and to the pupil. While the pupil still acquired the art of reading in the same laborious style, he very shortly entered upon a freedom which was quite as bewildering as had been the earlier tasks of imitation with no intelligent explanation. As indicated in the previous section, there came a great multiplication of textbooks in every subject, an elaboration of the curriculum, and a marked change of content in each subject. And this multiplication of texts exercised a determining influence on method. Noah Webster, the most voluminous contributor of texts, and perhaps one who contributed most greatly to the modification of method, said: "Indeed there is danger of running from one extreme to another and instead of having too few books in our schools we shall have too many."

With the great multiplication of texts came a method which yet characterizes American schools. The text gave a somewhat voluminous account of the subject to be mastered. A certain portion was assigned to the pupil for mastery and from time to time he was called up by the teacher to recite. At its worst the method was no better than the old *memoriter* plan, where the pupil simply memorized his textbook and repeated it to the teacher. The more closely the reproduction approximated the text the greater the satisfaction of the teacher. At its best it threw the pupil upon his own initiative, expected him to interpret material expressed in terms of an experience much broader than his own, and thus developed insight, originality, and ability to organize and control. Its usual result is implied in its characterization by a schoolman of the period as "the only sure method by which dullness can be effectually taught." With the ungraded or the district school and the untrained teacher, both then predominating, it was perhaps the only method available. Certain it is that the textbook method came into almost universal acceptance and still forms an essential factor in the procedure of the schoolroom.

In this early period, however, there were evils of which the present generation does not know, evils which intensified the individualism of the method. Not only was there a multiplicity of texts for the entire system and for the pupil, but there was a diversity for a given subject and for a given school or class. Each child furnished his own book and followed his own volition or that of his parent in selecting it. A curious confusion resulted. Mann's *First Annual Report* stated: "When a diversity of books prevails in a school there will necessarily be unfitness and maladjustment in the classification of scholars. Those who ought to recite together are separated by a difference of books. If eight or ten scholars in geography, for instance, have eight or ten different books, as has sometimes happened, instead of one recitation for all there must be eight or ten recitations. Thus the teacher's time is crumbled into dust and dissipated." Scarcely could a more striking illustration be found of the extremely individualistic method of the American school or of such complete dependence upon textbooks as to identify this dependence with method.

One of the early reforms accomplished by Mann was to give to the district boards the authority to select uniform texts for one school. This authority, however, they were long loath to use.

In 1846 the Connecticut secretary reported 215 different textbooks in use in the state, of which 92 were readers and 30 were arithmetics. This at least argues an improvement over the early part of the century where there were few subjects and a dearth of material. Writing of his own schooling in this period Peter Parley says: "The next step of my progress which is marked in my memory is the spelling of words of two syllables. I did not go very regularly to school, but by the time I was ten years old I had learned to write and had made a little progress in arithmetic. There was not a grammar, a geography, or a history of any kind in the school. Reading, writing, and arithmetic were the only things taught, and these very indifferently—not wholly from the stupidity of the teacher, but because he had forty scholars, and the standards of the age required no more than he performed."

The meager Colonial curriculum was reading and writing, usually with the simple processes of arithmetic. Massachusetts, possessing the longest experience and the best traditions and organization, led the march of improvement, but even this region made slow progress. The Law of 1789 required arithmetic as well as the reading and writing specified in the Colonial laws, and added the English language (grammar), orthography, and decent behavior. The effectiveness of the instruction in this last subject may be judged from the number of schools broken up each year as late as the middle of the following century. In 1827 geography was added to the curriculum; near the middle of the century, drawing and physiology.

The chief change, however, was in the content of the books. The earlier materials were the catechism, the *New England Primer*,

EDUCATION DEMOCRATIZED

the *Psalter,* the Bible. From the close of the Revolution a distinct type of American textbook began to be issued. Political material in the form of orations, patriotic appeals, and more or less exaggerated or distorted descriptions gradually replaced the somber religious materials of the earlier period. Undoubtedly the bombastic oratory, exaggerated style of speech, and rather flamboyant views and claims of the American citizens of these and succeeding generations were due largely to this change. However, this was but one means, perhaps a necessary one, by which provincialism vindicated itself, maintained its independence of "effete" European society, and developed in time a strong nationalism.

The earliest and most influential of the textbook writers of this period was Noah Webster, whose fame as a lexicographer has long outlived that as a textbook writer. In explanation of his earlier work he wrote, "In 1782 while the American army was lying on the banks of the Hudson I kept a classical school at Goshen, N.Y. The country was impoverished; intercourse with Great Britain was interrupted, and schoolbooks were scarce and hardly attainable." In 1783 he issued the first part of his *Grammatical Institutes of the English Language, comprising an easy, concise, and systematic Method of Education designed for the Use of English Schools in*

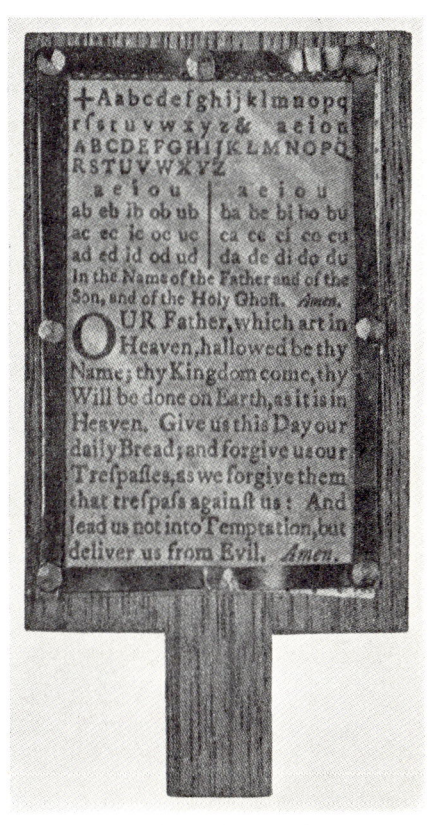

FIG. 65. A horn book.

America. This was a combination speller, reader, and grammar, which had patriotic as well as educational aims. Out of this volume grew various modifications, the most noted of which was the *American Speller.* This is the premier American textbook, of which more than seventy-five million copies have been sold, and which yet has its devotees. In 1806 appeared Webster's *Compendious Dictionary of the English Language,* which either in its school or in its unabridged form has ever since been a familiar and popular work of reference.

A	In ADAM's Fall We finned all.	G	As runs the Glass, Our Life doth pass.
B	Heaven to find, The Bible Mind.	H	My Book and Heart Must never part.
C	Chrift crucify'd For finners dy'd.	I	JOB feels the Rod, Yet bleffes GOD.
D	The Deluge drown'd The Earth around.	K	Proud Korah's troop Was fwallowed up
E	ELIJAH hid By Ravens fed.	L	LOT fled to *Zoar,* Saw fiery Shower On *Sodom* pour.
F	The judgment made FELIX afraid.	M	MOSES was he Who *Israel's* Hoft Led thro' the Sea.

FIG. 66. The alphabet from the *New England Primer.* (From an old edition.)

The only rival of Webster in popularity and fame was Lindley Murray (1745-1826), a Quaker educator of New York and New Jersey. In 1795 he published an *English Grammar,* in 1797 an *English Reader,* and in 1804 a *Spelling Book.* Somewhat more scholarly than those of Webster and, as became the work of an author English born, somewhat less narrowly nationalistic, these were also extremely popular, widely used, and strongly influential.

In 1784 Jedediah Morse issued his *Geography Made Easy,* the first American text on this subject. This was followed in 1789 by *American Geography, or a View of the Present Situation of the*

EDUCATION DEMOCRATIZED

United States, which was even more distinctly a means of political and nationalistic propaganda. In 1797 he published *Elements of Geography,* and in 1814 *Universal Geography.*

In 1788 Nicholas Pike issued his *New and Complete System of Arithmetic,* avowedly a patriotic or nationalistic endeavor. In its original form too bulky for simple school use, the many simpler scions of this work dominated American schools for half a century.

After these came a deluge of school texts, as became independent people, blessed with initiative, and groping for a democratic education. Many, however, attempted the synthesis of the old and the new. There were texts which began geographical studies with the exploration of the Red Sea by Moses and the study of ichthyology with Jonah. Many were yet cast in the old catechetical controversial style. Some adopted biblical phraseology, hoping that the form would keep alive, even if the spirit was gone. (See Illus. 70.)

MR. JOHN ROGERS, minifter of the gofpel in *London,* was the firft martyr in Queen MARY's reign, and was burnt at *Smithfield, February* 14, 1554.—His wife with nine small children, and one at her breast following him to the flake; with which forrowful fight he was not in the leaft daunted, but with wonderful patience died courageoufly for the gofpel of JESUS CHRIST.

FIG. 67. The burning of Mr. John Rogers, witnessed by his wife and nine children. A chapter in the *New England Primer.* (From an old copy.)

Perhaps the patriotic effort to conceal the real character and outcome of the War of 1812 was responsible for this particular passage; if so, later texts of more modern form have been even more successful.

The spellers, grammars, geographies, and arithmetics of the first generation of our nationalistic educators were the first of the distinctive type of American textbooks which have become one of the most characteristic features, perhaps even one of the best contributions, of American education.

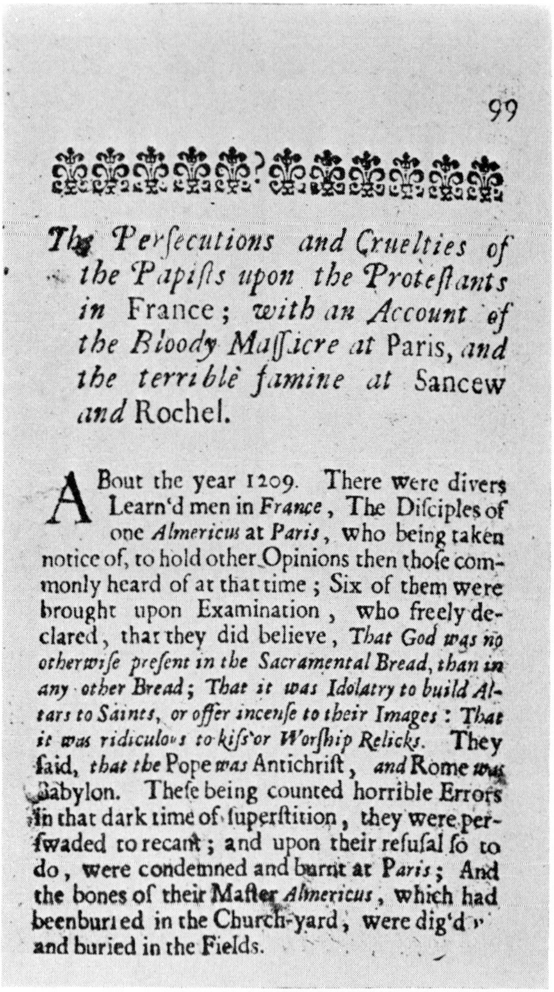

The Persecutions and Cruelties of the Papists upon the Protestants in France; with an Account of the Bloody Massicre at Paris, and the terrible famine at Sancew and Rochel.

About the year 1209. There were divers Learn'd men in *France*, The Disciples of one *Almericus* at *Paris*, who being taken notice of, to hold other Opinions then those commonly heard of at that time; Six of them were brought upon Examination, who freely declared, that they did believe, *That God was no otherwise present in the Sacramental Bread, than in any other Bread; That it was Idolatry to build Altars to Saints, or offer incense to their Images: That it was ridiculous to kifs or Worship Relicks.* They said, *that the Pope was* Antichrist, *and* Rome *was Babylon.* These being counted horrible Errors in that dark time of superstition, they were perswaded to recant; and upon their refusal so to do, were condemned and burnt at *Paris*; And the bones of their Master *Almericus*, which had been buried in the Church-yard, were dig'd v and buried in the Fields.

FIG. 68. Two pages from the *Protestant School Master,*

[350]

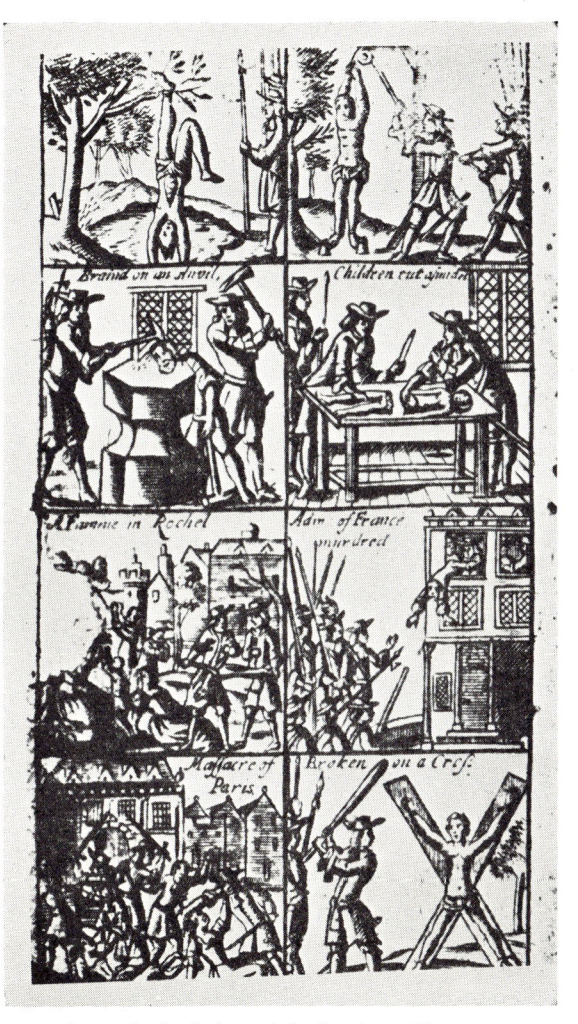

a popular textbook of the period. London, 1682.

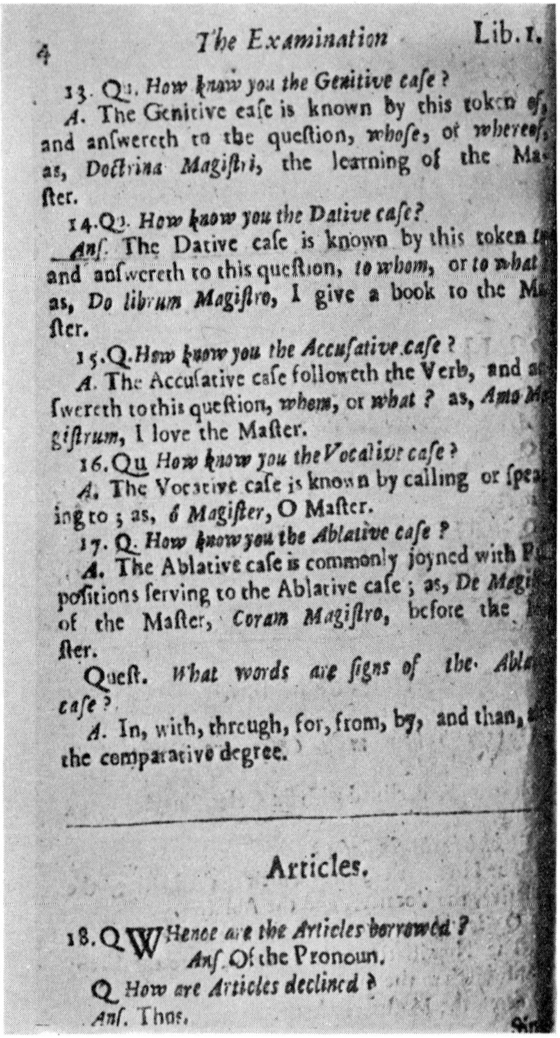

4　　　　　*The Examination*　　　Lib. 1.

13. Q. How know you the Genitive case?
A. The Genitive case is known by this token of, and answereth to the question, *whose*, or *whereof*, as, *Doctrina Magistri*, the learning of the Master.

14. Q. How know you the Dative case?
Ans. The Dative case is known by this token to, and answereth to this question, *to whom*, or *to what*, as, *Do librum Magistro*, I give a book to the Master.

15. Q. How know you the Accusative case?
A. The Accusative case followeth the Verb, and answereth to this question, *whom*, or *what*? as, *Amo Magistrum*, I love the Master.

16. Qu. How know you the Vocative case?
A. The Vocative case is known by calling or speaking to; as, *ô Magister*, O Master.

17. Q. How know you the Ablative case?
A. The Ablative case is commonly joyned with Prepositions serving to the Ablative case; as, *De Magistro*, of the Master, *Coram Magistro*, before the Master.

Quest. What words are signs of the Ablative case?
A. In, with, through, for, from, by, and than, the comparative degree.

Articles.

18. Q. WHence are the Articles borrowed?
Ans. Of the Pronoun.
Q. How are Articles declined?
Ans. Thus.

FIG. 69. Pages from a commonly used grammar, showing *amination of*

[352]

| Lib. I. | Of the Accidence. | 5 |

	Masc.	Fœm.	Neut.
Nom	Hic.	Hæc.	Hoc.
Gen.	Hujus.	Hujus.	Hujus.
Dat.	Huic.	Huic.	Huic.
Acc.	Hunc.	Hanc.	Hoc.
Voc.	ô	ô	ô
Abl.	Hoc.	Hac.	Hoc.

Singulariter

	Masc.	Fœm.	Neut.
Nom	Hi.	Hæ.	Hæc.
Gen.	Horum.	Harum.	Horum.
Dat.	His.	His.	His.
Acc.	Hos.	Has.	Hæc.
Voc.	ô.	ô.	ô.
Abl.	His.	His.	His.

Pluraliter

Genders of Nouns.

19 Q. **H**ow many Genders of Nouns be there?
Ans. Seven.
Q. *Which be the seven Genders?*
Ans. The Masculine, the Feminine, the Neuter, the Common of two, the Common of three, the Doubtful, and the Epicene.
Q. *With what Articles is the Masculine Gender declined?*

A 4 *Ans.*

the excessive analysis, e.g., seven genders. (From *The Ex-the Accidence.*)

[353]

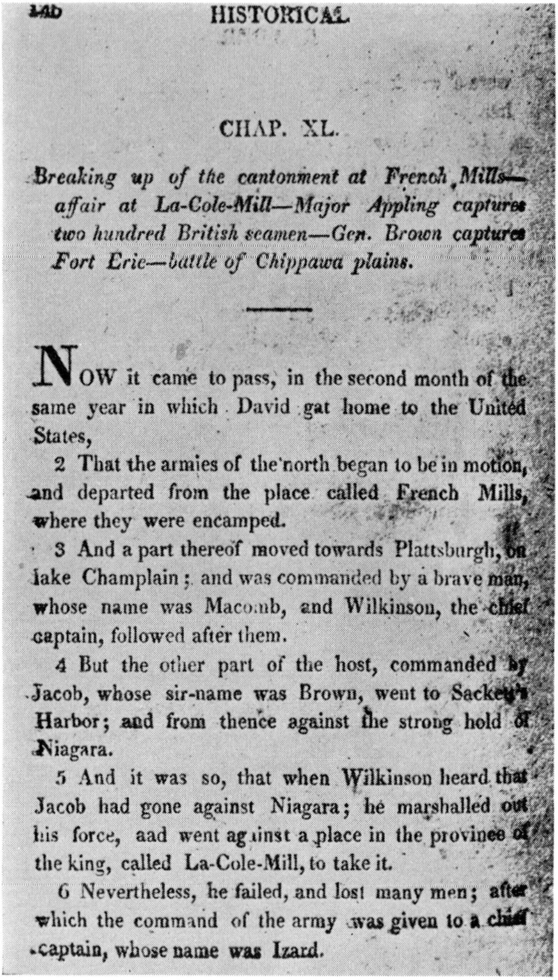

HISTORICAL

CHAP. XL.

Breaking up of the cantonment at French Mills—affair at La-Cole-Mill—Major Appling captures two hundred British seamen—Gen. Brown captures Fort Erie—battle of Chippawa plains.

NOW it came to pass, in the second month of the same year in which David gat home to the United States,

2 That the armies of the north began to be in motion, and departed from the place called French Mills, where they were encamped.

3 And a part thereof moved towards Plattsburgh, on lake Champlain; and was commanded by a brave man, whose name was Macomb, and Wilkinson, the chief captain, followed after them.

4 But the other part of the host, commanded by Jacob, whose sir-name was Brown, went to Sackett's Harbor; and from thence against the strong hold of Niagara.

5 And it was so, that when Wilkinson heard that Jacob had gone against Niagara; he marshalled out his force, and went against a place in the province of the king, called La-Cole-Mill, to take it.

6 Nevertheless, he failed, and lost many men; after which the command of the army was given to a chief captain, whose name was Izard.

FIG. 70. Imitation of biblical phraseology in ordinary textbooks.

READER.

7 In the meanwhile many of the evils of warfare were committed on and about the waters of Ontario and the great lake Erie.

8 And a gallant captain, whose name was Appling,* took about two hundred of the mariners of the royal navy of Britain, at a place called Sandy-Creek, by the waters of lake Ontario: being in the same month that the strong hold of Oswego was taken by the men of Britain.

9 Now on the third day of the seventh month, it came to pass, that Jacob, the chief captain of the host of Columbia, on the borders of the river Niagara,

10 Having prepared his men beforehand, crossed the river and captured fort Erie, and an hundred thirty and seven of the soldiers of the king, and some of the destroying engines;

11 And the next day being the anniversary of the independence of Columbia, after having left some of the men of war to defend the place,

12 He moved with his host towards the plains of Chippawa, where they rested for the night.

13 On the next day Jacob assembled his captains of fifties, and his captains of hundreds, and spake unto them, saying,

14 Lo! the army of the king are mighty men of valor, and their numbers are great, even those who fought in Spain, under the banners of Welling-

---

* *Major Appling.*

(From Hunt, *Historical Reader*, Chap. 40.)

FOUNDING OF AMERICAN SCHOOL SYSTEM

Content of the Textbooks.—The formality of schoolroom procedure, the absence of appeal to the pupils' interest, the emphasis on formal discipline, the excessive use of corporal punishment, the dependence of the teacher on classroom management instead of upon method of instruction, the change in the social and intellectual character of the people, all can be understood only by some further knowledge of the content of the texts.

Pike's *Arithmetic* is a volume of over 500 pages. It contains more than 350 rules, endlessly elaborated and illustrated with difficult problems. Seldom is there any reason for the rule or any explanation of it. Simple multiplication is presented through fourteen rules. The Rule of Three (proportion) was the limit of the usual schoolroom achievement, including however the rule of three inverse, the double rule of three, and conjoined proportion, each with its various cases, rules, and examples. For illustration, Case 9 under Practice, which is the application of the Rule of Three in business, is as follows:

> "*When the Price is any odd number of shillings under 40:*—Find the value of the greatest even number contained in the price, according to Case 5th, add thereto the value of the quantity at 1s. per yard &c., which sum will be the answer. *Or,* multiply the quantity by the price, according to the 1st or 2nd case in simple multiplication, and divide the product by 20, the quotient will be the answer; *Or,* lastly, if the price be under 13s. find the value of the quantity at 1s. per yard &c., and multiply it by the number of shillings in the price of 1 yard; the product will be the answer."

This is in English money. When it is recalled that at that time nine different kinds of currency were in use the task before the pupil may be imagined. The author being the schoolmaster of a New England seaport, much of the volume is devoted to interest, insurance, loss and gain, etc. Some of the rules are quite unintelligible to the school child or teacher of the present, as:

> "Deduct the tare and trett, divide the suttle by one hundred and sixty-eight, and the quotient will be the cloff, which subtract from the suttle, and the remainder will be the neat."

EDUCATION DEMOCRATIZED

The geographical writings of Morse were quite as oppressive in their way.

The significance of the change in the materials used in the readers is indicated in this passage from Martin:

> "The importance of this change in the New England schools cannot be overestimated. The substitution of the selfish and sordid aphorisms of Franklin for the Proverbs of Solomon and the divine precepts of the Sermon on the Mount; the declamations of Webster and Pitt for the lofty patriotism of Moses and Isaiah; the feeble reasoning in ethics of Mrs. Barbauld and Hannah More for the compact logic of Paul's Epistles; the tinsel glitter of Byron for the up-springing devotion of David; and the showy scene-painting in the narratives of Scott for the simplicity of the gospel story of the life of Christ—such a substitution could not take place without modifying, subtly but surely, all the life currents of the community."

Before accepting this opinion we should familiarize ourselves with the material used in the Colonial period. Reference has been made to the famous poem of Michael Wigglesworth on the *Day of Doom*. This poem was first published in 1662, and printed many times afterward. It is probable that no New England child for several Colonial generations was without familiarity with this poem,—such familiarity, in fact, that most of the 224 stanzas could be repeated verbatim by most of them. We select a few of them.

1.

"Still was the night, Serene and Bright,
when all Men sleeping lay;
Calm was the season, and carnal reason
thought so 'twould last for ay.
Soul, take thine ease, let sorrow cease,
much good thou hast in store:
This was their Song, their Cups among,
the Evening before.

5.

"For at midnight brake forth a Light,
which turn'd the night to day,

And speedily a hideous cry
   did all the world dismay.
Sinners awake, their hearts do ache,
   trembling their loins surprizeth;
Amaz'd with fear, by what they hear,
   each one of them ariseth.

166.

"Then to the Bar, all they drew near
   who died in Infancy,
And never had or good or bad
   effected pers'nally,
But from the womb unto the tomb
   were straightway carried
(Or at last e're they transgrest)
   who thus began to plead:

167.

"If for our own transgression,
   or disobedience,
We here did stand at thy left-hand
   just were the Recompense:
But Adam's guilt our souls hath spilt,
   his fault is charg'd upon us.
And that alone hath overthrown,
   and utterly undone us.

171.

"Then answered the Judge must dread,
   God doth such doom forbid,
That men should die eternally
   for what they never did.
But what you call old Adam's Fall,
   and only his Trespass,
You call amiss to call it his,
   both his and yours it was.

EDUCATION DEMOCRATIZED

180.

"You sinners are, and such a share
    as sinners may expect,
Such you shall have; for I do save
    none but mine own Elect.
Yet to compare your sin with their,
    who liv'd a longer time,
I do confess yours is much less,
    though every sin's a crime.

181.

"A crime it is, therefore in bliss
    you may not hope to dwell;
But unto you I shall allow
    the easiest room in Hell.
The glorious King thus answering,
    they cease, and plead no longer:
Their Consciences must needs confess
    his reasons are the stronger."

This selection properly belongs in Chapter VII on the New England School but is given here to indicate the change made in the early National period.

Other Defects of the District School.—These were of all sorts; it often had too many pupils (Quos. 488, 495), often too few (Quos. 489 and 501); too many teachers and too few teachers (Quos. 495, 496); too many textbooks (Quo. 493) and too few textbooks; too many inspectors and too few inspectors; there were many districts too large, many too small (Quos. 487, 488, 489). Many districts had 90 or 100 pupils, so that in the absence of a graded system the teacher found little time for each pupil. Many schools had fewer than five pupils, many even one or two. While in such cases as the last the individual pupil might receive sufficient attention, incentive was often lacking and the poorest of instructors were provided. Small number of pupils demanded small wage, and little competence on the part of the teacher. In 1855 Connecticut reported 45 districts with fewer than twelve pupils

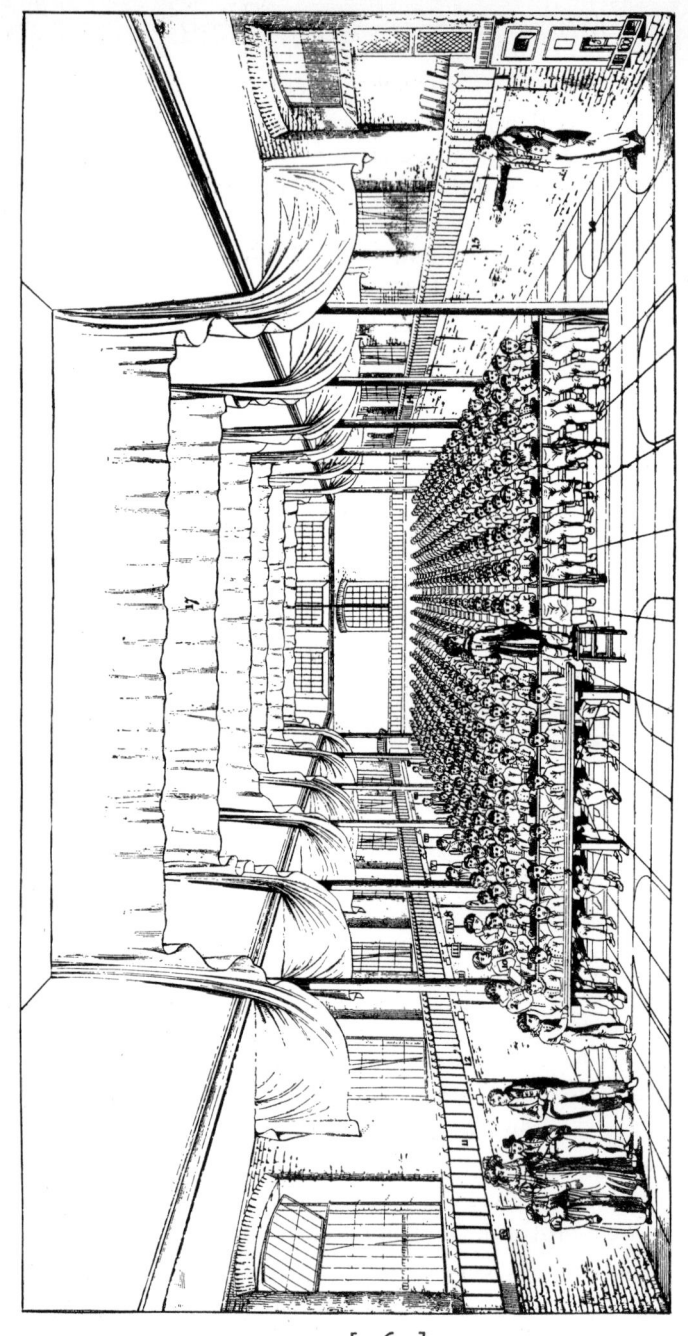

FIG. 71. Lancasterian schoolroom. One of these existed in New York City until the opening of the 20th century. The curtains hanging from the ceiling are to collect the dust and deaden the sound. Note the lesson boards hanging around the wall. (From the *Manual of the System of Primary Instruction*, 1831.)

EDUCATION DEMOCRATIZED

each. This meant that each of these districts had less than $15 per year for the support of schools. One Massachusetts school in 1844 had $5.60 for its year's schooling, and this after many years of Mann's efforts. Obviously the teacher secured must have been untrained and incompetent. The meager salary, oftentimes less than $1.00 per week, was supplemented by the "boarding round" of the teacher, a custom which often added materially to the discomfort and unattractiveness of the profession. At this time the schools of Connecticut were considered the best in the country. The Report of 1855 states: "For these schools a cheap teacher is almost invariably sought, and almost invariably a poor teacher is employed, a very poor teacher, or one quite inexperienced; and even the unprofitable serv-

FIG. 72. The Lancasterian school in operation. (From the *Manual of the System of Primary Instruction*, 1831.)

ices of these incompetent teachers must be speedily terminated. Few of these schools are kept more than four months in the year, the period required by law in order to be entitled to public money." As this report dates after the reform period, earlier conditions may be imagined.

Like the Lancasterian system the district school was a necessary step to the democratization of education.

The historian of the Massachusetts schools points out clearly the political and social evils caused by the district school system: "Questions involving the fate of nations have been decided with less expenditure of time, less stirring of passions, less vociferations of declamation and denunciation, than the location of a fifteen-by-twenty district schoolhouse. I have known such a question to call for ten district meetings, scattered over two years, bringing down from mountain farms three miles away men who had no children

FOUNDING OF AMERICAN SCHOOL SYSTEM

to be schooled, and who had not taken the trouble to vote in a presidential election during the period. Again, when a teacher has given dissatisfaction to a part of the district, possibly to a single family, a contest has arisen over the choice of a prudential committeeman. Into the discussion have been brought questions the most

FIG. 73. The Lancasterian school, methods of reward. (From J. Loos, *Enzyklopädisches Handbuch*, p. 113.)

remote; old family feuds have been revived, and new ones created; all the petty jealousies and rivalries, masculine and feminine, have been brought to the surface, until the whole district is by the ears. The poor little teacher, who was the innocent cause of all the disturbance, has been forgotten and a social war rages with the bitterness of a Kentucky vendetta and the protraction of an English suit in chancery."

EDUCATION DEMOCRATIZED

The Lancasterian or Monitorial Method (Quos. 524–550).—
The most distinctive method of teaching in vogue during the early National period was the monitorial system introduced under the name of Lancasterianism. This was a scheme of school support and of schoolroom organization as well as of method, but all three features were distinctive and very popular during a period extending over almost half a century. Several features of Lancasterianism

FIG. 74. The Lancasterian school, methods of punishment. (From J. Loos, *Enzyklopädisches Handbuch*.)

were particularly adapted to American conditions, especially to towns and cities. It was an elaborate social machine, and mechanical devices of all kinds were then in vogue. The new democracy, as yet an experiment, put great faith in such governmental machinery. There was a general belief that most social ills could be thus cured.

It was claimed that Lancasterianism also rendered the education of the masses possible because one teacher could instruct 500 pupils or even more. This made the plan very economical and thus overcame one of the great obstacles to the development of popular education. The fundamental feature of the scheme was the division of a school of perhaps 400 or 500 pupils, into a number of groups, usually of ten each, under the control of monitors. It was essentially the introduction of military organization and discipline into the school.

"The introduction of monitors, an extremely important part of the whole scheme, is as great an improvement in schools as the introduction of noncommissioned officers would be in an army which had before been governed only by captains, majors, and colonels; they add that constant and minute attention to the operations of the mass without which the general and occasional superintendence of superiors is wholly useless. An usher (*teacher*) hates his task and is often ashamed of it; a monitor is honored by it and therefore loves it; he is placed over those who, if their exertions had been superior, would have been placed over him; his office is the proof of his excellence. Power is new to him; and trust makes him trustworthy—a very common effect of confidence and exemplified in the most striking manner in Mr. Lancaster's school. Nor is the monitor at all detained by teaching to others what he has already learnt, at least not unprofitably detained; for if a boy be at the head of the first spelling class it is clear that a delay of six or eight weeks in teaching to others what he has already learnt will perfect him in his new acquirements and rivet them in his memory. After this he is made a private in some superior regiment, and his post becomes an object of honor and competition to the lads whom he taught. He is very wisely allowed to have a common interest with the boys whom he instructs, and to receive a prize equal in value with any prize obtained by any individual among them. In some instances, the monitor teaches and learns at the same time; for, in dictating the sum . . . the monitor is furnished with a key and therefore in dictating only reads what others have written for him, but in so doing it is plain his attention must be exercised and his memory impressed as much if not more than those of any boy in the class; and whatever good is produced in others by that mode of instruction must be produced in him in an equal or

EDUCATION DEMOCRATIZED

superior degree. The extraordinary discipline, progress and economy of this school age are, therefore, in a great measure produced by an extraordinary number of noncommissioned officers, serving without pay and learning while they teach."

This summary from the English essayist Sidney Smith, a contemporary of Lancaster, epitomizes the features and merits of the

FIG. 75. The Lancasterian schoolmaster as a handicraft man. (From Loos, *Enzyklopadisches Handbuch.*)

monitorial system as it appeared to that generation. There were the monitors and assistant monitors of the various classes in writing and arithmetic, supervising monitors being placed over all of the

FOUNDING OF AMERICAN SCHOOL SYSTEM

classes in a given subject. There were monitors of conduct, of slates, of playgrounds, and of every feature of school life.

Little attempt was made to teach more than the rudiments of reading, writing, arithmetic. These subjects were very minutely graded and the pupils passed from one group to another in each

FIG. 76. The Lancasterian schoolmaster as a farmer. (From Loos, *Enzyklopadisches Handbuch*.)

subject as they mastered the materials in the given stage of the organization.

Thus the advantages of individual promotion and promotion by subject, so difficult to obtain in the schools of today, were assured. The system also permitted great advance in the grading of schools. The classes in reading were as follows: 1st class, alphabet; 2d, words and syllables of two letters; 3d, words and syllables of three letters; 4th, words and syllables of four letters; 5th, reading lessons of one syllable; 6th, reading lessons of two syllables; 7th, the Testament; 8th, the Bible. In mathematics the classes were: 1st, addition and subtraction; 2d, addition and subtraction; 3d, multiplication and division; 4th, five first rules; 5th, reduction; 6th, rule of three; 7th, practice; 8th, interest. It is obvious that this scheme was superficial and quite different from a modern graded school system, since it covered but two or three years' work. But it popularized the idea of grading and of class recitation, so that it was often known as "the simultaneous method."

Methods were far more mechanical than the system of grading; most of the school work was purely *memoriter,* based upon dictation. The most uninteresting alphabetic and syllabic methods of learning to read dominated, alleviated by the use of the alphabet wheel and the sand board. The report of the New York schools for 1842 states: "The alphabet is taught by varied methods; by the printed lesson sheet, by single letters on binder's boards, and by tracing the letters in white sand, lightly covering a part of the writing desk painted black for the purpose. This is called the sand desk. This method, besides being a useful one in varying the exercises of the a-b-c-darians, is well calculated to aid mental development, calling into exercise analysis and comparison, and is a very intellectual method of teaching the alphabet."

Monitors were assisted by most minute directions which pupils were required to follow. The educational principles and insight involved may be judged by this sample from the illustrated manual used in the New York schools in 1850.

"While reading, as the eye rises to the top of the right hand page, the right hand is brought to the position seen in fig. 4, with the forefinger under the leaf, the hand is slid down to the lower corner, and retained there during the reading of the page, as seen in fig. 6. This also is the position in which the book is to be held when about to be closed; in doing which the left hand, being carried up to the side, supports the book firmly and unmoved, while the right hand turns the part it supports over on the left thumb, as seen in fig. 7. The thumb will then be drawn out from between the leaves and placed on the cover; when the right hand will fall by the side as seen in fig. 2. . . .

"In conclusion, it may be proper to remark that however trivial these minute directions may appear to some minds, it will be found on experience that books thus treated may be made to last double the time that they will do under the usual management in schools. Nor is this attainment of a correct and graceful mode of handling a book the only benefit received by the pupil. The use of this manual is calculated to beget a love of order and propriety and disposes him more readily to adopt the habit generally of doing things in a methodical and systematic manner."

This monitorial or simultaneous method involved a great gain over the old individualistic scheme in that all of the studying as well as reciting was done under the monitor, so that practically the entire school was in operation all the time. The attention of each child was held whether in study or in recitation, both being carried on by group effort. In place of the former schoolroom of fifty to one hundred pupils, of whom a dozen or so at most were receiving attention while the rest were allowed a great variety of occupations determined by individual choice or were not occupied at all, here was a schoolroom of several hundred children, all of them actively engaged.

As evident from old woodcuts, the method of the recitation was very distinctive. Lessons were printed on large battledores or charts, or written on movable (or portable) blackboards. These were suspended from hooks on the wall, and before each a group gathered under its monitor. One may judge of the impression these innovations made upon the times, quoting again from Sidney Smith:

"It must not be forgotten that in Mr. Lancaster's school every boy is every moment employed. It is obvious that in the class assembled round the suspended card for reading and spelling—the wand of the monitor pointing to the particular letter, the taking place, the hopes of obtaining a ticket—must keep the children constantly on the alert. When they read, spell, and write at the same time, *as in paragraph (A)*, or when the monitor dictates sums, *as in (C)*, it is impossible for any individual to be inattentive. In common schools the scholar is set to learn his spelling, or his cyphering, by himself; and after a certain time the master hears him his lesson, and judges of his attention by his readiness in performing it. The learning part of the

EDUCATION DEMOCRATIZED

business is left entirely to the boy himself, and his time often whiled away in every species of idleness. The beauty of Mr. Lancaster's system is that nothing is trusted to the boy himself; he does not only *repeat* the lesson before a superior, but he *learns* it before a superior. When he listens to the dictating process in arithmetic, and adds up as he is commanded, he does that, under the eye and command of a master, which in other schools he would be trusted to do by himself. In short, in these troops the appointed officer sees that the soldier shoulders his musket twenty times a day, who by doing it often cannot avoid doing it well. In other troops, the officer tells the soldiers how it is to be done, and leaves them to practice by themselves,—which they do, of course, very unwillingly and very imperfectly, if they do it at all. Such are the principles upon which Mr. Lancaster has planned his improvements in the education of the poor, and carried them into execution with such success *that one thousand boys may now be educated in reading, writing, and arithmetic,* by one person, at an expense not exceeding £300 per annum. A more beautiful, a more orderly, and a more affecting scene than the school of Mr. Lancaster, it is not possible to behold. The progress of the children is rapid beyond all belief and evinces in the most gratifying manner the extraordinary effects which are produced upon the human mind by the arts of cultivation."

Smith also justified the claim that "any boy of eight years old who can barely read writing, and numerate well, is by means of the guide containing the sums and the key thereto qualified to teach the first four rules of arithmetic, simple and compound, if the key is correct, with as much accuracy as mathematicians who have kept school for twenty years."

Lancaster's genius for organization showed itself in several mottoes which have since became almost proverbial: "Let every child at every moment have something to do and a motive for doing it" includes in the last phrase at least one principle of modern theory. Another epigram, "A place for everything and everything in its place" related both to schoolroom management and to method.

The popularity of the monitorial system as well as its general influence on method and its significance as a step in the development of the free public school is indicated by its very general adoption. Every region of the country was affected by it, though New England probably the least. It attempted to furnish free education to the great mass of children in the cities and towns where the opportunities offered by the church schools did not suffice. Virginia and the Carolinas had numerous organizations to support such schools. The schools of Cincinnati and other towns of the Middle West were thus begun, as well as those of the cities in New York, Pennsylvania, and the Central states in general. It was in the secondary schools or private academies, however, that the Lancasterian method was most generally adopted in the South and Middle West. Here the private schools which were built up by co-operative efforts to supplement the deficiencies of the public school system were very generally upon the Lancasterian plan. During the twenties Governor De Witt Clinton strongly advocated the establishment of a monitorial high school in each county of New York (p. 203). While this failed, yet the method was used freely by the academies subsidized by this and other states. One of the best known and most striking statements of the importance of the monitorial plan was that made by Governor Clinton in a public address. One paragraph gives the substance of his generous and somewhat visionary approval:

> "When I perceive that many boys in our school have been taught to read and write in two months, who did not before know the alphabet, and that even one has accomplished it in three weeks—when I view all the bearings and tendencies of this system—when I contemplate the habits of order which it forms, the spirit of emulation which it excites, the rapid improvement which it produces, the purity of morals which it inculcates—when I behold the extraordinary union of celerity in instruction and economy of expense—when I perceive one great assembly of a thousand children, under the eye of a single teacher, marching with unexampled rapidity and with perfect discipline to the goal of knowledge, I confess that I recognize in Lancaster the benefactor of the human race,—I consider his system as creating a new era in education, as a blessing sent down from heaven to redeem the poor and distressed of this world from the power and dominion of ignorance."

EDUCATION DEMOCRATIZED

The early Lancasterian schools confined themselves to the teaching of the three elementary subjects. However, in the third and fourth decades the principle was applied to the advanced subjects of the so-called high school of the day (p. 393). Here the plan soon showed its limitations. In this same period such subjects as geography, history, and grammar were introduced into the advanced grades of the Lancasterian schools of the cities. Here also the method failed. In New York the monitorial plan was abandoned in favor of paid and more mature assistant teachers. The methods, however, prevailed much longer, but after the middle of the century their inadequacy was clear to all. The Commissioner of Education of New York in 1871 stated: "Thousands of children leave school without being able to read or write. History and geography should be taught by reading books. Children read miserable twaddle. What I want to do is to make the children interested. I want the children to educate themselves. In our system of education we do not generate in the children a desire and love of self-culture. Without that they will go forth in the world without being educated and instructed at all." Even yet remnants of the influence of the Lancasterian organization and procedure can be detected in the work of many of our large city schools, particularly those of the East.

One other feature of school work was greatly influenced by Lancaster—that of discipline. Interest on the part of the pupil had been created in the old time school largely by fear of corporal punishment or by subservience to other external authority. Lancaster practically abolished corporal punishment, then perhaps the greatest evil of the schoolroom, the greatest deterrent to progress. In its place he substituted emulation, through a highly developed system of rewards. While this is not a satisfactory substitute for genuine interest, it at least marked an advance in motivation.

Along with the emphasis on emulation went the elaborate scheme of moral training developed by Lancaster as a substitute for the religious education then dominant. No feature of the system aroused more discussion during the period in which these schools flourished. But the question of emulation has been settled by the substitution of a genuine psychological interest, and the problem of religious education solved by its elimination from the scope of public school work. Hence the discussion of these phases of Lancaster's influence possesses no vital significance for the present generation.

The Infant School (Quos. Ch. XVI, Pt. IV).—The second and third decades of the century witnessed the introduction from England of another mechanical system of education, the so-called infant school. This institution flourished for a few years in most of the cities of the country, after which, like the Lancasterian and other schools, it was merged into the public school system. It left little permanent impress on the organization of the schools, though the primary department of the ward schools of New York maintained a separate principal until a very recent date.

The essential feature of the organization of infant schools was the massing of several score of small children under the direction of one man who directed their movements in schoolroom or playground by the use of group leaders. Instruction was in mass, chiefly by concert *memoriter* work, of a catechetical character. For this purpose the pupils were banked in raised seats, called a gallery; hence "the good gallery teacher" of the period. One such gallery remained in a school building of New York City until within the twentieth century, though long out of use.

The distinctive feature of the infant school was its emphasis on the content of education, while Lancasterianism emphasized the mastery of the formal elements. In stressing the value of information the infant school employed the method of question and answer, both of which were usually memorized by the child, and used the natural object or its picture as a means of instruction. In this latter feature it was greatly influenced by Pestalozzianism, from which it borrowed form without touching the fundamental psychological principles involved.

It is almost impossible now for us to realize the exaggerated importance then assigned to information and the exaggerated estimate of the capacity of the child to absorb knowledge.

Children were taken at two years of age or even less. The alphabet with all sorts of information, more or less congruous, tacked on was learned from blocks—in deference to Pestalozzianism.

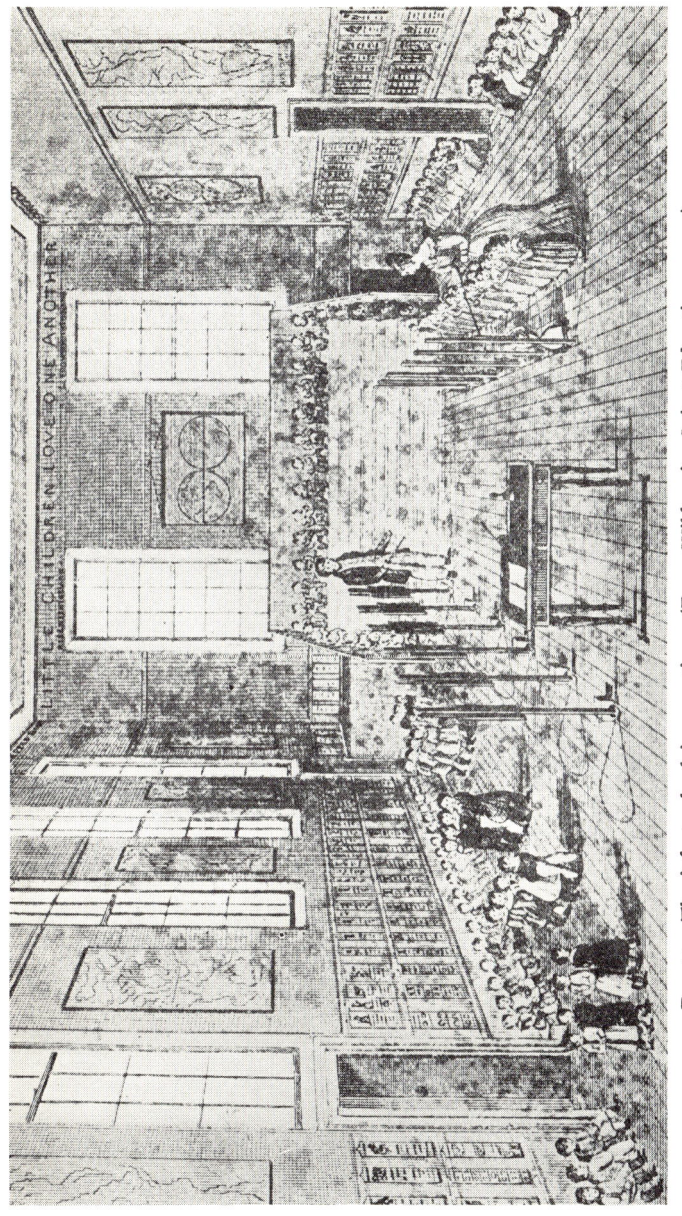

Fig. 77. The infant school in operation. (From Wilderspin, *Infant Education*, p. 44.)

Fig. 78. The infant school, a good gallery teacher. (From Wilderspin, *Infant Education*.)

EDUCATION DEMOCRATIZED

Here is a sample lesson from the volume by Wilderspin, the founder of the system:

"Q. What letter is this? "L.
A. Letter L., for lion, etc.
Q. Spell lion.
A. L-i-o-n.
Q. What is the size of a full grown lion?
A. A full grown lion stands four feet and a half high and eight feet long.
Q. How high do you stand?
A. Please, sir, some of us stand two feet, and none of us above three.
Q. Has the lion any particular character among beasts?
A. Yes, he is called the king of beasts on account of his great strength.
Q. When he seizes his prey how far can he leap?
A. To the distance of twenty feet.
Q. Describe some other particulars concerning the lion.
A. The lion has a shaggy mane, which the lioness has not.
Q. What other particulars?
A. The lions' roar is so loud that other animals run away when they hear it.
Q. Where are lions found?
A. In most hot countries; the largest are found in Asia and Africa."

After a chapter of twenty pages on arithmetic, including the multiplication and division tables and weights and measures, a chapter on higher mathematics for infants is given. The chapter is introduced with this philosophical observation:

"Useful knowledge can have no enemies, except the ignorant; it cherishes the mind of youth, and delights the aged, and who knows how many mathematicians there may be in embryo in an Infant School?"

A portion of one paragraph will serve as illustration:

"*Rhomboid*
"Q. What is this?
A. A rhomboid.
Q. What is the difference between a rhomb and a rhomboid?
A. The sides of the rhomboid are not equal, nor yet its angles, but the sides of the rhomb are equal."

Fig. 79. Another system of mechanical school organization. The circulating school. (From *A Description of the System of Inquiry*, by Steat, London, 1826.)

Fig. 80. Another system of mechanical school organization.

Undoubtedly many children did memorize a prodigious amount of such information, much of it in the form of definition.

The following lesson is taken from an examination of a ten-year-old boy in the New York schools of 1826:

"Q. What is the earth? A. It is a planet, and the third in the solar system.

FOUNDING OF AMERICAN SCHOOL SYSTEM

Q. What surrounds the earth? A. The atmosphere.
Q. Of what does the earth consist? A. Of land and water.
Q. What shape has the earth? A. It is round.
Q. How do you know it is round? A. Because we can see the tops of ships' masts first at sea.
Q. Does the earth stand still or move? A. It moves on its axis, and has its motion round the sun.
Q. What takes place from these motions? A. Its motion round the sun produces the change of seasons, and its motion on its axis, the succession of day and night.
Q. If the earth turns round, why are we not turned heels up at midnight? A. Because the attraction of gravity draws all bodies towards the center of the earth.
Q. Does any other planet obey the laws of gravitation? A. Yes, sir, Mars, as well as the other smaller planets, called asteroids, Jupiter, etc.
Q. Has the earth any satellite? A. Yes, the moon is the earth's satellite.
Q. Has any other planet a satellite, or moon? A. Yes, Saturn has seven and Jupiter has four, and they all gravitate towards their respective principals.
Q. Have we any antipodes? A. Yes, sir, they are the people directly under us; they have their feet opposite to our feet."

The magazines of the day record many instances of precocity as this, the product of the infant school idea. The following from the *American Journal* of 1828 is a condensation of a long account:

"Here is the life story of a bright boy nourished on the Infant School plan. Porter Brinsmade, born February 28, 1827, in Hartford, Connecticut. From the age of four months his eyes were directed to surrounding objects, until names of articles became familiar. At ten months he learned the alphabet from blocks. (He could not utter the sounds, but would pick out the letters called for.) He took no delight in toys, but in pictures and books. Geography was a favorite study before his second birthday. Then he became interested in geometry. His mother devoted herself to him. Love of knowledge was a passion. He was often told that to his Father in Heaven he was indebted for what he most loved; and with an affectionate earnestness

FIG. 81. An early form of Froebelian kindergarten, circle on the village green.

and graceful gesture of his little hand he would say 'Thank God.' . . . Porter died at the age of 2 years, 5 months."

The Introduction of the Pestalozzian Method (Quo. 429).
—The first genuine insight into the problems of method came to the American schools through the introduction of the teachings of Pestalozzi. This began with the efforts of William McClure previously mentioned (p. 235). McClure visited the school at Burgdorf in 1804 and 1805 and endeavored to persuade Pestalozzi himself to come to America. Failing in this he brought over Joseph Neef, one of Pestalozzi's teachers, who established a school near Philadelphia where he taught for some years. No clearer account or briefer summary of the Pestalozzian method has been given than the following by one of his pupils, who subsequently became famous as Admiral Farragut (Quo. 517).

"I accompanied my friend Captain Porter to Chester, where I was put in a school to a queer old individual named Neef. His method of instruction was simple in the extreme: he had no books but taught orally such subjects as he desired us to understand. The scholars took notes and were afterwards examined on these lectures. In the afternoon it was customary for us to take long walks, accompanied by our instructor. On these occasions Mr. Neef would make collections of minerals and plants, and talk to us about mineralogy and botany. The course of study was not very regular, but we certainly had an opportunity of gaining a great deal of useful information and worldly knowledge. We were taught to swim and climb, and were drilled like soldiers—branches of instruction to be accounted for, probably, by the fact that the old gentleman had been one of Napoleon's celebrated guards. I do not regret the time passed at this school, for it has been of service to me all my life."

Though this school was not a great success, Neef put the Pestalozzian ideas into a number of publications. The earliest of these, entitled *Sketch of a Plan and Method of Education Grounded on the Analysis of Human Faculties and Native Reason Fitted for the Offspring of the Free People and for all Rational Beings* appeared in Philadelphia in 1808. This was the first treatise on the theory of education published in the United States. Neef subsequently joined McClure and Robert Owen in the latter's communistic scheme at New Harmony, Indiana, in 1825. For the general public, however, the educational features of this experience were obscured by the economic and social ideas with which they were bound up.

During the third and fourth decades of the century there was a new movement in the popularization of the Pestalozzian ideas. This began in 1819 with the publication of John Griscom's *A Year in Europe*. Griscom was much interested in what he had seen of the Pestalozzian school, but he was more enamored of the monitorial scheme of organization as being better adapted to American conditions, but the early educational leaders in New England were more philosophically inclined and seized upon the Pestalozzian principle as one most in harmony with the growing democracy. Chief among these earlier advocates was William Russell, who in 1826 founded the *American Journal of Education*. In this magazine appeared Pestalozzi's letters to J. P. Graves, his one work published originally in English. For this and other periodicals many articles on Pestalozzianism were written. Another of these early advocates of Pestalozzianism was James G. Carter, who led the agitation for the founding of normal schools. Having failed in his earlier attempt to induce Massachusetts to establish such a school, he undertook a private normal school, as did also Russell at a later date. Working with Carter was Rev. Charles Brooks, also a leader in the normal school movement and a writer on Pestalozzianism. The early normal schools which resulted, founded in 1839 and 1840, really embodied the Pestalozzian idea and spirit. While in theory they adopted the principle enunciated by Neef,—"Books therefore shall be the last fountain from which we shall endeavor to draw our knowledge,"—they nevertheless depended very much in practice upon texts and textbooks. In fact out of this movement grew the earlier series of schoolbooks by which the Pestalozzian spirit was largely introduced. Chief among these are Woodbridge's works on geography, Colburn's on arithmetic; those of Josiah Brumstead and of John Russell Webb in reading. The first Mc-

10 HOOKER'S PRIMARY GEOGRAPHY.

LESSON II.

THE GEOGRAPHY OF THE SCHOOL-HOUSE.

On the previous page is a picture of the inside of a small school-house. You see the teacher's desk, and the desks and seats of the scholars. You see the stove in the corner, the door where you come in, and the three windows on the side.

Below this picture is a plan or map of this school-room. There is the wall all around it, with the open place in it to show where the door is. You see the places in the wall where the windows are. You see marked the place where the stove stands. There, too, are the places of the teacher's desk and seat, and of the desks and seats of the scholars.

We will now go outside. On the opposite page is the school-house itself, with its pleasant yard around it. There are four handsome trees in it, and you see some frames which the children use in their sports.

Below the picture is a plan or map of the lot and school-house. You see the shape of the school-house, and the walk up to it. The fence is marked, and you see the places of the trees.

This is the Geography of one school-house in the world. But the school-house that you are taught in may be very

FIG. 82. The introduction of the Pestalozzian method.

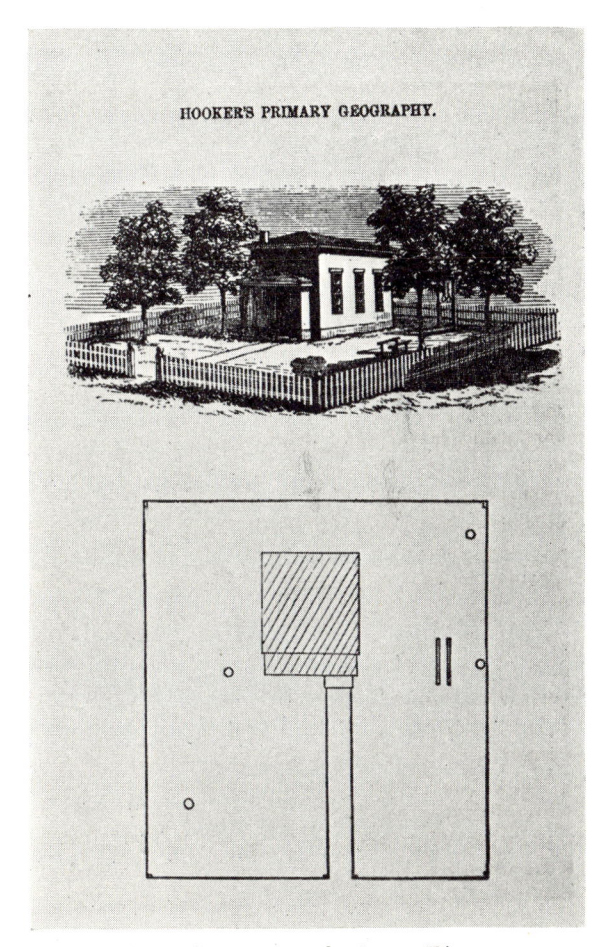

(From Hooker, *Primary Geography*, Lesson II.)

Guffey reader had appeared in 1836. While there were many features of the Pestalozzian method embodied in McGuffey yet he did not embody the most characteristic phases incorporated in other readers, namely the word method. The chief value of the McGuffey's readers was their introduction to a wide range of selections from the best literature.

Lowell Mason later introduced the same principles in the teaching of music.

Over against the textbook method was placed the object method as embodying the essence of the Pestalozzian teaching. Concerning this feature of the work of the early normal schools, one of their principals wrote: "This turned the attention of the school to collecting such objects, illustrative apparatus, and reference books as were necessary for a thorough system of objective teaching and study. The branches of learning required to be taught in the public schools were taken up, with special reference to teaching them to others in accordance with the laws of the human mind that control it in the acquisition of knowledge and development of its faculties. That the pupils of the normal school might have an opportunity of observing the application of their methods to real children, the town generally provided the school of observation, where they could add experience to their theories. The results of these things soon appeared in the professional spirit excited in the different departments of the normal school, in the improved work of its graduates, and in the new interest which their good example produced throughout the country in the study of the philosophy of education. The Westfield Normal School was the first to show that all branches of learning may be taught by the same objective method, and that elementary knowledge should be taught with special and constant reference to the scientific knowledge which is to be occasioned by it."

Horace Mann's *Seventh Annual Report* in 1843 (see p. 238) was the most important single influence in spreading the Pestalozzian ideas of method, discipline, school management, and curriculum. In subsequent years through the medium of the *Common School Journal,* he continued this effort and popularized through Massachusetts the work of the normal schools and the new educational ideas. One of the group of Massachusetts philosophers, A. Bronson Alcott, did much through his teaching, his writings, and his experimental school in making known ideas quite similar to those of Pestalozzi, though they may not have been drawn direct from him. While the Temple School existed only from 1834-39, and Alcott's teaching was much attacked, many of the experiences of this school were later made very much better known by his daughter, Louisa May, in her story *Little Men*. Thus these ideas entered into both the philosophy and the literature of this period. But the influence of these principles as well as that of the normal schools was chiefly local.

Through the work of Henry Barnard both in the *Connecticut Common School Journal* (1838-42) and in the *American Journal of Education* (1856-81) these ideas were much more widely disseminated. In the issues of these journals were published more of the Pestalozzian literature than is found probably in all other English sources. In 1858 appeared Barnard's *Pestalozzi and Pestalozzianism*, which yet remains the most extensive exposition of these ideas in English. However, their widespread dissemination in America awaited a movement subsequent to the Civil War.

Significant Aspects of the Influence of Pestalozzianism and European Experience on American Schools.—More important than the channels through which this influence came was its actual character. What is here termed Pestalozzianism is not to be distinguished from the general influence exerted by European experience and practice as these were reported to America in those days. But all these progressive principles had developed from the original ideas of the Swiss reformer or had been incorporated by his followers into the practice of the schools of the chief Swiss and German states of that period.

Most fundamental of all was the change in the atmosphere of the schoolroom, in the attitude and function of the teacher, in the greater freedom allowed the child. All of these came from the basal difference in the conception of education, viewed no longer as a process of acquiring information cast in an abstract form intelligible, interesting, and valuable, if at all only to the adult. Education is now conceived as a process of developing the child nature, through the enrichment of experience by means of widening activities. The harsh repressive attitude of the teacher disappears; corporal punishment is banished; instruction based on mastery of arbitrary forms as in reading and number work is minimized; child interest is consulted, child powers are considered.

This induced in the second place a new type of teacher, one instructed in psychology and trained in method. Teaching now comes to be based on certain psychological principles, not on the superficial knowledge and crude craftsmanship of the individual teacher. It is true that the statement of many of these principles has been greatly modified by the later progress of science, but as a basis they were then correct. The child was treated as a living, growing organism, the mind as a functioning entity, though much of the old Aristotelian terminology was yet used. A *general method* was in the process of formulation for the guidance of the teaching process.

This elaboration of a science of psychology, more or less empirical, upon which to found a general science of teaching, led to a third result, the formulation of detailed special methods for the various subjects taught in the schools. The vast importance which the subject of special method assumes in the training of the teacher dates from this day. The early reports in European schools did much to popularize it, the normal schools perpetuated and elaborated it. Of the 180 pages of Mann's *Seventh Report* 45 are devoted to special methods, particularly those in reading and in arithmetic. One of the chief recommendations was the abandonment of the alphabetic method, by which the child spent months or even years in memorizing the separate letters and then began to put them together in meaningless combinations. While the early schools of Pestalozzi continued to use some of these outworn methods, his followers developed the basal truth of his reforms. The so-called "mental arithmetic" was the appropriate development in that field. Actual numerical relationships, usually within the experience of the child, were substituted for the formal memorizing of symbols and the manipulation of these by arbitrary rule. Geography became the

EDUCATION DEMOCRATIZED

study of local environment; history the understanding of social institutions. Above all, as previously indicated, objects and experience instead of books became the basis of instruction. It is obvious that these reforms were not universally or even generally introduced into the American school. But the reform movement began.

A fourth gain was more universally realized, that of an enriched curriculum. More space is given to the consideration of this phase of reform than to any other by the various reports on European schools. Mann argues for language work, grammar, composition, drawing, geography, nature study, study of institutions, Bible study, music, physiology, and physical training. Ryerson's report to the Government of Ontario on the same topic three years later argues for a list of twenty-four subjects. A commentator on this report in 1912 writes, with just as much applicability to the neighboring states across the border,—

> "Indeed, as one reads the *Report* he is inclined to repeat the old adage: 'There is nothing new under the sun.' Almost every subject introduced into Ontario schools during the last quarter of the nineteenth century seems to have an insecure foothold, and are by many denominated 'fads.' These were included by Ryerson in his memorable report of 1846, and the arguments he uses in favor of their adoption would not seem out of place if used by an advanced educator of the present day. He pleads for music, drawing, history, civics, inductive grammar teaching, concrete number work, oral instruction, mental arithmetic, nature study, experimental science, bookkeeping, agriculture, physical training, hygiene and even political economy. He illustrates some German methods of teaching reading that many Ontario teachers fondly think were originated in their own country."

This trend toward an enriched curriculum may not all be traceable to Pestalozzian source, but it had its origin in the belief that education is the introduction of the child into the full life of the adult.

Summary.—If education may be said to have been nationalized through administration and system, it may be said to have been democratized through method, through curriculum and through schoolroom organization. In fact, it is difficult to distinguish between these three aspects of education. Method is most distinctive. In European schoolrooms, in general, subject matter is furnished to the pupil by the teacher. Textbooks are but outlines. The recitation is a collective reiteration of what the teacher has told previously. In American schools, material is furnished largely through the textbook. The pupil is the active factor, not the teacher. The pupil is thrown on his own initiative; develops self-reliance and independence of judgment. The extreme of this is found in the early national period, when each pupil furnished his own textbooks and practically all instruction was individual. The method of the collective recitation was not developed until quite recent times.

However, out of this condition grew one of the great merits of the American school, a superior body of textbook materials for the schools. Method and organization of subject matter were largely provided in the earlier decades through special systems of education such as the Lancasterian, Monitorial, the Infant Societies, the Pestalozzian schools, etc. However, Pestalozzianism largely influenced method, particularly, toward the middle of the century, through the introduction of object teaching and the use of the word method rather than the alphabetical method in reading.

In schoolroom method, the distinctive feature was the excessive use of corporal punishment. The custom of trying out the teacher by the older boys was quite an accepted feature of the school life during the earlier part of the century, even toward the middle of the century. The statistics given in the school reports indicate that in each state many scores of schools were broken up each year in conformity with this custom. Corporal punishment was all but universal in use. Such punishment was depended upon for incentive to study or even for deterrent example as well as to preserve discipline. In fact, this had the approval of the current interpretation of psychology as well as of morals. The opposition to corporal punishment and to religious instruction were the main causes for the marked opposition to the Horace Mann reforms developed during the middle of the century.

The contents of school books during the Colonial period had been almost altogether drawn from religious sources. From the Revo-

[388]

EDUCATION DEMOCRATIZED

lutionary period onward, political and nationalistic material was substituted. However, even in the early national period, many of the school books imitated Biblical language even though the material was of a modern nationalistic character.

The characteristic form of organization during this period was that of the District School, particularly in the rural regions. The District School in essence was the reduction of the control and support of schools to the smallest political unit which could be served by one school. Whereas the District School was all but universal throughout the country in the rural regions; in the cities, the Lancasterian, Monitorial, Infant Societies, and various mechanical measures for caring for large bodies of pupils, were adopted. The mechanization of education carried over into method as well in both the Infant School and the Lancasterian School. However, through the work of the various reformers of the many educational publications and of such movements as Pestalozzianism, a spirit of education which was freer and more rational was introduced, and finally triumphed over the more mechanical aspects.

Chapter XII

SECONDARY EDUCATION. THE DOMINANCE OF THE ACADEMY AND THE RISE OF THE HIGH SCHOOL

Transition from the Latin Grammar School to the Academy.—Though the Latin school had lost its vitality, much of its social significance, and its popular approval, the statement that it had disappeared before the National period began is entirely too strong. In Massachusetts these Latin schools were continued by legal requirement until 1827. By the law of 1789 the number of families required in a town to make the establishment of such a school mandatory was raised to two hundred. In 1790 there were Latin schools in 113 towns out of 270 having over 1000 population or presumably 200 families. No doubt many towns did neglect this requirement; but local records give many instances of the enforcement of the law, even against the will of the community. By 1810 there were 143 towns out of 288 that came under the provision of the law; in 1820, 172 towns out of 302. A law of 1824 practically exempted all but seven towns from maintaining such schools.

Meanwhile a transition had been going on which explains the seemingly sudden change made by the Law of 1824. The Colonial laws as well as that of 1789 required towns of the specified size to maintain a school in which Latin should be taught; but they left the problem of support to the towns. In most states except Massachusetts and later New York, such schools did not need the sanction of the state and were established in increasing numbers. Gradually the term Latin school ceased to be a name to conjure with, the term grammar school came to be applied to the English school, much as we use it now, and the term academy came into general use.

The academy movement, at least in New England, began with the founding of the Phillips academies, one at Andover in 1778,

SECONDARY EDUCATION

the other in Exeter in 1781. The definite occasion for these was the decline of the Latin grammar schools. Permanent teachers were no longer to be had, and the moral and religious influence of the Latin school had come to be of little significance. The Colonial Latin grammar school was supported in whole or in part by the town, was in most instances controlled by the town, and during the eighteenth century was usually free of tuition charges. However, from about the period of the Revolution the difficulty of maintaining these schools by public tax greatly increased, and private schools giving instruction in Latin and possibly Greek and supported by charges for tuition were established. Such schools enabled a town to comply with the law, relieved the inhabitants from one burden of taxation, suited the community by offering a much wider range of subjects of study, and afforded to individual enterprise an opportunity for gain.

Outside of New England the Latin grammar schools had never been very numerous and were seldom supported by the towns; there such schools as have just been described were often called Latin schools or grammar schools; but the usual name for them in all parts of the country was academy. Six such schools had been chartered by the legislature of Massachusetts in 1789 and thirty-four more by 1827. Because they were boarding schools these institutions possessed an influence and reached a clientele far beyond the borders of the town where they were situated and so replaced many grammar schools.

Characteristics of the Academy.—The chief distinction between the academy and the Latin school was the greater democracy of the former. It is true that the Latin grammar school was usually based on public support, but it was avowedly designed for a very restricted class with limited privileges, and for the training of leaders in one or two professions only—"in church and state" or often in church alone. The democracy of the academy is best indicated by the breadth of its curriculum, for it attempted to incorporate almost every subject then known and to meet every desire of its patrons or pupils. The method of support also accorded with the limited democratic ideas of the early nineteenth century,

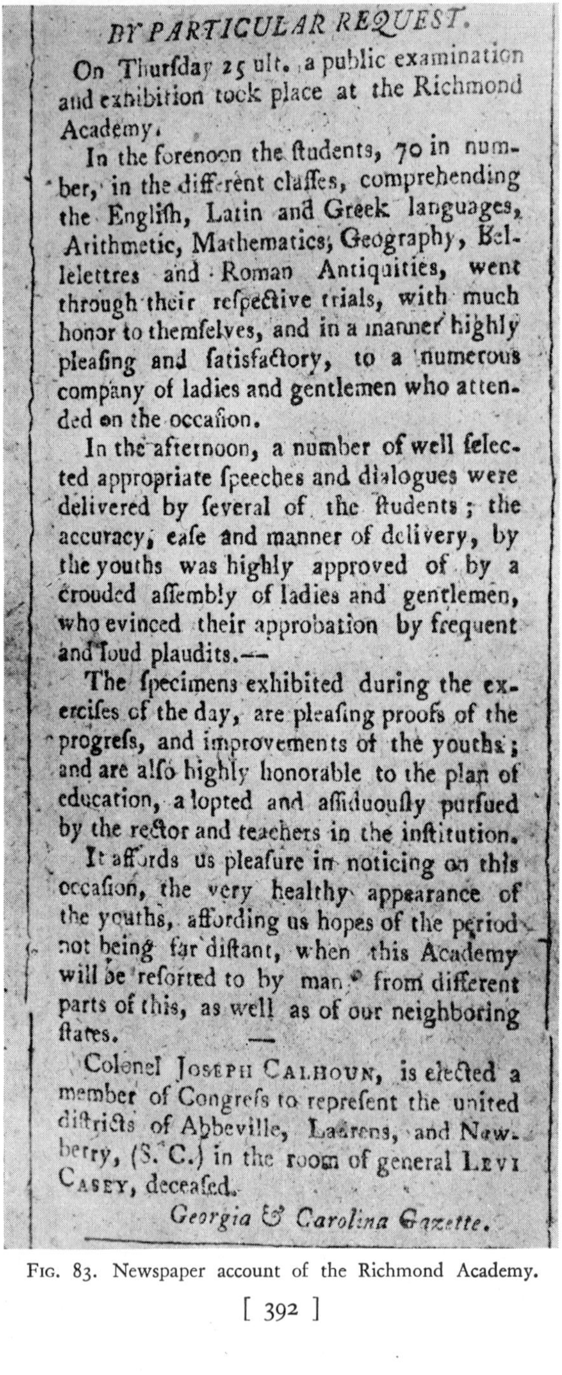

BY PARTICULAR REQUEST.

On Thursday 25 ult. a public examination and exhibition took place at the Richmond Academy.

In the forenoon the students, 70 in number, in the different classes, comprehending the English, Latin and Greek languages, Arithmetic, Mathematics, Geography, Bellelettres and Roman Antiquities, went through their respective trials, with much honor to themselves, and in a manner highly pleasing and satisfactory, to a numerous company of ladies and gentlemen who attended on the occasion.

In the afternoon, a number of well selected appropriate speeches and dialogues were delivered by several of the students; the accuracy, ease and manner of delivery, by the youths was highly approved of by a crouded assembly of ladies and gentlemen, who evinced their approbation by frequent and loud plaudits.—

The specimens exhibited during the exercises of the day, are pleasing proofs of the progress, and improvements of the youths; and are also highly honorable to the plan of education, adopted and assiduously pursued by the rector and teachers in the institution.

It affords us pleasure in noticing on this occasion, the very healthy appearance of the youths, affording us hopes of the period not being far distant, when this Academy will be resorted to by many from different parts of this, as well as of our neighboring states. —

Colonel JOSEPH CALHOUN, is elected a member of Congress to represent the united districts of Abbeville, Laurens, and Newberry, (S. C.) in the room of general LEVI CASEY, deceased.

Georgia & Carolina Gazette.

FIG. 83. Newspaper account of the Richmond Academy.

which placed much more stress on individual liberty than on equality. Anyone was entitled to found such a school and in many states not even the sanction of the authorities was required. Attendance was conditioned on fees and, since such schools were usually residence or boarding schools, upon large contingent expenses. Thus they were in full accord with the aristocratic democracy of the early nineteenth century. The establishment and operation of such schools as a form of individual enterprise, not to be limited or at least prohibited by the state, became customary. Even when they were chartered and supported by the community such institutions were able to maintain themselves for a long time on the basis of this strongly entrenched influence of localities or of leading families in the face of a growing democracy which denounced the aristocratic control of schools.

As opposed to the aristocratic Latin school which preceded it, and the democratic high school which followed, the academy was a middle class school, partaking of both aristocratic and democratic elements. In New York the academies were clearly set off against the colleges, the academies being considered colleges for the people. The democracy of the academy was probably best shown in the school life. Most of them were boarding schools established in small towns or even in rural regions. The Latin grammar school was usually a one-teacher school; at least the usher, if there was one, was distinctly subordinate. The teaching staff of most academies provided a "faculty," which associated with and exerted great influence over the student body. Usually consisting of both boys and girls, brought from rather restricted environment to the intellectually and socially stimulating surroundings of the academy, town, or dormitory life, the academy community developed a new democratic ideal whose influence spread far beyond its borders.

The support of the academies came from private gifts, local endowments, state subsidies, grants from religious bodies, contributions, but chiefly from students' fees. These last varied inversely with the amount of the former factors and depended usually upon the number and character of the subjects of study taken. From the point of view of the present, these rates were low. In New York, where we have accurate figures for this entire period, the average tuition for all academy students varied from $8 to $16. After the Civil War these fees increased rapidly and then averaged from five to ten times as high as during the early period. Notwithstanding the low rates of this early period, such fees furnished more than three quarters of the total support of the academies of New York throughout the period under discussion. During the same period the state government contributed from 12 to 20% of the total cost of support. Thus it is seen that private gift and endowment funds constituted but a small proportion of the whole. No such definite figures are available in other states but the general situation was much the same. Most commonwealths contributed by special appropriation for individual academies, but some provided by statute for a general scheme of support. In New York these funds were granted to the separate academies on the basis of the number of students and the subjects which they successfully carried as shown by state or "regents" examinations.

One feature of great significance was the inclusion of girls in the student body. The early Massachusetts academies, Dummer and Andover, were for boys alone. Leicester (1784), Westford (1792), Bradford (1803), were for both sexes, Ipswich Seminary (1825), and Abbott Academy (1829), were for girls alone. In Virginia, 69 of the 255 academies incorporated up to 1860 were for girls and 20 were co-educational. Nearly all of the female or co-educational academies were established after 1840. In Pennsylvania there were 37 "female seminaries" among the 103 academies or similar institutions founded by 1842.

Extent of the Academy System (Quos. 573–582).—Only general estimates and impressions of the extent of the academy system for the entire country can be given. As previously shown (p. 205), Winterbottom in his survey of 1796 (Quo. 359) mentions by name 50 academies in the thirteen original states and speaks in a general way of numerous others. In 1833 a survey made by the secretary of the American Education Society included information from 497 academies in fourteen states. Of these states eleven were of the original group. During the period from 1830 to 1870 the academy

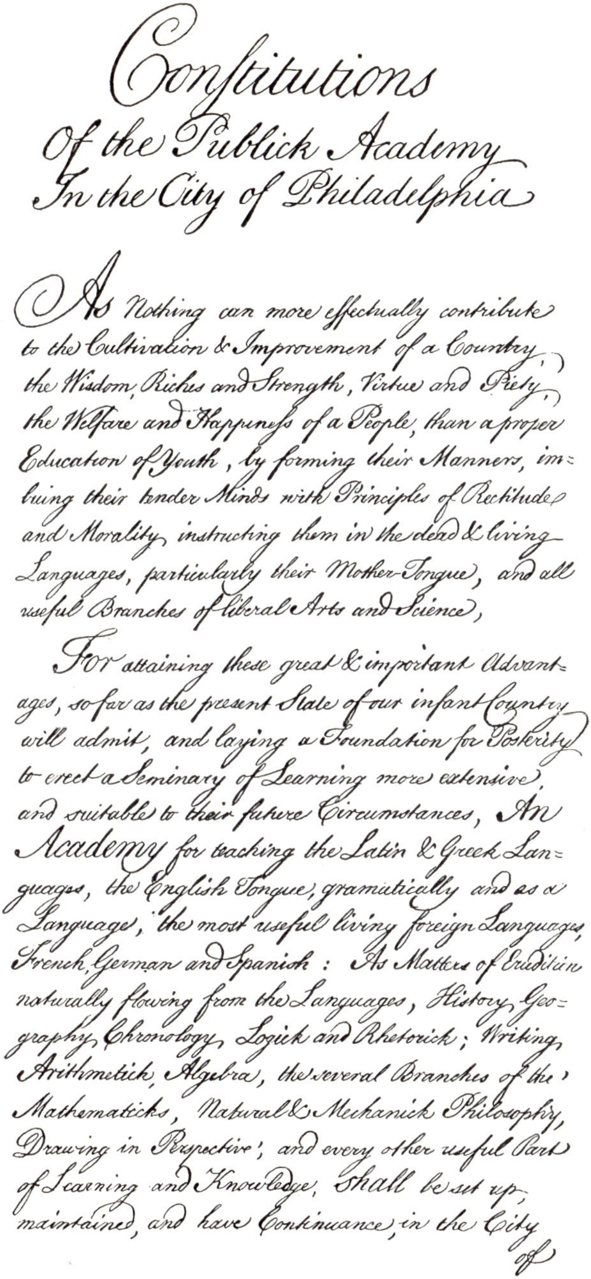

Constitutions
Of the Publick Academy In the City of Philadelphia

As nothing can more effectually contribute to the Cultivation & Improvement of a Country, the Wisdom, Riches and Strength, Virtue and Piety, the Welfare and Happiness of a People, than a proper Education of Youth, by forming their Manners, imbuing their tender Minds with Principles of Rectitude and Morality, instructing them in the dead & living Languages, particularly their Mother-Tongue, and all useful Branches of liberal Arts and Science,

For attaining these great & important Advantages, so far as the present State of our infant Country will admit, and laying a Foundation for Posterity to erect a Seminary of Learning more extensive and suitable to their future Circumstances, An Academy for teaching the Latin & Greek Languages, the English Tongue, gramatically and as a Language, the most useful living foreign Languages, French, German and Spanish : As Matters of Erudition naturally flowing from the Languages, History, Geography, Chronology, Logick and Rhetorick ; Writing, Arithmetick, Algebra, the several Branches of the Mathematicks, Natural & Mechanick Philosophy, Drawing in Perspective; and every other useful Part of Learning and Knowledge, Shall be set up, maintained, and have Continuance, in the City of

FIG. 84. Constitution of the Philadelphia Academy, drawn up by Benjamin Franklin. (From the original manuscript.)

FOUNDING OF AMERICAN SCHOOL SYSTEM

system attained its greatest extent and influence. The schools existed in considerable number in every region of the country. From the very nature of the institution—its individualism, its freedom from state control, its dependence on local and private support—it is impossible to get an accurate statement of its extent. However, a survey of the three typical states previously discussed, Massachusetts, New York, and Virginia, will serve as an index for the entire country.

In Massachusetts the work actually began with Dummer academy, opened in 1763 but not incorporated until 1782. Andover was founded by Samuel and John Phillips in 1778 and chartered in 1780. By 1797 fourteen such schools had been chartered by the state and three of them had received land from the legislature. In 1797 a general policy regarding these schools was adopted by the state. Grants of land were recommended to all academies that met certain conditions as to funds and location. Each academy should serve from thirty to forty thousands of population; every portion of the commonwealth was to be favored; grants from the state were for permanent funds alone. Under this system the number of academies incorporated increased to 17 in 1800, 36 in 1820, 68 by 1830, 114 by 1840, and 154 by 1860. In addition to these incorporated academies, there were many private schools of academy grade or at least teaching many of the academy subjects. From the information extant concerning these it is possible to distinguish some of them from private schools of more elementary character. In the first year (1838) that Horace Mann collected the statistics of Massachusetts schools there were found to be 1100 such private schools and 73 incorporated academies. The number of pupils in the incorporated academies was over 3500 and in the private schools nearly 25,000. In 1860 the incorporated academies had decreased to 65 and the private schools to 640. The number of pupils in the incorporated academies was the same as in 1830 but attendance in private schools had decreased by 10,000. Meanwhile the population of the state had doubled. This period of the ascendancy of the academy is also the period of the rise of the high school. After the Civil War the high school became the typical secondary school,

[396]

SECONDARY EDUCATION

though in Massachusetts academies continued to thrive, chiefly, however, as institutions serving many communities outside the state.

In New York the academy system began with the founding of the Board of Regents in 1785. The grant made in 1782 from public lands in each township, called "gospel and school lots," formed a basis for grants to academies. From 1796 the legislature passed occasional acts favoring grants to local academies, either in lands, in funds, or rarely in permission for local tax. A portion of the money raised by the state lottery of 1801 was for some years set aside for academies. With the common school fund established in 1805 was also established the Literature Fund, the proceeds of which were distributed by the regents to academies. This fund was built up from various sources. Much of the Surplus Revenue Fund of 1837 was devoted to this purpose, and in 1846 the new constitution set aside all of this fund for the support of academies.

The growth of the academies in New York closely paralleled their development in Massachusetts. The *Annual Reports* show this development both in total numbers existing and in the actual incorporation by five-year periods. A graph of Massachusetts academies very closely parallels these. By 1800, 19 academies had been incorporated, and 8 were in operation. By 1828, 48 had been incorporated and 34 were in existence. In 1827 the Literature Fund was greatly increased. During the following three years as many academies were incorporated as during the previous twenty years. A similar leap is noted after the next great increase of the fund in 1833. In 1830, 75 academies had been admitted by the regents and 57 were in existence. By 1840, 143 had been admitted and 126 were in existence. By 1860, 292 had been admitted and 170 were in existence. This is the largest number reported in operation for any five-year period. From this time on the academies declined in numbers and influence until about 1890, when there was a revival due to wholly different circumstances from those which prevailed during the first half of the century.

Virginia may be taken as a type of the Southern states. The activities of the various Protestant denominations were responsible for practically all the academies of these regions. Aside from the

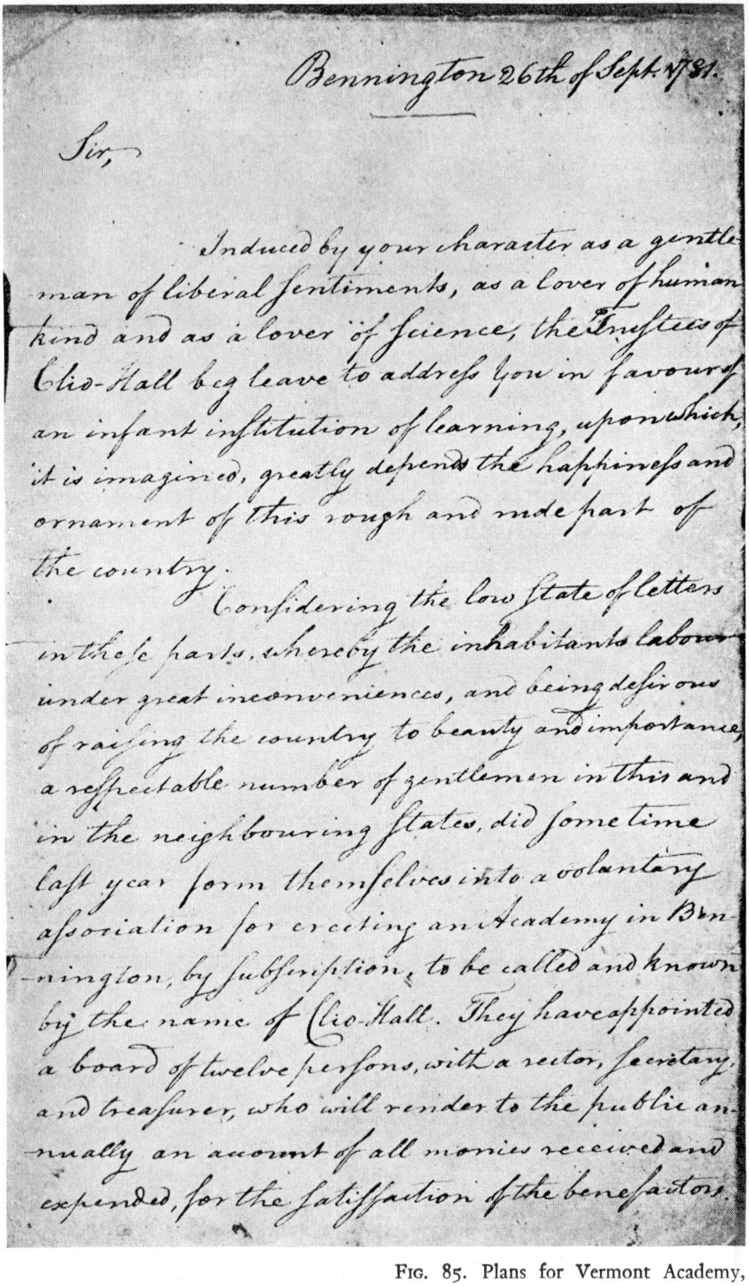

> Bennington 26th of Sept 1781.
>
> Sir,
>
> Induced by your character as a gentleman of liberal sentiments, as a lover of human kind and as a lover of science, the Trustees of Clio-Hall beg leave to address you in favour of an infant institution of learning, upon which, it is imagined, greatly depends the happiness and ornament of this rough and rude part of the country.
>
> Considering the low state of letters in these parts, whereby the inhabitants labour under great inconveniences, and being desirous of raising the country to beauty and importance, a respectable number of gentlemen in this and in the neighbouring states, did some time last year form themselves into a voluntary association for erecting an Academy in Bennington, by subscription, to be called and known by the name of Clio-Hall. They have appointed a board of twelve persons, with a rector, secretary, and treasurer, who will render to the public annually an account of all monies received and expended, for the satisfaction of the benefactors.

FIG. 85. Plans for Vermont Academy,

Anxious that no time be lost in carrying our design into effect, we have already circulated subscriptions through various parts, not without success. — But we still need cash. And as the Academy depends entirely upon Charity for its existence, to whom can it look with so much propriety as to its rich Neighbours, who love to encourage noble designs?

The object of this address is therefore Sir, humbly to request your Patronage to young Clio Hall, which looks up to You with respect and honour. — The least favour will be received with gratitude, and the kind donor will be had in lasting remembrance.

If the idea of this address shall be so fortunate as to gain your approbation, we shall be much obliged if You will communicate it to the gentlemen of your honourable circle. We are,

Sir,
With great respect,
Your most obedient
humble Servants,
by order,
David Avery.

The Honourable
Phil. Schuyler Esqr.

1781. (From the original manuscript.)

[399]

preparatory school of the university and one or two endowed schools, there were no institutions for secondary education surviving from the Colonial period. Many private schools flourished from time to time. Following the Revolution several "classical schools" were opened by ministers, chiefly from Princeton and Yale, and fostered by the religious bodies. Until the establishment of the Literary Fund, the state gave no aid. The legislature chartered many of these schools and often gave permission to raise funds by lotteries

FIG. 86. A New England village academy and its environs. (From *New England Magazine*.)

or by other means. Among the earlier of these institutions were Prince Edward Academy (1775), later Hampden Sidney College; Liberty Hall Academy (1776), now Washington and Lee; Fredericksburg Academy (1783), later Fredericksburg College. By 1800, 21 such institutions had been chartered and there were others existing without the support of the legislature. By 1820, 39 others had been chartered; by 1840, 55 more; and by 1860, 100 more. Some 225 in all were chartered before 1860, though there is no means of telling how many existed at any one time. The less significant and unchartered institutions bearing the name and doing the work of academies would no doubt bring the total actually in operation to

SECONDARY EDUCATION

this number. So it is apparent that the Southern states were quite as well supplied with these institutions as were those of the North.

Such schools were even more individualistic in the South than in the North. The state of Virginia did little to help them. Of the entire number 17 were assisted at times by the state legislature out of the Literary Fund which had been designed for free public schools, but the flourishing condition of the academies was a most effective argument against any state aid to education.

Other states gave encouragement to academies in one of two ways: (1) by charter, by subsidy, or both, to individual institutions; or (2) by the enactment of general laws providing for some system of extending these institutions throughout the state. The former

FIG. 87. The Norwich, Conn., Academy. The first of the free academies. (From Barnard's *American Journal of Education*, Vol. II, p. 696.)

individualistic method was most common, but it resulted in no organized system. The academies were national in their universal distribution and in the fact that they were the commonly accepted form of secondary education during this period. Under the second type of help actual state systems were elaborated, which might be either similar to that of Massachusetts, where general principles were laid down for the encouragement of such institutions by the state, or similar to that of New York where a central body was created, with power to authorize or incorporate academies and to sanction their participation in the distribution of state funds. In 1785 Georgia adopted the latter plan; each county was to have an academy, these to constitute component parts of the state university. Little developed from this, however, except a college and later a state university. Louisiana adopted a similar scheme immediately after its admission into the Union, and academies were formed in at least twelve counties. This plan, however, was abandoned in 1821 and the component institutions were left to local support, assisted in a few instances by state subsidies. Michigan adopted a similar centralized institution in 1817, which later (1827) was elaborated to require a grammar school (Latin and French) in each township of 200 families. When the present state university was founded in 1837, branch preparatory schools or academies were by the same scheme to be established in various parts of the state. At least nine such were established, but in 1849 the system was abandoned in favor of local subsidies and support for the individual academies or for the establishment of high schools. In Maryland the Colonial system of Latin grammar schools for each county was gradually transposed into a similar system of academies. By 1812 such a system had been worked out. In Pennsylvania the plan of the state subsidy for institutions under private control—colleges, academies, normal schools—had been in favor from the first. Before the middle of the century over one hundred academies were receiving state assistance in this manner. Despite the continued state appropriations and the multiplication of these schools, they did not flourish except in numbers. In 1838 a law was passed including the following provisions:

"To each university and college now incorporated, or which may be incorporated by the Legislature, and maintaining at least four professors and instructing constantly at least one hundred students, one thousand dollars. To each academy and female seminary now incorporated, or which may be incorporated by the Legislature, maintaining one or more teachers capable of giving instruction in the Greek and Roman classics, mathematics, and English or English and German literature, and in which at least fifteen pupils shall constantly be

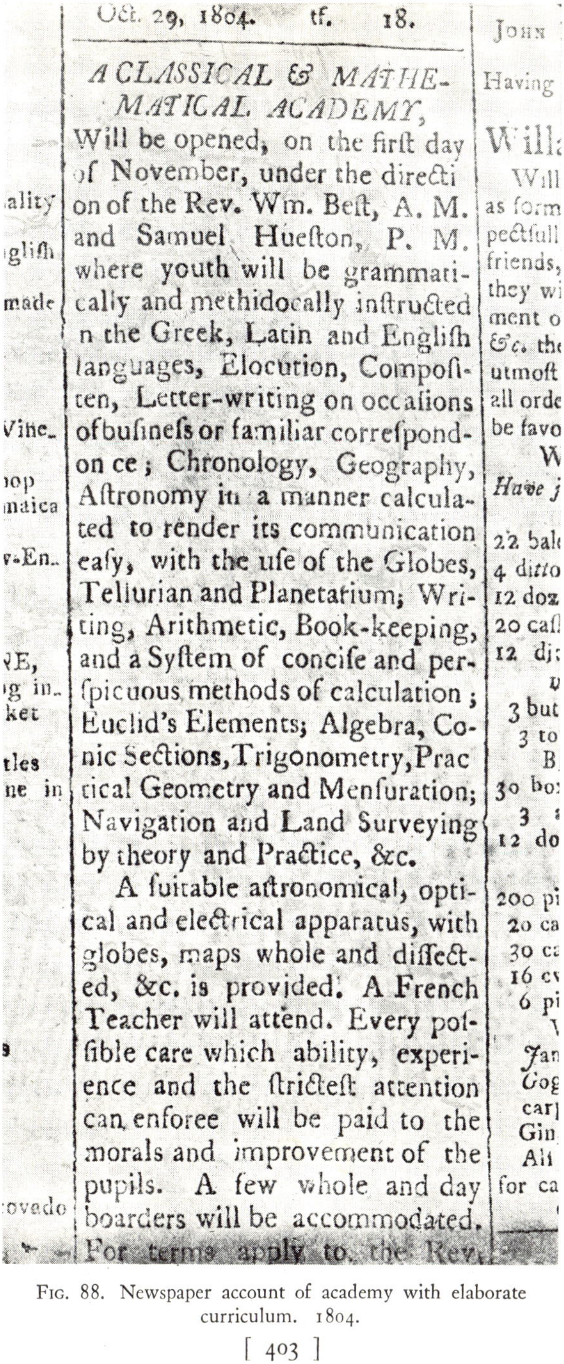

Oct. 29, 1804.   tf.   18.

*A CLASSICAL & MATHE-
MATICAL ACADEMY,*
Will be opened, on the first day of November, under the direction of the Rev. Wm. Best, A. M. and Samuel Hueston, P. M. where youth will be grammatically and methidocally instructed n the Greek, Latin and English languages, Elocution, Composition, Letter-writing on occasions of business or familiar correspondonce; Chronology, Geography, Astronomy in a manner calculated to render its communication easy, with the use of the Globes, Tellurian and Planetarium; Writing, Arithmetic, Book-keeping, and a System of concise and perspicuous methods of calculation; Euclid's Elements; Algebra, Conic Sections, Trigonometry, Practical Geometry and Mensuration; Navigation and Land Surveying by theory and Practice, &c.

A suitable astronomical, optical and electrical apparatus, with globes, maps whole and dissected, &c. is provided. A French Teacher will attend. Every possible care which ability, experience and the strictest attention can enforce will be paid to the morals and improvement of the pupils. A few whole and day boarders will be accommodated. For terms apply to the Rev.

FIG. 88. Newspaper account of academy with elaborate curriculum. 1804.

[403]

taught in either or all of the branches aforesaid, three hundred dollars. To each of said academies and female seminaries, where at least twenty-five pupils are taught, as aforesaid, four hundred dollars; and to each of said academies and female seminaries, having at least two teachers, and in which forty or more pupils are constantly taught, as aforesaid, five hundred dollars."

Curriculum and Method.—One of the most striking characteristics of the academy was the breadth of its curriculum. In striking contrast was the Latin grammar school which limited its course to two or three subjects. The flexible system of the academy permitted the introduction of almost every subject. The dominant idea in the education of the Latin grammar school was discipline; that of the academy curriculum was culture, which was interpreted to mean the introduction of almost every element that forms a part of the intellectual life or achievement of the race. Drawing their first students from a wide range of territory, from every class in society, these schools met the needs and interests of these various localities and social groups by a wide offering of subjects of study. The core of academy education yet remained the old classical curriculum of Latin, Greek, and mathematics, just as the core of the student body in the more flourishing academies remained the group preparing for college. But even the college curriculum had responded to the same influences, and the requirements of entrance had been much broadened. Among the additional subjects required for admission were those of geography beginning in 1807, English grammar in 1817, algebra in 1820, geometry in 1844, ancient history in 1847. Once introduced by the leading colleges (most of those were first required by Harvard) such subjects soon became generally prescribed.

But it was the new subjects of the natural science group which during this time came into greatest prominence and offered the greatest attraction to the educators of the time. They formed a large part of the offerings of the academy and undoubtedly proved one of their great attractions. Astronomy was easily the most popular of these and the most widely introduced. Natural philosophy followed closely, and in fact astronomy was frequently included

SECONDARY EDUCATION

under this title. It was the new discoveries in physics, especially electricity and electro-magnetism, that were the most novel and offered the greatest stimulus to the imagination. Chemistry, geology, botany, and zoology were likewise popular. The systematic organization of these latter made them attractive subjects for presentation. The very general use of *memoriter* methods, together with an exaggerated idea of the value of systematic knowledge, or rather of information systematically classified, was largely responsible for the great vogue of these subjects and of science in general. The extended enterprises of the day in the way of internal improvements and economic development, such as mining and canal and railroad building, had all offered a stimulus to the study of the systematic sciences, and to the practical application of mathematics and physics through the rudimentary engineering sciences. Speculative and practical interest united in greatly increasing the popularity of these subjects.

From the first, beginning even with Franklin's academy in the middle of the eighteenth century, the study of the vernacular language and literature had been greatly emphasized. English grammar had been greatly elaborated and in America, especially through the text of Lindley Murray (first published in 1795), came to rival Latin in popularity. Similarly the study of the English classics, especially those of Milton, Pope, and the classicists of the seventeenth and eighteenth century, came to be considered as possessing value equal or superior to that of the masterpieces of Latin and Greek literature. National pride and political aspiration had much to do with this. Rhetorical study and the declamatory arts were greatly fostered. Readers with oratorical selections were multiplied for use not only in the elementary schools but especially in the academies. In addition to such subjects, religious literature played an important part in the curriculum of the academy. Many if not most of these schools gave definite instruction in religion. Many of them were under ecclesiastical control; most of them owed their inception to denominational zeal. The moral influence of these institutions was fostered partially through the subjects in the course of study but more especially through the community life and the

FOUNDING OF AMERICAN SCHOOL SYSTEM

oversight and direction of the student body by the faculty. Manners were usually united with morals as a part of the curriculum; the female seminaries especially devoted great attention to these finishing subjects. Sometimes these accomplishments were carried to absurd extremes. The following advertisement quoted from a newspaper published in Norfolk, Va., in the late eighteenth century is one of the best illustrations of this tendency:

"E. Armston (or perhaps better known by the name of Gardner) continues the school at Point Pleasant, Norfolk Borough, where is a large and convenient house proper to accommodate young ladies as boarders; at which school is taught petit point in flowers, fruit, landscapes, and sculpture, nun's work, embroidery in silk, gold, silver, pearls, or embossed, shading of all kinds, in the various works in vogue, Dresden point work, lace ditto, catgut in different modes, flourishing muslin, after the newest taste, and most elegant pattern waxwork in figure, fruit, or flowers, shell ditto, or grotesque, painting in water colors and mezzotinto; also the art of taking off foliage, with several other embellishments necessary for the amusement of persons of fortune who have taste. Specimens of the subscriber's work may be seen at her house, as also of her scholars: having taught several years in Norfolk, and elsewhere, to general satisfaction. She flatters herself that those gentlemen and ladies who have hitherto employed her will grant their further indulgence, as no endeavors shall be wanting to complete what is above mentioned, with a first attention to the behavior of those ladies intrusted to her care.

"Reading will be her peculiar care; writing and arithmetic will be taught by a master properly qualified; and, if desired, will engage proficients in music and dancing."

The most accurate impressions of the curriculum of the academies can be gained from a study of those of New York where the regents' reports offer a detailed account covering more than a century. No curriculum requirements were made for thirty years after the formation of the board of regents, but in 1817 it was required that all academies receiving state aid should teach the ancient classics together with all subjects required for admission for the colleges. A state law of 1827 made a definite enactment for con-

SECONDARY EDUCATION

trolling the curriculum, which remained in force for a half century. This specified that the state subsidies to the academies should be distributed on the basis of the number of students enrolled in the classical or the advanced English studies or in both. This prescribed a fundamental curriculum and definitely placed English on the same basis as the classics. The requirements in English made by the regents were composition and declamation. It is interesting to note that declaiming thus came to be regarded as an art essential to the free American citizen. While this was the minimum requirement, the records of these years indicate that at least 22 different subjects were offered by the academies. From this time until near the middle of the century the curriculum constantly expanded. During the half century more than 100 different subjects are listed as having been taught in the academies. From 1787 to 1870 the regents' reports show 149 different academic subjects. Of these 23 appear before 1826 and 26 after 1840; while a full 100 appear during the short 15-year period from 1826 to 1840. The offering of any one year is quite as significant. The list for 1837 includes more than 60 subjects and is as follows: arithmetic, algebra, architecture, astronomy, botany, bookkeeping, Biblical antiquities, biography, chemistry, composition, conic sections, Constitution of the United States, constitution of New York, elements of criticism, declamation, drawing, dialing, English grammar, evidences of Christianity, embroidery, civil engineering, extemporaneous speaking, French, geography, physical geography, geology, plane geometry, analytic geometry, Greek, Grecian antiquities, German, general history, history of the United States, history of New York, Hebrew, Italian, Latin, law (constitutional, select revised statutes, criminal and mercantile, Blackstone's *Commentaries*), logic, leveling, logarithms, vocal music, instrumental music, mapping, mensuration, mineralogy, mythology, natural history, navigation, nautical astronomy, natural theology, orthography, natural philosophy, moral philosophy, intellectual philosophy, penmanship, political economy, painting, perspective, physiology, English pronunciation, reading, rhetoric, Roman antiquities, stenography, statistics, surveying, Spanish, trigonometry, topography, technology, principles of teaching.

It will be seen that many of these are simply branches of a more general subject. As for instance, history may be divided into Greek history, Roman history, French history, history of the United States, history of New York, and so on. However, from the point of view of the organization of the curriculum, each constituted a distinct unit with little or no connection with or reference to other units.

Following the state law, most of the teachers were divided into two departments, the classical and the English. As a matter of fact, the curricula of the two were almost identical except that the classical departments taught Latin and Greek, while the English substituted French or a combination of French, German, and Spanish. The period of the great multiplication of the subjects of study followed 1830. Up to that time the subjects were comparatively few. But during this following period there developed the new interest in education and the very much broader conception of its scope and function.

In this great number of subjects there is a substantial core consisting of Latin, English, French, and algebra, which appears continuously from the closing years of the eighteenth century to the opening years of the twentieth; but there is also a very much larger group of studies introduced at the beginning of the second quarter of the nineteenth century but vanishing within half a century. Many of these were incorporated into more comprehensive subjects. These belong particularly to the natural sciences, as anatomy, electricity, natural philosophy. But some have disappeared altogether. The most conspicuous of these is logic; many, such as calculus and Hebrew, have simply been relegated to the higher institutions. Within a half century about seventy subjects appear and disappear. This half century covers the latter part of the period we have under consideration. The most surprising thing about this entire development of the curriculum is that in the decade preceding 1835 are recognized and introduced into the various academy curricula more than eighty new subjects. This does not mean that all of these subjects are found in any one curriculum, but that they should be represented within the limits of one state is quite as

SECONDARY EDUCATION

significant. No better evidence of the individualizing tendency of the education of the period could be given.

As to method, individualism controlled quite as markedly as in the curriculum. There were no demonstrated principles or formulated science of teaching; each institution followed its own ideas as did each teacher his own devices. Since, however, so much was determined by traditional views, there was fairly general agreement as to principles of procedure. The theory of mental discipline largely controlled. The aim of most of the formal subjects was to teach the children to reason, "to develop the intellect" or "to train the mental faculties." But with the great variety of new subjects, especially the sciences, it was clearly recognized that their chief value was in giving information. "The great purpose of education was to store the mind (which in this sense is but another name for memory) with useful knowledge; and in the process of doing so to give increased energy, activity, and precision to the mental faculties." This quotation from the *Regents' Report* of 1839 gives very concisely the entire theory of method of this period. Determined by both of these points of view, much of the work of the academy was purely *memoriter*. Great stress was laid on the examination as a test of these attainments. Preliminary to the examination, and in fact a prominent phase of work throughout, was abundant drill. The prominence given to spelling and to the spelling match is a typical illustration of this feature. The regulations of the regents in New York require that all pupils be frequently practiced through "regular exercises in spelling, pronunciation, and all elementary subjects." In the advanced subjects, especially the new sciences, the lecture method was largely used. In connection with this, especially in "natural philosophy," demonstration experiments were common. Laboratory experimentation had not yet developed.

Individualism in method showed itself conspicuously through the great development of devices. Teachers' magazines devoted a large part of their space to the presentation and defense of such devices. In the absence of definitely formulated principles and methods many teachers came to look upon such devices as the essential features of method. Toward the middle of the century, after the formation of normal schools, a more scientific conception of method began to prevail.

Origin and Characteristics of the High School (Quos. 591–603).—During these early decades of the nineteenth century, there had been a very marked movement towards public control of higher education. In the second quarter of the century this change in public opinion began to affect the institutions of secondary education. This movement revealed itself in two ways: first, in the formation of the so-called free academies; second, in the establishment of high schools. As has been seen, very many of the academies received public aid. Where this aid was derived directly from taxation very strong sentiment was frequently aroused against fees for tuition. In fact, many challenged the right of an institution which shared in the public taxes to levy charges for instruction. Many academies in Pennsylvania and the states to the south received a part of their patronage and of their support through the scheme of charity education in vogue there (p. 296). In some regions the state required that, in return for the aid given, academies should educate a stipulated number of pupils free of tuition charges. In other regions where a local area contributed through taxation to the support of an academy the institution was open to all pupils from that area without charges for tuition. Such an academy became a "free academy." An especially notable controversy occurred in Connecticut during the late forties over the establishment of the free Academy at Norwich. Such an institution was hailed by many as distinctly superior to the high school which was just then in the early stages of formation. In 1847 New York City established a free academy, as did also Philadelphia, Baltimore, and most of the leading cities of the East at about the same time. These institutions resembled the old time academy in that they were controlled by a board of trustees and not by a public school board. While most of their support was drawn from public sources yet individual contribution was of importance. The essential feature was that they were free of tuition for the local area.

Meanwhile, especially in New York, another attempt had been

SECONDARY EDUCATION

made to establish a free secondary school of the Lancasterian or monitorial type. Borrowing the name of a very popular institution in Edinburgh, Scotland, these have been called high schools. In control and support they were essentially academies. In breadth of curriculum they were similar to the academies. The novel feature of these institutions was the adoption of the monitorial scheme of instruction and discipline borrowed from the Lancasterian system of elementary schools. Such a scheme had been carried to a high degree of efficiency in Edinburgh in the parent institution. In 1825 such a high school for boys was founded in New York City by John Griscom. This proved so successful that later (1826) one was opened for girls. Many friends of education contributed to these schools, but they proved so successful that they became practically commercial ventures instead of philanthropic institutions. Change in educational sentiment and the development of the higher grades of the public schools on the same plan brought about their speedy downfall. Meanwhile Governor De Witt Clinton, during the decade of the twenties, had urged upon the legislature on several occasions the desirability of establishing a county system of such schools throughout the state. This plan found little favor; while one or two such schools were initiated, none ever flourished. However, the private or quasi-public forms of secondary institutions were much more popular. The first of these were stock companies; the second were organized, partially at least, on a philanthropic basis. The number, character, and name of those in New York are instructive and may be taken as indicative of what was going on in other states, where records are not so accurate as those furnished by the regents. These, in the order of their founding, were: New York High School Society, 1825, a stock company, dissolved in 1833; Livingstone County High School, 1827, a stock company, became an academy in 1846 and a normal school in 1866; Rochester High School, 1827, became a collegiate institute in 1839 and was the first school to receive for a time aid from local taxation; Buffalo High School Association, 1827, a stock company, changed to an academy in 1830; Gouveneur High School, 1828, a stock company but in receipt of aid from local taxation; Utica High

School for Boys, 1827, a stock company, known from 1833 as a gymnasium; Warren County High School, 1828, a stock company, not organized, but probably initiated as was the Livingstone County institution in response to Governor Clinton's messages; Palmyra High School, 1829, a stock company, extinct in 1850; Newburgh High School, 1829, in receipt of local support and merged in the common school system, 1852; Ontario High School, 1830, a stock company, school not organized; Clyde High School, 1834, under trustees, assisted by local tax, made free in 1874; Preble High School, 1834, under trustees, legalized but not organized; La Fayette High School, 1836, a stock company, school not organized; Sandy Hill High School, 1836, under trustees, not organized; Lewiston High School Academy; Troy High School, a stock company receiving local aid; Ellenville High School, 1856, a stock company.

This long list is given in full partly because the statement is so frequently made that high schools did not exist before the Civil War; partly because it illustrates the rather vague use of terms not definitely fixed by custom; and finally because it shows the actual evolution of the high school as a public-supported institution. It is probable that in New York the term high school was commonly used during this period to indicate the monitorial system of instruction, while academy referred to form of control and support. Hence the occasional use of both terms by an institution.

Meanwhile the founding of a new type of institution had actually begun in Massachusetts. If the free academy was a step beyond the ordinary academy in the democratization of secondary schools, the new institution soon to be called high school was a much more pronounced step. In 1821 the Boston town meeting voted to establish an English classical school as a parallel to the Latin grammar school of ancient origin. The name indicates that the school was to be distinguished from the English grammar school, as that term was coming into use for the stage of common education generally known as the grammar grades, and on the other hand from the Latin grammar school of ancient standing. The new English classical school was to be parallel to the Latin classical school but the curriculum was to consist of the entire range of modern sub-

SECONDARY EDUCATION

jects, substituting English literature, mathematics, the sciences, logic, and history for the Latin and Greek of the old school. Three years later the term English High School is employed in the official vote to designate this school, and thus is introduced the specific use of the name which has since become universal in the United States. It is probable that the term was here, too, borrowed from the Scottish institution, a general knowledge of which had been made common through Mr. Griscom's publications and through the discussion of the proposed institution in New York. In 1826 Boston established a similar high school for girls (p. 464). This proved so great a success that the numbers applying for admission really constituted a factor in its dissolution. Two years later the course of study in the grammar schools, or upper grades, as we would now call them, was elaborated and became a substitute for the high school for girls, which was abandoned. Following upon this the Massachusetts Law of 1827 made provision for institutions throughout the commonwealth similar to those of Boston. In time similar institutions bearing the name of high schools were founded in the leading cities of most of the Northern and Western states. By this time, however, the Massachusetts system had attained effective operation so that other parts of the country could profit by the earlier experiences of this state. Following the adoption of the new state system in Pennsylvania in 1836, Philadelphia developed its central high school in 1838. Baltimore founded one the following year, which later became the city college. Charleston, South Carolina, established a similar school in the same year. Though bearing the name of high schools these institutions charged tuition and were essentially of the city college or academy type. The same year saw the addition of the high school to the newly founded graded school system of Providence, R.I.

The essential features of these early high schools, which remained their outstanding characteristics, were, first, their support through public taxation, and second, their control through publicly elected officials. This control by the public might be two or three steps removed from direct election but ultimately the controlling body was responsible to public authority. In the academy and even in some of the free academy type, control was through a self-perpetuating board. In the free academies and city colleges the boards of control were not self-perpetuating, but were created by acts of public authority. These institutions, however, had no connection with the public school system. But the high schools formed an integral part of the public school system and were almost invariably controlled by the same board. These institutions, with the few exceptions noted, were open to all pupils without the payment of any charges. This in time came to be an absolutely essential feature. The high school thus early became "the poor man's college" and in control, support, and student body was the last step in the democratization of secondary education.

The curriculum of these early institutions as compared with that of the academies was restricted. Individual whim or caprice was now subject to public control and checked by the fact that it constituted a public charge. Determination of the subjects of study by public enactment was carried much further than in the preceding stage (p. 161). This represents a development of the democratizing process beyond the individualism of the academy period, for it is a recognition of the social significance of education and the importance of social choice. The narrowing of the curriculum arises not so much from the theory of social responsibility as from the very practical experience of a social cost of education.

In method the early high schools show no significant development beyond the academies. Increased numbers, larger class groups, and a systematized course of study produced a greater formalism in method, through the development in class instruction, which was quite in accord with the tendencies revealing themselves in other phases of education.

Development of the High School System before the Civil War Period.—The Massachusetts Law of 1827 laid the foundation for a system of high schools in this state, the only one to develop thoroughly previous to the Civil War. This law does not contain the term "high school" but it provides that every town or district containing five hundred families should maintain a school for at least ten months of each year, in which should be taught in

SECONDARY EDUCATION

addition to the subjects of the elementary school, the history of the United States, bookkeeping, geometry, surveying, and algebra. Every town or city containing four thousand inhabitants was compelled to add to this curriculum Latin, Greek, general history, rhetoric, and logic. Schools of both types should be for the benefit of all the inhabitants and supported by public taxation. By the Census of 1830, 35 towns would have been compelled to support schools of the lower type, and by that of 1840, 44 towns. By the latter date, however, Horace Mann estimates that only thirteen towns did maintain such schools. This low attainment, however, was due to the reactionary measure of 1829 which practically made this provision of the Law of 1827 merely permissive. The provision again became mandatory in 1835, but in 1840 towns were once more relieved from the support of such schools if they would raise 25% more for their other schools than had ever been raised before. This provision was repealed in 1848, but the Statute of 1850 lowered the former standard by providing that the offering of these subjects for shorter terms in a number of schools would be considered equivalent to maintaining one school for the entire year, provided the combined terms of the several schools amounted to the full twelve months. In 1857 this law was repealed and the original enactment of 1827 made operative. By this law algebra and the history of the United States were added to the curriculum of the elementary school, physiology and hygiene were made permissive, and natural philosophy, chemistry, botany, civil government, and Latin were added to the requirements of the high school. High schools of the higher grade were required to offer in addition French, astronomy, geology, intellectual and moral

FIG. 89. First high school building, erected in Boston in 1821. (From Grizzell, *Origin and Development of the High School in New England before 1865*.)

FOUNDING OF AMERICAN SCHOOL SYSTEM

science, and political economy. These laws showing action and reaction are mentioned in order to indicate the difficulties that even the most advanced communities met in developing a system of free secondary schools.

By the Census of 1850 there were 76 towns that would have been obliged to maintain high schools of the lower standard and 46 of the higher, while by 1860 the number of towns large enough to support a high school of the lower standard had increased to 128 and 61 of these were of sufficient size to come within the provisions of the law requiring an institution of the higher grade. By 1840, 16 towns of the 44 had complied with the law. By 1850, 42 of the 76, and by 1860, 86 of the 128 actually had the schools which their population required. The discrepancy between the number of towns having over 500 families and those supporting high schools would indicate a number entirely neglecting the law or taking advantage of the privilege of exemption. On the other hand some towns below the minimum requirement of population had voluntarily established high schools. Of these there were two in 1840, five in 1850, and sixteen in 1860. Thus by the date last named there were more than one hundred high schools in the state of Massachusetts. One of the estimates published by the Commissioner of Education in 1900 allows only forty for the entire country. The facts just stated show that the statement frequently made concerning the small number of high schools in the United States at this time have taken into account only those in the larger cities and have omitted many less conspicuous but no less effective institutions.

New York High Schools (Quos. 583–588).—In the list given on pages 411–12 it will be seen that two or three of the early high schools were organized on the county basis and were to receive public aid. These were established in response to Government charters in advocacy of a county system of monitorial high schools. But none of them succeeded. Others of these were the result of a union of district schools, having a joint board of trustees at least partially representative of the local districts and receiving some support from local taxation. This status was not very definite, as in Rochester

SECONDARY EDUCATION

the trustees were required to report to the common council, "as trustees of a school district"; nowhere was it permanent. But in 1853 the legislature passed the union school law which legalized this consolidation of districts and which provided for a unification of wards in cities and districts in towns, eliminating the grosser evils of the district system, insuring a graded system of schools, and in many places securing the organization of a high school as a part of the public system. Permission for such union frequently had been given by the legislature to certain cities then rapidly gaining in population. The act extended this permission throughout the state. Agitation for such legal provision had been going on for fifteen years, but the dual system in New York state, in which the regents of the university supervised, controlled, and subsidized from the Literary Fund all academies and secondary schools, while the superintendent of public instruction and local trustees performed similar functions for the public common schools, created many difficulties in the expansion of the latter system to include secondary education.

In 1847 the New York Free Academy was incorporated under special trustees, but supported by local funds. In the same year the Lockport Union School Board was authorized, to consist of representatives of each of the co-operating districts and to support advanced studies out of tax funds. Thus the public high school system was definitely legalized.

By 1853 eight other towns or villages received the same privilege, later made general. Special legislation continued particularly where the property of a local academy was to be transferred to public school authorities and it was desired to guarantee the continuance of free secondary instruction. Twenty-three such cases were acted upon before the Union Free School Act of 1864.

For some years no uniform usage developed regarding the name to be applied to these free, tax-supported, publicly controlled institutions of secondary education. Of the twenty-two established by 1860 only one bore the title high school, while free academy was applied to ten, institute to two, and classical or union classical school to three. Occasionally the terms academy and high school were combined. Legislature enactments generally employ the phrase "academy or high school" in referring to secondary education. In 1889 the legislature defined the word academy to include "high schools, academical departments of union schools and all other schools of higher education not possessing degree-giving powers."

In towns and villages the name union school continued in preference to academy, but after 1860 the use of the term high school in cities inclined general usage to the designation now commonly accepted. By 1860, 12 such institutes had been founded *de novo,* and 4 organized from previously existing institutions; by 1870, there were 36 new and 40 reorganized; by 1880, 86 new and 88 reorganized or a total of 174 institutions recognized by the regents and classified as high schools.

High Schools in Other States.—Previous to the Civil War institutions for secondary education were established either by special enactment for the individual city or on the basis of the union school districts as provided for in New York. Some states, such as Iowa and Michigan, had permissive laws permitting communities to establish such institutions contingent upon the demand indicated by a stipulated majority either of popular vote or of the board of education. It is quite obvious that the estimates given in the published lists do not take account of a great number of such schools. The lists have been limited usually to schools in cities of very considerable size. Evidently to make any fair comparison with the number of high schools at the present, those in the small communities should have been included also. It is also evident, by the Civil War period, that the high school was a well established institution in many states, though it reached the effectiveness of a system in only one or two, and that even in these it still had to compete with the academy as the dominant and the most popular type.

Summary.—Progress towards the nationalizing and democratizing of secondary education was made during this period first through the academy. The essential feature of the academy was its individualism, hence increasing nationalization is seen not in

SECONDARY EDUCATION

the enactment of state systems, though there were a few, but in the establishment of these institutions in considerable numbers in every state. There were few regions which did not have access to an academy. Democratization was evidenced by the fact that they were chiefly finishing schools and appealed to the great middle class rather than to the small class preparing for college and for the few learned professions; also by the curriculum, which was all-inclusive; by the freedom in choice of subjects; by the individualistic methods of instruction; and by the democratic community life of teacher and students.

The early high schools constituted another step towards nationalization and democratization. Previous to the Civil War a complete system of high schools was worked out in only one state—Massachusetts. Elsewhere the academy still predominated or existed exclusively; even in Massachusetts the academy excelled in popular esteem, though the high schools had begun to predominate in amount of public support and in attendance. The high school represented triumphant democracy above all in complete support by taxation and in control by publicly elected officials. It had become a component part of the public school system though still subordinate in importance to the academy. In New York the two institutions came into a direct conflict in which the academy was victorious.

As to curriculum, the high school offered a more restricted course of study, as this was now brought under public control and made responsive to public needs rather than individual preference or even whim. The process of democratization was shown in both institutions in the admission of girls. In the academies this step was at first taken by only a few institutions; this broadening of scope or clientele was further supplemented by institutions for girls alone; then the predominant type came to be coeducational. The first high schools were for boys or girls alone. With few exceptions, however, they soon came to be coeducational.

Chapter XIII

HIGHER EDUCATION

General Characteristics.—In Chapter VII it was indicated that the break in the Colonial traditions in the field of higher education came with the founding of King's College in 1754. In Pennsylvania, however, the radical departure marked in the proposals of Benjamin Franklin in the University of Pennsylvania, by Provost Smith in his College of Mirania (Quo. 286), and by President Johnson in the first announcement of King's College were not realized (Quo. 278). Though attempts were made both at Kings and at Pennsylvania to initiate these radical educational proposals, yet a few years saw the colleges in operation along the narrow traditional lines. The successors to President Johnson and to Provost Smith were quite of the conventional type. The student body was reduced to the smallest compass, the collegiate work to the narrow classical and mathematical routine. The Revolutionary War intervened and brought the work of most of the American colleges to a standstill. After the Revolution the period of stagnation continued except at William and Mary, where the fertile genius of Jefferson had brought consideration to many new proposals. In general the number of students greatly diminished. In many institutions buildings and records had been destroyed. There was no time or energy left for consideration of plans of alteration or improvement of methods. After the war the institutions were satisfied to re-establish their work. The question of mere existence was of dominating importance. Books were scarce and costly. The sciences were new and timid. The romance languages especially were considered under the influence of popery or tinctured with the danger of heresy, religious or social. The Teutonic languages were considered uncouth and the culture represented of no importance. Yet before the opening of the nine-

[420]

HIGHER EDUCATION

teenth century numerous signs were evident of a new era in higher education. There was little in the college life to indicate that a new national life had come into being and needed the guidance and the inspiration of university trained men and of college leadership. Gradually, however, new ideals were formulated and in a number of important characteristics the colleges underwent a slow but persistent change. Briefly to survey these new forces as they developed through the decade of the early National period is the purpose of this chapter.

The most important of these changes were (1) the marked broadening of the curriculum, showing the new social demands; (2) the development of professional schools, indicating an expansion of public interest; (3) a reorganization of collegiate administration necessitated by the two previous changes; (4) a general change from religious to secular control; (5) a development of state universities.

Expansion of the College Curriculum (Quos. 604–606).— The abortive attempts of Kings and Pennsylvania to break away from the traditional Oxford and Cambridge curriculum, followed by all of the early Colonial colleges, was repeated with a slightly greater success by William and Mary under the leadership of President Madison in 1779. These changes were chiefly due to the influence of Thomas Jefferson (Quo. 611), who undoubtedly was influenced by broad political considerations as well as educational. The professorships of divinity and Oriental languages were abolished, and in their place were established the professorships of law and politics, one of anatomy, chemistry, medicine, and one of modern languages. Provision was made for additional instruction in the field of international law, fine arts, biological science (natural history), and the physical sciences (natural philosophy). During the process of the French Revolution Jefferson attempted to have transplanted bodily from Europe the University of Geneva with its broad scheme of universal studies and the free organization of the Continental institutions. This idea being opposed by Washington and proving impracticable, the college gradually fell back under the traditional ecclesiastical control, though the old ecclesiastical curriculum was not re-established. With the creation of the University of Virginia shortly afterwards the old college lost much of its influence.

Even before the close of the Revolution changes began to occur at Harvard. In 1780 the study of the French language was made permissible to students who brought the consent of their parents or guardians. This, however, was as an extra. In 1785 the course of study was as follows: in addition to the classics required

FIG. 90. Architectural plans of the University of Virginia, drawn up by Thomas Jefferson. (From Adams, *Thomas Jefferson and the University of Virginia*, p. 68.)

of all, the freshman year offered Greek and Latin, rhetoric, arithmetic and the art of speaking; the sophomore year offered algebra, and the higher mathematics; the junior year evidences of Christianity; the senior year logic, metaphysics and ethics. The freshman and sophomore years had a choice between Hebrew and French, while declamation was required of all. A professorship of chemistry had been established in the previous year: in 1804 one in rhetoric and oratory (held for a time by John Quincy Adams); in 1805 a professorship of natural history.

Naturally the most conspicuous addition to the college curriculum was in the line of the natural sciences. While astronomy had been in the old college curriculum it was not until 1830 that

HIGHER EDUCATION

the first observatory was erected at Yale. The other leading colleges soon followed. Geology was introduced by Professor Silliman at Yale in 1802, though the distinct chair in this subject was not created until 1850 under Professor Dana. Field work had begun in this subject as early as 1827 growing out of the work of Rensselaer Institute and the interest developed through the construction of the Erie Canal. Early in the century extensive field work was undertaken by the students at Williams. Natural history was introduced at Harvard in 1788 and at Columbia in 1792. Chemistry had been introduced in connection with medical study preceding the Revolutionary War. Collegiate instruction in chemistry was offered at Harvard in 1782 and at Dartmouth in 1798. At Princeton in 1795 was established the first individual chair; Columbia followed in 1800, Yale in 1801 (under Silliman).

Another group of new subjects was that of the modern languages. French had been permitted even before the Revolution as a subject outside of the ordinary curriculum and with the consent of parents. The first chair of the French language was established in Columbia in 1784. Previous to the Revolution, however, instruction had been given. Instruction at William and Mary dates from 1776; the professorship at Harvard from 1815. All of this instruction was quite elementary. It was not until 1825 that more advanced work was offered at Harvard. The organization of the University of New York in 1831 provided for four chairs in modern languages. With the introduction of these modern languages, attendance on Hebrew was made optional both at Yale and at Harvard and this subject thus tended to disappear.

With the reorganization of Kings, now Columbia, in 1784, three professional faculties were established in addition to the old arts faculty. The latter consisted of seven professorships covering the field of Latin, Greek, moral philosophy, rhetoric and logic, mathematics, natural philosophy, astronomy, and French. The first four and the seventh were given a salary of £100, the fifth £50, the sixth £200. This in addition to the "emoluments of the classes."

At Princeton the change began in 1775 when President Smith succeeded Witherspoon. In that year a professorship of chemistry was established, held by McLane, under whose leadership the physical sciences found their way into the American college. In 1802 a chair of modern language was founded. In 1818 chairs of experimental philosophy, chemistry, and natural history were established.

This expansion of the curriculum overcame the old problem of narrowness and conventionalism but brought new problems of its own. When the University of the City of New York was organized in 1830 sixteen departments were created. The course of study in all institutions had so expanded as to be unrecognizable to the collegian of a previous generation. Moreover, it was proving to be unattainable by the students and unmanageable by the faculty. Some new scheme of organization must replace the traditional one in which one fixed curriculum had been set for all students. Consequently, during the second quarter of the century many schemes were proposed for the alleviation of the burden placed on the student by the great expansion of the course of study. To a certain extent these difficulties were met by the very general expansion of the college course to cover four years instead of three, quite common during the Colonial period, and further by an expansion of the secondary or preparatory course of study. This meant in general a greater maturity upon the part of the students, but the two combined did not solve the problem. An approach to an elective system was made when the older colleges permitted the substitution of a modern language for Hebrew.

In 1825 the University of Virginia opened under a novel scheme of administration. There was no fixed curriculum of studies and no definite control of the students' program of studies. Candidacy for a degree, however, was yet determined by the satisfaction of requirements of a somewhat rigidly prescribed course. Jefferson's ideas controlling this plan were derived from the knowledge of European customs. This knowledge came through his early experience with the French universities and more recently through the knowledge of German university customs reported to him by Professor Ticknor of Harvard.

At the latter institution Ticknor brought about a limited trial

HIGHER EDUCATION

of freedom of election of certain subjects during the few years following 1825. Then and again under President Quincy in the early 1840's an experiment was made in allowing to the three upper classes certain freedom of selection regarding at least one half of their course. The early experiment was connected with the opening of the university courses to students not candidates for a degree, and especially to those who desired to study in a particular department only. This again was an expression of new social demands on education as well as a reflection of European customs. In 1841 President Quincy, summarizing this experience, stated that the scheme was adopted with great expectations but, as events proved, without any important success. During the sixteen years only eighteen students attended the college under this permission.

Throughout this period there was much discussion of the organization of the college curriculum and the function of a college education. A general report to the trustees of Amherst College in 1826 (Quo. 617) states that the "American public is not satisfied with the present course of education in our higher seminaries. It is not sufficiently modern and comprehensive to meet the exigencies of the age and of the country in which we live." The complaint was made partially against the classical languages but more generally "that while everything else is on the advance our colleges are stationary." The report advocated a provision for parallel courses to supplement the classical course. It provided for an addition to the "present classical and scientific four years' course of a new course equally elevating with this but distinguished from it by more modern and national aspects and by a better adaptation to the trades and future pursuits of the large class of young men who aspire to the advantage of a liberal education."

In this new course English literature and language was made of prominence. French, Spanish, German, Italian were to be substituted for Greek and Latin. Practical mechanics was added; chemistry was emphasized; natural history, modern political history, political law, civics, drawing, and civil engineering were recommended. The common elements left in the various curricula were ancient history, geography, rhetoric, and oratory, mathematics, physics, intellectual and moral philosophy, political economy, and theology.

Again the only result was as at Harvard, a few special students for several years. But the entire complaint sounds very familiar to the contemporary ear, and the futile outcome seems familiar to the modern administrator.

In 1827 a very extensive report on the organization of the curriculum was made by the faculty of Yale College (Quo. 618). The committee was appointed "to inquire into the expediency of so altering the regular instruction in this college as to leave out of said course the study of the dead languages, substituting other studies therefor and either requiring a complete knowledge of said language as a condition of admittance to such college or providing instruction in same for such as shall choose to study these after admittance." This report, which makes in its entirety quite a volume, rejected the recommendation and gives probably the most effective defense extant of the traditional disciplinary view of education. Various other attempts were made to solve the problem created on the one hand by the rapid expansion of human knowledge and by the growing social demands for a broader and more practical curriculum, and on the other by the unwillingness of the student to limit himself to the conventional subjects and by his inability to compass them all.

In 1829 the University of Vermont abolished the class system, established a scheme of examinations on each subject and in the languages on each author, permitted the students to pursue single studies or any course of study in any department, and granted degrees only to those who had mastered the old classical mathematical course. This was essentially the scheme of the University of Virginia and was only another way of getting at the problem which Harvard attempted to provide for by admitting the special student, and Amherst by creating the parallel courses of study. Here as at the other institutions, the plan met with little success.

In 1850 Brown under President Wayland attempted a similar reform. The fixed term of four years was in that period abolished. Students were to pursue as many or as few courses of study as they chose. There were to be no general examinations for admission, and a variety of degrees were to be provided for. Its fate was similar to that of the other experiments.

All of these experiments were attempts to break away from the traditional course. President Wayland had early asserted that the studies in all of the Northern colleges were so nearly similar that students in one institution found little difficulty in being admitted to any other. President Barnard in 1856 said that the obligatory studies are such as are universally regarded as furnishing the best discipline for the mind and such as are indispensable to a man of liberal education. It was against this kind of uniformity testified to by the Amherst faculty in 1826 (Quo. 617), the Yale faculty in 1827 (Quo. 618), President Wayland in 1847 (Quo. 619), President Barnard in 1856 (Quo. 620), that all of these experiments were made; yet all of them were but experiments and it was not until the period following the Civil War that effective measures were taken to escape from this situation. The remedies which were made effective during the pre-Civil-War period were (1) those of a new type of college founded and controlled by the states, and (2) the establishment of a variety of types of professional schools. Before these two movements are to be considered, one other aspect of collegiate development during this period demands attention.

Change from Ecclesiastical to Secular Control.—One phase of the transition of the college from an ecclesiastical to a secular institution has been indicated in the expansion of the curriculum. In 1784 special concession regarding attendance on classes in the ancient languages was made to those with whom "law, physics or politics were the objects of their future expectation." This discovery that every student was not intended for the Christian ministry was due to the very great change in the professional distribution of the college graduates. During the first century of the existence of the college about 70% of all graduates entered the ministry. In the period following the Revolution it dropped to about 20%; from 1840 on it was 10% or less. This did not so much indicate a lessened demand for the ministry as a very greatly increased demand for adequate training in the other professions

FOUNDING OF AMERICAN SCHOOL SYSTEM

and a broadening of the social conception of education. Nevertheless it is also indicative of the decreased importance of the ecclesiastical influence.

Another indication of this is seen in the student life itself. In the late eighteenth and early nineteenth century the conduct of the student body had come to be a problem of no little significance. Insubordination was common, open rebellion not infrequent. Especially after the Revolution was there a marked change. Many of the old customs fell into disuse. For instance, the requirement of not wearing the hat on the college campus was considered offensive to the new republicanism. So it was dropped along with the custom of listing students according to the position of their fathers. At Harvard the custom of examination of the students by committees of the corporation of overseers was rebelled against, and in 1790 such a committee engaged in examining a freshman class was attacked with stones. In Yale the old service of malted drink had been discontinued but that of cider, which of the proper vintage is quite as efficacious, was continued until 1815. The conduct of the students in commons is indicated by the statement that in a single term six hundred tumblers and thirty coffee pots were carried off. Of one of the presidents of Yale, Lyman Beecher narrates: "One evening he brought a foreign ambassador or other dignitary with him to prayers, but, being rather late, the students were in a row, stamping, etc. all over the chapel. This mortified him exceedingly. He reached the stage, tried to speak to quell the tumult. Couldn't be heard: then up with his cane and struck on the stage, shivering it to splinters and broke out into a rage." The same author writes: "College was in a most ungodly state; the college church was almost extinct. Most of the students were skeptical, and rowdies were plentiful. Liquors were kept in many rooms. Intemperance, licentiousness and gambling were common. That was the day of infidelity of the Tom Paine school. Boys that dressed flax in the barn used to read Tom Paine and believed him. Most of the class before me were infidels and called each other Voltaire, Rousseau, D'Alembert, etc."

In Princeton the disturbance of the students was so great that

HIGHER EDUCATION

the trustees were called in. The Commencement season was especially one of boisterous behavior. In numerous instances the assistants of the local government had to be called in, which at one time led to a migration of the student body somewhat similar to that of the medieval university.

These, however, were only superficial indications of a far more significant process that was going on in the public mind, which led to profound change in the character of the institutions themselves. At Harvard the conflict between theological and religious conservatism and liberalism had been going on throughout the eighteenth century. Out of this conflict had grown the establishment of Yale and later on of Williams. The new Constitution of Massachusetts in 1780 confirmed the University organization of the seventeenth century and in the same year James Bowdoin was elected a member of the corporation, the first one who was neither clergyman, professor, nor tutor. Early in the first decade of the nineteenth century a non-clerical president was elected, though he did not serve. Successive acts by the legislature changed the composition of the board of overseers, decreasing the ecclesiastical element. In 1820 a constitutional convention provided that the members of the board of overseers should not be confined to the Congregational Church, but the provision was defeated by the people. In 1843 clergymen of all denominations became eligible. In 1851 a large proportion of the membership of the board was chosen by the general convention. In 1865 the electoral power was placed in the hands of the alumni of the institution. Meanwhile in 1825 the faculty had been made the immediate governing body of the institution, and later ecclesiastical allegiance had been removed. Practically the college severed its official relations with the Congregational Church with the change in composition of the governing board in 1843.

At Princeton in the second decade of the century the problem of ecclesiastical control was solved by the establishment of a theological seminary. The college agreed not to appoint any professor of theology, and an independent theological school was established, with different trustees, though under the same president. This left the college technically independent of ecclesiastical control, though in reality its sympathies and policies were closely identified with the Presbyterian Church. At Columbia the change involved in the organization of the University of the State of New York marked the transition. The first organization in 1784 gave the dominant control of the higher education in the state to the faculty of Columbia College. This institution was closely affiliated with the Episcopal Church, so that a conflict with the extreme republicanism and non-sectarian factors arose which in 1787 resulted in the reorganization of the State University forbidding any representation on the board of regents from the faculties of the constituent institutions, and placing the election of these regents in the hands of the state legislature. Thus while Columbia was left with a close ecclesiastical affiliation which it could perpetuate, through its right of co-optation, the State University itself was entirely freed from ecclesiastical affiliations.

Organization of Professional Schools (Quos. 612–616).—Previous to the Revolution both theology and medicine had been recognized in the university organization. Theology as a distinct subject from the founding of the Hollis professorship at Harvard in 1721, medicine from the organization of the Medical school in the University of Pennsylvania in 1767, and at Kings College in 1767. Following the Revolution these two, with law, received general recognition. From the outgrowth of the tendency towards secularization came the organization of distinct theological institutions. That at Princeton in 1812 has been mentioned. Since Columbia failed to provide for this professional interest, the General Theological Seminary was organized in New York in 1819. Separate faculties were organized in Harvard in 1818 and at Yale in 1822.

The Revolution, with its great emphasis upon the importance of common law, from which the revolutionary patriots drew most of their arguments, together with the founding of the new nation with its ramification of local government, now all industriously concerned in the manufacturing of laws,—created a demand for an academic study of this subject to supplement the apprenticeship training then in general vogue. This began with the estab-

HIGHER EDUCATION

lishment of a professorship of law at Columbia in 1792 under James Kent. Pennsylvania followed immediately. The first faculty of law with degree-conferring powers was established at Harvard in 1817.

The organization of the technical scientific lines was due to the great expansion of the natural sciences during the early nineteenth century, and to the notable triumphs of the application of science to practical problems. The first attempt at the organization of such a school was by Rensselaer at Troy, New York. This was largely the outgrowth of the interest created by the construction of the Erie Canal. The founder said "my principle object is to qualify teachers for instructing sons and daughters of farmers and mechanics, by lectures or otherwise, in the application of experimental chemistry to natural philosophy, and natural history to agriculture, domestic economy, the arts, and manufactures. These are not to be taught by seeing experiments and hearing lectures according to the usual method, but they are to lecture and to experiment by turns under the immediate direction of the professor or competent assistant. Thus by a term of labor like an apprentice to a trade, they are to become operative chemists." The far-reaching importance of the principle here involved is evident. It is clearly the first attempt, at least on this continent, to organize the application of the experimental method in science as a means for training technical experts. In 1847 both Harvard and Yale followed and this year the Lawrence Scientific School was established in connection with the former school and the Sheffield Scientific School in connection with the latter. The Chandler School was established at Dartmouth in 1851.

The Establishment of State Universities.—The most definite expression of the desire for a national institution or system of university instruction is found in the growth of the American state universities. These are institutions founded by the various commonwealth governments, governed indirectly by them through boards of regents or trustees, the members of which are usually selected through some branch of the state government and which are supported in entirety or for the most part by state appropriations; the privileges of which are open to all and free from any charges for tuition; which are free from all ecclesiastical relationships and make no religious requirements on the part of instructors or students. This type of institution was a very different thing from the Colonial college which, while created and subsidized at least to a considerable extent by the Colonial governments, were under self-perpetuating boards of trustees and were closely affiliated with some ecclesiastical organization.

The new institutions were the immediate outgrowth of the political theory of the times and an expression of the one definite educational view of the political leaders. In other words it was a definite realization of the conception of the national system of education as far as such a view had then developed. Provision for such a university was made in a number of the early state constitutions. Those commonwealths belonging to the original group of thirteen which had not developed a university in Colonial times early provided for this type of institution. These were the three Southern colonies. Similar provision was made by all of the newer institutions to the west and south. In time such an institution becomes the most distinctive feature of the American system of education. These institutions were of two distinct types. First, the inclusive administrative type, which did not provide for instruction directly, and second, the instructing university. The former type was a clear imitation of the French ideas then prevalent, though not realized in the concrete by Napoleon until somewhat later than the earlier American experiments.

The Administrative University.—The clearest and the most effective one of this type was the University of the State of New York, which indeed is the only one of these earlier creations which has persisted. In 1784, two months after the British had evacuated New York, the legislature began the consideration of a proposal to re-establish higher education. The early scheme was a compromise of views held by the conservative English party powerful in the city and made up largely of the friends of the old Kings College, of the Episcopal church, and of the aristocracy of the English element. The other party, chiefly recruited from the representa-

HIGHER EDUCATION

tives of the state in general, was democratic in its leanings and influenced strongly by French ideas. The outcome was the University of the State of New York, in which all authorities were vested in the board of regents, which included representatives of the state, city, and county governments, of each of the religious denominations, of the founders of any collegiate institution, of the fellows, professors, and tutors of the representative colleges. These regents were given the power to found schools and colleges in any part of the state, to endow them and to grant degrees. As the reorganized Kings, now Columbia College, was the sole existing institution and possessed of all the property which belonged to the newly created university, the Columbia faculty had an undue influence. On the other hand, the political, especially the upstate, appointments constituted the majority of the board and placed the legal control of the one existing college in the hands of men who were not its particular friends. Consequently this scheme soon revealed its defects, and in 1787 the University was reorganized in the form which has persisted down to the present century. The new organization made a clear distinction between the administrative university and the component parts, or the teaching colleges. The University itself was to be controlled by the board of regents who were now to be elected by the state legislature, with the exception of the governor and lieutenant-governor, who were ex-officio members. To the regents was given the power of conferring upon institutions the privilege of granting degrees. On the other hand it could offer no instruction itself, nor could any members of the teaching staff of the component institutions become members of the governing board. This was in direct opposition to the original plan, in which all such instructors were made ex-officio members of the board of regents. To the board of regents was given the control of secondary as well as higher education, the authority of incorporating and recognizing institutions of either grade, and in general of directing the state policy concerning higher education. This consistent, continuous, judicious, and intelligent oversight has been perhaps the largest factor in determining the development of education in the Empire state. It has given the state a more definitely organized system of higher instruction than any other state, and has made the educational forces more amenable to centralized authority and to professional direction than those of any other state.

The University of the State of New York, however, was the only successful one of these attempts to create the administrative university. However, there were many other attempts in this early period.

The University of the State of Georgia preceded that of New York in its organization by a few weeks. By legislation in the following year (1785) the entire public system of education in the state was organized as the University. The spirit of individualism was too strong, however, to permit the central institution to exercise any great control over the isolated parts. The fund which was accumulated was distributed among the various counties, which thereupon multiplied the academies with little reference to the judgment or authority of any central board.

Maryland in 1784 also organized its higher education under the title of the Convocation of the University of Maryland. The rivalry of the component institutions, together with the political and social conditions of the times, rendered the scheme unworkable and soon the individual colleges were left to pursue their own policies without centralized control. In a similar way Louisiana organized all of its institutions of higher education under the board of regents. Here the fact that the population was largely French in origin and tradition would seem to have made the conditions of the experiment most favorable, but the population was very sparse, the interest in higher education slight, the subsidies necessary were large and altogether the difficulties too numerous and great to make the proposed plan more than a temporary experiment. Others of the Southern states followed a similar plan, but for a short time only. That of the State of Kentucky really had its origin in the Virginia legislative act of 1780, but the elaborate system of county academies provided by this scheme was far ahead of the needs of the times.

Next to the state of New York the most conspicuous attempt to establish an administrative university was that of the state of Michi-

HIGHER EDUCATION

gan. Here again the early French influence, through its presence in the composition of the population, was an important influence. As early as 1817 an administrative university was organized under the name of Catholepistemied, or the University of Michigania. This body was to consist of a central instruction institution together with such "colleges, academies, schools, libraries, museums, laboratories and other useful literary and scientific institutions as it might desire to create." It had the power to appoint teachers and other school officers in all the counties, towns, and cities of the territory. The expense of all was to be borne by the central government. This remained, however, a legislative dream. Michigan was admitted to the Union as a state in 1835. The school law was enacted in 1837 and again was largely modeled on European ideas. The State University which was then created proved one of the strongest and most influential of these institutions, but it was a teaching institution only and retained none of the old centralizing administering functions.

These various attempts are of interest in revealing the ideas of the leaders of the times and also the inadequacy of these theoretical schemes to meet the hard conditions of these newer communities and to accord with the natural individualism of a people fostered now by the crude conditions of frontier life.

The Teaching State University.—If the administrative state university was a failure in all but one instance, the teaching university soon developed a conspicuous place in the American educational system. Though the original idea of the University of Georgia proved abortive, the central institution began its instruction in 1800. North Carolina, Tennessee, and Kentucky also authorized state universities before the close of the eighteenth century. Mississippi, Louisiana, Alabama, South Carolina followed shortly afterwards in the early years of the nineteenth century. Ohio, Indiana, and the other states of the Northwest Territory made provisions for a state university in their original constitutions. In fact the land grants of Congress laid the foundation of these.

Most of these early state universities existed merely in a provision of the state constitution or of the state legislature. Few of them were operative until the second quarter of the century. Those which were operative were supported, but most inadequately, through irregular subsidies of the legislature, through gifts of land, or through contributions of private parties. The consistent support through a tax levy was yet in the future. Meanwhile, through the profound struggle which revealed the popular ideas and interests against which these new state institutions had to contend, the state university which first made popular the institution, as we have it now, was being formed in Virginia. Here Jefferson (Quos. 610–611) had early attempted to secularize higher education by removing William and Mary from ecclesiastical control. In 1779, as previously noted, he succeeded in secularizing the curriculum of the institution. In the same year he proposed a general scheme of education for the state in which William and Mary was to become the state university. This failing and the institution yet remaining under ecclesiastical control, he next proposed the removal of the University of Geneva to Richmond. This proving impracticable, he later labored for the removal of William and Mary to the capital of the state and thus to sever its ecclesiastical connection. Finally, despairing of securing this result, Jefferson with other friends of education turned to the creation of a new institution made on novel lines. The institution itself was authorized in 1816 but did not open for instruction until 1825. There were many novel features, few of which were reproduced in the succeeding state universities. These features were all due to the influence of Jefferson and marked the contrast between the new type of institution and the old. There were to be no prescribed studies, there was to be no governing executive authority within the institution, aside from the control of the board of visitors and the general legislation of the faculty. The conditions of entrance were very general and liberal; students could follow any course of study desired. Degrees, however, were conferred only after fulfilling very strict requirements. The student body was self-governed, the internal administration of the institution was in the hands of the faculty, without executive head. The organization of the institution was along seven independent lines, namely, ancient languages, modern language, natural philosophy, moral philosophy,

HIGHER EDUCATION

chemistry, medicine, and law. The success of the institution was marked. Its novel features brought into high relief many of the limitations of the traditional college institution; its influence was profound and widespread, especially in the South.

Of the institutions in the North, the University of Michigan, though not the earliest, was the most adequately supported, and of the widest influence. Here at the middle of the century were introduced certain ideas of instruction prevailing in the universities of continental Europe, and thus began the movement in higher education which characterized the latter half of the nineteenth century.

The Endowed College.—Though the state universities are the distinct creation of this early National period, the endowed college of private benefaction or of ecclesiastical dominance yet remained the dominant type. One great factor in developing these institutions and in drawing a sharp line between them and the state universities was the famous Dartmouth College Decision which must be given some special attention.

The Dartmouth College Case.—No legal or political conflict has had so great an influence on the institutions of higher learning and few court decisions have been of greater importance to the social and economic development of the country than the famous Dartmouth College Case of 1817 (Quos. 608, 609). The conflict arose over the attempt of the legislature of New Hampshire to gain control of Dartmouth College, which had been founded and endowed by private parties, and was controlled by a self-perpetuating board of trustees. This organization was the one prevailing in all colleges. The rights of these trustees had been confirmed by royal charter. However, a division of interest had existed among the authorities of the college for some years. The arbitrary government of the President, Wheelock, who had practically inherited his position from his father, the founder, led to the public controversy and an appeal to the legislature. Partisan antagonism between the Federalists and the Democrats, which were then very bitter indeed, entered in. On the recommendation of the Governor, the legislature modified the charter of the institution, appointed a large number of new trustees most of whom were ex-officio representatives of the state government, and also appointed a board of visitors having revisory powers over all acts of the trustees. The case was decided against the college by the state courts, carried to the Supreme Court of the United States, where it was argued by the most famous lawyers of the time, before perhaps as distinguished a bench of judges as the American courts have ever had. The argument of Daniel Webster (Quo. 608) and the decision of Chief Justice Marshall (Quo. 609) have become classics. The decision was that the charter granted to the college was a contract in the sense of the Constitution of the United States, and that the state legislature was forbidden by the Constitution to pass any law impairing the obligation of contracts; though nearly all state constitutions adopted subsequent to this have contained a provision retaining the right of the legislature to modify such a charter as a part of the contract, yet this can be done only on the basis of general interest or the public welfare.

Upon this decision has been built up the structure of modern economic law, since the corporation which here finds its legal defense has become the chief instrument of modern business. Its educational significance is two-fold, in that it confirmed the privately endowed institutions in all of their rights and privileges, and on the other hand revealed to the commonwealths of the Union that if they desired to build up educational institutions directly under their control they must be created to that end and supported by the state. Hence the line between the endowed college and the state university was made distinct and the creation of the institution of the type of the latter became a part of the political scheme of every new commonwealth and of most of the older ones.

Privately Endowed Institutions.—If the Dartmouth College Decision did not furnish the stimulation essential to the multiplication of these institutions, it did give the necessary assurance of legal and political security. Stimulated by the distribution of population, by the promises of vast national wealth, the zeal of denominational propaganda, the individualism and initiative of the new democracy, that local pride so characteristic of the new American communities,—a pride which is more largely composed of exuberant hope than of a judicious estimate of actual conditions—

these institutions were greatly multiplied. In the years following the Dartmouth decision more than 500 such institutions have been created. From the Revolution to the Dartmouth controversy, only about twelve such institutions had been established if the component units of the state university are omitted. Most of these were outgrowths of previous academic foundations. From the Dartmouth controversy to the close of the Civil War more than two hundred of such institutions which are yet surviving were established. This is almost as great a number as those established from the close of the Civil War to the present time. No denomination was without its institution, no local community of any considerable area was without its college. In fact most of all the stronger denominations aimed to develop a college in each state, and many local communities boasted more than one institution. Such institutions furnished the most conspicuous feature of our educational system of this period and constituted one of the most characteristic products of American life. Whatever may be the fate of the small college or the present function of the denominational institution, there can be no doubt as to the essential part which it played in developing the life, the intellectual interest, and the character of the people during this middle National period. Most of these colleges grew from the germs of academies. Many of them remained such in reality though they bore the more pretentious name. All of them made contributions to our national life which but for them would have remained undeveloped. Many of them were made conspicuous because of the great personalities at their head. Among these were Dwight of Yale, Nott of Union, Wayland of Brown, Hopkins of Williams, and a multitude of others only less well known.

The Fellenberg Institute (Quo. Ch. XVI, Sec. 111).—A conspicuous but ephemeral phase of higher education during this period was the great popularity of the manual labor institutes. These were in imitation of the institutions founded by Emanuel von Fellenberg at Hofwyl, Switzerland. Fellenberg labored in connection with Pestalozzi and attempted to apply his educational ideas in the field of advanced education. The essential idea was a combination of manual and intellectual activity for the advantage of both mind

FOUNDING OF AMERICAN SCHOOL SYSTEM

and body. The institution which he built up and which flourished from about 1810 to 1844 included in addition to a classical college an industrial school, household arts, agricultural school, and a number of trade shops. The institution was organized to cover the whole range of social activities, and was designed to be if not self-

FIG. 91. Manual Labor Institute, the original school in Switzerland. (From *Blätter von Hofwyl bei Emanual Fellenburg*, Bern, 1843.)

supporting at least representative of society in microcosm. In European societies, yet organized on the class basis, it was possible to train the representative of these various classes for the specific positions they were to occupy in life. The theories embodied had a philosophical and psychological basis as well as a sociological one. Believing that all knowledge came primarily through the senses and

HIGHER EDUCATION

that the learning process was best formulated in connection with the industrial and social activities, this school embodied many radical, modern, social, and educational principles. The nearest approach to the parent school we have had in this country were the institutes at Hampton and Tuskegee developed after the Civil War for the training of the Negroes and Indians.

Transferred to American soil in the early National period practically all of the theoretical basis of the scheme was lost sight of

FIG. 92. Fellenberg Institute as transferred to America. Robert Dale Owen's experiment at New Harmony, Ind. (From Podmore, *Robert Owen*, p. 86.)

except in the few professional publications. On the other hand two phases of the scheme attracted particular attention, since they fitted into the life of the times. The first was the economic feature, which promised to make it possible for the student to earn his support while he was acquiring his intellectual equipment. At a time when athletics and physical training had yet found no place in college life, when the students were drawn largely from active life of rural occupation to a very sedentary academic life, in which close devotion to study was fostered by the somewhat ascetic ideals of the initiated student, this feature had great promise and received great emphasis.

Few of these institutions, especially in the newer frontier communities, had any adequate endowment. Support came chiefly from student fees. While the economic demand was at a minimum and the cost of food was from the present point of view ridiculously low, yet the actual expense demanded was, relative to the means, much greater than it is today. It is small wonder that the great educational principles involved were completely cast aside in the face of the pressing economic demands. It is safe to say that the great majority of academic institutions founded in the third, fourth, and fifth decades of the century embodied this manual labor ideal. Such institutions as Oberlin in Ohio, Wabash in Indiana, Knox in Illinois, as well as a multitude of others were started on this basis. In many cases the earlier college buildings were the product of student labor. In most, however, agricultural labor was the chief measure adopted. But at a time when the most strenuous agricultural endeavor but afforded to keep a thrifty pioneer family alive, with the possible margin sufficient to send one son to college, it is obvious that no farm, however well managed, would suffice to support the entire student body. Moreover, it was quickly found that manual labor wholly for the purpose of economic gain, left little time, energy, or interest for academic pursuits. In most instances the experiment was soon dropped and the manual labor scheme went to join the great multitude of abortive educational ideas. Only later, when vocational training came to be recognized as a legitimate and essential part of an educational scheme as an end in itself, was the idea revived with any success.

Summary.—The break from the conventional Oxford-Cambridge type came in the middle of the eighteenth century with the founding of Kings and Pennsylvania. In practice, however, no successful break was made until long after the Revolution. The Revolution itself produced a period of stagnation in college life. Following this there came a wave of radical ideas fostered chiefly by French influence. The Revolutionary spirit of the times found expression in student life, where exuberance bordered closely on license. In the early National period, with the growth of modern science and the spirit of freedom which soon began to express itself in the intellectual life and in fields of investigation, the college curriculum began to expand. The most conspicuous as well as earliest additions were in the fields of the physical and biological sciences, and in the social sciences as represented by political economy and history and international law. Modern languages and literature, especially French, also received gradual recognition. This expansion of the curriculum demanded new organization and administration, and various attempts approaching the elective system were made during the early half of the nineteenth century, but none succeeded except the scheme of the University of Virginia. Similar attempts to popularize the college through the introduction of unclassified students or the building up of the student body not interested in degrees, or through the breakdown of the class system, likewise failed. The general outcome was a greatly augmented curriculum, yet based on the old disciplinary idea, which now entailed a very much more superficial study of the large number of subjects. In the field of administration the most important change was that from ecclesiastical to secular control. The most marked conflict was that at William and Mary, where Jefferson made a prolonged but unsuccessful attempt to secularize the institution, and at Harvard, which finally resulted in the fourth decade of the century in freeing the institution from the control of the orthodox religious interest. The outcome at Harvard, though not reached until after the Civil War, was the transferring of the ultimate source of control to the alumni of the institution itself. In Virginia the conflict was settled by the establishment of a state university. In general all of the commonwealths sought to establish institutions where the direction of the policy was ultimately determined by authority selected through politics rather than ecclesiastical channels. Further reaction against the narrowness of the traditional institution was the founding of various professional schools. Medical schools which started before the Revolution were now multiplied. Law schools were added very shortly after. The institution of industrial technology was added in 1825, and by the middle of the century three of the larger New England institutions had founded scientific schools of the modern technological type. The result of all of these forces was found in the establishment of state universities proposed in New York and a number of Southern states even before the adoption of the National Constitution. Most of these earlier ones were of the purely administrative type. These, however, soon proved inadequate to American conditions and the only one which has continued with success is that of the State of New York, founded in 1784. State universities of the teaching type were early provided for but none largely successful before that of the University of Virginia, which began work in 1825. The Dartmouth College Decision of 1817 confirmed the privately endowed or ecclesiastical institutions in all of their privileges. This resulted in greatly multiplying such institutions as well as strengthening the political force in the establishment of state institutions. All of the new states, and all but one of the original thirteen which did not have chartered collegiate institutions within their borders, developed a state university. On the other hand in the period from 1817 to the close of the Civil War the private institutions were multiplied until they numbered over two hundred. With most meager economic support many of these adopted the scheme of combining manual labor with academic pursuits in the hopes of enabling the students to support themselves while obtaining an education. Practically all of these schemes proved abortive. The close of this early National period found every American commonwealth fully equipped with a system of higher educational institutions, both state and endowed, sufficient in number at least to meet all existing demands, and expressive of the varied interests and the intense individualism characteristic of the democracy of the times.

Chapter XIV

THE EDUCATION OF GIRLS AND WOMEN

Ideas and Practices Concerning the Education of Women and Girls during the Eighteenth and Early Nineteenth Centuries.—The processes of democratizing and nationalizing education are both evident in the development during this period of the higher education of women. The first two or three decades of the century had been fertile in the propounding of radical ideas; the fourth and fifth decades were fruitful in radical attempts to carry them out. In no phase of education were these innovations more productive of change or more fraught with important consequences for society in general than in the recognition of the distinct right of women to free access to education of every degree and of every kind.

As our own generation has witnessed the political enfranchisement of women, so the early nineteenth century, particularly the generation from 1825 to 1865 saw their admission to educational privileges substantially equivalent to those of men. It is not easy for us to realize the conception of women then prevalent (Quo. 563). To judge from the literature of the times, particularly that relating to her education, woman was considered either a drudge or a doll. Neither attitude was complimentary to her intelligence, nor provocative of worthy educational activities. In one case she was to be trained as a servant in the practical household duties; in the other she received the artificial, superficial polish of the "finishing schools" of the day.

While this was the popular attitude or public pose in which all but a few, both men and women, acquiesced, yet no doubt in private then, as in practice always, feminine worth and merit, intelligence and affection exerted a determining influence and operated, though

FOUNDING OF AMERICAN SCHOOL SYSTEM

more quietly and unobtrusively than at present, not only in the control of all private affairs but in the guidance of public activities and social morals.

Even in the Colonial period there was considerable opportunity and activity in the field of woman's education. Women, even of the apprentice or servant class, were commonly taught to read, and were always carefully trained in the practical, social, and economic duties of the home. Beyond this, opportunity and achievement varied with time, place, and person. The dame school was always accessible to the girls. Occasional town schools conferred the great favor of tuition, usually in special and inconvenient hours (Quos. 552-553). Private schools were always willing to sacrifice social prejudice for a consideration; while a multitude of them in every community catered to the popular fashions of the finishing process. From the early eighteenth century occasional private academies offered the opportunity of higher intellectual training.

But at no time previous to the period under consideration is there revealed any adequate recognition of the truth that the education of women presents the same problems, is based on the same rights, involves the same privileges and processes, and works toward the same ends, as the education of men. All this, however, came during the early nineteenth century. Consequently, while there is an interesting history of the education of girls and women in the Colonial period, it is unnecessary to consider in detail the earlier conditions in order to trace the process of the intellectual enfranchisement of women.

The announcement in 1825 of the *Journal of Education,* the first important periodical of its class in the United States, stated that "above all, the subject of female education will be considered of unspeakable importance." Thus spoke the leader with vision. Evidence of how "unspeakable" the importance of the subject was is offered by the large volume of matter printed on this subject during this period. True, an apologetic attitude was usually assumed by the reformer; and his somewhat heretical views were usually buttressed by a statement of the importance of the advocated reforms to the welfare of the male element in society. The official report

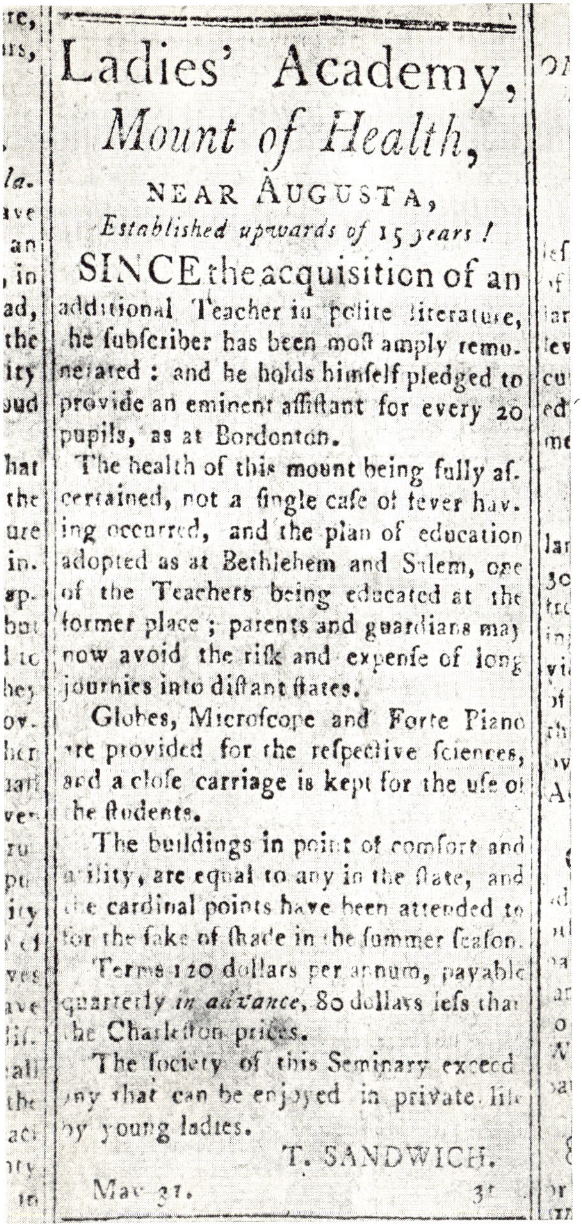

Ladies' Academy,
Mount of Health,

NEAR AUGUSTA,
Established upwards of 15 years!

SINCE the acquisition of an additional Teacher in polite literature, the subscriber has been most amply remunerated: and he holds himself pledged to provide an eminent assistant for every 20 pupils, as at Bordenton.

The health of this mount being fully ascertained, not a single case of fever having occurred, and the plan of education adopted as at Bethlehem and Salem, one of the Teachers being educated at the former place; parents and guardians may now avoid the risk and expense of long journies into distant states.

Globes, Microscope and Forte Piano are provided for the respective sciences, and a close carriage is kept for the use of the students.

The buildings in point of comfort and utility, are equal to any in the state, and the cardinal points have been attended to for the sake of shade in the summer season.

Terms 120 dollars per annum, payable quarterly *in advance*, 80 dollars less than the Charleston prices.

The society of this Seminary exceed any that can be enjoyed in private life by young ladies.

T. SANDWICH.

May 31.

FIG. 93. Newspaper account of a women's academy in the south.

of the High School for Girls in Boston which was established in 1826 reads:

> "In the first place, in regard to the *general* expediency of placing women, in respect to education, upon ground if not equal at least bearing a near and an honorable relation to that of men in any community, your committee think that no doubt can at this day be entertained by those who consider the weight of female influence in society, in every stage of moral and intellectual advancement; and especially by those who consider the paramount and abiding influence of mothers upon every successive generation of men, during the earliest years of their life and those years in which so much or so little is done towards forming moral character and giving the mind a direction and an impulse towards usefulness and happiness in after life. As to the general expediency, then, of giving women such an education as shall make them fit wives for well educated men and enable them to exert a salutary influence upon the rising generation, as there can be no doubts, your committee will use no arguments at this board, but will confine themselves to the particular expediency of provision for a higher education of our daughters at the public expense."

The dominant finishing type of education is well illustrated by the announcement quoted on page 66. This sort of education was usually justified both as a development of social graces and as an employment for time which otherwise would be devoted to the vanities and the petty vices of the leisured classes in general and of the sex in particular. "Ignorance," says Fenelon, "is often the cause of *ennui* to a young girl, and prevents her from finding an innocent employment for her leisure." The antidote to this was the emphasis on practical or household duties, chiefly "as a means of preventing young girls from occupying their thoughts with foolishness and of turning them towards useful things."

By the time of the reforms of the thirties and forties this view was quite generally recognized as inadequate. However, these intellectual opportunities were to be strictly guarded, in the opinion of the great majority of educators. One of the most enlightened and

EDUCATION OF GIRLS AND WOMEN

influential of these expressed as follows the conservative view yet prevailing in the middle of the century:

> "Culture in young women should never develop into learning; for then it ceases to be delicate feminine culture. A young woman can not and ought not to plunge with the obstinate and persevering strength of a man into scientific pursuits, so as to become forgetful of everything else. Only an entirely unwomanly young woman could try to become thoroughly learned, in a man's sense of the term; and she would try in vain, for she has not the mental faculties of a man. In opposition to these sentiments I may be directed to learned ladies, a second-rate article which, thank God, is extremely rare."

Even when stating principles of education for girls acceptable from the present point of view there was ordinarily a curious inability to see such principles equally applicable to the education of boys. The same writer adds:

> "The studies of girls should be intended not to make them know much, and still less to make them as it were hang about themselves scraps of knowledge, like lifeless and tasteless ornaments, trying to look splendid in them; but that they should thoroughly assimilate whatever they do learn with their whole being and make it a well-chosen and valuable ornament of their minds. Such a mode of studying will secure them the permanent possession of what they learn, to their own pleasure and the pleasure of all around them."

This discussion led to a common prejudice against sending girls to school, particularly to those following the plan of boys' schools, and above all to co-educational schools.

> "A regular order for the daily occupations should be prescribed for them; but they must also be accustomed from early childhood to leave books or piano at any moment when necessary to assist a smaller child or to be of use to their parents. Such cases can not of course be provided for in the order of the day; they are the exceptions to the rule. But girls should also be trained, as soon as the exceptional service is over, to return at once to books or instrument and go quietly on with their studies as if nothing had interrupted. School instruction is inferior, for girls, to home instruction because it affords no interval for these services of love, and if the studying for several

hours, one after another, is the one chief thing sought, then the school is unsuitable for girls."

The words of Goethe, while expressing no doubt the German estimate, were substantially the popular view of the early nineteenth century:

"Early let woman learn to serve, for that is her calling;
For by serving alone she attains to ruling,
To the well-deserved power which is hers in the household.
The sister serves her brother while young and serves her parents;
And all her life is still a continual going and coming,
A carrying ever and bringing, a making and shaping for others;
Well for her if she learns to think no road a foul one,
To make the hours of the night the same as the hours of the day
To think no labor too trifling, and never too fine the needle,
To forget herself altogether, and live in others alone.
And lastly, as mother, in truth, she will need every one of these virtues."

The idea of protest against this view was taking shape in America at this time. Emma Willard, in her address to the New York Legislature in 1819, stated the evils in the existing theory of woman's education as follows:

"Not even is youth considered in our sex, as in the other, a season which should be wholly devoted to improvement. Among families so rich as to be entirely above labor the daughters are hurried through the routine of boarding school instruction and at an early period introduced into the gay world, and thenceforth their only object is amusement . . . Mark the different treatment which the sons of these families receive. While their sisters are gliding through the mazes of the midnight dance they employ the lamp to treasure up for future use the riches of ancient wisdom, or to gather strength and expansion of mind in exploring the wonderful paths of philosophy. When the youth of these two sexes has been spent so differently, is it strange or is nature in fault if more mature age has brought such a difference of character that our sex have been considered by the other as the pampered, wayward babies of society who must have some rattle put into our hands to keep us from doing mischief to ourselves or others? Another difference in the treatment of the sexes is made in our country which though not equally pernicious to society is more pathetically unjust to our sex. How often have we seen a student who, returning from his literary pursuits, finds a sister who was his equal in acquirements while their advantages were equal of whom he is now ashamed. While his youth was devoted to study and he was furnished with the means, she, without any object of improvement, drudged at home to assist in the support of the father's family and perhaps to contribute to her brother's subsistence abroad, and now, a being of a lower order, the rustic innocent wonders and weeps at his neglect. Not only has there been a want of system concerning female education but much of what has been done has proceeded upon mistaken principles.

"One of these is that without a regard to the different periods of life proportionate to the importance, the education of females has been too exclusively directed to fit them for displaying to advantage the charms of youth and beauty. Though it may be proper to adorn this period of life, yet it is incomparably more important to prepare for the serious duties of maturer years. Though well to decorate the blossom it is far better to prepare for the harvest. In the vegetable creation nature seems but to sport when she embellishes the flower, while all her serious cares are directed to perfect the fruit.

"Another error is that it has been made the first object in educating our sex to prepare them to please the other. But reason and religion teach that we too are primary existences, that it is for us to move in the orbit of our duty around the Holy Center of perfection, the companion not the satellites of men; else, instead of shedding around us an influence that may help to keep them in their proper course we must accompany them in the wildest deviations. . . .

"Neither would I be understood to mean that our sex should not seek to make themselves agreeable to the other. The error complained of is that the taste of men, whatever it might happen to be, has been made a standard for the formation of the female character. In whatever we do it is of the utmost importance that the rule by which we work be perfect. For if otherwise what is it but to err upon principle? A system of education which leads one class of human beings to consider the approbation of another as their highest object teaches that the rule of their conduct should be the will of beings imperfect and erring like themselves, rather than the will of God which is the only standard of perfection."

A more general and less radical view held by progressive educators working towards a gradual improvement and influenced largely in their views by the best of current practice, was that expressed by Noah Webster, almost a generation earlier:

> "The women in America—to their honor it is mentioned—are not generally above the care of educating their own children. Their own education should therefore enable them to implant in the tender mind such sentiments of virtue, propriety, and dignity as are suited to the freedom of our government. But the influence of women in forming the dispositions of youth is not the sole reason why their education should be particularly guarded; their influence in controlling the manners of a nation is another powerful reason. . . . But a distinction is to be made between a good education and a showy one; for an education merely superficial is a proof of corruption of taste and has a mischievous influence on manners. . . . In all nations a good education is that which renders the ladies correct in their manners, respectable in their families, and agreeable in society. That education is always wrong which raises a woman above the duties of her station.
>
> "In America female education should have for its object what is useful. Young ladies should be taught to speak and write their own language with purity and elegance—an article in which they are often deficient. The French language is not necessary for ladies. In some cases it is convenient, but in general it may be considered as an article of luxury. As an accomplishment it may be studied by those whose attention is not employed about some more important concerns. Some knowledge of arithmetic is necessary for every lady. Geography should never be neglected. *Belle lettres* learning seems to correspond with the dispositions of most females. A taste for poetry and fine writing should be cultivated, for we expect the most delicate sentiments from the pens of that sex which is possessed of the finest feelings.
>
> "A course of reading can hardly be prescribed for all ladies, but it should be remarked that this sex cannot be too well acquainted with the writers upon human life and manners. The *Spectator* should fill the first place, in every lady's library. Other volumes of periodical papers, though inferior to the *Spectator*, should be read and some of the best histories. With respect to novels, so much admired by

EDUCATION OF GIRLS AND WOMEN

the young and so generally condemned by the old, what shall I say? Perhaps it may be said with truth that some of them are useful, many of them pernicious, and most of them trifling. A hundred volumes of modern novels may be read without acquiring a new idea. Some of them contain entertaining stories and, where the descriptions are drawn from nature and from characters and events in themselves innocent, the perusal of them may be harmless.

"In the large towns in America music, drawing, and dancing constitute a part of female education. They however hold a subordinate rank, for my fair friends will pardon me when I declare that no man ever marries a woman for her performance on a harpsichord or her figure in a minuet. However ambitious a woman may be to command admiration abroad, her real merit is only known at home. Admiration is useless when it is not supported by domestic worth, but real honor and permanent esteem are always secured by those who preside over their own families with dignity."

Importance of the Development of Education for Women.—Few aspects of education were more frequently discussed than its application to girls and women. But this discussion

FIG. 94. Moravian Women's Academy at Bethlehem, Pa. One of the earliest institutions for women's education. 1786. (From Reichel, *Bethlehem Seminary,* p. 32.)

was carried on so largely by men in terms of condescension and by women in terms of apology that it now arouses chiefly amusement or indignation, the resulting emotion perhaps being dependent upon the sex of the reader. It is not that the need and right of woman to education was not recognized, but that its nature was considered as determined—whether as a need or as a right—by some condition of dependency, as that of daughter, sister, wife, mother. For all these relationships, generally considered from the point of view of their importance to the welfare of men, were but forms of status which woman might render more useful for others, but from which she might never escape to be considered in the light of her own personality.

Nor can it be charged that there was lack of actual attention to the education of girls during this period, or a deficiency of institutions for them. It was often pointed out that girls quite as frequently as boys were sent from home to school; that they remained away from home quite as long; that schools for girls were as numerous as those for boys; that very frequently both sexes were admitted to the same institution. The difficulty lay in the kind of education given to them and this was due to the prevalent conception of woman's status. The education considered appropriate was one of adornment, which was satisfied with "a capacity of writing a decent note, or at most of holding a very limited communication in French," or with the production of a few mediocre paintings, largely the work of the instructor's brush.

The great educational accomplishment of the period was the establishment of the belief that women are possessed of the same capacity, interests, and obligations as men, and are entitled to similar opportunities. The Scottish philosopher, Stewart, failed to see how education offered a solution of the problem, yet clearly formulated its basic principle as related to social welfare and progress. It is woman to whom "nature has intrusted the first development of our intellectual and moral powers, and who may therefore be regarded as the chief medium through which the progress of the mind is continued from generation to generation."

The rapid progress and the idealism of the American people are due quite largely to this early recognition of the significance of adequate education for women. To the neglect of education of women

EDUCATION OF GIRLS AND WOMEN

along intellectual lines many peoples such as the Orientals or the Balkan nations owe the tardiness of their progress.

In these middle decades of the nineteenth century the form of this question most frequently discussed was whether women's higher education should be directed chiefly to the formal mastery of the classical languages and of higher mathematics just because that was the dominant form of the higher education of men at that period. Indeed, the whole problem of the higher education of women still appears to many in this guise, which means that the problem is merely transferred from the conventional and traditional view of education.

The real problem is far more fundamental than conventional mastery of the formal content of a traditional education. It is the recognition of the equality of women with men as to intellectual capacities, social responsibility and influence, vocational opportunities, and right to personality. Such recognition is necessarily slowly achieved, and even slower is the evolution of an adequate education. But in the process the progressive influences of the home will reinforce those of society, while the conserving influences of the home counteract the materialistic and sordid tendencies of business and politics, in shaping the activities of these more general social institutions.

The Great Leaders in the Movement for the Higher Education of Women.—No account of the development of higher education for women can be accurate even as to essential facts, nor can it reproduce at all the spirit of this great social movement, without some note of the great personalities which took the lead. There were scores of women teachers in the seminaries and academies of the time, exerting profound influence through their force of character, keen intelligence, and wide learning. However, a few of these stand out because of their achievement in the organization of a more advanced type of education for girls than that which then prevailed.

Among these Mrs. Emma Hart Willard (1787–1870) was the most prominent (Quos. 570–573). Educated in the district schools and the rudimentary academies for girls in Connecticut, she began her career of forty years' teaching at the age of seventeen. After a short experience in the district school she opened a school for girls in Connecticut, which she conducted with great success. This was followed by similar service to other communities in Connecticut and Vermont. The character of these and other schools of the same nature may be judged from Mrs. Willard's textbooks in geography and history, worked out as courses in these schools and used very extensively during the following years in schools of all types. These texts would correspond to those now found in the upper grammar grades.

Believing in the possibility of a type of education for girls comparable to the collegiate work of boys, she drew up in 1816 an "Address to the Public, particularly to the Legislature of New York,

Fig. 95. Troy Seminary in an old tobacco factory. (From *New England Magazine*, Vol. XXV, p. 563.)

proposing a Plan for Improving Female Education." Recognizing in De Witt Clinton, then Governor of New York, the one public official with a broad educational outlook, and possessing great political ability herself, she determined in 1818 to present her scheme to him. As a first step in the realization of her hopes her academy in Vermont was removed to Waterford, N. Y., on recommendation of the Governor. The institution was incorporated and a law was passed entitling it to share in the apportionment of public funds made by the regents of the State University. This law was claimed as the first whose sole purpose was to improve female education, "and indeed the first case of government appropriation for the higher education of women."

However, the latter effort failed of realization at the time, for the regents refused to apportion funds to the Academy. In 1820 Governor Clinton again recommended this enterprise in his message: "As this is the only attempt ever made in this country to promote the education of the female sex by the patronage of government, as our first and our best impressions are derived from maternal affection, and as the elevation of the female character is inseparably connected with happiness at home and respectability abroad I trust that you will not be deterred by commonplace ridicule from extending your munificence to this meritorious institution." But both legislators and regents were "deterred" and rejected the proposition offered in successive years.

In 1821 the academy was moved to Troy, which community gave assistance by public grant and private gift. In this institution the ordinary branches of a common education were taught together with the traditional languages, music, and painting of the girls' finishing schools. But great stress was laid upon natural, mental, and moral philosophy and upon the higher mathematics, particularly algebra and geometry, the inclusion of which Mrs. Willard regarded as marking a "leading epoch in female education." Mrs. Willard always regarded this introduction of the mathematical branches as the chief cause of the strong intellectual power and leadership shown by American women in the later years of the century. At this time such subjects were rejected by common opinion as unimportant or, more commonly, improper for girls. The offering of them in an institution organized for the education of girls undoubtedly did constitute an epoch, whether or not the state actually fulfilled its agreement to subsidize the new movement.

Mrs. Willard was largely instrumental in building up an advanced curriculum, that is, in opening to women so-called "masculine subjects," though a number of others share with her the credit of this achievement. Yet there were other factors in her great influence on women's education. Perhaps no one thing was more important than her insistence upon thoroughness; her effort to discredit the prevailing superficiality of women's education by demonstrating that the customary lack of thoroughness was not essential. Furthermore she held that "communication" is essential to the completion of the learning process, and advocated that her pupils should teach the subjects they studied. She herself had trained her own staff of teachers most efficiently. Believing that one great purpose of the seminary was to furnish adequately trained teachers for the academies and the common schools of the country she added a training department. The expenses of the pupils preparing to teach were so frequently cared for by the head of the school that this philanthropy threatened the very existence of the institution. Through several decades her influence and that of the school were disseminated by the unfailing streams of teachers going out to all parts of the country, so it is easy to understand how the Troy Female Seminary became the most influential establishment in women's education during the first half of the century. Its public examinations became notable occasions, visitors coming from such distant places as Cincinnati and New Orleans.

In 1838 Mrs. Willard resigned from the Seminary to devote her time to improving the preparation and the condition of women teachers. In 1840 she was elected by the voters of the town of Kensington, Conn., as "Superintendent" of the common schools of the town for one year. Thus she was not only the first woman to hold such a position but one of the first persons to perform this function in the country (see p. 271). It is to be noted that she served gratuitously as well as efficiently. Her biographer fittingly writes:

"The selection of Mrs. Emma Willard to occupy a place in this gallery of eminent American teachers was not so much because of her accomplished work, immense as this has been; not because she had by unsurpassed energy established the first scientific female seminary; not because as an author a million of her books were circulated; nor because she has published various addresses on the subject of educa-

EDUCATION OF GIRLS AND WOMEN

tion, presented by invitation before various important bodies in various parts of the country; nor because she has enlisted wide discussion and general interest by the results of investigations in physiology; nor because she has done much disinterested work for the improvement of the public schools; nor because she initiated in her own seminary a system for the special education of teachers; but because she is pre-eminently a REPRESENTATIVE WOMAN, who suitably typifies the great movement of the nineteenth century for the elevation of woman; because her life has been consecrated to the education and advancement of her sex; rather we might say that the Christian elevation of woman has been the life itself."

During the fourth decade of the century Mrs. Willard traveled extensively throughout the country promoting the general cause of education and particularly the education of women. She lived to see the triumph of the cause to which her life was devoted.

Mary Lyon (Quos. 569-571).—Perhaps the most striking personality of all these woman educators was Mary Lyon. Born in 1797 on a sterile mountain farm of western Massachusetts, she was left at the age of five one of a large family of children with a widowed mother. Assisting on the farm, sharing in the laborious activities of a rural household, devoting to spinning, weaving, and the making of garments such leisure hours as these other duties afforded, she still found time to study. Her struggle for knowledge reads like a romance not to be paralleled in more recent generations. Home duties left little time to gain such scant knowledge as was offered by the district school, two miles away. The entire management of farm and family falling on her shoulders at the age of fifteen, what opportunity had she to attain any insight into the wider aspects of knowledge? Yet this insight she did gain and in an astonishingly brief time. By accepting service in a family when she was twenty she entered an academy; and by service of this kind alternating with teaching, which she began at the wage of seventy-five cents per week, she managed in a few years to acquire what few could accomplish by continuous application—brilliant intellectual achievement, superior skill in teaching, and a great life purpose.

This purpose was to found in an institution of higher learning

FOUNDING OF AMERICAN SCHOOL SYSTEM

which should offer to young women the full measure of the intellectual life of the times which colleges offered to men. To this broad cultivation of the mind should be added the domestic training anticipated from a community dormitory life, and the deep religious fervor of the times. This school must be endowed, in order to remove its management from the dangers and limitations of profiteering, and to open its opportunities to the poorest girls. It must be independent of direct sectarian control, for its all-controlling motive was to be found in the advancement of women.

FIG. 96. An early building of Mount Holyoke College popularly called, "The Ministers' Rib Factory." 1837. (From *New England Magazine*.)

These purposes were fully evolved through several years of alternating study and teaching, followed by sixteen years of continuous experience on the staff of academies and in a select school of her own. Thus Miss Lyon became familiar with the work and organization of the popular New England academies, with the best teachers and the most far-sighted education, as well as with the defects and limitations of existing practices. Much of this experience was with Miss Grant, who first formulated the idea of a seminary for girls comparable to the colleges for men. After some unsuccessful attempts the plans for the seminary were matured, its location at Mount Holyoke, in the valley of the Connecticut River, chosen, its body of trustees secured, the arduous task of raising funds accomplished, and in 1836 its incorporation achieved. The school opened late in the following year. This work was accomplished by almost

EDUCATION OF GIRLS AND WOMEN

incredible effort and sacrifice. The spirit, though not the magnitude of the achievement can be judged from the facts that the funds raised, about $15,000, were expended for the building and that Miss Lyon served as Principal for a salary of $200.

In these present days of prosperous institutions, of great educational philanthropies, of large student bodies, and of the popularity of the higher education of women, it is hard to appreciate the difficulties of this task and the value of its accomplishment at a time when prejudice against the appearance of women in public made it difficult for Miss Lyon even to address her own board of trustees, when many of the gifts to the institution were in sums less than one dollar, and when no more money being available it was necessary to collect support for the students in the form of food and clothing. Nor can the merits of the institution be adequately measured by the modern method of statistics; for its largest result was probably the profound influence of the personality of Miss Lyon on the character of hundreds of girls. As stated in the original announcement of the seminary by Miss Lyon, "Here we trust will be found a delightful spot for those 'whose heart has stirred them' to use all their talents in the great work of serving their generation and of advancing the Redeemer's kingdom. In the same manner, we doubt not, that the atmosphere will be rendered uncongenial to those who are wrapped up in self, preparing simply to please and to be pleased, whose highest ambition is to be qualified to amuse a friend in a vacant hour." Trained intelligence, household or technical efficiency, democratic sentiment, social comradeship, moral devotion, spiritual insight, religious conviction, were her ideals, realized in large measure in the lives of numbers of girls and women.

Other Leaders.—Every state, in fact many communities, furnished leaders of this type, perhaps less able, certainly less influential, but no less devoted and within their narrow circles no less worthy of gratitude for their contribution to the progress of society and to the cause of the intellectual and social enfranchisement of their sex. Among these at least one must be mentioned—Catherine Beecher, who had as a most promising pupil in her school at Hartford in 1822 her sister, Harriet Beecher (Stowe). In the state of Connecticut

Miss Beecher rendered quite as great a service as did Miss Lyon in Massachusetts or Mrs. Willard in New York, though no institution has survived to perpetuate her memory.

Many able men also contributed to the advancement of women's education. Among these the most conspicuous was William Woodbridge of Connecticut, whose influence was exerted through the magazines (p. 240) as well as through his teaching; Reverend Joseph Emerson of New York, John Kingsbury of Rhode Island, and James M. Garnett of Virginia.

The actual development from the condition described by Webster in 1788 (p. 207) to the establishment of a fully developed college for women and to equal privileges for both sexes in colleges hitherto exclusively for men will now be traced briefly. It is substantially the history of the first half of the nineteenth century.

The Early Education of Girls.—That in every generation there have been numbers of educated women needs no argument. To give any accurate estimate of conditions at any one time or at various periods is difficult. A few studies of the literacy of women in the Colonial period have been made. For the most part these have been based upon signatures to deeds and hence represent the propertied class only, or upon other legal papers which might be executed by other classes but not representative of society in its entirety. On this basis it has been established that about 75 per cent of the women of Virginia in the seventeenth century were illiterate; among the Dutch of New Amsterdam the percentage was about sixty; while similar studies in New England show about 58 per cent in the middle of the century and about 38 at its close to be unable to sign their names. These figures are not conclusive, but they indicate a widespread degree of illiteracy among women. Moreover, conditions in these respects seem to have improved with time, while the illiteracy of men, tested in the same manner by the number who make their marks in signing legal papers, increased.

The art of writing was acquired by most women in the home or in the dame school. In the middle colonies girls frequently if not usually attended the church or parish schools. In New England the situation is not clear. The question was at times discussed and

EDUCATION OF GIRLS AND WOMEN

referred to the selectmen. But until the dame schools were incorporated into the town system during the middle and latter part of the century, it is probable that girls did not attend the town schools except on rare occasions.

The formal institutional education of women began in the groups that carried this custom with them from Europe. Of this type was the school opened in 1727 by the Ursuline nuns brought from France to establish a convent for the French of Louisiana. The convent and school are still in existence and the memory of their earliest location is perpetuated in Nun Street and Religious Street, while the building begun for them in 1727 is standing now. The great interest in education characteristic of the Moravians, the original Bohemian Protestant body, is best typified in their great bishop, Comenius. Under their Pennsylvania leader, Count Zinzendorf, a school for girls was founded in Germantown in 1742; this was later transferred to Bethlehem, where it yet exists. The following year another one was founded at Nazareth and later moved to Frederickstown. Linden Hall Seminary, founded in 1746, was permanently established in Letitz in Pennsylvania. These and others by the same sect were the earliest girls' schools in the Colonies and exerted an influence extending beyond the limits of the sect.

Admission of Girls to the Town Schools of New England (Quos. 552–553).—It will be recalled that as early as 1639 the question of the admission of girls to the town schools of Dorchester was raised. While in this case the answer was left to the selectmen, there is no statement of their decision. Similar records show that the question was considered from time to time in various towns and that in some it was answered in the affirmative under certain restrictions. But there was no general movement of this kind until near the close of the eighteenth century. In most towns where any record of this point is made—and these can be taken as indicative of the attitude of the majority—it was not until after the Revolution, in fact in many cases not until the nineteenth century, that girls were admitted on equal terms, or even on any terms, to the town schools. Previous to this time they obtained their instruction in reading and writing, much more rarely in ciphering, in dame schools, in private schools, or in the home, rarely in the town school but during special hours.

In Boston where some dame schools had been incorporated earlier, the first specific recognition of girls was in 1789. In the reorganization of the town schools it was stated, "that in these schools the children of both sexes shall be taught writing and also arithmetic in the various branches of it usually taught in town schools, including vulgar and decimal fractions." These were the writing schools. Of the reading schools it was stated "that in these schools the children of both sexes be taught to spell, accent, and read both prose and verse, and also be instructed in English grammar and composition." To the latter schools girls were admitted only during the half year from April to October, and it was not until 1826, after the experiment with the "Girls' High School" (p. 413) that they were put on a basis of equality. It will also be recalled that in Boston children were not admitted to the early town schools until they were about seven years of age and had acquired the rudiments of reading; and that after 1818 a system of primary schools on quasi-public basis was established, providing for children under this age. These schools were not incorporated with the town school system until the middle of the century.

The first step in the admission of girls to the town schools was usually the granting of this privilege for only certain months of the year or certain hours of the day. Plymouth in 1793 made a special appropriation for a girls' school, "kept by the teacher of the grammar school, for six months in the year, one hour in the forenoon and one in the afternoon at the close of the regular daily session." The school committee of Charlestown, Mass., reported in 1791 that "it is their opinion that females be admitted into the public schools within the Neck for six months in the year, viz., from May to October inclusive. That their hours of instruction be from eleven to one o'clock, and from four to six. That they be admitted at seven years of age or more. That until nine years of age they be taught reading and spelling. That after that age they also be taught writing and arithmetic."

EDUCATION OF GIRLS AND WOMEN

The Haverhill, Mass., school regulations in 1790 proposed "That from May to September one hour in the forenoon and the same in the afternoon be specially appropriated for the instruction of the young misses or females; that of consequence the common school be dismissed daily for such a period at 11 o'clock in the forenoon and a like hour in the afternoon to give time for that purpose." The quotation of such records as these could be multiplied indefinitely.

With the establishment of the divided or the district school, the incorporation in many places of the old dame schools with the town school system, the introduction of district summer and winter sessions, and the employment of women teachers for the summer session, there came a general admission of girls into the summer session. In the early nineteenth century even this distinction broke down. Hingham, Mass., voted in 1791 that "There shall be five female schools for six months"; and in 1800 voted "that girls of twelve years of age and upwards might attend certain of the male schools in the winter months, and boys under nine might attend certain female schools in the summer months." These records reveal what was rapidly coming to be the general practice.

With the admission of girls to the common schools came in time the union of reading and writing schools, the grading of schools, and the expansion of the curriculum. The general process is typified in Northampton, Mass., which after a long and checkered policy in the schooling of girls decided in 1803 "that school mistresses should be provided for female children under the age of ten years for five months, from the first of May to the first of October, one mistress to thirty scholars or thereabouts; that a committee should be appointed by the town to employ such mistresses and apportion the scholars among them; that female children between the ages of ten and fourteen should have liberty to go to the town schools under the direction of the selectmen for three months of the year, to wit, from the first of May to the first of August, for the purpose of being instructed in writing and the higher branches of education."

In general it may be said that in the district schools of the small towns girls were admitted on an equality with the boys in the period immediately following the Revolution, as in fact they had been, under certain restrictions, in some towns before the Revolution. But in the large towns it was almost or quite half a century after the Revolution before the plane of equality was attained.

Girls in the Grammar Schools.—If such was the attitude toward the admission of girls to the elementary schools, there was as a matter of course much stronger opposition to their attending the grammar or Latin schools. The Hopkins Grammar School of New Haven in 1680 made a rule "that all girls be excluded as improper and inconsistent with such a grammar school as the law enjoins and is the design of this settlement." Concerning Dorchester Grammar School it was voted in 1784 "that such girls as can read in a Psalter be allowed to go to the grammar school from the first day of June to the first day of October." A few years later this privilege was extended to six months of the year. By this time, however, the grammar school had become more or rather less than a Latin school and it is probable that girls were admitted chiefly if not exclusively to the English branches.

Either because of prejudice against the education of girls or because of lack of sufficient preparation on their part there are few records on the question of the admission of girls to the Latin grammar schools. Undoubtedly it was this condition which favored the building up of private schools offering the higher subjects, and which inclined the officials to sanction them. An excellent type of these was the famous school opened by Caleb Bingham in Boston immediately after the Revolution. The record of 1784 reads, "Mr. Caleb Bingham approbated by the selectmen to keep a private school for the instruction of young ladies in the useful branches of reading, writing, etc." Later authorization of such schools provided for the teaching of higher branches. But it was not until 1826 that Boston made public provision for the education of girls beyond the common grades. It may be assumed that the Latin or grammar schools, such as survived in modified form into the National period, made no provision for girls except in rare cases, usually those of exceptional ability or special tutoring.

EDUCATION OF GIRLS AND WOMEN

Girls' Education in Private Schools.—The earliest and most common form of the private school was the dame school. To these girls were admitted and in them throughout the eighteenth and the early nineteenth centuries the vast majority of girls obtained all the formal education which they received. About the period of the Revolution these schools in rural New England had been quite generally incorporated in the town school system and consequently are included in the discussion of that topic (p. 121). Throughout the other colonies and until public school systems were established in the National period they continued to flourish. A record of Medford, Mass., in 1819 indicates the general custom in New England. The school committee reported "that the town contains 158 girls over the age of seven years ... and 117 children of both sexes over four years of age and under seven years of age that require to be taught in the summer season by women teachers; that the Committee be authorized to employ these women teachers for six months beginning about the first of May, who are to teach the girls of all ages from four years old and upwards, and the boys from four years old to seven, unless they are sufficiently qualified to go to the master's school."

But the dame schools were for the most part under private management and hence do not appear in the public records. On this account it is impossible to give any accurate estimate of their extent or of the part they played in the education of girls.

During the early National period as well as immediately preceding the Revolution the scope of these dame schools was expanded to include the rudiments of the more advanced subjects, so that many of them, perhaps most of them in towns and cities, became finishing schools as well as dame schools.

The conception of education remained much the same. Woman was considered largely, so far as education was concerned, either a doll or a drudge, and she was educated accordingly.

The advertisements found in the newspapers in very great numbers throughout this period from the middle eighteenth to the middle nineteenth centuries indicate the extent of this system of female schools and the prevalence of this type of education.

Schools of the more advanced type were often kept by men. A Salem, Mass., advertisement of 1782 announces, "Nathan Reed has commenced a school near the town house for young ladies for reading, writing, arithmetic, English grammar, elocution, composition, and geography." Quite often the masters of public schools held private schools for girls before and after the public school hours. A Salem announcement of 1796 states that: "Mr. Jackson notifies that he shall have a morning school from six to eight o'clock for young ladies, in the common and higher studies." Sometimes the hours were even earlier. Nathan Hale, the patriot, wrote of his school at New London, Conn., at the opening of the Revolution, "I have kept during the summer a morning school between the hours of five and seven, of about twenty young ladies; for which I have received six shillings a scholar by the quarter."

The newspapers of the Colonial and the early National periods abound in advertisements of such schools, and afford the chief information we have of them. These institutions existed in every center of population, were flexible in their offerings, more or less superficial in their work, and ephemeral in their existence. The early use of the term "high school" among them should be noted.

The Girls' High Schools (Quo. 564).—Probably the earliest usage of this term was to designate the monitorial high schools opened in New York in 1826. For several years John Griscom, associated with a number of persons interested in public education, had conducted a similar school for boys. This proving very successful financially as well as professionally, a High School for Girls was instituted on the same plan. For a time the school had an attendance of about 500. Mr. Griscom remembers "that the lady placed in it as principal was chiefly remarkable for her skill in flower painting," so the experiment was short-lived.

Of a different character was the Girls' High School of Boston (Quo. 553–556) which flourished for the two years, 1826–28. The chief incentive to the establishment of this school probably came from the marked success achieved by the English Classical or High School for Boys, established in 1821. The committee which recommended its establishment emphasized as reasons: first, that many

EDUCATION OF GIRLS AND WOMEN

girls of fourteen or over were then included in the classes of the grammar schools, which would be made more efficient by the change, while the older girls would be better educated; second, that teachers would thus be furnished for the expanding system of primary schools; and third, that the monitorial system of instruction could be tested preliminary to its adoption in the other schools of the city.

The very success of the school defeated it. In abandoning the scheme the committee declared, "no funds of any city could bear the expense" of giving a higher education to every girl as well as boy. It deemed education for girls more impracticable than for boys because the girls, not being drawn away from the college by preparation for a profession or trade, would have nothing except their marriage to prevent their parents from availing themselves of it. As an alternative, advanced subjects were added to the curriculum of the grammar schools. The High School for Girls was re-established after the middle of the century, chiefly as a training school for teachers.

In a similar way girls were provided for in New York, first by the expansion of the graded school curriculum to include advanced subjects, and after the middle of the century through the establishment of a normal training school for girls. In Providence, Rhode Island, a girls' high school founded by John Kingsbury in 1828 continued under his direction with notable success for over thirty years. This, however, was again a private institution, differing from the academies only in name.

Girls in the Quasi-Public Schools of the Public School Societies.—It was with the organization of a "Female Association" to maintain a school for the education of girls who were not cared for in the numerous church charity schools of the time that the public education of girls in New York city may be said to have begun. This was in 1802 when the population of the city was over 60,000 and when there were only the private schools and the charity schools of the various denominations. Later, when buildings were erected by the Free School Society, a room was reserved in each one in which a school for girls was maintained by the

Female Association. In 1814 about 300 girls were in attendance; in 1820 about 750. After 1816, when the revenue for the state school fund was first distributed, the Female Association shared in these allotments. Gradually the work of the association was transferred to the Public School Society, and in 1845, it having become obvious that the city would thereafter adequately provide for the education of poor children, the Female Association gave its remaining school to the Public School Society. While at first the girls were instructed by Lancasterian methods the association soon adopted the method of the Infant School. And in general it may be stated that outside of New England the education of girls was first provided for on a public foundation by the Lancasterian or the Infant School methods.

In Philadelphia an Association for the Instruction of Poor Children opened a school for boys in 1807, and one for girls in 1812. These were merged in the public school system in 1818. This system, as will be recalled (p. 208), was still a quasi-public rather than a public system. The law made provision for the free education of girls between the ages of five and thirteen, "children of indigent parents."

In Boston a survey made in 1817 showed 2365 children in the public schools, of whom 736 were girls; and 3767 children in private schools, 2288 being girls. There were then about 80 dame schools. The following year it was shown that 552 children between four and seven, the majority of them being girls, were in no school. Consequently in 1819 a Primary School Committee was formed, distinct from the School Committee but supported by public funds, for the development of primary schools. In ten years a system of 53 schools was built up, with more than 3000 pupils, of whom a considerable majority were girls. About the middle of the century these schools were amalgamated with the other public schools into a complete system.

In smaller communities where schools were supported by means of quasi-public or philanthropic societies, the custom regarding the admission of girls varied with the locality. Sometimes separate societies for the founding of girls' schools were established, particularly where the Lancasterian plan was followed. More frequently provi-

EDUCATION OF GIRLS AND WOMEN

sion was made for girls along with boys, at first usually in separate classes. The general introduction of the infant school idea during the thirties included boys and girls without discrimination.

The schools kept by the various religious sects, often with paying pupils from the wealthier members of the congregation, but intended especially for the poor, and hence known as charity schools, should here be noted. They form an intermediate type between private schools and those supported by philanthropic societies. As a rule such schools admitted both boys and girls. Records of individual institutions show that now girls and now boys predominated. There was no great difference in the work of the sexes other than that found in all the schools of the day—domestic and needlework for the girls, arithmetic and higher subjects for the boys.

Education of Girls under the New State Educational Systems.—The early state system founded on general statute made no distinction between boys and girls, though often specifying that both sexes should be provided for.

In Massachusetts the statutes uniformly stipulate that provision be made for all children in the elementary schools as for youth in the grammar schools. The report of the Secretary of the State Board, when such reports appear (1839 and after) refer continuously to the increasing number of women teachers employed (p. 246) and significantly argue for their employment in the teaching of boys as well as of girls. No discrimination having been made between the sexes it is impossible to make any quantitative estimate of the number of each.

The early New York statutes established schools "in which the children of the inhabitants" shall be instructed. The question whether girls should be sent to school was then left to the parents. No doubt prejudice still played a large part and, since these schools were all tuition or rate schools, economic conditions played a yet larger one. Reports concerning the operation of the Law of 1795 do not indicate that girls attended, but the local records do. Even after the permanent establishment of the public school system it is not possible to tell how generally girls attended. Certainly there was no legal hindrance. By the third and fourth decades of the century school enrollment nearly equalled the school population between the ages of six and fifteen, so there could have been no great discrimination against girls in the common or district schools. No doubt in general the shorter period, the summer school, and the most poorly equipped teachers fell to their lot.

The Pennsylvania Law of 1818 distinguished between boys and girls in the matter of age, providing permissive education for poor children, boys from six to fourteen and girls from five to thirteen, but made no other discrimination.

During the earlier decades of the century, before systems of tax-supported or assisted schools were established, the states to the north and west made extensive provision for subsidies to schools privately initiated—usually under the name of academies. There seems to have been no discrimination against institutions for girls alone or against those open to both sexes. Where systems were established wherein funds from state tax or school funds were restricted to specific uses no legal discrimination was made. Consequently the extent of the use of these privileges by girls depended on custom or circumstances alone. While it is recorded that in this early period many citizens "objected to their daughters' studying arithmetic or learning to use the pen," yet when schools were made free, or substantially so, this prejudice undoubtedly disappeared. The state supported school certainly proved an influential factor in establishing the equality of the sexes in education.

Girls' Education in the Academies (Quos. 554–565).—Under this caption various types of institutions must be included. First there were the numerous private schools, operated for commercial reasons and open to girls (p. 406). Second, there were the numerous female seminaries which offered the superficial finishing type of education. Third, there were the public academies, though the name was not always distinctive, which aimed to give girls much the same education as similar institutions gave to boys. Fourth, there was the co-educational academy.

Many private institutions adopted the high-sounding name of academy, but more frequently they chose that of seminary. Some

EDUCATION OF GIRLS AND WOMEN

such schools had existed from the early part of the eighteenth century, even before Franklin in 1743 applied the term to the institution which he developed later in Philadelphia, under quasi-public control. But it is the academies controlled by boards of trustees and operated, not for private benefit, but for the public good, that are here under consideration.

How closely the two types were allied is indicated by one of the earliest of these institutions. In 1787 a Harvard graduate, John Poor, opened "The Young Ladies' Academy of Philadelphia" in that city. After fifteen years of successful service it was incorporated by the legislature and was claimed at that time to be the only incorporated institution for young ladies in the United States. The curriculum offered reading, history, arithmetic, grammar, composition, geography with the use of globes and maps, rhetoric, and vocal music.

Pennsylvania, dependent during Colonial times upon religious denominations and private enterprise for her schools, was the home of great members of academies and seminaries. The historians of the state number these by the hundred; consequently the public free schools developed tardily, and the state followed the plan of subsidizing many of these academies. In 1834 this policy was reduced to a system and a relatively small number of schools, of a given standard, were subsidized. By 1842 the state was subsidizing 65 academies and 41 female seminaries. When it is recalled that many of the academies of a private character taught girls as well as boys, it will be seen that extensive provision for the education of girls was made in this state. Of these numerous institutions, however, a report to the legislature in 1834 stated: "Most of the academies have fallen to the grade of common schools. This is a melancholy truth, so that very few of them can be used as seminaries for training teachers." Unfortunately one cause for this decline in the standards of the academies was the admission of girls who were ill prepared for any higher work because of the lack of any other educational provision.

In the South the situation was somewhat similar to that in Pennsylvania except that the development of the free school system being still more retarded the compensating development of the academies continued until after the Civil War. In Virginia during the period from 1800 to 1860 of 194 academies founded 69 were for girls and 20 were co-educational. However, the great increase in the provision for girls took place after 1840. While but six "female" and one co-educational institution had been chartered before 1820, from 1840 to 1860 charters were granted to forty-eight academies for girls and to twelve for both sexes. During that period only forty institutions were chartered for boys. Aside from the incorporated institutions great numbers of private schools of lower standards flourished. It is obvious that during this latter period the opportunities for girls in institutions of secondary education were quite as abundant as for boys. But the fact that such institutions were chartered does not imply that the state necessarily granted funds or took any further interest in them. Indeed out of a total of more than two hundred the state subsidized only seventeen and these for boys alone.

Co-educational Collegiate Education (Quo. 572).—It remained for the freer, less conventional society of the new West to break down the conservatism and prejudice long dominant in this field. Many academies in various parts of the East and South had demonstrated that girls have both ability and interest in academic subjects above the elementary branches and not merely decorative in character. Some few schools in the North and East had demonstrated that girls could receive this education on the same basis and in the same institution as boys. The success of the Troy Female Seminary had shown that both patronage and financial support could be obtained for an institution that taught the higher branches and even aspired to make its work equivalent to that of the colleges of the period.

The Middle West solved the problem and destroyed the prejudice against both women's collegiate education and co-education by founding colleges admitting men and women without any distinction. Oberlin College, Ohio, founded in 1833, was the first of these. It must be noted, however, that its exact title was collegiate institute not only because of a large preparatory or academic department

FIG. 97. Public examination in the Troy Academy. (From *New England Magazine*, Vol. V, p. 564.)

and several other innovations, but in recognition of the fact that it was not the conventional college. Although the institution possessed degree-granting powers and offered a college course standard for those days the college charter was not obtained until 1850. Long before this, however, the co-educational feature was an acknowledged success. *The American Annals of Education* for 1838 stated: "We consider it now fully established that the sexes may be educated together. The discovery is one of the most important ever made. The benefits which are likely to flow from it are immense. Woman is to be free. The hour of her emancipation is at hand." Of the total attendance of 391 in this year 126 were girls, and 105 of these were in the collegiate school. This was a much larger percentage than the men students could show. However, most of the women pursued the "ladies' course," which required but one preparatory year. Up to 1865 only 79 women had received the degree of the college course.

In 1853 Antioch College, also in Ohio, was opened, under the presidency of Horace Mann. The attendance here was very small, and the stormy experience resulting from the adoption of a number of innovations kept the institution an academy rather than a college for some years. Meanwhile many sectarian schools had been founded in Ohio, most of which opened their doors to women either on an equality with men or by means of an annex or seminary. At least nine of these were in existence by 1855, several of them earlier than Antioch. Lombard and Knox set similar examples in Illinois. By 1855 or 1860 all the Northern and Western states had similar co-educational institutions. Both religious and political motives as well as economic conditions exerted influence toward this end, and by the close of this period sentiment in favor of co-education in these denominational colleges was all but universal.

During the same period the trans-Mississippi region began to develop educationally, throwing all its influence to one side of this controversy. In these regions the public school had developed without any traditional restrictions from private school conventions. Democratic support demanded democratic opportunity without limitation of sex. Woman's part in the development and enrichment of frontier life had been such that there could be no thought of excluding her from any of its privileges. Sparseness of population, remoteness from centers of culture, difficulties of transportation, financial limitations, all rendered the development of a dual system impossible. State universities were developed from the very inception of each state and practically all of these admitted women on an equality with men.

These colleges in the order of their opening as co-educational institutions are: Utah, 1850; Iowa, 1856; Washington, 1862; Kansas, 1866; Nebraska, 1871. Most of these in their early years were little more than academies. The most influential and highest grade state university of the period was that of Michigan, founded in 1838. In 1870 it admitted women on an equality with men, offering to them, probably for the first time, opportunity for a collegiate education of full grade and scope. With this step the controversy may be said to have been settled and the custom of co-education in higher institutions definitely established.

With the exception of the endowed colleges of New England, and many endowed as well as a few state institutions in the South, practically all institutions of higher training are co-educational. However, there is an exception to co-education in the last type, now to be reviewed. For with the recent development of colleges for women there have come into being as many institutions, denying their privileges to men as deny them to women.

Collegiate Education of Woman (Quos. 563-574).—In this period came the complete success of the struggle for the higher education of women, in the establishment of institutions of full collegiate grade for women only, and in the opening of universities to women. If the point at issue lay in the use of the term college, or even in the giving of collegiate degrees, the earlier decades of the century were as worthy of note as the mid-century. But these earlier institutions represent educational ideals rather than accomplishments and the somewhat vague use of scholastic terms, not yet definitely fixed in their meaning, or unrealized social and educational aspirations. The use of the term academy or seminary being preferred in the North, most of these earlier colleges or "collegiate institutions" were found in the South and West. In these regions educational institutions for girls were numerous and popular. Most of them having the traditional labels, usually that of seminary, were devoted to education of the finishing type. Those stressing the academic studies of advanced character often assumed the title of college without having actually attained the standards maintained by the best colleges for men—a practice common then, affecting institutions for men or women or both, and not uncommon even yet in various parts of the country.

Among those early institutions may be noted Elizabeth College in Mississippi in 1817; Mississippi College, 1830; Queensboro College, North Carolina, 1838; Greenville College, 1854; Salem Academy, made a college in 1866. Ohio had two Wesleyan Female Colleges before 1855, one as early as 1842. Before 1860 practically every Southern and most Western states had educational institutions admitting women, with degree-conferring power and termed colleges. The more popular degree in the early years seems to have been *Domina Scientarium*. Only one or two of these Southern institutions yet exist; in few is there any record of the early curriculum left to prove its collegiate character. Most of them were sectarian institutions, many of them were private, some even of the degree-granting class were proprietary. In the Mid-western states co-educational institutions were more numerous than colleges for women alone. In none of these regions, perhaps in but a few institutions of the country, could girls obtain a preparatory education sufficient to equip them for standard collegiate work.

In 1855 Elmira Female College was chartered in the state of New York. Guarded by the requirements of the Regents of the State University, this institution was probably of standard college grade. But, as in the preceding five years it had been both an academy and a "Female University," its early status was perhaps not the most secure. While many of the co-educational institutions had attained the recognized college standard previous to this time, Elmira was probably the first institution distinctly for women to set a standard equivalent to that of colleges for men. As with all the earlier insti-

EDUCATION OF GIRLS AND WOMEN

tutions its influence was local. The limitations which had hampered all these pioneer attempts were insufficient funds and lack of properly prepared students. These limitations were removed in the case of Vassar Female College, chartered in 1861 and opened in 1865. Whether this was the first woman's college it is needless to discuss. It was not the first to bear the name; nor the first to grant degrees; nor the first to formulate and attempt the ideal. It was the first to possess adequate means, students, staff, and prestige.

Even after the possibility of the higher academic education for women had received many demonstrations and co-education in the collegiate field had proved a success in two or three flourishing institutions, the practicability, even the desirability, of offering to women alone the collegiate education then given to men was still an open question.

It remained for a practical businessman to render possible the attempt, and to go to the heart of the whole problem. In his letter to the first board of trustees Matthew Vassar wrote (Quo. 563): "Woman, having received from her Creator the same intellectual constitution as man, has the same right to intellectual culture and development." Having thus disposed of the sophistries which had precluded the discussion of this problem for many decades, he states just as succinctly the sound arguments for the innovation. "I considered that the mothers of the country mold the character of its citizens, determine its institutions, and shape its destiny. Next to the influence of the mother is that of the female teacher, who is employed to train young children at a period when impressions are most vivid and lasting. It also seemed to me that if woman were properly educated some new avenues to useful and honorable employment, in entire harmony with the gentleness and modesty of her sex, might be opened to her. It further appeared, there is not in our country, there is not in the world, so far as is known, a single fully-endowed institution for the education of women. It was also in evidence that for the last thirty years the standard of education for the sex has been constantly rising in the United States; and the great, felt, pressing want has been ample endowment to secure to female seminaries the elevated character, the stability and permanency of our best colleges." This gift of 1861 permitted the opening of the college in 1865. Its successful operation was the first demonstration of the feasibility of an institution for women of the same grade and character as those for men.

The subsequent founding of institutions similar to Vassar falls in the next period of educational development. Wellesley and Smith, both in Massachusetts, were opened in 1875. The collegiate education offered by these institutions has been more rigidly academic than the somewhat more practical one suggested by the founder of Vassar. This exclusion of the more practical aspects of higher education, in the applied forms of the various sciences, has remained characteristic of the other colleges for women founded even later on the Vassar model. While these colleges for women have grown somewhat more "academic" than their founders had planned, the administration of the curricula of colleges for men and of co-educational colleges has grown much more flexible, through connection with professional schools, introduction of applied sciences and semi-professional subjects in medicine, sanitation, education, and social science. Consequently there has sprung up a wide divergence between the college for women and that for men, in which the former demonstrates the intellectual equality of the sexes by maintaining a more rigidly academic and traditionally conservative education than is enforced in other institutions.

Summary.—A radical achievement of this educational period was the general change both in ideas concerning the education of girls and women and in the institutional opportunities for such education. The intellectual and educational rights of women were substantially achieved between 1825 and 1865. The conception of woman's education as either a practical training for the household or a process of adornment to fit its subject for a life of idleness or frivolity gave way to one which considered the purposes, processes, and problems of the education of women as substantially the same as those for men. The leaders in this great movement were numerous, both men and women. Chief among them were Emma Hart Willard and Mary Lyon. During the earliest decades of the National period the town schools of New England gradually removed

EDUCATION OF GIRLS AND WOMEN

all restrictions on the attendance of girls, though this process was not fully accomplished in some of the larger cities until later. Opportunities equal to those for boys were not furnished in many of the more populous communities until after the middle of the nineteenth century. Consequently private schools for girls flourished. Dame or elementary schools for girls were incorporated in public school systems as these were founded. But in all regions of the country opportunities for girls were largely furnished by private institutions; in the South this was almost exclusively so. In the cities the education of children of the poorer and middle classes, then more clearly differentiated from the well-to-do and the wealthy than now, was cared for by quasi-public philanthropic societies. In the largest cities, as often in smaller ones, special organizations existed for the care of schools for girls. Otherwise girls were admitted with boys. In rural regions co-education came earlier. The early state laws providing for public education made no discrimination against girls. Even before the beginning of the nineteenth century some New England academies opened their doors to girls. By the second quarter of that century co-educational academies and seminaries for girls alone became quite numerous in all parts of the country. State aid was first voted to the academy founded by Mrs. Willard in 1819 in New York. Some of these institutions in cities where day pupils replaced boarders were called high schools, though private in control and support. In 1826 the city of Boston opened a public high school for girls, which was abandoned after two years. With the establishing of publicly supported high schools or union schools came the admission of girls on terms of equality. In the colleges co-education began with Oberlin in 1833, and in the Middle and Far West it soon became the normal status. All state universities west of the Mississippi admitted women from the first. The University of Michigan admitted them from 1870. The first adequately endowed institution of collegiate grade for women was Vassar, opened in 1865.

Chapter XV

THE TEACHING PROFESSION

Democracy and Professional Training (Quos. 544-545).—
The stability and the efficiency of a democracy is conditioned upon the discovery, development, and dependence upon specialized ability, trained for expert service. Belief in such a principle has even yet no very general acceptance, but its recognition is a constantly growing one. As long as the belief prevails that anyone can teach school, or even that anyone can farm, or can fill a public office without special training, there is not much hope for progress in any of these great fields of social activity. The belief in the universality of ability was an outgrowth of the democratic sense of equality established in our country during the early National period. The political life of the country was founded upon such a belief, and from 1830 on the belief was given full expression in action. The only limitation to this belief that had any popular support was the view, at that time being vigorously emphasized by the leaders, that intelligence was a necessary condition to such equality.

A similar popular view prevailed regarding teaching. With development of public systems of education and the general adoption of the district system, schools were greatly multiplied: this called for a very large increase of the teaching staff. The popular view throughout this period was that, given ordinary intelligence and the necessary information on the subject taught, anyone could teach. Even should there be a deficiency in the latter the supply of textbooks then being furnished in great abundance would meet this want. The leaders of education, however, were coming to see that something further was demanded and that a successful teacher needed not only the possession of the requisite information but also some specialized knowledge of the forces dealt with and of the technical methods of securing the desired results. With the first steps toward the realiza-

THE TEACHING PROFESSION

tion of these views came the earlier stages of a specialized training for teachers, which formed the only secure basis of a teaching profession. Before considering the successive steps in the early evolution of the profession, two other considerations profoundly affecting the teaching class need to be mentioned.

The Woman Teacher (Quos. 559–562).—The first of these is the growing number of women in the teaching class. By the close of this period women teachers came to dominate in numbers so far as the elementary school was concerned. It has been seen during the Colonial period that, aside from the dame school and the summer school or woman's school introduced in New England, the vast majority of all school teachers were men. This introduction of the woman school or of the woman teacher in the summer session in New England was due, as we have seen, to the parceling of the school among the small districts, the holding of two or more sessions, the one in the summer being attended by the small children only (Ch. V). This division of the school required many more teachers, which necessitated a very much reduced rate of payment. The only class that could afford to take this work was one which did not have competitive opportunity in other employments. Therefore women were drawn in continuously larger numbers into the work of teaching. Accurate estimates of actual numbers engaged during this period are of course very difficult to obtain.

The annual reports of all of the early state superintendents, particularly of New England and New York, give continuous attention to the phenomenon of the increase of women teachers. Each year showed a marked increase in the number of women teachers compared with the increase of men. While in general the male teacher predominated in the winter session, the woman teacher was in great majority in the summer session. Horace Mann notes (Quo. 557), however, the very rapid increase in the number of women teachers even during the winter term, so that in the very first year of his administration women came to predominate. By 1855 the woman teacher was twice as numerous as the male in all of the New England states except Vermont. Here, however, they composed only one fifth of the teaching staff. In general the woman teacher

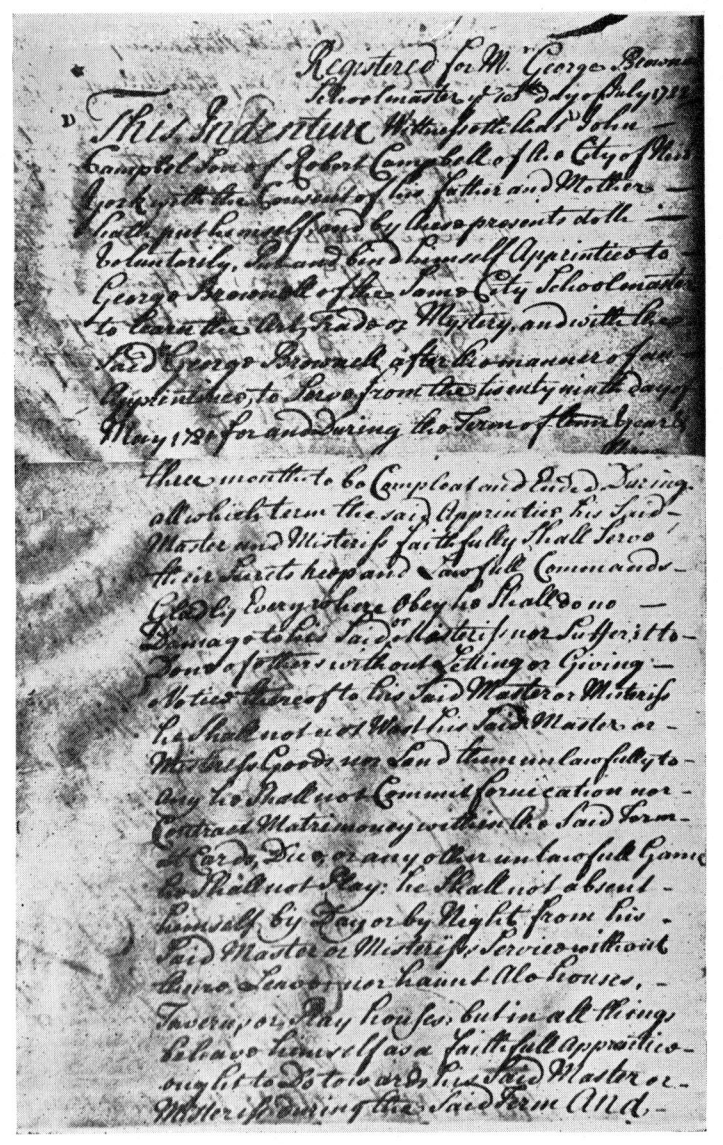

Fig. 98. An indenture of a youth to a schoolmaster.

Evidences the earliest form of professional training.

came to predominate in the Eastern states earlier than in the newer states of the Middle West.

Much of the discussion of this important change in the composition of the teaching profession given by the early state superintendents relates to the significance of this change and the characteristic advantage of the woman teacher. Governor Seward of New York, commenting on this change in 1839 (Quo. 561), wrote:

> "He, it seems to me, is a dull observer who is not convinced that they are equally qualified with the other sex for the study of the magnificent creation around us, and equally entitled to the happiness to be derived from its pursuit; and still more blind is he who has not learned that it was the intention of the Creator to commit to them the higher and greater portion of responsibility in the education of youth of both sexes. They are the natural guardians of the young. Their abstraction from the engrossing cares of life affords them leisure both to acquire and to communicate knowledge. From them the young more willingly receive it, because the severity of discipline is relieved with greater tenderness and affection, while their more quick apprehension, enduring patience, expansive benevolence, higher purity, more delicate taste, and elevated moral feelings qualify them for excellence in all departments of learning, except perhaps the exact sciences. If this be true, how many a repulsive, bigoted, and indolent professor will, in the general improvement of education, be compelled to resign his claim to modest, assiduous, and affectionate woman. And how many conceited pretenders who may wield the rod in our common schools, without the knowledge of human nature requisite for its discreet exercise, too indolent to improve and too proud to discharge their responsible duties, will be driven to seek subsistence elsewhere."

This somewhat exuberant statement of the politician summarizes the main arguments advanced by the educational leaders.

The entrance of women into the teaching profession and their rapid rise to dominance in this field is one of the most marked social features of the period (Quo. 557-562). It reflected but another phase of the growing democracy in which the caste lines of sex were dissolved by the growing tolerance and intelligence of the time. When special opportunity for preparation for the profession was afforded, the women quickly seized control of it. The normal

THE TEACHING PROFESSION

training classes in the academies were largely composed of women. The first normal school in Massachusetts was for women alone. Those which followed in that and adjoining states showed in their earliest years about an equal division in attendance between men and women. However, the proportion of women rapidly increased till they came to predominate even more largely than in the teaching profession itself.

In the newer settled regions of the Middle West men still predominated in the teaching profession throughout this period. It is estimated that as late as 1855 less than one fourth of the teachers in Indiana were women. By 1870 they held 40% of the teaching positions: in 1880, 42%; in 1890, 49%. Not until after 1890 did they come to hold the majority of the teaching positions. In these regions the women came into the schools largely through the city and town systems. At the period when more than 50% of the teachers of the state were men, less than 14% of the teachers of the 58 cities and incorporated towns of the state were men. The change in this state was probably slower than in many other communities of the Middle West, for at the time when in Indiana more than one half of the teachers were men, the number in Michigan was less than one fourth, in Illinois less than one third; only in Ohio were they nearly equally divided. This extensive employment of women in the schools attracted the attention of all foreign observers. The Swede, Siljestrom, who published a work on American Educational Institutions in 1853, writes:

> "The second point to which I desire to draw particular attention is, the frequent employment of women as school teachers. This custom is becoming more common every year. In Massachusetts there were in 1837, according to the official returns, 2370 male and 3591 female teachers, while in 1850 the numbers were 2437 of the former, and 5238 of the latter. In this period the proportion of female teachers had thus increased from 60 to 70 per cent. The same has been the case in all the States. In Maine, the latest official returns bearing on this subject show the proportion of the male to the female teachers to be as two to three, in New Hampshire as one to two, &c, &c.
>
> "Experience has shown that, as regards the education of youth,

women are not only equal to men, but that in many respects they are much more qualified for the task; and in America this is so fully received as an axiom, that it is not uncommon to find the proportion of female teachers employed in the schools considered as a criterion by which to judge of the efficiency of popular education in the various states. The facilities for preliminary preparation being equal, there is indeed no reason why, in point of knowledge and of capacity for teaching, women should be inferior to men; and in America in particular, where even among the lower classes the weaker sex is generally exempt from hard labor, and where men of all classes are mostly engaged in arduous practical pursuits, women are in a peculiarly favorable position as regards the acquisition of that knowledge and general mental cultivation which is obtained from books.

"But supposing the alternative to lie only between men and women equally ill prepared for the calling of teacher, I would in this case, without hesitation, give the preference to women. If the art of instruction has made any progress of late years, it is undoubtedly chiefly owing to the more extended cultivation of the perceptive faculties. Now it is generally acknowledged that, in natural quickness of perception, women have always surpassed men; and it hardly admits of a doubt that this, I may almost say intuitive power, will in most cases lead the former to adopt more effective and quickening methods of teaching than can be expected from men, otherwise on a level with them in point of mental cultivation.

"In addition to this, it cannot be denied that women in general are greatly superior to men as regards conscientiousness and punctuality, patience and perseverance, equanimity and order, refinement of manners and of taste, and consequently they are so much the more qualified to awaken and maintain that spirit and order which every one must desire to see prevail in the schools; and it is remarkable to observe how, by means of the domestic spirit thus introduced, young women of 18 or 20 years of age are enabled to maintain discipline among a number of pupils of both sexes, and some of whom are as old as themselves. It is, however, probable that the respect which the laws of society in America enjoin towards females, in some measure contributes to keep the male pupils under proper restraint."

Teachers' Wages. (Cf. Chart VIII).—Coincident with the multiplication of schools through the district system and the employment

THE TEACHING PROFESSION

of the woman teacher came the very great decline in the rate of payment. It is very commonly held by teachers that the development of their profession and the recognition of its standing and of its rights depend upon an increase of remuneration for professional services. It is true that the development of the profession and of its growth in public esteem is indicated by an increased wage, but it is not the increased wage which makes the profession: the fact is that both wage and professional recognition are effected by common causes. With the disappearance of the professional schoolmaster, especially of the grammar school type in the later Colonial period, what little public repute pertained to the profession disappeared. The crude conception of democracy had its effect upon the teaching profession, if it can be called a profession, as well as upon other aspects of the life of the time. The remuneration for teaching decreased at an almost astonishing degree. The diagram, page 281, shows the conditions in the State of Connecticut. The figures upon which this is based differentiated between the salaries of men and women so that the diagram throws light upon both aspects of the subject. The year when we first get these figures, 1837, the average monthly salary of the women teachers of Connecticut was $5.75, that for the men was $14.50. While these figures must be given in averages, the average here is very much more significant than it frequently is because the range of distribution was not great. Ten years later the average salary for women had been increased 75 cents a month, that of men $2.25 per month. Ten years later, by 1857, the average monthly salary of the women teachers was $17.25, that for the men was $29.00. This was not greatly changed until the period following the Civil War, when there was a material increase. Since that time the improvement has been gradual but steady. In the Middle West the situation was not far different. In 1847 in Michigan the average salary for women teachers was $5.74 per month, and for men $12.87 per month. In the early years of the Civil War this rate was practically doubled in each case, and as in New England the substantial increase came in the five-year period immediately following the Civil War. In Indiana the average monthly wage for the women in 1850 was $6.00, that for the men was $12.00. In Massachusetts in

1848 the average monthly salary for women was $8.07, for men $24.51. In Maine the average salary for women teachers was $4.80 and for men $15.40. New Hampshire and Vermont were below Connecticut. The average in New York at this time was $6.99 for women and $15.95 for men. This is almost as high as that of Massachusetts, as was also that of Pennsylvania. In Ohio the average wage for women teachers was $8.73 and for men $15.42. In Indiana $6.00 for women and $12.00 for men. This will indicate the general condition all over the country. When it is borne in mind that the schools frequently did not last more than three or four months the economic status of the individual teachers can be readily imagined. It is true in many if not in most of these regions the custom yet prevailed of the teacher receiving his board from the patrons of the school. That the range of distribution was not great was shown for the State of Maine. For the year mentioned above there were 4000 women teachers, only 29 of which received as much as $16.00 and upwards, while 67 received less than $4.00, with the average wage for all of $4.80.

Training of Teachers in the Monitorial Schools.—The earliest recognized form of a specific training for the teacher was given in connection with the Lancasterian monitorial schools. If school teaching itself was not recognized as a special professional art the management of the monitorial school was. So intricate was this mechanical device that its attainment might well be termed a "mystery" after the manner of the old crafts. Consequently in the earlier years the Public School Society of New York attempted to provide for this need through the apprentice system. A few boys were actually indentured to the monitorial teacher, required to serve as monitors under the apprentice law and given a certificate of the mastery of their trade. This, however, was too cumbersome. The society later allowed a number of the older monitors to continue their assistance to the teacher in the discharge of his duties, and after a successful period of such training to be certificated by the officers of the society. For some years this school of apprentices or monitors was held from six to eight o'clock each morning. Later on in the twenties advanced classes in the higher subjects were established for the training of these pupil teachers, which classes developed in time into the grammar grades of the city schools. When the monitors were dropped from the schools, during the decade of the thirties, these advanced grades were continued for the general pupils. With the development of the city school system after 1843 they were continued as advanced grades. So it happened that the city schools of New York developed a system of nine or ten grades but of no high schools.

The work begun in New York City was advocated by Governor Clinton for the entire state. In his message to the legislature in 1818 the Governor advocated this idea and continued his efforts to this end for the ten years of his governship. In 1820 in his message to the legislature he said:

> "There are probably twenty schools in the State conducted on the Lancasterian system exclusively, and several others which follow it partially, but not so far as to give it a distinctive character. In some of these establishments several young men have lately been instructed as Lancasterian teachers, and it is to be hoped that the system will be carried into the most extensive operation. There are now upon an average about 50 scholars for every schoolmaster under the present plan of the common schools, and whether the number be great or small, the introduction of the Lancasterian method is of importance, for, admitting in all cases the competency of the teacher to attend to all his pupils, yet when we consider the rapidity of acquiring instruction under that system, and reflect on the useful habits it forms and the favorable impression which it makes on the minds and the morals of those who participate in its benefits, we cannot hesitate to give it a decided preference."

In 1828 he advocated a monitorial high school in each county designed primarily for the training of teachers. At no time, however, was he able to persuade the legislature to his view.

The monitorial schools of Philadelphia and other cities as a part of the system trained their own monitors. Many of these monitors received sufficient preparation to become effective teachers in similar schools. Nowhere else, however, was there an attempt to elaborate this into a system for the common schools as in New York. The monitorial schools served as training schools only to the extent that the mechanical idea of education involved in the schemes of Lancaster or Bell were adopted and proved feasible. Dr. Bell had said: "Give me twenty-four pupils today and I will give you back twenty-four teachers tomorrow." And if we allow that this scheme of memoriter work was education, his claim was a valid one. Just judgment was passed on this scheme when Horace Mann said:

> "One must see the difference between the hampering, blinding, misleading instruction given by an inexperienced child and the developing, transforming, and almost creative power of an accomplished teacher—one must rise to some comprehension of the vast import and significance of the phrase "to educate"—before he can regard with a sufficiently energetic contempt that boast of Dr. Bell."

The Academy and the Supply of Teachers (Quos. 546–547).

—The significance of the academy as a source of supply of teachers

> ROBERT SAVAGE,
> From Monmouth-County in New-Jersey;
> HAS hired the School-Room where the noted Mr. Gatehouse formerly taught, and intends to open School on Monday the 17th Instant; which School-Room is at the House of Mr. Samuel Foster, jun. Silk Dyer, in Princes-Street. Whoever is pleased to favour him with the Tuition of their Children, shall be carefully taught true Spelling, Reading, Writing, Arithmetic, &c. Also, the Rudiments of the Latin and French.

FIG. 99. The private schoolmaster advertises his wares. (From *New York Mercury,* Sept. 10, 1759.)

for the common schools has been previously noted. Even for Franklin's academy in the middle of the nineteenth century it was indicated that one of its chief purposes was "that a number of the poorer sort might hereby be qualified to act as schoolmasters in the country, to teach children reading, writing, arithmetic and the grammar of their mother tongue." While later institutions were not quite so frank, their actual operation did not vary greatly from this standard. Some of the earlier academies which were on the most stable foundation, and which were chiefly concerned with preparing students for colleges, also recognized their obligation to the common

THE TEACHING PROFESSION

schools, and opened departments usually called English departments for the education of prospective teachers. Even the greatest of Massachusetts academies at Andover opened such a department in 1830. It was because of this service in many states that the legislature granted subsidies to such schools.

Many of the Pennsylvania academies had special departments for teachers beginning with that of the Moravian School at Nazareth Hall in 1807. The regents of New York in the report of the legis-

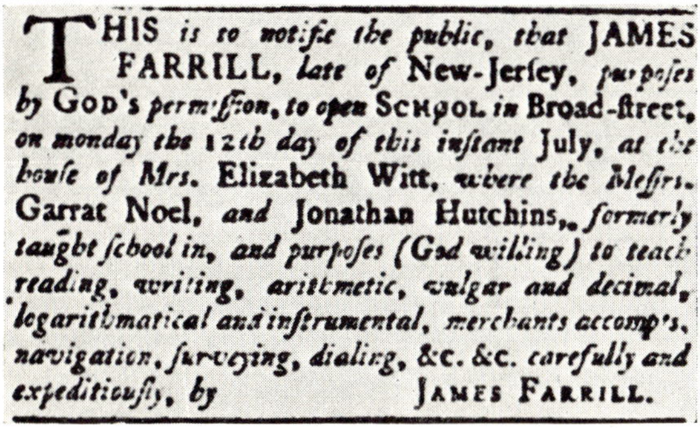

> THIS is to notify the public, that JAMES FARRILL, late of New-Jersey, purposes by God's permission, to open School in Broad-street, on monday the 12th day of this instant July, at the house of Mrs. Elizabeth Witt, where the Messrs. Garrat Noel, and Jonathan Hutchins, formerly taught school in, and purposes (God willing) to teach reading, writing, arithmetic, vulgar and decimal, logarithmatical and instrumental, merchants accomp's, navigation, surveying, dialing, &c. &c. carefully and expeditiously, by JAMES FARRILL.

FIG. 100. A private schoolmaster and his authorization. (From *New York Mercury*, July 12, 1756.)

lature in 1821 state: "And when it is recollected that it is to these seminaries that we must look for the supply of teachers for the common schools, as well as for the occasional rescue of humble merit from obscurity, the regents trust that they should be able to extend this sphere of their bounty and of their usefulness by such additional appropriation . . . as the resources of the state may warrant." It was in this period that Governor Clinton repeatedly made his suggestion of monitorial high schools for the training of teachers. The regents did not agree with the Governor and through their continuous reports to the legislature won it to their view that "our great reliance for the nurseries of teachers must be placed on our colleges and academies." In 1827 and following years both the legislature and the regents repeatedly declared their purpose of assisting the training of teachers through academies, and finally, 1834, passed a law making additional appropriation for the maintenance of teachers'

[493]

departments in a number of academies. Eight were selected by the regents and for a number of years constituted the source of supply of the teachers trained for the common schools. These to all intents and purposes became normal schools, and therefore deserve the recognition of the first of such institutions established in our country. After six years the control of these schools was transferred from the regents to the State Superintendent, where it continued for six years more, when it was abandoned in favor of the state normal school. Meanwhile so popular had these become that by the Law of 1838 every such school which received as much as $700 from the

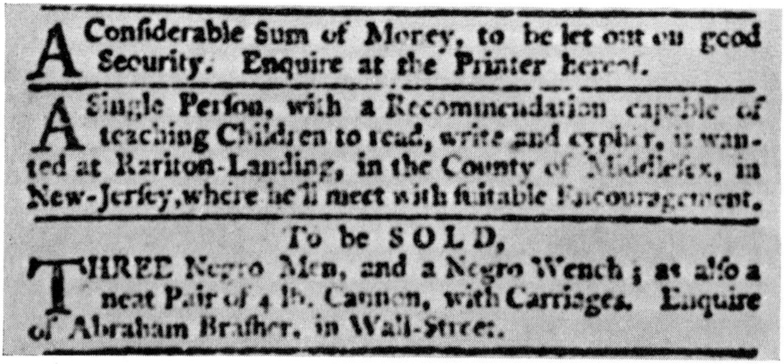

A Confiderable Sum of Money, to be let out on good Security. Enquire at the Printer hereof.

A Single Perfon, with a Recommendation capable of teaching Children to read, write and cypher, is wanted at Rariton-Landing, in the County of Middlefex, in New-Jerfey, where he'll meet with fuitable Encouragement.

To be SOLD,

THREE Negro Men, and a Negro Wench; as alfo a neat Pair of 4 lb. Cannon, with Carriages. Enquire of Abraham Brafher, in Wall-Street.

FIG. 101. Advertisement for a private schoolmaster. (From *New York Mercury*, July 31, 1758.)

state was required to maintain a teacher training department. This requirement, however, was too vague to be effective in many instances. The entire period from 1820 to 1850 was one of controversy between the advocates of various schemes for the training of teachers. First, the academies contended successfully against Governor Clinton's monitorial high school scheme. After this suggestion was killed and teachers' departments actually established (1834), the advocates of a separate normal school arose in opposition to the academy scheme. These in turn won and such a school was established at Albany in 1844. Following this the special state aid for teachers in academies was withdrawn and the supporters of the common school system united in their effort to build up a system of normal schools. While teachers' departments continued in many

THE TEACHING PROFESSION

of the academies the more important ones were gradually taken over by the state department of public instruction as normal schools, leaving the academies to follow their individual wishes regarding this phase of their work. During this period twenty-five different academies reported to the regents concerning their work for the training of teachers. Twelve of these twenty-five received special appropriation for their work. The number of pupil teachers enrolled varied from 300 in the earlier years to as many as 950 in the later years. If the number reported in smaller academies without special departments is included the total is considerably increased. The importance of this very considerable system of schools for the training of teachers is very frequently overlooked. It undoubtedly

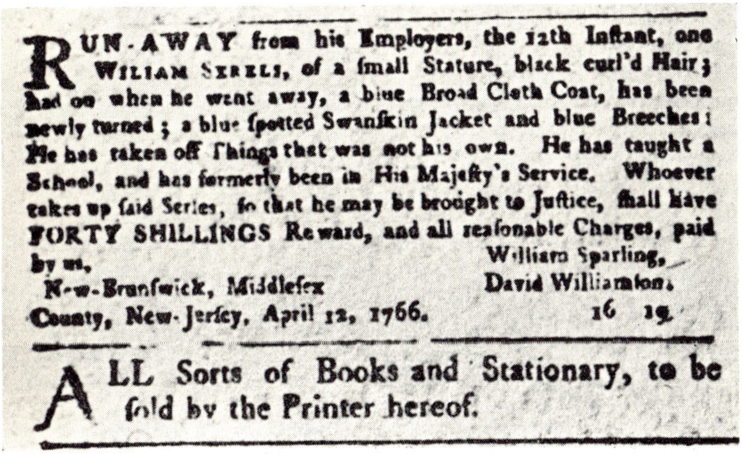

> RUN-AWAY from his Employers, the 12th Instant, one WILIAM SIRELS, of a small Stature, black curl'd Hair; had on when he went away, a blue Broad Cloth Coat, has been newly turned; a blue spotted Swanskin Jacket and blue Breeches: He has taken off Things that was not his own. He has taught a School, and has formerly been in His Majesty's Service. Whoever takes up said Series, so that he may be brought to Justice, shall have FORTY SHILLINGS Reward, and all reasonable Charges, paid by us,
>   William Sparling,
>   New-Brunswick, Middlesex   David Williamson,
> County, New-Jersey, April 12, 1766.   16 19

> ALL Sorts of Books and Stationary, to be sold by the Printer hereof.

FIG. 102. Character of the Colonial schoolmaster, indicated by an advertisement. (From *Weekly Post Boy*, May 1, 1766.)

was an important factor in placing the New York system in the van of educational progress in the second quarter of the century. Nor can the statement that the training offered in these academies was purely academic be borne out. In some years at least fourteen of the number reported using the same textbook in the principles of teaching. But at best the professional spirit could be but poorly developed in institutions which were not primarily designed for this purpose.

However, many of the arguments used against them were unsupported. The chief one was that they could supply but a small proportion of the teachers needed by the state. Fully two thousand new teachers were needed each year at the time when the combined teachers' department contained not more than five hundred or at most nine hundred pupils. It is to be recalled, however, that not until very recently did the normal schools of any state furnish a much more adequate supply.

The Origin of the Normal School Idea (Quo. 548).—From time to time in the period from 1789 articles had appeared in the public press advocating the special training of teachers. With the founding of our first reputable educational magazine in 1826 (p. 240) by William Russell, a definite organization for the advocacy of this idea was established. In earlier publications Russell had been one of the advocates of such a school. The most persistent of these agitators through the press was James G. Carter of Massachusetts, who has been given the title of the "father of the normal school." In persistent discussion in the public press he emphasized what came to be the three characteristic features of the American normal school. First, a course which should give a thorough preparation in the subjects to be taught in the common schools; second, a preparatory course on the science and the methods of teaching; and third, practice schools. In 1827 Mr. Carter opened a school for the training of teachers and petitioned the legislature for aid. Even previous to this time a similar private school had been opened in Vermont by Samuel R. Hall, an agent for a missionary society. In 1827 appeared Hall's *Lectures on School Keeping,* the first of a multitude of publications upon this topic. Although Mr. Hall changed his location from time to time yet he maintained such a private normal school from 1823 until 1840. Carter's practical effort was not so successful, but he continued his agitation through the press and founded the American Institute of Instruction, which became one of the most effective factors in educational progress in Massachusetts during the ensuing decades. Later, becoming a member of the legislature, Carter continued his advocacy, and in 1837 the legislature adopted his bill providing for a State Board of

Education, and in the following year the one for the establishment of normal schools. Meanwhile similar agitation had been going on in Connecticut, in New York, and in Pennsylvania. The educational press (p. 240) had now come to be an effective and constant advocate of the normal school idea. The official heads of the public school, whether called state superintendents or secretaries of boards, had now become leaders of educational opinion in these respective

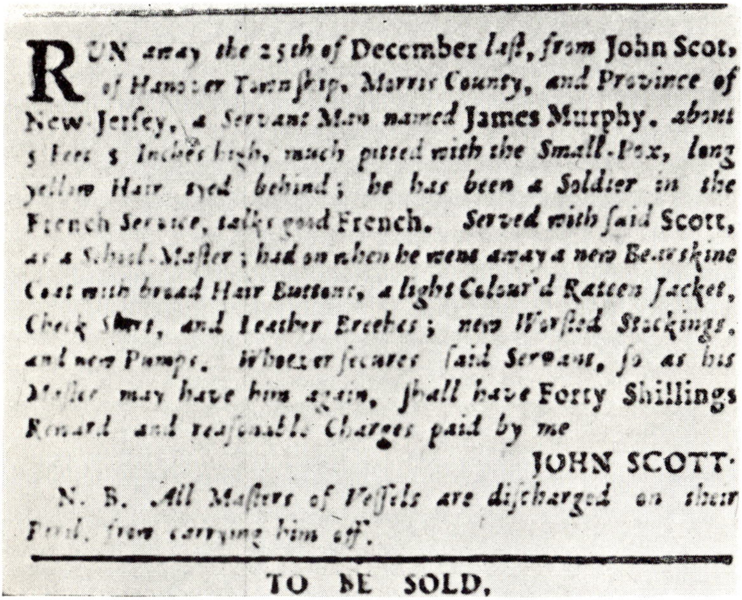

RUN away the 25th of December last, from John Scot, of Hanover Township, Morris County, and Province of New Jersey, a Servant Man named James Murphy, about 5 Feet 5 Inches high, much pitted with the Small-Pox, long yellow Hair tyed behind; he has been a Soldier in the French Service, talks good French. Served with said Scott, as a School-Master; had on when he went away a new Bearskine Coat with broad Hair Buttons, a light Colour'd Ratteen Jacket, Check Shirt, and Leather Breeches; new Worsted Stockings, and new Pumps. Whoever secures said Servant, so as his Master may have him again, shall have Forty Shillings Reward and reasonable Charges paid by me

JOHN SCOTT.

N. B. All Masters of Vessels are discharged on their Peril, from carrying him off.

TO BE SOLD,

FIG. 103. The teacher runs away from school. (From *Weekly Post Boy*, Jan. 14, 1754.)

states. One and all they advocated such institutions. Meanwhile popular information concerning European systems of schools, especially the Prussian, had given prominence to the normal school idea (p. 235).

Russell, editor of the *American Journal of Education*, beginning in 1825 (p. 240), and Woodbridge in the *Annals of Education* from 1831, did much to popularize the idea of the Prussian seminary for the training of teachers. As did Cousin's volume from 1835 (p. 237); in the West Calvin E. Stowe's *Report to the Ohio Legislature* (Quo.

FOUNDING OF AMERICAN SCHOOL SYSTEM

428); Bache's *Report to the Trustees of Girard College,* and in fact all of these publications having to do with education in Europe or attempting to stimulate educational endeavor in the United States, laid stress upon the importance of the training of teachers through professional institutions.

These common efforts at popularization finally bore fruit. What was needed to bring this about was a definite instrument of authority and a leader with vision and influence. The Massachusetts Board of Education was established in 1837 with Horace Mann as

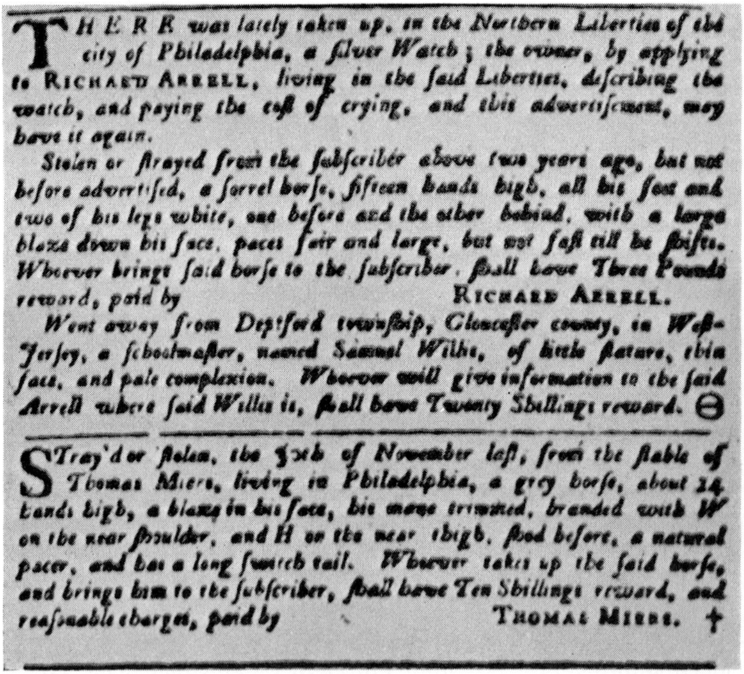

FIG. 104. A schoolmaster breaks his contract. (From *Pennsylvania Gazette,* Dec. 16, 1756.)

its first secretary. One of the men greatly interested in the improvement of the teaching profession offered $10,000 if the state would appropriate a similar amount for the establishment of a normal school. This was approved in 1838 and a school established at Lexington. Though the school met with great opposition—that proved

[498]

almost fatal in the following legislature—yet it shortly demonstrated its worth, and two others were established almost immediately, one in the western (Barre, later Westfield), the other in the southern (Bridgewater) part of the state.

Merits and Conflict among the Various Schemes for the Training of Teachers.—The training of teachers in the academies in New York had been continued with success for some years. But

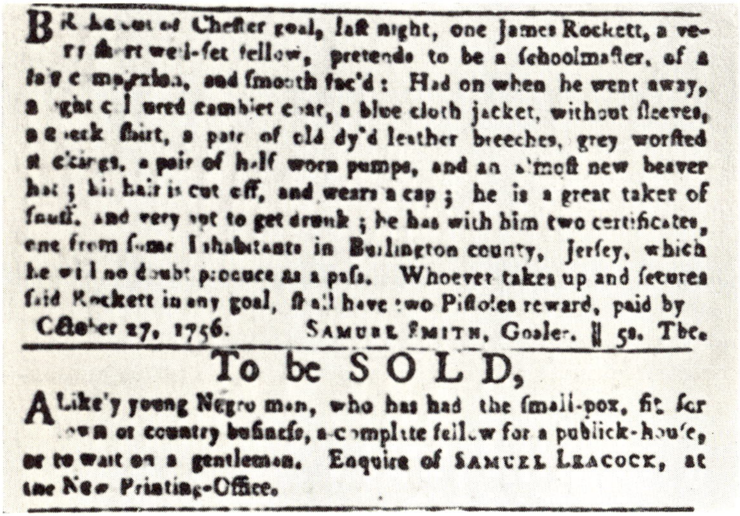

> Broke out of Chester goal, last night, one James Rockett, a very short well-set fellow, pretends to be a schoolmaster, of a fair complexion, and smooth fac'd: Had on when he went away, a light coloured cambler coat, a blue cloth jacket, without sleeves, a check shirt, a pair of old dy'd leather breeches, grey worsted stockings, a pair of half worn pumps, and an almost new beaver hat; his hair is cut off, and wears a cap; he is a great taker of snuff, and very apt to get drunk; he has with him two certificates, one from some Inhabitants in Burlington county, Jersey, which he will no doubt produce as a pass. Whoever takes up and secures said Rockett in any goal, shall have two Pistoles reward, paid by
> October 27, 1756.   SAMUEL SMITH, Goaler. 5s. The.
>
> **To be SOLD,**
>
> A Likely young Negro man, who has had the small-pox, fit for town or country business, a complete fellow for a publick-house, or to wait on a gentleman. Enquire of SAMUEL LEACOCK, at the New Printing-Office.

FIG. 105. A schoolmaster escapes from jail. (From *Pennsylvania Gazette*, Nov. 25, 1756.)

this in itself would never have developed a teaching profession. The training was almost wholly academic. The difference between teachers' training departments and the other departments of the academies lay chiefly in the fact that in the former much time was devoted to the study of the subjects taught in the common schools. There was much drill and memoriter work. In addition to this they gave brief attention through lectures to the theory of teaching. President Potter of Union College in 1840 made a study of the training of teachers in the academies and reported as follows:

"I. The students in these departments make good proficiency in their studies, but pursue the higher branches to the neglect of those which are elementary.

II. They remain at the institutions about one-third of the time originally contemplated.

III. They are not generally exercised in teaching in the presence of their instructors; most of them, however, have taught common schools.

IV. They usually expect to teach after leaving the department, but not for a long time.

V. The departments have contributed indirectly but materially to the improvement of the common schools, viz.:

(1) They have led employers to consider the importance of having better qualified teachers.

(2) They notify trustees where they may apply for teachers.

(3) They create an intimate and salutary connection between academies and common schools.

(4) They multiply the number of persons who make teaching a temporary pursuit and render such persons better qualified for their duties.

(5) They increase the number of better informed citizens, especially of such as will take an interest in common schools and make good inspectors."

In contrast to this work the Massachusetts normal schools and those shortly after founded on these models gave little attention to academic subjects outside of those taught in the common schools. To these they gave great attention, emphasizing not only the drill and memoriter work of the academies but attempting a psychological analysis and approach of the Pestalozzian ideas embodied in the Prussian normal schools. In addition to this they gave great attention to the art of teaching, not then recognized in any other source as an art. That is, both by practical observation and the study of psychology and of Pestalozzian method prospective teachers were trained "in the most effectual way of reaching the untaught mind." Much attention was also given to the schoolroom management, which also became recognized as an art, though its treatment was quite mechanical and formal, as it has remained until recent times. As a means to making effective these three purposes, the normal schools established the practice school. Here the young teacher had the advantage of actual experience in the art of instruction under

THE TEACHING PROFESSION

expert guidance and with scientific criticism. The respective merits of these various types of institutions, as urged by their advocates, may be summarized as follows.

The arguments against the academy plan were briefly, first, that only a very small number of teachers could be thus educated—probably not more than one tenth of the number needed; second, that the academies were primarily concerned with general education and only incidentally with professional teaching; third, that the expense of attendance was too great and that the salary of the common school teacher would not then and would probably never justify such an investment in professional training. It may be noted in passing that this argument still has much validity though the improvement in the teacher's salary has been great. Those defending the academies as a means of professional education argued, as against both the monitorial school and the normal school, that because of the low salary and the temporary employment of teachers special institutions for their training were not justified, and could not be supported. Second, particularly those in favor of the academies held that these later institutions already existed in great numbers, had been subsidized by the state, and therefore the state should use them for this purpose. Fourth, one practical objection, whether directly voiced or not, was that these new types of schools would have to be supported by direct tax as an addition to the common school charge, whereas the academies were supported out of the established literary fund. Fifth, much was made out of the fact that the academies possessed the advantages of the higher course of study together with the laboratories, museums, and so on, which would prove of much assistance to prospective teachers.

General Establishment of the Normal School (Quo. 550).—Following the establishment and the successful operation of the Massachusetts normals, leaders of the public school system in various states began definite agitation for the establishment of such institutions. With the re-establishment of a State Superintendent in New York, the movement for the professional training school took definite shape. Though the management of the training department of the academies had been taken from the regents and placed in the hands of this official, the superintendent saw clearly that the effectiveness of the common school system depended upon a specialized professional institution. Consequently in 1845 such a school was established at Albany, following the same general plans as the Massachusetts normals. Teacher training classes in academies were continued. A great number of these institutions continued to be subsidized by the regents for such work, though the subsidy was limited to an appropriation of no more than twenty-five pupils in each institution. Meanwhile a similar movement had been going

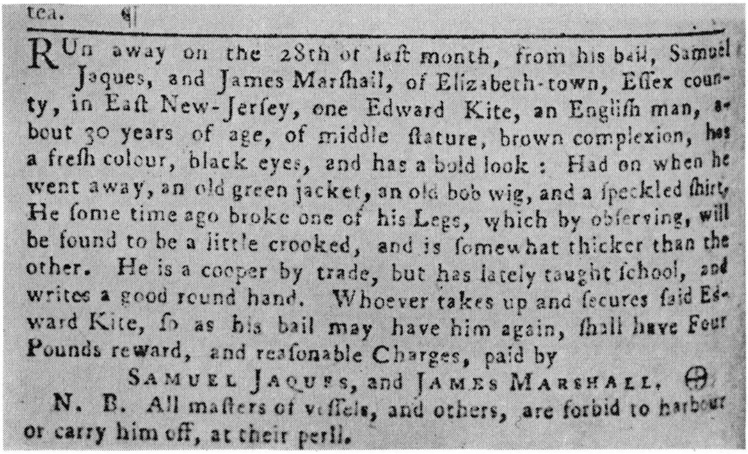

> tea. ¶
> RUn away on the 28th of laſt month, from his bail, Samuel Jaques, and James Marſhall, of Elizabeth-town, Eſſex county, in Eaſt New-Jerſey, one Edward Kite, an Engliſh man, about 30 years of age, of middle ſtature, brown complexion, has a freſh colour, black eyes, and has a bold look : Had on when he went away, an old green jacket, an old bob wig, and a ſpeckled ſhirt. He ſome time ago broke one of his Legs, which by obſerving, will be found to be a little crooked, and is ſomewhat thicker than the other. He is a cooper by trade, but has lately taught ſchool, and writes a good round hand. Whoever takes up and ſecures ſaid Edward Kite, ſo as his bail may have him again, ſhall have Four Pounds reward, and reaſonable Charges, paid by
> SAMUEL JAQUES, and JAMES MARSHALL.
> N. B. All maſters of veſſels, and others, are forbid to harbour or carry him off, at their peril.

FIG. 106. A schoolmaster "jumps his bail." (From *Pennsylvania Gazette,* June 6, 1751.)

on in Connecticut. The agitation for such a school had covered the entire period of agitation in Massachusetts, beginning as early as 1825. When a State Board was established in 1838 and Henry Barnard made secretary, this agitation was redoubled. Through the Connecticut *Common School Journal,* through frequent reports and constant reports of the legislature, the idea was popularized. It was not until 1849 that the legislature established the school. Mr. Barnard was very familiar with the European systems of training of teachers and in 1851 published his extensive work on Normal Schools—the most elaborate and detailed source of information on this subject then available.

THE TEACHING PROFESSION

Meanwhile the previous year the first normal school in Pennsylvania had been organized out of the Lancasterian training school, which had been in operation for many years. This, however, later developed into a high school, and the first state normal school was not established until 1857. Michigan followed with the school at Ypsilanti in 1850, and from that time on the establishment of such schools became quite general. These institutions were practically all of a type following the Massachusetts model. The only new department in this field during this period was that represented by the normal school at Oswego, N. Y., in the early sixties. This grew up as a local training school for the city teachers and was more directly concerned with the work of the graded city schools than any of those previously founded. It was also more distinctly Pestalozzian than were the others in that it laid great stress upon instruction through objects. The earlier normals had incorporated much of the Pestalozzian idea of school management and of the Pestalozzian method in teaching arithmetic, geography, and the common branches in general. In Oswego the work was much influenced by the object teaching, as elaborated by the English Pestalozzians, and did much to lessen the dependence upon the textbook in the elementary grades. Elaborate training in sense perception through various activities tended to replace much of the old recitation work. The Oswego school was largely responsible for the starting of a new type of normal—the city training schools. These, however, did not develop until after the Civil War, and thus fall beyond the period under consideration.

Training of Teachers in Service (Quo. 550).—It was speedily recognized by the friends of education and even by the leading advocates of the normal schools that they were wholly inadequate to reach the entire teaching body, and that something must be done of a more general character looking towards the improvement of the teaching profession. In the third and fourth decades of the century a number of societies had been organized of friends of popular education. These had as their purpose the agitation for the founding of a public school system and the improvement of the character of the teachers. Among these were the Society for the Improvement of Common Schools, founded in Connecticut in 1827; a similar one in Pennsylvania in 1828; the Western Academic Institution at Cincinnati in 1829; the American Institute of Instruction in Boston in 1830; and the American Common School Society in New York in 1838. Such societies popularized the idea for general meetings of teachers in which professional interest should be stimulated and professional knowledge disseminated through lectures, conferences, and demonstrations. Out of these grew the institute idea.

The Cincinnati organization developed into a college for teachers in 1834 and held annual institutes for several years. Henry Barnard instituted such meetings as soon as he was made Secretary of the Connecticut Board. Horace Mann did much of his earlier work by indefatigable labor in educating the public and in training his teachers through his own addresses. He called to his aid a number of men interested in the public aspect of education and soon also a number having special knowledge of the various school subjects. A group of these public speakers made an informal institute, the first distinct use of the term, and thorough organization of the work occurred in New York in 1843.

In New York county organizations of teachers had been early formed. In the decade of the forties, even before the establishment of the normal schools, these county organizations had instituted professional programs. Some of these had been organized as definite schools of instruction with the regular program and class meetings. This plan proved so helpful that it soon became popular. In two years' time such institutions had been organized in seventeen counties varying in length of session from two to eight weeks and enlisting the attendance of more than one thousand teachers. Shortly after the legislature began to make annual appropriation for their encouragement. While the establishment of the normal school developed, a professional group of teachers was made available for the service of instruction in the institute. Before the close of this period this new method of reaching the common school teacher had developed until it covered most of the states and had proved a very effective supplement to the normal school idea and an efficient

FIG. 107. The ideal schoolroom and teachers of the Centennial year. (The *American Educational Monthly*, 1876.)

factor in promoting the ideal of a free common school as well as the teaching profession.

Local organization of teachers into teachers' associations constituted a further factor in their professional training. These local organizations, which in time grew statewide, were different from the more general education associations mentioned earlier in that they included only the teachers of the common schools and took into consideration subjects not of general public interest but solely of technical professional concern. A development of the teachers' institutes out of the earliest of these in New York has just been mentioned. While this is the most notable instance of their professional service, and while they did not become of general prevalence or of great significance until the latter half of the nineteenth century, yet their rise, even if in somewhat ephemeral form during this early period, was one of the most important indications of the developing consciousness of a new profession. This class consciousness, concerned as it was with the rights, privileges, and duties of teachers, but also of their specific need of training and information, gave additional strength and influence to the developing profession.

Summary.—A democratic society is slow to recognize the necessity for expert service and for professional preparation. The popular view regarded teaching as an art that almost anyone could practice. Experience soon showed, however, that specialized training was highly desirable if not essential. This view gradually won acceptance and constituted an important factor in the development of a definitely recognized teaching profession. Two changes of importance in shaping the character of the teaching profession were taking place at this time. One was the rapid increase of the number of women employed in teaching. This was a phenomenon peculiar to American conditions. The development of the public school system, the adoption of the district system of organization, and the common resort to separate winter and summer terms greatly increased the number of teachers demanded. So that the woman with the necessary education, to whom entrance to other employment was denied, rapidly crowded into the work of teaching. By the

THE TEACHING PROFESSION

middle of the century they constituted at least the majority of the teaching staff in the New England and the Middle States.

The second factor was the low salary rate of the profession during this period. In 1840 the average salary rate for women teachers in a number of the states was not over six or seven dollars.

Out of these early conditions developed the earlier attempts for the professional training of teachers. The first of these was in connection with the monitorial schools founded on the Lancasterian plan. These affected the cities only. The second stage was found in the academies from the student body of which was drawn a great number of the better prepared teachers of these early decades. Occasionally New England academies organized a teachers' department. In New York the state systematized this and from 1834 on elaborated a system of academies having teachers' training departments. However, the advocates of a special institution for the training of teachers succeeded in establishing their idea in the neighboring states. These institutions generally received the name of normal school and were an imitation of the similar schools established in France and Germany. Advocacy of such institutions had begun even in the eighteenth century. The first private one to materialize was in 1826 and the first state one was established by the Massachusetts legislature in 1838. Neighboring states soon followed and by 1860 practically all the states of the East and North had developed such institutions. However, these institutions, then as now, only affect a small proportion of the actual teaching staff. Consequently methods for the training of teachers were early developed. The earliest of these was the General Education Society, which had in view the development of public sentiment as well as specific knowledge for the teacher. This was early followed by the organization of teachers' institutes which first appeared early in the forties. Shortly after teachers' organizations of a more advanced professional character followed. All of these institutions exercised a very definite influence in building up the teaching profession and through this in strengthening the public school system itself.

INDEX

A

ABC-darian, 128
Abducted children, 38
Academia Virgeniensis et Oxoniensis, 166
Academician, The, 240
Academies and training of teachers, 160–64, 283, 391–411, 492–94
  characteristics of, 391
  curriculum of, 391–92, 395, 399, 404
  for ladies, 446–47
  free academies, 401, 412–13, 417
  girls in academies, 472–74
  method in, 404–5
  rise of, 160–63
  support of, 393
  systems of, 394–400, 402
Accipies, 139
Adams, Charles Francis, 205
Adams, John, 201–2, 211
Adult education, 266–69
Adventurer, 35
Advertisements of indentured servants, 41, 51
Agriculture, 190
Alabama, University of, 435
Albany, schools in, 77
Alcott, Bronson, 385
Alcott, Louisa M., 385
American Institute of Instruction, 241
American Journal of Education, 240
Amherst College, 425–26
Amsterdam, New, 69–77
Annals of education, 240
Antioch College, and education of women, 476
  and Horace Mann, 476

Apprentice system of education, 7–9, 11, 34–52
  character of, 34–35
  decline of, 209
  indenture, 44, 46
  in Boston, 47
  in Maryland, 43
  in Massachusetts, 105–7
  in New England, 41, 46–50, 105–7
  in New York, 45, 46
  in Pennsylvania, 43–45
  in Virginia and the South, 42–43, 55–58
Aristocracy in Virginia, 55
Aristocratic character of education in the colonial college and in the early 19th century, 186–87
Aristocratic character of society, 122
Arithmetic, required for college entrance, 156
Arithmetics, 349–56
Arizona, 199
Arminius, 31
Artificers, statute of, 7, 9, 18

B

Bache, Alexander, 238
  report of, 498
Baptists, 71, 117, 166–67, 261
Barnard, Henry, 239, 244–45, 319, 385
Barnard, President, 427
Barracks, public, for school children, 233
Barring out the school master, 340
Beecher, Catherine, 461
Berkeley, Governor of Virginia, 53
Bible, King James version of, 266
Bishop, Nathan, 271

[509]

INDEX

Blair, James, 167
Board of school teachers, 283
Book of Discipline, 24
Book, education of the, 4
Boston Latin school, 112, 136
Boston Latin grammar school, 154, 208–9
Boston News Letter, 41
Boston schools, 464
Brethren of the Common Life, 30
Brinsley, 20–21
Brooklyn, school in, 77
Brooks, Rev. Charles, 381
Brown University, 153, 169, 272, 426
Bushwick school in, 77

C

Cabell, Joseph, 218–19
Cabots, 3
Calvin and education, 31–32
Calvinists, 6
   see also Scotland, Switzerland, Puritans, Pilgrims, Knox, etc.
Cambridge, Mass., schools in, 106–7
Cambridge, University of, 21, 30, 154
Canals and communication, 227
Canons, ecclesiastical, 16–17
Carter, James G., 231, 245–47, 381, 496
Catechizing of children, 15–16, 57–59, 77
Census, U. S., of 1790, 187
Certification of teachers, 95
Chandler Scientific School, 431
Channing, William Ellery, 231
Chantry foundation of schools, 10
Chantry schools, 10, 14, 15, 30, 296–99, 316–20
   see also Poor Law
Charity schools, 57–58, 80–81, 87, 90, 94–95, 110, 163, 209, 296–99
   equipment for, 92
Charleston, schools in, 113
Cheever, Ezekiel, 154–55, 354
Chemistry 423
Church and education, 15, 17–21, 57, 91
   see also English church and education, and S.P.G.
   control of schools, 93

Church and state, separation of, 153
Cincinnati, 273
Circulating school, 376
Cities, population of, 223–25
   see also Urban population
City school system, 270–74
Civil War and education, 229, 414–15
Classification in schools, 256–57
Clinton, Governor DeWitt, 203, 215, 370–71, 411, 493–96
   and women's education, 456–57, 490–91
Clinton, Governor George, 203, 214, 370
Co-education, 474–77
   at colleges, 474
Colleges, 140, 437
   admission to, 156, 177
   entrance to, 177
   expansion of curriculum, 420–24
   in the 18th century, 420–21
Colleges, belief in, 165
   age of entrance, 180–81
   age of graduation, 177–79
   control of, 173–74
   curriculum, 176–77, 421
   entrance requirements, 156
   method of training in, 176–79
   motives for founding, 170–72
   student life, 180–81
   subjects of disputation, 178
   support of, 172–73
   the endowed, 437
Collegiate education of women, 477–80
Colloquies, 158
Colonization, 5
Columbia College, 102, 170, 423, 430–31
   see also Kings College
Columbus, Christopher, 3
Comenius, 157
Commerce, 190
Committee, school, control by, 114–16
Common School Journal, Mass., 240–41
   New York, 241
Commons, students', 180
Commonwealth and education, 14
Communication, means of, and education, 89–90, 189–91, 226–28

[510]

INDEX

Compulsory education, 105-7
  attendance, 249
Concord, Mass., 128
Conduct, see Rules of
Congress and education, 306
  see also National institutions and education
Connecticut, schools in, 23-24, 123, 126-27, 207, 210, 212-13, 308
  district school system, 277
  establishment of free schools, 327
  Latin grammar school, 150-51
  support of, 313-15
Consistory of Dutch Reformed Church, 75
Consolidation of schools, 258-59
Constitution of U. S. and education, 194
Constitutional convention and education, 199
Constitutional provisions for education, 210-11, 290
Control of schools, 93, 114-15
Copernicus, 3
Corderius, 158
Cordwainer, 8
Corlett, Elijah, 154-55
Corporal punishment, 339
Cost of public schools, 325-28, 329
Cousin, Victor, 236-37
County superintendent of schools, 282-83
Covenant, Halfway, 117
Crabbe, on the Dame School, 129
Craft, see Trade, 7
Cranshaw's sermon, 53
Criminals, 37-38
  extensive list of 18th century crimes, 37
Cromwell, 37
Curriculum, 338, 346, 362, 421
Curriculum of academies, 159

D

Dana, Professor, 423
Dame school, 120-21, 127, 129, 132, 446
Dartmouth College, 169, 423
Dartmouth College Case, 437-39
"Day of Doom," 357-60

Debt, imprisonment for, 192-93, 228-29
Dedham, Mass., early schools, 107, 114-15, 132, 147
De La Ware, Lord, 53
Delaware, colony of, 73, 100-1
Delaware, education in, 78, 100-1, 210-11, 216, 308-9
  Dutch schools in, 77
Democracy and education, 86-87, 192-93, 338-87
Democratic government, 108, 114-15, 122-23, 228-30
Descartes, 31
"Determining," 139
Development of education, factors in, 185
Disputations, 175
  in Harvard, 178
Dissenters and education, 21
District school, beginnings of, 121
  defects of, 359
  development of, 275-77
  enrollment of pupils, 288
  evils of, 279-80
  in Connecticut, 277
  in Indiana, 277
  in Michigan, 277-80
  in New York, 277
  in Vermont, 277
  limitations of, 279-80
  origin of, 116-18
  system, 274-79
District vs. union schools, 259
Divided school, 118-19, 150
Divinity students, 155
Dock, Christopher, 99
Dorchester, Mass., schools of, 113-15, 130, 134, 147-48, 150
Dort, Synod of, 28-29
Dummer Academy, 394-97
Dunkards, numbers and schools, 86, 96
Dutch colony and education, 69-71
  character of, 78-80
  schools in, 70-77, 100-1
  schools under English rule, 80-81
Dutch influence on American schools, see Holland

[511]

INDEX

Dutch precedents, 25
Dutch Reformed Church, 29, 80–82, 169
  and education, 261

E

East India school, 64, 140
Eaton free school, 65, 140
Ecclesiastical control of colleges, 427–29
  of schools, 109
Economic conditions in the early 19th century, 190–92
  changes, 226–27
Edinburgh high school, 411
Edinburgh, University of, 62–63
Education, nature of, 232–35
Edward III and education, 7–14, 63
Eighteenth century, 12, 19, 36
Election, freedom of, 424–26
Eliot, John, 136
Elizabeth, Queen, 7, 11, 13
Elmira College, 478
Emerson, Joseph, 462
Endowed schools, 63, 139
English church and education, 15, 17
  in Virginia, 53–55
English government and education, 13
English, influence on founding of American schools, 6–13
English Statutes, 7
Episcopal church and education, 430
Erasmus, 27, 158
Erie Canal, 423, 431
European ideals, influence of, on America, 235–41
Evening schools, 83, 267

F

Farming, *see* Husbandry
Farragut, Admiral, 380
Fellenberg, Emanuel von, 235, 244, 439
Fellenberg Institute, 439–42
Fenelon, on education of women, 448–49
Fifteenth century, 12, 36
Forefathers, 3

Fourteenth century, 7, 12, 36
Francker, university of, 30
Franklin academy, 394–95, 405
Franklin, Benjamin, and apprentice education, 50, 201, 420
  and secondary education, 162–63, 199
Freedom, municipal, 25
  indenture, 25
Free schools, 53, 63, 110–13, 138–39, 160, 295–337
  final establishment of, 324–32
  forces for and against, 334–36
  support of, 309
French, influence on founding of American schools, 13
  in colleges, 22, 423
Funds, school
  loss of, 311
  significance of, 313
  see Permanent school funds.

G

Garnett, James M., 462
General Theological Seminary, 430
Geneva, Calvin school in, 6, 32
  University of, 32, 421, 436
Gentry, education of, 21
Geography, 348–49
Geology, 423
Georgia, education in, 219, 287, 306
  state university, 434–35
German population, 96
German religious sects and their schools, 95–97, 100–1
  education, 13, 222–24
  immigration, 224
  influence on trading, 254–58
Gilbert, Sir Humphrey, 4
Girls, education of, 445–81
  admission to town schools, 462–63, 466
  high schools for, 448–49
  in private schools, 467
  see also Women, education of
Girls in school, 130–31
  in grammar schools, 466–67
  in high schools, 468–69

[512]

INDEX

in private schools, 467–68
in public school societies, 469
in state public school systems, 471
Gloucester, 150
Goethe, on education of women, 450
Government, origin of representative, 108
Grading and classification in schools, 255–59
Graduation, age of, from college, 179
Grammar schools, 20, 24, 136–64
  girls in grammar schools, 467–68
  school master, 154–56
  see also Latin schools
Grammatical Tower, 152
Grant, Miss Zilpah, 460
Grants in aid, 197
Graves, J. P., 381
Great Awakening, The, 160, 169
Great Remonstrance of New Amsterdam, 70, 82–83, 136
Greek, study of, 20, 137
Greene, Samuel S., 271
Gresham, Sir Richard, 9
Gresham, Sir Thomas, 9
Griscom, John, 236, 411–13
Gronigen, University of, 31
Grotius, 31
Guild, see Gild, 8, 9, 10
  outline of system, 51–52

H

Hall, Samuel R., 496
Hampton Academy, 65, 85
Hampton Institute, 441
Harlem, 77
Harrower, John, indentured school master, 38–39, 61
Hartford, 151
Harvard College, 134, 149, 157, 165–67, 422–35
  control of, 174
  graduation from, 178–79, 181
  support of, 172–73
Hawley, Gideon, 215–16
Head rights, 56
Hebrew, study of, 20, 138

Henry VIII, 11
High schools, 19–20, 410–18
  character of, 413–14
  girls in, 468–69
  system of, 414–15
  see also Latin schools
Holland, influence of, on American schools, 3, 6, 13, 25–28
Holyoke College, 460
  see also Lyon, Mary
Holy Roman Empire, 25
Hopkins grammar school, 151, 466
Horn Book, 347
Hours of labor, 39
Huddlestone, school master, in New York City, 86–87
Huguenots, French, 71
Husbandry, 9
Hutchison, Anne, 71

I

Illinois, education in, 291
  establishment of free schools in, 330
Immigration and education, 224
Immigrants, 37
Indentures, 37–49
  advertisements of, see Apprenticeship
  and education in servant class
India, route to, 5
Indiana, establishment of free schools in, 290, 323, 330
  schools in, 277, 290–92
  university of, 435
Indians, conversion of, 5
Indian school, 140
Indian school in Virginia, 64
  at Dartmouth, 169–71
  attendance, 117
  see also Moore's Indian charity schools, motives for settlement
Individual instruction, 240–41
Industrial education, 11–13, 34–51
Industry, 180
Infant schools, 372–80
Inns of Court, 62
Instruction, institutes of, 241–42

[513]

INDEX

Inventions, 226
Iowa, free schools in, 331
Ipswich Latin schools, 149
Irish, 224

J

Jamestown, 13
Jefferson and education, 199, 201–3, 436
   educational bill, 202, 218–19, 420–21
Jews and education, 89
Johnson, President, 420
Johnson, "Wonder-working Providence," 41
Jones, Hugh, "Description of Virginia," 62
Justices of Peace and education, 13

K

Kentucky, state university of, 435
Kepler, 3
Kilpatrick, 75
Kindergarten, 378
King James, *see* Bible
Kingsbury, John, 462
Kings College, 102, 145, 168, 175–76, 420
   see also Columbia College
Kingston, 77
Kitchen school, 129, 280
Knox, John, influence on education, 24

L

Labor, organized, and education, 230–55
Lancaster, monitorial system, 254, 299–303, 360–71
Lancasterian system, 254–55, 260
Lancasterianism, 244
   and training of teachers, 490
Land grants for education, 197
Land holdings in Massachusetts, 107
   in Virginia, 7
Land system, 55
Land trusts for schools, 307–15
Latin, use of, 155–59
Latin grammar schools, 19–20, 127
   in Massachusetts, 146–47
   in New Jersey, 146

   in New Netherlands, 144–45
   in New York, 145
   in Pennsylvania, 146
Latin, study of, 20–21, 30, 62, 101, 110, 127, 136–64, 156, 158–59, 390–94
Lawrence Scientific School, 431
Law schools, 430–31
Learning, 137
Leisure, education for, 21
Leyden, university of, 27, 30–31
Liberal education, 138
Liberty, development and spirit of, 50–52
Licensing of school teachers, 93, 103
Literary education, 18, 105
Literary fund, 218, 287, 298–99, 308
   see also Virginia, education in
Little schools, 60
Local taxation for support of schools, 320–24
Locke's treatise on education, 204
Log College, 162–64
London Company, 64
Lotteries, support of schools by, 304–6
Louisiana, university of, 435
Louvain, university of, 30
Lovell, John, 155
Lutherans, numbers, 96
   schools, 98–99
Lyceums, 268
Lyon, Mary, 459–62

Mc

McClure, William, 235, 380–81
McLane, Professor, 423–24

M

Madison, James, views on education, 202
   President and William and Mary, 421
Magazines, educational, 240–41
Magellan, 3
Maine, school laws of, 126, 153, 204–5, 213
Mandeville, 19

[514]

INDEX

Manhattan, 69-73, 77
Mann, Horace, 231, 238-55, 476, 504
  reforms of, 238-40
  results of reform, 247-49
  results of religious controversy, 262-65, 384, 386-87
Manual labor, 439-42
  see also Fellenberg Institute
Manufacturing, 190
  see also Industry
Marshall, Chief Justice, 438
Martin, 274
Maryland, Latin grammar schools in, 141-44, 206-7, 218
  state university of, 434
Mason, Lowell, 384
Massachusetts and education, 105, 112-13, 126-27, 212, 277, 281-82
  academies in, 396-97
  high schools in, 413
  Latin grammar schools in, 146
  support of, 148-49, 153, 205-6, 210-11, 212-13, 270-71, 321
Masses, education of, 16
Mather, Cotton, 136, 154
Mechanical schools, system of, 374-80
Mechanics Institutes, 266-67
Medicine, schools of, 430
Menonites, numbers and schools, 86, 96
Merchant guilds, 9
Method in education, 338-39, 342-45
Methodist Episcopal church and education, 261
Michigan act for funds for education, 195, 198-99, 292-93
  district schools in, 277
  free schools, 327
  university of, 434-35, 437
Middle Ages, 7
Mirania, College of, 420
Mississippi, and education, 435
Missouri, and education, 331
Monasteries and education, 10
Monitorial system and education, 360-70
  and training of teachers, 480-82
Moon free school, 140-41
Moore's Indian charity school, 169

Moore's school in Virginia, 140
Moravians, numbers and schools, 86, 96-97, 99
  education of women, 452-53, 493
Morse, Jedidah, 348-49
Motives for settlement, 5, 15
Mount Holyoke College, 460-62
Moving school, 118-19
Mr., 155
Mulcaster, Richard, 16
Murray, Lindley, 405
Muscovy, Grand Duke of, 76
Mystery, *see* Trade

N

National improvements, 227
National University, 199
Nationalism and education, 185-87
Nationalization of education, 185-95, 272
  through States, 194-95
Natural history, 423
Negro slaves, 55
  education of, 300-1
Newark, 77
Newbury, 149
New England Primer, 132-33, 212-23, 346-49
New Hampshire schools, 124-26, 207, 213
  Latin grammar schools in, 150-51, 213
New Harmony, Indiana, school at, 441
New Haven colony, schools in, 123-24, 151
  college of, 165
New Jersey, schools of colonial, 89, 95-97
  free schools in, 329
  Latin grammar schools in, 145, 216
  colleges in, 169
New Mexico, 199
New Netherlands of the U. S., 69, 72
  Latin grammar schools in, 143
New Orleans, 273
New Utrecht, 77

[515]

INDEX

New York, academies in, 396–97, 416–17
  district school systems, 214–16, 277, 283, 325
  enrollment of free school, 325–29
  free academy, 410–17
  high schools, 416–17
  Latin grammar schools in, 145, 206–7
  University of the state of, 430, 432–33, 435
New York City, 208, 214–15, 272, 300–1
  schools of, 208–9, 214–16, 269–71, 282–83
  University of the City of, 423–24
Newspapers, 189
Nineteenth Century, 12, 36
Normal schools, 283
  origin of, 496–502
Northampton, Mass., 465
North Carolina, Latin grammar schools in, 150
  academies in, 140, 206–7, 210, 218–19, 287, 306
  University of, 434–35
Northwest Territory, 192–93
Norwich Academy, 401
Notitia Scholasticia of the S.P.G., 88
Nursing Schools, 97

O

Oberlin College, 474–76
Ocean trade, 226–27
Ohio Act of 1802, 198, 290–91
Ohio and education, 287
  free schools in, 329
  university of, 435
Ohio Company, 198
Oklahoma, 199
Old field schools, 60
Ordinance of 1785, 195–96
Ordinance of 1787, 192–93, 195–96
Oregon Act, 199
Organization, *see* School room organization
Organization of teachers, 504–6
Orphans, 55

Owen, Robert, 235, 380–81, 441
Oxford, 21, 31, 162, 174

P

Papacy, 10
Parish system, 57–58
Parochial school systems, 75
  function of, 80–83
Patroon system, 72–73
Pauper schools, 296
  see also Charity schools
Peck, Gideon, 216
Penn Charter School, 102
Penn, William, 91, 93
  see also Quakers
Pennsylvania, apprentice education in, 43, 93, 95–97, 100–1, 216, 272, 285
  academies in, 402
  establishment of free schools, 327, 331
  Latin grammar schools, 137, 296–98
  schools in, 93–101, 287, 308
Pennsylvania, University of, 162–63, 165, 170–71, 420, 430–31
Permanent school committee, 115
Permanent school funds, 307–15
Pestalozzi, 235, 245, 250–51, 338–40
Pestalozzianism, 380–87
Philadelphia, schools of, 208, 302–3
Physicians, education of, 134, 345
Pike, Nicholas, 348–49
Pilgrims and education, 25
Plymouth, 13, 124
Poor, schools for, 111
  law and schools, 110–11
  see also Charity schools
Poor law, connection with school law, 9–10, 11–13, 47
Population, composition of, 187–89, 222–25, 288
  density of, 288
  dispersion of, 112, 118–19
  in early 19th century, 222, 283–89
  in New Amsterdam, 73
  in Pennsylvania, 96
  in Virginia, 55
  urban and rural, 288–89

INDEX

Post offices, 189
Presbyterian Church and education, 29, 141, 162, 166, 430
Press, educational, 240
Princeton, tutors from, 61, 156–57, 168–69, 423, 428–29
Printing, 53
Private schools, 59–61, 66, 83, 97, 127, 244–45, 296–99, 332–34
Professional schools in universities, 430–31
Professions, education of, 137
Professors, 179
Property qualification for suffrage, 192–93, 228–29
Protestants, and education, 3, 5, 13, 29, 260
Protestant Tutor, 350–51
Providence, R. I, 271, 413
Prudential men and schools, 114–15
Public schools, 63, 102, 138–39
Public school societies, 299, 304
  of New York City, 254, 301–3
  of Philadelphia, 303
Public school system, founding of, 105
Puritans, 5, 6
Puritans and education, 14–15, 91, 139

Q

Quakers, 71, 86, 89, 91, 93–99, 117
Queens College, 169
  see also Rutgers
Quincy, President, 424, 25

R

Railways, 228–29
Rate Bill System, in support of schools, 316–20
Readers, in the church, 58
  methods of beginning, 342–44
Reading, *see* Literary education
Rebels, political, 37
Reform, educational, 241–55
Reformation, 3–5, 10–11

Religion and education, 18–57, 132
  control of education, 260, 262–66
  freedom in, 91
  in Virginia and the south, 53, 76–77, 197
  see also Reformation and education, and Horace Mann, 262–66
Religious instruction in schools, 251, 260–66, 345–59
  controversy, New York and Pennsylvania, 262
  New England, 263–65
Religious persecution, 71
Renaissance, 3
Rensselaer Institute, 31, 423
Resources for education, 324
Revenues, school, 309
  see also Permanent school funds and School support
Revolution, American, and education, 195, 204–5
Revolution, right of, 31
Rhode Island, abolition of Rate Bills, 331
Rhode Island, and education, 126, 153, 331
Richmond, Va., academy, 392–93
Roelantsen, Adam, 74
Roman Catholic, 261
Rousseau, treatise on education, 204
  influence of, 204
Roxbury, Mass., schools of, 112, 128, 148
Rules of conduct, 98
Russell, William, 497
Rutgers College, 168–69

S

Salem, 13, 131
  and indentured servants, 51
Saline lands, 198
Savages, education of, 35, 62
Scaliger, 31
School dame, 132
School, first in North America, 73–75
School house, 38–39

INDEX

School law, first in Colonial America, 5, 6, 10, 148
School master, duties of, 80
School master, indentured, for sale, 51
School master, indentured, for training, 47–50
School room organization, 338–39
School teachers, salaries of, 131, 276–78, 281–83
Schools, origin of American, 6
Schools, support of, 110–11
  sources of support, 320–24
Schools, term of, 78
Scotch-Irish, 24, 33, 37
"Scotchmen," 71
Scotland, 5
Scotland, influence of in founding of American schools, 6, 23–25
  population in Colonial America, 37
Scots, contribution to secondary education, 162–64
  population, 287–88
Scriptures, 4
Secondary education, 19, 136–63, 390–419
Secondary education and schools, 103
Secretary of State, Board of Education, 280–81
Sects, religious, 85–87, 98
Secular control of colleges, 427
Selectmen and schools, 114–15
  see also Prudential men
Servant class, 35, 137
  origin of, 35
Service, training of teachers in, 503
Seventeenth century, 12, 19, 35–36
Seward, Governor, of New York, 486
Sheffield Scientific School, 431
Silliman, Professor, 423
Sixteenth century, 11, 12, 13, 19, 36
Slaves, 55, 224–25
Smith, Provost, 420
Smith, Sidney, on Lancasterianism, 363–65, 368–69
Society for Propagation of the Gospel in Foreign Parts, 59, 85–95
  character of, 87–88, 92–93

South Carolina, 219
  University of, 435
Spinoza, 31
"Spirits" or kidnappers, 38–39
Squadroning out schools, 150
Staats General of Holland, 69–77
State or commonwealth functions in education, 194–95, 210 11
  systems of education in, 211
State Superintendent of schools, 280–81
State support of education, 172–73
State systems of education, 269–71
  state superintendents, 268–69
State universities, 431–33
  see also Universities
Statute of apprenticeship, 7
Statute of artificers, 7
Stowe, Calvin, 237
Stowe, Harriet Beecher, 237, 460–61
Stuart monarchy, 53
Student life, 180–81, 428–29
Suffrage, 228
  educational qualifications for, 192–93
Summaries, 33, 52–53, 67–68, 103, 134, 164, 182, 219–21, 293–94, 336–38, 387–89, 418–19, 442–44, 480–81, 506–7
Superintendent of schools, 270–73
Support of schools, 9–13, 110–13, 295–337
  sources of, 321–23
Swiss, influence on founding of American schools, 6
Symmes School, 65, 140, 150

T

Taxation, direct, for support of schools, 112
Taxation, for schools and schooling, 10, 11, 13
Tax resources for education, 324–27
Teachers, character of, 134, 154–55, 158–59
  professional training of, 482–507
  supply of, 492–94

[518]

INDEX

the indentured teacher, 484–85
training in academies, 492–94
training of, 283–490–92
training of, in service, 503–6
wages, 488–90
Teachers' organizations, 504–6
Teaching, profession of, 47–51, 79, 98
   see also Monitorial schools, 490
Telegraph, 228
Tennants, father and son, 162–64
   contribution to education through the Log College, 162–64
Tennessee, state university of, 435
Textbooks, importance of, in American education, 344–45
   variety of, 345–46
Textbooks, prescribed for the S.P.G., 90
Thackeray, William, 19
   The Virginians, 62
Theology, schools of, 430
Thirteenth century, 13, 36
Tichnor, George, 424–25
Tisbury, 149
Town meeting and schools, 112–13, 275
Town schools, 109–10
Township system of schools, in Indiana, 277
Town, the New England, 107–8
Trade, craft or mystery, 7
Travel and education, 81
Trimium, 140
Trinity Church, New York City, 56
Troy Seminary, 456–59, 474–77
   see also Willard, Emma Hart
Tuition schools, support of, 112–13
Tuskegee Institute, 441
Tutorial education, 61–62
Tycho Brache, 3

U

Union Schools, 259
Universality of education, 25, 185
Universities, influence of, 22–23
   administration of, 431–35
   Dutch, 30–31
   state, 431–34
   teaching, 435
University, belief in, 165
   National, 199–200
   see also Colleges, belief in
Urban or city population, 188–89, 222–23
Utah, 199
Utrecht, university of, 31

V

Vassar College, 479–80
Vassar, Matthew, 479–80
Vermont, 126, 210–11, 213, 277
Vermont, University of, 210, 426–27
Vestry Boards, 57–58
Village, central town, 108
Virginia, education in, 202–4, 207, 217, 285–86, 298–99
   academies in, 396–97
Virginia, education in Colonial, 53–67
   English attitude of Virginia Company, 54–55
   Latin Grammar schools in, 140
Virginia, University of, 422–24, 425–27, 436
   see also Jefferson, Thomas
Visitation, articles of, 18
   inquiries, 58
Voorleser, 76, 82
Vorsanger, 76, 82

W

Waldenses, 31
Wales, 14
Warrants for the Rate Bill System, 318–19
Washington, President, and education, 199–201
Watertown, 131
Wayland, President, 426–27
Wealth, influence of national, 50–52, 63
Webster, Daniel, 196, 251, 438–39

[519]

INDEX

Webster, Noah, 207, 347
  on education of women, 452–53
Western Literary Institute, 252–53
  committees of, 252–53
West India Company, Dutch, 69–72, 74–78
West Jersey, education in, 91
Wigglesworth, Michael, 357–60
Wilderspin, Samuel, 372–80
Wiley, Caleb, 287
Willard, Mrs. Emma Hart, 236–37, 271
  on education of women, 450–53, 455–59
William and Mary, 118
  College, 140–41, 166–67, 169, 173, 176–77, 178–79
William and Mary University, 64, 67, 420–21, 436
Williams College, 429
Winchester School, 22
Winterbotham, Rev. W., Summary of Education, 205
Winthrop, Governor, 112
Women, education of, 445–481
  collegiate education of, 477–80
  leaders for, 455–62
Women's colleges, 477
Women teachers, 119–21, 483–88
Women's education, Governor Seward on, 486
  women as teachers, 483
Woodbridge, William C., 236, 462
Workhouse schools, 13
  in Virginia, 55–57
Working class, influence of, on education, 37–41, 230–35

Y

Yale, 149, 167–68, 423, 426, 429–30

NOV 2 0 2006

MAY 1 3 2013